Explaining Mormonism

Explaining Mormonism

A Believing Skeptic's Guide to the Latter-day Saint Worldview

GREGORY STEVEN DUNDAS

WIPF & STOCK · Eugene, Oregon

EXPLAINING MORMONISM
A Believing Skeptic's Guide to the Latter-day Saint Worldview

Wipf & Stock
An Imprint of Wipf and Stock Publishers
199 W. 8th Ave., Suite 3
Eugene, OR 97401

www.wipfandstock.com

PAPERBACK ISBN: 978-1-6667-4183-4
HARDCOVER ISBN: 978-1-6667-4184-1
EBOOK ISBN: 978-1-6667-4185-8

VERSION NUMBER 072522

To my mother

"A man should look for what is, and not what he thinks should be."
—ALBERT EINSTEIN (ATTRIBUTED)

"He who has never changed his mind has never learned anything."
—ADVERTISING CAMPAIGN FOR A DUTCH NEWSPAPER[1]

---

1. Quoted in van Lommel, *Consciousness Beyond Life*, 325.

Contents

Abbreviations

ANF	Roberts and Donaldson, *Ante-Nicene Fathers*
D&C	The Doctrine and Covenants of the Church of Jesus Christ of Latter-day Saints
HOTC	Roberts, *History of the Church*
KJV	King James Version of the Bible
NOAB	Coogan, *New Oxford Annotated Bible*
NPNF	Schaff and Wace, *Nicene and Post-Nicene Fathers*
OTP	Charlesworth, *Old Testament Pseudepigrapha*

Preface

EXPLAINING MORMONISM IS AN attempt to examine the belief system of the Church of Jesus Christ of Latter-day Saints from a broad cultural and intellectual perspective. Although it deals with a variety of theological matters, it is not strictly speaking a work of theology. It is rather an analysis of a *worldview*. A worldview has been defined as "a framework or set of fundamental beliefs through which we view the world and our calling and future in it."[1] And because the Latter-day Saint (LDS) worldview is founded on ideas about such diverse matters as the nature of God, the history of the Christian church, and the significance of marriage and the family, it will be necessary to approach our subject from a variety of vantage points, and to draw from the work of a wide variety of experts, including theologians, philosophers, historians, social scientists, and even physicists.

But why is it described as "a believing skeptic's guide" to Mormonism? It is because although I am a believing Latter-day Saint of many years, I continue to regard myself a skeptic by nature. Many readers might well wonder how such a combination is possible. The seeming paradox in the phrase "believing skeptic" comes from the modern notion of a skeptic as one who rejects all notions of religious faith—an atheist, or an agnostic. A more traditional definition of the word "skeptic," however, is simply an individual who is inclined to doubt or question all accepted opinions. The fairly obvious connection between the two definitions is the assumption that one who doubts will, above all, doubt the existence of God. But the sincere skeptic should be willing to doubt the atheist's disbelief as much as the believer's belief.

I believe my credentials as a dyed-in-the-wool skeptic and contrarian are as convincing as anyone's and go back to my earliest childhood. I was not born a Latter-day Saint or religious believer of any kind, but was raised in a home that valued education and rational, critical thought. Moreover, I seem to have been born with a fundamental desire to question and to challenge. My mother was a dedicated optimist, almost a Pollyanna, and as a born contrarian I always felt a burning need to challenge her rose-tinted view of the world. Hence, one of my favorite tropes as a young child went as follows:

---

1. James H. Olthius, quoted in Sire, *The Universe Next Door*, 18.

> My mother: (to me) Isn't it a gorgeous day today? Look at the beautiful blue
> sky! (we lived in San Diego, so this was a common occurrence)
> Me: (to the sky) Sky . . . are you beautiful? (to my mother) No—so see?

Among many other classical virtues possessed by my mother, she was clearly a model of patience, as I am still alive to write this book.

My mother was a woman of almost Victorian sensibilities and held to a strong moral code. But her moral sense was based on notions of utility and duty rather than on a belief in God or the Bible. She was also dedicated to the proposition that one should think for oneself and not allow one's independence of mind to be hijacked by what some group taught. Consequently, she was not overly pleased with my decision to convert to the Church of Jesus Christ of Latter-day Saints at age eighteen. Yet, for me the decision to become a "believer" never meant abandoning my independence of thought. I was simply, as the famous atheistic philosopher-turned-deist Anthony Flew has put it, following where the evidence led.[2]

I served a Latter-day Saint mission at nineteen and married inside a Latter-day Saint temple and have been a more-or-less active participant in my local Latter-day Saint ward (i.e., congregation) ever since. But I also continued to develop the skeptic within me, attending college to hone my mental tools, and eventually obtaining graduate degrees in ancient history and law. In both those fields one is trained to be highly analytical and to question the *evidentiary basis* of all claims of fact and truth and take all truth claims with a grain of salt. I have never abandoned my inborn skepticism or my childhood disposition to challenge assumptions and ask questions. I don't believe in accepting superficial answers in religion or in any other area of life, and even when after much hard thought and study I have finally settled on a resolution of a matter that has piqued my curiosity, I try never to entirely stop questioning my own assumptions.

It's quite possible that I would have been a much better "believer" had I been raised in a Latter-day Saint home and inculcated in the faith from my earliest days. In any case I am, whether by nature or nurture, for better or for worse, a compulsive questioner: Is that proposition (on any given subject) true? Is it plausible? What is the evidence in favor of it? What is the evidence against it? Which of alternative propositions is the more plausible? Does a given opinion fit with everything else I know (or think I know) about the world? Is there a third scenario that should be considered? Is there any real proof one way or another? (I am skeptical that there is *absolute* proof for any general proposition.) This dual approach of belief combined with skepticism would perhaps drive other people crazy. In my case, I suppose it keeps me sane, because it reassures me that I am not being deceived by someone else or even by my own mind.

This book is directed in the first instance at readers, whether believers or not, who come to religion with a mildly to moderately skeptical eye—i.e., those who feel

---

2. See Flew, *There is a God.*

inclined to doubt others' declarations and assertions. It is also aimed at Latter-day Saints who do not consider themselves skeptics per se, but who nevertheless find it helpful to reinforce their faith with reasoned justifications for their beliefs. Modern-day scripture recognized from the beginning that not all believers would have a perfect faith, and it would therefore be necessary to study "all good books" and to seek learning by "study" as well as "faith."[3] One of the most striking convictions of LDS theology is that there is no fundamental divide between "spiritual" and "secular" knowledge. Joseph Smith taught that "all truth" can be encompassed in "one great whole." And three church leaders declared in 1840:

> We consider it perfectly consistent with our calling, with reason and revelation that we should form a knowledge of kingdoms and countries whether at home or abroad, whether ancient or modern, or whether of things past present or to come; whether it be in heaven, earth or hell, air or seas; or whether we obtain this knowledge by being local or travelling, by study or faith, by dreams or by visions, by revelation or by prophecy, it mattereth not to us; if we can but obtain a correct [view of] principles, and knowledge of things as they are, in their true light, past, present, and to come.[4]

Latter-day Saint beliefs have come under concerted attack of late from rationalists of various stripes, and it is natural for even strong believers to feel the need for discussions that respond to such arguments. There has been much written in recent years in the vein of defensive apologetics, direct responses to discrete challenges raised by critics of the church; for example, historical questions relating to Joseph Smith's use of a seer stone, or the practice of polygamy, or questions of DNA analysis in connection with the Book of Mormon.[5] But our efforts should go beyond such narrowly focused analyses to examine the positive strengths of the Latter-day Saint position in its broad outlines vis-à-vis alternative worldviews. Even if one has a fairly secure intuitive appreciation of the teachings of the church, it can be reassuring to consider at some length just how strong a logical case can be made for one's faith.

It is my sincere conviction, as a result of lifelong study (both religious and secular), that the principles of what is commonly called "Mormonism," or what Latter-day Saints refer to as "the restored gospel of Jesus Christ," have a remarkable inner logical coherence and make remarkably good sense intellectually when seen in their entirety—although they may seem at first acquaintance to be quite bizarre. I also believe that the LDS worldview has an extraordinary ability to provide philosophically intelligent and spiritually satisfying answers to many of the most profound human questions of existence.

---

3. *Doctrine and Covenants* (abbreviated hereafter *D&C*) 88:118; see also 90:15.

4. *HOTC*, 4:234. The statement is by Heber C. Kimball, Wilford Woodruff, and George A. Smith.

5. See, for example, Hales, *A Reason for Faith*; Ash, *Shaken Faith Syndrome*.

Nevertheless, this book makes no attempt to address the question of ultimate truth; I am not in any way attempting to prove that Mormonism is true. That feat is effectively impossible, and I am certain it never will be achieved, despite the hopes of some amateur Mormon archaeologists and other optimists.[6] As I discuss later, most answers to questions in life are not susceptible of objective, scientific proof, whether one is seeking the best restaurant in town, trying to find the ideal job, or hoping to repair a damaged marriage. What I *am* trying to do is to make the case that the LDS view of the world does indeed makes sense *from the inside*, so that the curious reader will better be able to understand the appeal of this still-young religion to millions of people worldwide.

Some readers may suppose that in arguing in favor of my own beliefs, and discussing what I perceive to be the shortcomings of others' beliefs, I am somehow disparaging those other religions and beliefs. Let me assure you that I have no such intention. My hope is that no reader will feel that his or her own beliefs are being slighted or denigrated in any way. I have only respect for people of all beliefs—in particular for anyone who devotes time and effort, in a world where entertainment and triviality seem to reign supreme, to trying to understand this often crazy world in which we live. Voltaire is popularly credited with the declaration, "I disapprove of what you say, but I will defend to the death your right to say it."[7] Joseph Smith put it a little differently: "If it has been demonstrated that I have been willing to die for a 'Mormon,' I am bold to declare before Heaven that I am just as ready to die in defending the rights of a Presbyterian, a Baptist, or a good man of any other denomination."[8] Even more strikingly, he described his benevolent attitude toward other religions:

> If I esteem mankind to be in error, shall I bear them down? No. I will lift them up, and in their own way too, if I cannot persuade them my way is better; and I will not seek to compel any man to believe as I do, only by the force of reasoning, for truth will cut its own way. Do you believe in Jesus Christ and the Gospel of salvation which he revealed? So do I. Christians should cease wrangling and contending with each other, and cultivate the principles of union and friendship in their midst.[9]

No one likes to have their beliefs, their fondest assumptions, questioned and challenged. We all become emotionally wedded to certain principles around which we have ordered our lives, and there is a very natural tendency to go into a defensive crouch whenever we feel that they are under attack. My intent is not to criticize anyone else's belief system in a spirit of disapproval or disparagement, but merely to

6. See Welch, "The Role of Evidence," 273–74.

7. The quotation is not Voltaire's at all, but that of Evelyn Beatrice Hall (writing under the pseudonym of S.G. Tallentyre) attempting to summarize Voltaire's views.

8. *HOTC*, 5:498.

9. *HOTC*, 5:499.

present my own honest views of the world in a spirit of truth-seeking—a spirit which hopefully I share with anyone who would crack open a book like this one.

A NOTE TO NON-LATTER-DAY SAINT READERS:

I have tried to write a book that is approachable by interested readers and seekers from outside the LDS faith. Most books dealing with LDS teachings can be off-putting to the average reader, filled as they are with Mormon jargon and concepts and terms foreign to most people, including terms like "eternal salvation," "exaltation," "godhead," or even "Melchizedek Priesthood." And even when the terms themselves are clearly explained, the basic religious concepts can be quite puzzling especially to the reader not raised in the Christian tradition. It is a simple fact that large numbers of people today have little or no acquaintance with the Bible and biblical concepts. They do not spend their days wondering which church has the proper "priesthood authority," whether infants should be baptized, or whether one is truly saved by "faith" rather than "works." This book, then, while it may occasionally touch on these or similar issues, focuses its lens instead on such basic spiritual questions common to all of humanity as whether life has a purpose or meaning, and what that meaning is; whether God exists—and if he does, why he allows evil and suffering to exist; whether there is a life after death, and if so, what it consists of; what the meaning of human sexuality is and what its proper role in our lives is; and so on. These are questions that all human beings can relate to, questions that we all ask at some point in our lives, if perhaps only in the darkest moments of our private thoughts.

Introduction

That Mysterious, Menacing World of Mormonism

I am in no position to judge Joseph Smith as a revelator, but as a student of the American imagination I observe that his achievement as national prophet and seer is clearly unique in our history. Ralph Waldo Emerson and Walt Whitman were great writers, Jonathan Edwards and Horace Bushnell major theologians, William James a superb psychologist, and all these are crucial figures in the spiritual history of our country. Joseph Smith did not excel as a writer or as a theologian, let alone as psychologist and philosopher. But he was an authentic religious genius, and surpassed all Americans, before or since, in the possession and expression of what could be called the religion-making imagination.

—HAROLD BLOOM[1]

THE CHURCH OF JESUS Christ of Latter-day Saints, known better to the world as the "Mormon Church," was founded on April 6, 1830 in the tiny town of Fayette, New York, with only six official members and maybe a couple of dozen additional followers. Today it is a worldwide faith counting some sixteen million members in more than 80 percent of the world's countries. During much of the later twentieth century it was widely cited as one of the fastest-growing churches in the world. Yet its beliefs still seem to be shrouded in mystery and, despite its proclaimed devotion to Jesus Christ in its very name, many people still insist that it does not qualify as a proper Christian church.[2]

---

1. Bloom, *The American Religion*, 96.

2. There are countless denunciations of Mormons as cultists and non-Christians, both online and in print, of widely varying degrees of subtlety and sophistication, and a smaller number of defenses by Latter-day Saints. Perhaps the best example of the former is Blomberg, "Is Mormonism Christian?" For the LDS position, Robinson, *Are Mormons Christian?* Jan Shipps, a highly respected scholar of Mormonism, presents an in-depth response to the question whether Latter-day Saints are Christians and whether Mormonism is a form of Christianity (which she points out are two quite different questions). Like countless other sophisticated intellectual discussions, she ultimately "withholds judgment" on the question, which she (as a believing Methodist) says will someday be resolved by a much Higher Court. See Shipps, "Is Mormonism Christian?"

In 2012, at the end of the second presidential campaign by Mitt Romney, despite widespread media coverage about the LDS church over the course of the campaign, large numbers of Americans seemed still to feel that they knew little or nothing about the religion. However, this did not seem to be only a matter of straightforward lack of knowledge or understanding. For many it was also, one might say, an ignorance sprung from discomfort and apprehension, a sneaking suspicion that there is more to Mormonism than meets the eye, and even the possibility that something about it is somehow sinister.

The musical show *The Book of Mormon* opened on Broadway in 2011 and since then has become a mainstay of popular culture. During its first year, the show was consistently one of the top five best-selling shows on Broadway. Its run on Broadway continues more than a decade later, and there have also been two national touring productions, as well as productions in the UK, in Australia, and in several other countries. The show won nine Tony awards, including for Best Musical, and the Broadway album not only won a Grammy award for Best Musical Theater Album but reached number three on the Billboard charts and became the highest-charting Broadway cast album in over four decades.

What has driven this show's remarkable success? Doubtlessly its popularity can be traced in part to its own artistry and cleverness, but a major factor has surely been the public's perennial fascination with Mormonism, dating back to the lurid nineteenth-century depictions of Mormon patriarchs and their many wives. Even today, Mormonism remains shrouded in mystery and is viewed with suspicion by many people. In a recent in-depth survey, although three-fourths of respondents viewed Mormons as trustworthy and good people, nearly half described them as "mysterious" and having "weird beliefs."[3] This "weirdness" is something virtually unique with Latter-day Saint beliefs. While other non-mainstream religions might be described as odd or foreign, they are unlikely to be deemed "weird."

Similarly, it is difficult to imagine a hit musical—no matter how cleverly produced—mocking Buddhists or Baptists, Muslims or Methodists, Jews or even Jehovah's Witnesses. Unlike all those faiths (with the partial exception of Islam), Mormonism is inherently associated in the public mind with bizarre beliefs and practices, with such things as secret temples, peculiar undergarments, and, of course, polygamy. For some people, there is even a strong underlying sense that Mormonism's very wholesomeness is simply a cover for underlying forces that are malign, menacing, dangerous.

Perhaps the most notable book of recent years relating to the theme of menacing Mormonism is Jon Krakauer's *Under the Banner of Heaven: A Story of Violent Faith*. Originally published in 2004, the book continues to sell well. According to the publisher's website, it examines an "appalling double murder" along with "a multilayered, bone-chilling narrative of messianic delusion, polygamy, savage violence, and unyielding faith." Although the book focuses primarily on one small breakaway sect of

---

3. Lawrence, *How Americans View Mormonism*, 36.

apostate Mormons, it also discusses the origin of the LDS faith and suggests that the roots of that violence are found in mainstream Mormon theology itself.

Yet, despite its widespread reputation for weirdness (or worse!), one of the most astonishing things about Mormonism is that it has been for years one of the world's fastest-growing religions. Today the Church of Jesus Christ of Latter-day Saints has sixteen million members, a fourfold increase in membership in approximately forty years. From 1997 to 2017 it grew by 60 percent, from ten million to sixteen million members. The question naturally arises, what is the broad appeal of such a peculiar religion to millions of people, not only in the U.S. but worldwide?

And in addition to their sheer growth in numbers, Latter-day Saints are known for their high levels of education and their success in business and in many other walks of life. As Stephen Mansfield has written, "Mormons are disproportionately represented as corporate CEOs and board members, in senior government jobs, in top university jobs, and among the nation's wealthiest."[4] They have been particularly prominent in business. Among the best-known CEOs of recent years are J. Willard Marriott (Marriott), Nolan D. Archibald (Black & Decker), Jon Huntsman Sr. (Huntsman Corp), Mitt Romney (Bain Capital), David Neeleman (Jet Blue), Kevin Rollins (Dell), and Dave Checketts (Madison Square Garden). Kim Clark was the dean of Harvard Business School before accepting a request from the president of the LDS church to become president of Brigham Young University's Idaho campus, and then to become a full-time member of one of the church's presiding councils. Until his death in 2020, Clayton Christensen was for years a leading Harvard Business School professor and consultant for numerous top corporations.[5] Apart from stars in the business world, one can name eminent figures in a variety of other fields: Orson Scott Card, Stephenie Meyer, Anne Perry, Brandon Sanderson, Stephen Covey (writers); Lindsey Stirling, Gladys Knight, Brandon Flowers, The 5 Browns, The Tabernacle Choir at Temple Square (formerly The Mormon Tabernacle Choir), David Archuleta, Donny and Marie Osmond (musicians); Bryce Harper, Steve Young, Eric Weddle, Danny Ainge, Dale Murphy (sports); Harry Reid, Orrin Hatch, Jon Huntsman Jr. (government). Many other well-known individuals in a wide variety of fields could also be named.

The question naturally arises, what would draw individuals of such manifest talent and ability to Mormonism? Many of them, to be sure, were born and reared in LDS families, but to my knowledge they have remained in the church and identify as Latter-day Saints.[6] Many of them would attribute much of their success to their religious beliefs—not merely to their belief in God, but specifically to the unique

---

4. Manfield, *Mormonizing of America*, 221. See also Haws, *The Mormon Image*, 195–199.

5. On the LDS success in the business world, see Benedict, *The Mormon Way*.

6. There are, of course, a number of other show-business celebrities, e.g., Katherine Heigl and Amy Adams, who are not currently practicing Latter-day Saints but express their regard for the general values they were raised with as children.

teachings and practices of their church regarding the nature of God, the purpose of life, the importance of families, and so on. And why would they be willing—particularly those in business, where reputation is everything—to be identified with a wacky "cult" associated with irrational, mind-controlling beliefs?

The most obvious solution to this quandary is that most of the perceived weirdness of Mormonism is based on simple misunderstanding. Where there is lack of understanding, *mis*understanding and prejudice naturally abound. But while the suspicion of political conspiracy by the LDS church may be outlandish,[7] it is not at all surprising that even people who are acquainted with Latter-day Saint teachings find them mysterious and confusing. Indeed, it must be admitted by all honest observers that it is a highly peculiar religion, one full of unusual beliefs and paradoxes. One prominent paradox is that Mormonism, while on the one hand highly Christian in its theology, is also in many ways very unlike traditional Christianity.

A religious studies professor from UNC has observed that this mixture of the familiar and the odd has given rise to what she calls the "invasion of the body snatchers syndrome," saying:

> But just as Mormons seem to be ideal Americans, they also provoke typically American fears. While Mormons embody the economic and moral success embodied by the American Dream, they also subscribe to beliefs that, to many, seem peculiar—even bizarre. Mormon beliefs . . . and practices such as temple rituals or a legacy of polygamy . . . all provoke unease and distrust. How can these people, so *like* many other Americans, be so *different*? I call this double legacy the "invasion of the body snatchers" syndrome: no matter how much Mormon behavior conforms to what most consider admirable (and maybe *especially* because they look so wholesome), some Americans are convinced Mormons secretly await an opportunity to take over the world.[8]

Latter-day Saints as a group are generally perceived as conservative, both politically and socially, but this view obscures the more important underlying reality that Mormonism is quite a radical religion, certainly the most radical form of Christianity in existence today. To take only two examples, Latter-day Saints believe that human beings are *literally* made in the image of God and that they are ultimately capable of becoming gods themselves. Most Christians—indeed, most theists in general, including Jews and Muslims—believe that God is a purely *spiritual* being, with no corporeal existence of any kind, while Joseph Smith proclaimed that "the Father has a body of flesh and bones as tangible as man's; the Son also."[9] Similarly, for most believers the idea that men and women can themselves become gods seems appallingly blasphemous: how can there ever be more than one God?

---

7. See, for example, Holan, "The Mormon Religion."

8. Quoted in Haws, *The Mormon Image*, 277.

9. D&C 130:22

And in addition to its odd mixture of the familiar and the new, Latter-day Saint theology tends to be quite complex. Students of Mormonism have often expressed surprise at its depth and sophistication. Stephen H. Webb, a Catholic theologian, declared himself "astounded" when he first began investigating LDS beliefs, which he described as intellectually audacious and "like looking into a mirror that, upon closer inspection, turns into a maze."[10] The anthropologist Melvyn Hammarberg has described Mormonism as "awesome in its magnitude and power and detail."[11] And Jan Shipps, a historian of religion, has observed: "Mormonism is a really complex theological system. All its parts fit together beautifully. But if you just know a little bit about one of them, or part of them, it seems weird."[12]

This book, then, is an attempt to dispel the mystery surrounding Mormon doctrines by exploring some of the complexities of Latter-day Saint theology for the benefit of the non-specialist reader, to explore its inner logic and to demonstrate how remarkably well its complex parts fit together. It does not attempt to address all the potential questions that skeptics might raise about the Mormon faith. It has little to say about such highly topical subjects as the place of women in the church or technical questions like the genetics of Native American peoples—a subject far beyond my competence.[13] Instead, it focuses on what I judge to be the core doctrines of the restored gospel, those foundational ideas on which the imposing structure of Mormonism is based. This includes, above all, the church's fundamental teachings regarding such basic human questions as the meaning and purpose of life, the nature of deity, and the nature of the eternal reality which stretches far beyond this earthly existence.

Our exploration of Mormonism will begin with a brief outline of the story of Joseph Smith himself and briefly introduce some of his unusual teachings. As will be seen, numerous visitors to the pioneer prophet found him much more intelligent, engaging, and normal than rumor had led them to believe. The second chapter comprises an excursus on what it means to be a skeptic, the limits of human reason, and the importance of keeping our minds open to the unexpected as we search for ultimate reality. I will then go on in the succeeding four chapters to examine and discuss the implications of what Latter-day Saints call the "plan of salvation," the basic paradigm of humanity and how we all fit into God's plan for mankind. This subject is at the heart of the Latter-day Saint worldview, and I will show how it presents a complex yet highly coherent account of the meaning and purpose of human existence. Indeed, I will argue that the entire picture of human salvation as taught by Joseph Smith proceeds logically from the basic principle that God is our literal Father, i.e., that we are

10. Webb, *Jesus Christ, Eternal God*, 243–70.

11. Hammarberg, *Mormon Quest for Glory*, 2.

12. Luo, *Crucial Test for Romney*.

13. Some have argued that DNA analysis has shown that there is no genetic connection between Native Americans and ancient Israelites, as apparently portrayed in the Book of Mormon. In response to this argument, see Perego, "The Book of Mormon."

his children rather than merely his creations, and that he loves us profoundly as only a father can. His plan for our happiness consists of three parts, addressing in very specific terms the basic questions of where we came from, how we came to this existence, and what we are supposed to accomplish while we are here (and why), and what all this is ultimately leading up to.

I will then move on to consider certain basic aspects of the Latter-day Saint lifestyle, particularly their attitudes toward sexuality and family. I will propose a justification for the church's strict teaching regarding sex by linking it directly to the fundamental principles of God's plan for humanity. Next comes a discussion of the historical basis of the Latter-day Saint teaching of the so-called Great Apostasy from earliest Christianity, and of the need for a "restoration" of Christ's church. The subsequent chapter discusses the Book of Mormon, and I will propose arguments for why Joseph Smith's remarkable account of the origin of the book is in fact the most plausible one. Finally, I will explore the bedrock Mormon belief in divine revelation, the idea that it is possible to acquire knowledge through spiritual, as opposed to purely intellectual, means. Throughout this treatise, in attempting to help the reader understand Latter-day Saint views, I will not narrowly limit the discussion to citing LDS teachings and writings, but will explore ideas from a wide variety of multidisciplinary sources, comparing and contrasting where useful. From these citations it will become evident, among other things, that individual ideas and doctrines taught by the Church of Jesus Christ of Latter-day Saints are not quite as unique or strange as one might think. What is in fact most original with Mormonism is not the individual teachings but the overall picture—how the pieces fit together to constitute a unique whole.

Every honest person, whether believer or skeptic, will admit that Mormonism offers an extraordinary picture of the world—so far out of the ordinary, indeed, that one feels almost compelled to call it "bizarre." Joseph Smith himself declared that if he had not experienced what he had, he would not have believed his story himself. Mormonism is in certain ways a worldview that seemingly has no place in the modern world of science and technology, of iPhones and iPads. Well over a century ago, Charles Dickens accused the Latter-day Saints of fanaticism and "seeing visions in an age of railways."[14] In 1964, the writer William Whalen questioned how Mormons, as they became increasingly well educated over time, could possibly continue believing in the historicity of the Book of Mormon and other doctrines so far from modern rationalism.[15] Nonetheless, many millions of people have found and continue to find in Latter-day Saint theology a compelling view of reality that drives them to devote countless hours to making the Latter-day Saint vision a reality in their own lives. That fact in and of itself makes Latter-day Saint theology a subject worthy of attention.

14. Charles Dickens, "In the Name of the Prophet."

15. See Bushman, *Contemporary Mormonism*, 181. As we shall see in chapter 2, there is actually a *positive* correlation between Mormons' educational level and their level of devotion to their religion.

Scientists often refer to the concept of elegance as an indicator of the value of a theory. String theory, for example, is often referred to as an "elegant" theory. Just what *elegance* means in this context is hard to define, but it has something to do with simplicity and comprehensiveness. An elegant theory in physics can explain and tie together many aspects of reality with just a few principles.[16] To those on the inside, Mormonism is such a theory. Of course believers will call it "truth" rather than "theory," but one of the reasons they are so convinced of its truthfulness is its ability to explain so much about human life—particularly the meaning of our existence and the purpose of suffering and death—with just a few tweaks, as it were, to the traditional Christian scenario. Elegance in a religion, just as in physics, does not prove that the theory is true. But the ability of a worldview to illuminate the darkest recesses of reality is surely a powerful indicator of its merit. As the French philosopher Simone Weil declared:

> If I light an electric torch at night out of doors, I don't judge its power by looking at the bulb, but by seeing how many objects it lights up. The brightness of a source of light is appreciated by the illumination it projects upon non-luminous objects. The value of a religious or, more generally, a spiritual way of life is appreciated by the amount of illumination thrown upon the things of this world.[17]

16. Patrick House, "What is Elegance in Science?"
17. Quoted in McGrath, *Surprised by Meaning*, 9.

1

Joseph Smith and the Radical Claims of Mormonism

This Joe Smith is undoubtedly one of the greatest characters of the age. He indicates as much talent, originality, and moral courage as Mahomet … or any of the great spirits that have hitherto produced the revelations of past ages. In the present . . . irreligious . . . age of the world, some such singular prophet as Joe Smith is required to preserve the principle of faith, and to plant some new germs of civilization that may come to maturity in a thousand years. While modern philosophy, which believes in nothing but what you can touch, is overspreading the Atlantic States, Joe Smith is creating a spiritual system, combined also with morals and industry, that may change the destiny of the race.

—JAMES G. BENNETT, EDITOR, *NEW YORK HERALD*, APRIL 3, 1842[1]

Do I personally believe? No. [Joseph Smith] may have believed that he did [see God]. But whether he saw, I have no evidence for that. And since I'm not a Mormon who by an act of faith believes it, even though it can't be proved, I have to then make a judgment on the basis of the evidence. However, you can say, look what he did. Is one human being capable of doing [all that he did]? Without divine help and intervention?[2]

—ROBERT REMINI[3]

IN 1844, A VISITOR to the Latter-day Saint city of Nauvoo, Illinois wrote a letter to the local paper describing his impression of Joseph Smith, the Mormon leader. In the letter he described himself as utterly astonished at how different Smith was from the negative accounts that were widespread at the time.

1. See note 35 below.

2. Consider the following summary of Joseph's accomplishments: "His people marveled that he did so much when he was just one of them, and his accomplishments—translations, cities, missions, gatherings, priesthoods, temples, cosmologies, governments—are astonishing by any standard." Bushman, *Rough Stone Rolling*, 560.

3. Quoted in Swinton, *American Prophet*, 46.

From many reports, I had reason to believe [Smith] a bigoted religionist as ignorant of politics as the savage, but to my utter astonishment . . . I have found
him as familiar with the cabinet of nations, as with his Bible . . . [He] appears
perfectly at home on every subject and his familiarity with many languages
affords his ample means to become informed concerning all nations and principles, which his familiar and dignified deportment towards all must secure
to his interest the affections of every intelligent and virtuous man that may
chance to fall in his way; and I am astonished that so little is known abroad
concerning him . . . Free from all bigotry and superstition, he dives into every
subject, and it seems as though the world was not large enough to satisfy his
capacious soul, and from his conversation, one might suppose him as well
acquainted with other worlds as this.[4]

As we shall see, this anonymous traveler was by no means the only person to
find himself surprised by the enormous gap between the Joseph Smith of popular
imagination—a foolish and ignorant country yokel and religious fanatic—and the
man himself. And in a similar way, the doctrine Joseph taught, popularly referred to
as "Mormonism," developed a reputation as being foolish and nonsensical—as well as
unbiblical—which can only be dispelled through closer examination.

Already by 1832, at the tender age of twenty-seven, Joseph Smith had proclaimed
a series of doctrines that upended traditional views of God, mankind, and reality in
general. He taught, for example, that:

- God had not ceased communicating with mankind after the Bible, but still declared his living will through prophets, including Joseph himself;

- all of God's revealed word is scripture, whether it was found in the Bible or
  elsewhere;

- angels—literal messengers from God—still appeared to mankind;

- Christian doctrines had been altered so dramatically over the centuries that true
  Christianity no longer existed on the earth;

- God had commanded Joseph to restore his original church to the earth, with its
  original organization and rituals;

- mankind's free will to choose good and evil was fundamental to God's plan;

- knowledge of God's plan for mankind, including the role of Christ, was taught to
  all the early prophets, dating back to Adam himself;

- the afterlife was not a matter of heaven or hell, but consisted of several different
  levels of divine *glory*; hell in the sense of eternal torment existed only for a few,
  the most incorrigible of all, while everyone else, even the ordinary wicked, would
  end up in some degree of heaven.

4. *Nauvoo Neighbor*, 3.

In the next dozen years, before his assassination at age thirty-eight, Joseph would teach even more radical doctrines, among them:

> that mankind had lived as spirit-beings in a spirit world long before the creation of this earth—indeed, that men and women had in some sense existed eternally;

> that God was not merely an incorporeal mind, or spirit, or essence, but was an actual being possessing a physical body;

> that the salvation and exaltation of mankind ultimately implied becoming like God—i.e., becoming divine;

> that marriage—eternal marriage—was a fundamental part of becoming like God.

Perhaps without being fully aware of it, Joseph had implicitly answered many of the most intractable questions of mankind, such as:

> Does God really exist?

> What is his will for all of us?

> What is the purpose of life?

> Why does God allow suffering and evil in this life?

None of these ideas altered the fundamental Christian truths that Jesus of Nazareth was the Son of God, that he had died on the cross and atoned for the sins of mankind, and that salvation could be had only through faith on his name. But Joseph's teaching cast this traditional Christian doctrine into an entirely new context, a context that spanned eternity extending in both directions, past and future.

THE RISE OF MORMONISM

The teachings of Mormonism originate, remarkably, with a young farm boy in Upstate New York, Joseph Smith. He was born in Vermont in 1805, but moved with his impoverished family to the Finger Lakes region of New York, to a town called Palmyra. There, as he tells the story in his own words, at the age of fourteen, he became passionate about matters of the soul and intently curious to figure out which of the various competing churches, or sects, he should join.[5] His mother and sister and two brothers had become Presbyterians, but his father, though a believer, preferred to stay aloof from all churches and worship God according to his own conscience. This was during the so-called Second Great Awakening in the young American republic, and Joseph

---

5. Joseph wrote more than one account of his early years and his calling as a prophet of God. The most thorough account, and the one accepted by the LDS church as official, was authored in 1838 and can be found in many places, including the church's volume of scripture known as The Pearl of Great Price. All the accounts have been studied thoroughly by Steven C. Harper in *Joseph Smith's First Vision*. See also Welch and Carlson, *Opening the Heavens*, 1–75.

felt thoroughly conflicted among the various claims of the different churches, each one claiming to have the correct version of Christ's teachings.

Joseph appears to have begun as something of a skeptic himself. He attended various revival meetings and developed "some desire to unite with" the Methodists, but was keenly aware of behaviors among the various clergy which manifested competitiveness rather than godly love and devotion. "All their good feelings one for another (if they ever had any) were entirely lost in a strife of words and a contest about opinions." He may have doubted for a while the existence of God, and he ended up maintaining his independence from organized churches along with his father. He nonetheless had an intense desire to be forgiven of his sins and to "get Religion too [and I] wanted to feel & shout like the Rest but could feel nothing."[6]

As a result of this intense spiritual seeking, and after some perusal of the Bible, the young Joseph resolved to seek wisdom directly from God, as the Bible itself instructed (see James 1:5), and he retired to the woods outside his log house to utter his first heartfelt, vocal prayer. The result was, to say the least, spectacular. He received a direct visitation (that is, not a dream, but a waking vision) of God and Jesus Christ, who told him his sins had been forgiven, but that he should join none of the existing churches, for they had all "gone out of the way." Instead, he was told, he should wait for further instructions, and that at some later point the fullness of the gospel would be revealed to him.

As it turned out, Joseph waited three years, at which point another heavenly visitor—an angel who identified himself as Moroni, an ancient American prophet—came to call, this time at his house, late at night while his family was asleep—and told him that he should go the next day to a nearby hill, where he would find a set of ancient gold plates buried in a stone box in the ground. In fact, Joseph did find the plates exactly where the angel had instructed him. He was not permitted to remove the plates for several years, but when he was finally able to take possession of them, he was instructed to translate the contents of the plates (with divine assistance, since they were written in a language unknown to any living person) and publish them to the world. This he did, with scribal assistance, over a period of more than a year, and the results were published in 1830 as *The Book of Mormon.*[7]

Word of this endeavor leaked out, and even before publication Joseph's "golden bible" was mocked in the local press. Various articles denounced the work as

6. Bushman, *Rough Stone Rolling*, 37. On skepticism in Joseph's environment, see Bushman, *Joseph Smith and the Beginnings*, 6.

7. Roughly 21 months passed between the time Joseph received the plates from the angel and the production of a full-length manuscript. But detailed research has shown that the actual number of days in which the dictation of the full text took place was limited to about 90. The rest of the time was filled with many other workaday activities, including travel. There was also an initial period of translation and the ensuing loss of the first 116 pages of manuscript, which was never redictated and is not found in the current text of the Book of Mormon. The huge majority of the text was set down during April and May 1829, roughly at an astonishing pace of over 3,500 words per day. See Welch, "Miraculous Translation."

"blasphemy" and "fanaticism."[8] Shortly after the appearance of the Book of Mormon, a local minister declared that it was "the greatest fraud of our time in the field of religion." A local newspaper called it "the greatest piece of superstition that has come within our knowledge." [9] The *Rochester Daily Advertiser* declared that "[a] viler imposition was never practiced. It is an evidence of fraud, blasphemy, and credulity, shocking to both Christians and moralists."[10]

Undaunted, Joseph and a small group of followers organized themselves into a new church, the Church of Christ.[11] They began preaching that this church was not just another church, not another "reformation" of existing Christianity, but rather a brand-new "restoration" of the ancient church of Christ as it had existed in the early decades after the crucifixion. They proclaimed that the ancient church, with the passage of time, had fallen away from the truth through a general *apostasy*, and hence that none of the other existing churches, no matter how well meaning they might be, had the correct doctrine or the legitimate authority of God. God, fulfilling the hopes and expectations of many, had finally set his hand to restore the ancient doctrine and organization in its purity, through the instrumentality of Joseph Smith.[12]

Joseph received numerous revelations in the ensuing years, many of which were written down and later compiled into a volume originally known as the *Book of Commandments*, while later editions were published as *The Doctrine and Covenants of the Church of Jesus Christ of Latter-day Saints* (abbreviated D&C). Some of these revelations were about practical matters, such as where the fledgling church's proselyting efforts should be focused. But many of them taught new doctrine—or rather, old doctrine that had presumably been lost as a result of the Great Apostasy.

The purpose of all this new revelation was presented by God in the revelation which now serves as the preface to the entire volume:

> Prepare ye, prepare ye for that which is to come, for the Lord is nigh; and the anger of the Lord is kindled, and his sword is bathed in heaven, and it shall fall upon the inhabitants of the earth. . . for they have strayed from mine ordinances, and have broken mine everlasting covenant; they seek not the Lord to establish his righteousness, but every man walketh in his own way, after the image of his own god, whose image is in the likeness of the world, and whose substance is that of an idol, which waxeth old and shall perish in Babylon,

8. Bushman, *Rough Stone Rolling*, 82.

9. Bushman, *Rough Stone Rolling*, 82.

10. Kirkham, *New Witness*, 2:40.

11. The church was later renamed, by divine revelation, as The Church of Jesus Christ of Latter-day Saints. See D&C 115.

12. Among others, Roger Williams, founder of the state of Rhode Island, had actively looked for God to send new apostles to reestablish his church on the face of the earth. Many others, as early as the Middle Ages in Europe, had perceived corruption in established Christianity and sought for some kind of renewal of the church. For further detail, see chapter 8 below. For the early teaching regarding the apostasy and the need for a restoration, see Givens, *Wrestling the Angel*, 23–41.

even Babylon the great, which shall fall. Wherefore, I the Lord, knowing the calamity which should come upon the inhabitants of the earth, called upon my servant Joseph Smith, Jun., and spake unto him from heaven, and gave him commandments . . .[13]

Other revelations presented entirely new teachings, for example, that there was more than one level of heaven prepared for God's children. The afterlife was not merely a matter of heaven and hell, but there were three kingdoms of glory, each of which was specifically for those willing and able to live according to the suitable degree of righteousness. The highest, or celestial, kingdom, would in fact be found on the earth itself:

> Therefore, [the earth] must needs be sanctified from all unrighteousness, that it may be prepared for the celestial glory; for after it hath filled the measure of its creation, it shall be crowned with glory, even with the presence of God the Father; that bodies who are of the celestial kingdom may possess it forever and ever; for, for this intent was it made and created, and for this intent are they sanctified. And they who are not sanctified through the law which I have given unto you, even the law of Christ, must inherit another kingdom, even that of a terrestrial kingdom, or that of a telestial kingdom. For he who is not able to abide the law of a celestial kingdom cannot abide a celestial glory. And he who cannot abide the law of a terrestrial kingdom cannot abide a terrestrial glory. And he who cannot abide the law of a telestial kingdom cannot abide a telestial glory; therefore he is not meet for a kingdom of glory. Therefore he must abide a kingdom which is not a kingdom of glory.[14]

From the first time that he reported his original vision to the clergymen he knew, Joseph reports being mocked and criticized. The Protestant clergy of that day insisted that God did not appear to men in visions, for all that needed to be known was in the Bible. This criticism grew quickly into active persecution, which plagued the fledgling church from its first days. On the other hand, significant numbers found Joseph's message of divine restoration and revelation deeply appealing. Of those who embraced the book and joined the new church, Parley P. Pratt can be taken as representative. Pratt, who had been searching for the true church of Christ for several years, tells the story of his first encounter with the Book of Mormon:

> We visited an old Baptist deacon by the name of Hamlin. After hearing of our appointment for evening, he began to tell of a *book*, a STRANGE BOOK, a VERY STRANGE BOOK! in his possession, which had been just published. This book, he said, purported to have been originally written on plates either of gold or brass, by a branch of the tribes of Israel; and to have been discovered and translated by a young man near Palmyra, in the State of New

13. D&C 1:12–17.
14. D&C 88:18–24.

York, by the aid of visions, or the ministry of angels. I inquired of him how or where the book was to be obtained. He promised me the perusal of it, at his house the next day, if I would call. I felt a strange interest in the book. I preached that evening to a small audience, who appeared to be interested in the truths which I endeavored to unfold to them in a clear and lucid manner from the Scriptures. Next morning I called at his house, where, for the first time, my eyes beheld the "BOOK OF MORMON"—that book of books—that record which reveals the antiquities of the *"New World"* back to the remotest ages, and which unfolds the destiny of its people and the world for all time to come;—that Book which contains the fullness of the gospel of a crucified and risen Redeemer;—that Book which reveals a lost remnant of Joseph, and which was the principal means, in the hands of God, of directing the entire course of my future life.

I opened it with eagerness, and read its title page. I then read the testimony of several witnesses in relation to the manner of its being found and translated. After this I commenced its contents by course. I read all day; eating was a burden, I had no desire for food; sleep was a burden when the night came, for I preferred reading to sleep.

As I read, the spirit of the Lord was upon me, and I knew and comprehended that the book was true, as plainly and manifestly as a man comprehends and knows that he exists. My joy was now full, as it were, and I rejoiced sufficiently to more than pay me for all the sorrows, sacrifices and toils of my life. I soon determined to see the young man who had been the instrument of its discovery and translation.[15]

As word of the new restoration of God's work upon on the earth began to spread, and the "Saints" (as they called themselves, based on New Testament usage) carried out proselyting missions, the church began to grow and expand, first into northern Ohio and soon thereafter into Missouri, at that time a frontier territory of the United States. In Kirtland, Ohio they encountered a group known as "Campbellites," followers of Thomas and Alexander Campbell, who were also seekers of a reversion to New Testament Christianity. The Mormons obtained numerous converts from Campbellite congregations, most notably Sidney Rigdon, a well-educated minister who soon became an intimate associate of Joseph Smith, and Parley P. Pratt, who became the church's most spirited missionary and who has been called the "Apostle Paul of Mormonism."[16]

Missouri at that time was a rough-and-ready frontier land, but Joseph declared that he had received a revelation that Jackson County, Missouri was destined to become a new land of Zion—a promised land which God had declared would ultimately become the central territory of a new establishment of his kingdom upon the earth. The Missourians undoubtedly resented the growing political power of the Latter-day

15. Pratt, *Autobiography*, 36–37.
16. See Givens and Grow, *Parley P. Pratt*.

Saints as they migrated into the area at a remarkable pace. But they resented Mormon theology just as much. Various leaders of a fast-growing anti-Mormon movement there declared that the Mormon religion was a "delusion" and the Book of Mormon "a farrago of nonsense." Mormons "blasphemed the Most High God and cast contempt on His holy religion, by pretending to receive revelations direct from heaven, by pretending to speak unknown tongues, by direct inspiration, and by divers pretenses derogatory to God and religion and to the utter subversion of human reason."[17] The Latter-day Saints countered that such theological opposition (which was not, of course, limited to Missouri) was simply a result of deep-seated but mistaken historical traditions of Christianity. There was nothing in the Bible, for example, that forbade the receipt of further revelation outside the Bible. To the contrary, it was simply a matter of human tradition, developed in medieval Europe, that God's word was forever limited to that one volume.

The persecutors, whatever their motives, ultimately became violent and drove the Saints first into the less-populated areas of Missouri and finally out of the state altogether. The governor of the state notoriously passed an "extermination order," an executive order to the state militia declaring that "the Mormons must be treated as enemies and must be exterminated or driven from the state, if necessary, for the public good. Their outrages are beyond all description."[18] Partly in response to this order, seventeen unarmed Latter-day Saints were killed by members of a local militia at a place known as Haun's Mill. Shortly thereafter the Mormons were completely driven out of Missouri in mid-winter and took refuge in Illinois.

They settled on the banks of the Missouri River, in a malarial swampland where prior attempts to settle had failed.[19] Out of virtually nothing they built a city which they called Nauvoo (meaning "to be comely or beautiful" in Hebrew), and which quickly grew into the second largest city in the state. With a new central location for gathering, the Saints rapidly grew into a thriving community, enjoying a level of prosperity they had not previously known. In Kirtland, although scarcely able to afford a plow, they had built a temple through great financial sacrifice, reportedly even contributing their china and glassware, which was crushed and added to the plaster walls to make them glisten. Having been forced to abandon that building when they were driven out of Ohio, they now commenced building another temple, more than 50 percent larger than the first. Joseph introduced a series of spiritual rituals in connection with that temple, which were designed to teach of the relationship between God and man and to prepare men and women to reunite with God after this life.

17. See Arrington and Bitton, *Mormon Experience*, 47.

18. The order was not formally rescinded until 1976.

19. The Saints found a few abandoned houses from previous attempts at settlement, and a few houses that were still inhabited and known as Commerce, Illinois. They managed to drain the swamps in spite of the constant threat of malaria. There were numerous cases of miraculous healings, but also many deaths. Joseph Smith pitched a tent in front of his house and lived in it after giving up the house for the use of the sick. See Rollins et al., "Transforming Swampland."

The hardiness and resilience of the Saints in the face of their repeated persecutions drew forth a certain sympathy and respect from some observers. One writer wrote favorably of their achievements, referring to the "energy, industry, and self-denial with which the community is imbued."[20] The *Daily Missouri Republican*, like so many reports from disinterested observers who actually met Joseph and his associates, declared itself surprised by the Mormon prophet:

> We had supposed from the stories and statements we had read of "Jo Smith" (as he is termed in the papers) to find him a very illiterate, uncouth sort of a man; but from a conversation, we acknowledge an agreeable disappointment. In conversation he appears intelligent and candid, and divested of all malicious thought and feeling towards his relentless persecutors.[21]

A lengthy missionary expedition to England was launched, which resulted in a great harvest of converts, many of whom emigrated across the Atlantic and provided a strong foundation for the future of the church. Other missionary efforts were conducted in Canada, in American Indian territories, in various European countries, in the isles of the Pacific, and even in Palestine, where the land was dedicated for the return of the Jews.

Among Joseph's boldest endeavors was his presidential campaign, launched in 1844. His main concern was to publicize the plight of the Saints and to obtain redress for their grievances in Missouri after President Van Buren and Congress had refused to do anything to help them. But he circulated a lengthy and serious pamphlet declaring his views on a variety of issues and controversies of the day. Most notably, he favored the abolition of slavery by 1850; slaves, he said, should be purchased from their owners (with funds acquired from the sale of public lands) and set free. He was essentially opposed to the use of prisons for those convicted of crimes apart from murder. He said that prisons should be turned into "seminaries of learning" because "rigor and seclusion will never do as much to reform the propensities of man, as reason and friendship." He did not favor the doctrine of states' rights, in light of how the state of Missouri had treated the Saints, but he was no lover of the federal government either, and endorsed a reduction in the size of Congress by two-thirds, and a reduction of their pay at the same time to "two dollars and their board per diem (except Sundays.) That is more than the farmer gets, and he lives honestly . . ."[22]

This platform drew forth some significant praise in the non-Mormon press. The *Springfield Register* declared that Smith "ought to be regarded as the real Whig candidate for President until Mr. [Henry] Clay can so far recover from his shuffling and dodging to declare his sentiments like a man." The *Iowa Democrat* actually supposed that Smith had a chance of being elected, based on his "superior talent, genius, and

20. Quoted in Marvin S. Hill, *Quest for Refuge*, 105.
21. Quoted in Mulder and Mortenson, *Among the Mormons*, 111–12.
22. On the presidential campaign, see McBride, *Joseph Smith for President*.

intelligence, combined with virtue, integrity, and enlarged views," while the *Quincy Herald* scolded the *New York Tribune* and other papers for publishing articles that contained "slanderous falsehoods" against the Latter-day Saints.[23]

In June of 1844, Joseph, his brother Hyrum, and several other close associates were jailed (not for the first time) in a small two-story stone structure in Carthage, Illinois. By this time, opposition to Joseph and his church had reached a fever pitch, and the jail was assaulted by a mob of about one hundred men. Some members of the mob were part of the militia that had been charged with protecting the Smith brothers, but who nonetheless had sworn that they had "had too much trouble to bring Old Joe here to let him ever escape alive." In the ensuing brief fight, Joseph and Hyrum were killed.

Many of the church's enemies assumed that it would shrivel and die with the death of Joseph, but that of course was not the case. Following the assassinations of Joseph and Hyrum, which the church called the "martyrdom," the mantle of leadership was assumed by Brigham Young, a man of very different abilities and temperament but who regarded himself as Joseph's most faithful disciple.[24] He was responsible for leading the difficult migration westward to Utah. As previously, they were driven out of their homes in wintertime. But this time, under Brigham's powerful leadership, they were able to spend a difficult winter in Iowa, just across the Missouri River, before beginning a thousand-mile trek and ultimately settling in an utterly desolate territory near the Great Salt Lake. There, in the midst of the Rocky Mountains, they established a strong, independent community. Although they had fled beyond the limits of the United States into Mexican territory, the expanding national boundaries of the United States quickly overtook them.[25] The territory of Utah was officially organized in 1850, and the state of Utah in 1896.

23. *HOTC* 6:268; Leonard, *Nauvoo*, 338.

24. During a period in 1837 when a large percentage of the leadership of the church deserted Joseph Smith at least temporarily, Brigham Young remained faithful. He later stated, "I feel like shouting Hallelujah, all the time, when I think that I ever knew Joseph Smith, the Prophet whom the Lord raised up and ordained, and to whom he gave keys and power to build up the Kingdom of God on earth and sustain it" (Young, *Discourses of Brigham Young*, 456). On another occasion he said, "I can truly say, that I invariably found him to be all that any people could require a true prophet to be, and that a better man could not be, though he had his weaknesses; and what man has ever lived upon this earth who had none?" (*Teachings of the Presidents: Brigham Young*, 343). There are two solid biographies of Brigham Young: Arrington, *Brigham Young*, and Turner, *Brigham Young*.

25. Parley Pratt said that at this point, "The struggle now was over, our liberties were gone, our homes to be deserted and possessed by a lawless banditti; and all this in the United States of America." Brigham Young said with only slightly less bitterness, "The exodus of the nation of the only true Israel from these United States to a far distant region of the West, where bigotry, intolerance, and insatiable oppression lose their power over them—forms a new epoch." See Bowman, *Mormon People*, xviii–xix. Despite their extreme disillusionment with the United States, in 1846 church leaders issued a formal statement that "Our patriotism has not been overcome by fire, by sword, by daylight or by midnight assassinations which we have endured; neither have they alienated us from the institutions of our country" (Mackay, *Mormons or Latter-day Saints*, 185). That same year Brigham volunteered five hundred men from the pioneers to serve in the war against Mexico. Of course, the men would be paid, and the Saints were desperately in need of money. Thus, ironically, the Saints participated in the very

The church has undergone considerable change, of course, since 1844. Anti-Mormonism, already quite pronounced, became much more widespread throughout the nation when it came to light that the Mormons, in addition to their peculiar beliefs, practiced polygamy or plural marriage.[26] The Saints clung fiercely to that practice for decades in the face of imprisonment (over 1,300 men went to prison for the practice) and confiscation of property, and even loss of voting rights.[27] Plural marriage was officially renounced by the president of the church in 1890 in response to a divine revelation, though some members refused to give up their most peculiar practice for a number of years.

The pioneer ethos of the LDS church endured for many decades, but is now finally dwindling. Church leaders no longer command with the same degree of authority that Brigham Young did. For example, in Brigham's day men were regularly called on proselyting missions by having their names announced publicly in a church meeting without any warning, and were expected to leave their families forthwith. Today, married men are normally not called as missionaries, except following retirement, when they volunteer to serve brief missions with their wives, and a large majority of missionaries are young men—and, increasingly, young women—under the age of twenty-six who volunteer by applying months in advance.

Programs and practices have also changed. The church's health code, known colloquially as the "Word of Wisdom," ceased being merely a wise counsel and became a binding rule. The church's famous welfare program began during the Great Depression. Remarkably, following the end of polygamy, the church's reputation began a long and surprising climb from seeming almost anti-American to becoming almost "quintessentially American."[28]

Yet despite all these changes, doctrinally the church is still very much Joseph Smith's church. His revelations are still the fountainhead of church doctrines and his writings continue to be greatly revered as an authoritative source for understanding doctrine.[29] And although his sixteen successors as church president have also car-

---

war that would result in their new homeland being absorbed, four years later, into the United States.

26. Thomas Fitch, a member of Congress, on the blight of polygamy: "I am not unmindful of the deep disgrace to the nation that the barbarous social practices of the Asiatic should be unblushingly pursued among a Saxon people in this noon of the nineteenth century." Quoted in Fluhman, *Peculiar People*, 115.

27. The Edmunds-Tucker Act, passed in 1887 and upheld as constitutional by the Supreme Court in 1890, was an authoritarian law that clearly was aimed at destroying the church entirely. It disenfranchised any citizen who was convicted of polygamy or who refused to take an anti-polygamy oath. It also dissolved the church as a legal corporation and mandated confiscation by the federal government of all church-owned properties over the value of fifty thousand dollars.

28. The phrase comes from columnist George Will, quoted in Moore, *Religious Outsiders*, 43. On the myriad changes in the church in the early twentieth century, see Alexander, *Mormonism in Transition*; Mauss, *Angel and the Beehive*.

29. In recent years the church has undertaken a massive effort to publish an exhaustive edition of all Joseph Smith's papers, including documentary and administrative records, known as *The Joseph*

ried the title of "prophet," Joseph is still considered in every way *the* prophet of Mormonism. But it is important to keep in mind that for Joseph and his followers the term "prophet" meant something rather different from the common understanding. Doubtless many people would be inclined to imagine someone like Charlton Heston as Moses—a bearded man of immense *gravitas* who goes around making solemn pronouncements in ringing tones in the name of God—or perhaps a man of papal piety and dignity. Joseph was quite different and was occasionally criticized by some of his followers for his lack of *dignitas*. He was described by one young man who met him as "a friendly, cheerful, agreeable man," but "a queer man for a prophet of God."[30] He ran a dry-goods store in Nauvoo for a while, though he was never a successful businessman. He described himself as being of a "native cheery Temperament," and was athletically talented, being known in particular for his skill as a wrestler. Some observers were even inclined to doubt his prophethood because of his lack of solemnity, while they saw his older brother, Hyrum, a more serious and sedate man, as a better candidate for a prophet.[31] Joseph occasionally lamented how the Saints took him more seriously than he took himself. He complained that he often felt unable to speak freely and give his personal opinion, because his words would end up being garbled and then declared to be the word of God merely because they came from him.[32] Whatever one may think of the doctrines he presented to the world, there is no doubt that Joseph Smith was a remarkable man of remarkable accomplishments. According to the *New York Sun*:

> It is no small thing, in the blaze of this nineteenth century, to give to men a new revelation, found a new religion, establish new forms of worship, to build a city, with new laws, institutions, and orders of architecture, to establish ecclesiastic, civil and military jurisdiction, found colleges, send out missionaries,

---

Smith Papers. It currently consists of some two dozen volumes and is not yet completed. All the material from these volumes is available online at www.josephsmithpapers.org. In contrast to the high level of continuity with Joseph Smith found in the LDS church, one might consider the church which today calls itself the Community of Christ, but which for over a century was known as the Reorganized Church of Jesus Christ of Latter Day Saints, or RLDS. Of the many breakaway groups that sprang up following the death of Joseph, it is the only one that can still be considered as significant today in terms of membership (around a quarter of a million). Although from the beginning they rejected the doctrine of polygamy and the temple rituals such as baptism for the dead (in which church members are baptized vicariously for their deceased ancestors), they preserved many of the distinct teachings of Joseph, such as the Book of Mormon, the dual order of priesthood, and the open canon of scripture—i.e., ongoing revelation to living prophets. In recent years, however, the church has tended to deemphasize many of the doctrines from their LDS heritage, including the Book of Mormon. In turn, they have established more ecumenical ties with protestant Christianity, including adoption of the traditional notion of the Trinity, and emphasize such "soft" religious doctrines as "world peace" and ending poverty and hunger. See "Our Beliefs."

30. Bushman, *Rough Stone Rolling*, 190

31. Baugh, "Joseph Smith's Athletic Nature."

32. Givens, *Wrestling the Angel*, 19.

and make proselytes in two hemispheres: yet all this has been done by Joe Smith, and that against every sort of opposition, ridicule and persecution.[33]

Quite notably, Joseph did all this between 1828 and 1844, when he was assassinated, a total of sixteen years. But to his followers, he did much more than all that. In the words of Brigham Young, "He took heaven, figuratively speaking, and brought it down to earth; and he took the earth, brought it up, and opened up, in plainness and simplicity, the things of God."[34] Joseph introduced an entirely new way of looking at the relationship between God and man. The traditional view of Christianity was to posit a massive and uncrossable gulf between the human race and God. As we will see later on, this was not so much the view of the earliest Jews and Christians as it was the result of Christian thinkers in the second century and later, who assimilated their beliefs to the cultural ideas of the time, based in large part on Greek philosophy.

According to thinkers such as Plato and Aristotle, God was utterly absolute and self-existent, unchanging and unchangeable in nature, indeed existing entirely outside the world of change. Mankind, by contrast, belonged to a contingent state of being in a world of constant change and instability. This view profoundly shaped the thinking about God of such influential Christian thinkers as Augustine and Thomas Aquinas. Not only did they conceive of God as an utterly different kind of being from mankind, but they also greatly emphasized the sinfulness and depravity of man that had resulted from the fall of Adam. This belief in an unbridgeable gulf between man and God, between earth and heaven, was magnified by the reformers, such as Martin Luther and John Calvin, and was a fundamental attitude of the Puritan ancestors of the United States. Today it remains a basic doctrine of Reformed Christians but also, in less extreme form, of Protestants and Catholics in general.

Joseph Smith, in contrast, declared that God was literally our Father, and that we all had lived with him in a spiritual state before we were born. As our Father, he loved each of us deeply and sent us to earth to succeed, not to fail, and he had no interest in condemning mankind to hellfire. In fact, Joseph denied the traditional notion of hell altogether, and taught that even the wicked would mostly be saved in a glorious kingdom, though on a far lower level than the righteous. Although he did teach the fall of Adam, he insisted that this was a positive and necessary step in God's plan of redemption, not an unfortunate failure.

Numerous visitors who came to meet the prophet and his followers out of curiosity found themselves pleasantly surprised at their openness, civility, and lack of fanaticism. James G. Bennett, the editor of the *New York Herald*, declared that

> This Joe Smith is undoubtedly one of the greatest characters of the age. He indicates as much talent, originality, and moral courage as Mahomet…or any of the great spirits that have hitherto produced the revolutions of past ages.

33. *New York Sun*, September 1843, quoted in *HOTC* 6:30.

34. Brigham Young, *Discourses*, 458.

. . Joe Smith is creating a spiritual system, combined also with morals and industry, that may change the destiny of the race."[35]

One English traveler wrote an extensive letter to various newspapers of what he discovered:

> Joseph Smith, the Mormon Prophet, is a singular character; he lives at the 'Nauvoo Mansion House,' which is, I understand, intended to become a home for the stranger and traveler; and I think, from my own personal observation, that it will be deserving of the name. The Prophet is a kind, cheerful, sociable companion. I believe that he has the good-will of the community at large, and that he is ever ready to stand by and defend them in any extremity; and as I saw the Prophet and his brother Hyrum conversing together one day, I thought I beheld two of the greatest men of the nineteenth century. I have witnessed the Mormons in their assemblies on a Sunday, and I know not where a similar scene could be effected or produced. With respect to the teachings of the Prophet, I must say that there are some things hard to be understood; but he invariably supports himself from our good old Bible. Peace and harmony reign in the city. The drunkard is scarcely ever seen, as in other cities, neither does the awful imprecation or profane oath strike upon your ear; but, while all is storm, and tempest, and confusion abroad respecting the Mormons, all is peace and harmony at home.[36]

Perhaps the most detailed and balanced description of Joseph himself comes by way of Peter H. Burnett, an attorney who defended him at a trial in Missouri:

> Joseph Smith, Jr., was at least six feet high, well-formed and weighed about one hundred and eighty pounds. His appearance was not prepossessing, and his conversational powers were but ordinary. You could see at a glance that his education was very limited. He was an awkward but vehement speaker. In conversation he was slow, and used too many words to express his ideas, and would not generally go directly to a point. But, with all these drawbacks he was much more than an ordinary man. He possessed the most indomitable perseverance, was a good judge of men, and deemed himself born to

---

35. As found quoted in the Joseph Smith Papers; see Bennett, "Mormons." James Gordon Bennett is one of the most interesting journalists in the history of the early LDS church. He published hundreds of articles on the Latter-day Saints throughout his career, and in 1841 the city council of Nauvoo passed a resolution (at the behest of Joseph Smith) expressing "lasting gratitude" and "appreciation" to "that high-minded and honorable editor of the New York Weekly Herald, James Gordon Bennett, Esq., . . . for his very liberal and unprejudiced course towards us as a people, in giving us a fair hearing in his paper, thus enabling us to reach the ears of a portion of the community, who otherwise would ever have remained ignorant of our principles and practices." But his very first, very early piece on the "Mormonites" was not quite so complimentary, referring to Mormonism as "the latest device of roguery, ingenuity, ignorance and religious excitement combined." See Arrington, "James Gordon Bennett."

36. Longer quotations of these and many other commenters can be found in Cannon, *Joseph the Prophet*, 344–60.

command, and he did command. His views were so strange and striking, and his manner was so earnest, and apparently so candid, that you could not but be interested. There was a kind, familiar look about him, that pleased you. He was very courteous in discussion, readily admitting what he did not intend to controvert, and would not oppose you abruptly, but had due deference to your feelings. He had the capacity for discussing a subject in different aspects, and for proposing many original views, even on ordinary matters. His illustrations were his own. He had great influence over others. As evidence of this I will state that on Thursday, just before I left to return to Liberty, I saw him out among the crowd, conversing freely with every one, and seeming to be perfectly at ease. In that short space of five days he had managed so to mollify his enemies that he could go unprotected among them without the slightest danger. Among the Mormons he had much greater influence than Sidney Rigdon. The latter was a man of superior education, an eloquent speaker, of fine appearance and dignified manners; but he did not possess the native intellect of Smith, and lacked his determined will.[37]

Joseph Smith himself was fully aware how outlandish his own story was: "No man knows my history," he declared near the end of his life. "I cannot tell it: I shall never undertake it. I don't blame anyone for not believing my history. If I had not experienced what I have, I would not have believed it myself."[38] He was also aware of his own personal imperfections but separated those from his formal teachings: "I never told you I was perfect; but there is no error in the revelations I have taught."[39]

It is easy enough to dismiss the claims of Mormonism based on common sense. Angels do not appear to people, and mysterious books written on gold plates are the stuff of fantasy. As a good skeptic might say, it is one thing to keep an open mind, but not so open that our brains fall out. Surely we cannot live our lives considering every bit of nonsense as *possibly* true. Perhaps not, but there are countless examples of

37. Quoted in Allen and Leonard, *Story of the Latter-day Saints*, 132–33. For a similar but more modern retrospective of Joseph Smith, see the following statement by Stephen H. Webb (Webb was a Roman Catholic professor of religion and theology): "By any measurement, Joseph Smith was a remarkable person. His combination of organizational acumen with spiritual originality and personal decorum and modesty is rare in the history of religion. He was so steadfast in his ability to inspire men and women through times of great hardship that none of those who knew him could claim to fully understand him. He knew more about theology and philosophy than it was reasonable for anyone in his position to know, as if he were dipping into the deep, collective unconsciousness of Christianity with a very long pen. He read the Bible in ways so novel that he can be considered a theological innocent—he expanded and revised the biblical narrative without questioning its authority—yet he brusquely overturned ancient and impregnable metaphysical assumptions with the aplomb of an assistant professor. For someone so charismatic, he was exceptionally humble, even ordinary, and he delegated authority with the wisdom of a man looking far into the future for the well-being of his followers. It would be tempting to compare him to Mohammed—who also combined pragmatic political skill and a genius for religious innovation—if he were not so deeply Christian." Webb, *Jesus Christ, Eternal God*, 253.

38. *HOTC* 6:304–5.

39. *HOTC* 6:366.

"nonsense" that have turned out to be true, particularly in science. What seems absurd in one age may appear much less so in another.

In the following chapter we will make a slight detour into matters of the intellect and questions of human logic and knowledge. This discussion will be on a purely pragmatic level rather than a theoretical excursion into formal epistemology. In other words, we are not interested in such philosophical conundrums as how we are we able to know anything at all. Instead, we will examine, on a pragmatic and concise level, such questions as how much confidence (i.e., faith!) we can realistically have in the fruits of our own logical thought and the conclusions of scientists and other experts. The reader who prefers to get on with the analysis of the Latter-day Saint worldview may prefer to skip over it, but hopefully it will provide many readers with food for thought about how to think about the claims of this book (or of any other) in their own quest for a greater understanding of ultimate things.

2

Skepticism, Rationality,
and the Search for the Truth

If one regards oneself as a skeptic, it is a good plan to have occasional doubts about one's skepticism.

—Sigmund Freud[1]

Common sense is nothing more than a deposit of prejudices laid down in the mind before age eighteen.

—Albert Einstein (attributed)[2]

WHAT IS REALITY? How do we discover it? And how do we know when we have found it (or when we have not)? The skeptic may pride himself on his use of such tools as logic, evidence, and critical thinking, but how far can these actually take us? Are there limits to the utility of such methods when it comes to ferreting out ultimate truth? To what extent can we rely on the findings of science? And even if the results of scientific research were entirely reliable, how far could they actually take us in our quest for the ultimate?

Latter-day Saints do not reject science, logic, or critical thinking as valuable human endeavors, but they do acknowledge that ultimate reality—God's reality—transcends our ability to fully understand it. This does not mean that we should cast reason out the window and simply go with our intuition or wishful thinking; even less does it imply that we should simply accept the declarations of parents or ecclesiastical leaders on blind faith. It does mean, however, that we must temper our judgments about the world by an awareness of how transitory, conditional, and prone to error human knowledge is.

1. Freud, *New Introductory Lectures*, 48.

2. Calaprice, *Ultimate Quotable Einstein*, 481. This may not be a direct quotation from Einstein, but he apparently approved of the attribution. See "Common Sense."

Before proceeding to a discussion of specific Latter-day Saint doctrines in the next chapter, it may be useful to examine briefly what skepticism is—or should be. We will consider briefly such matters as the limits of logic and the scientific method in the quest to understand ultimate reality, i.e., what this life is really all about. We will also touch very briefly on various seeming absurdities in the realm of physics that are commonly accepted by scientists today as true. Most importantly, we will emphasize how limited human knowledge is. Religious skeptics have often pointed out how our planet, contrary to the traditional Christian view of the Earth as the center of all creation, is in reality but an insignificant dot on the face of the universe. Equally significant, however, is the unfortunate fact that all the magnificent, hard-won knowledge that has been accumulated by human beings over millennia is but an insignificant drop of water in the giant bucket of reality.

WHAT IS A SKEPTIC?

The term "skeptic" is often equated today with "non-believer" or even "atheist," but it was not always so. The word comes from the ancient philosophical school known as skepticism. The original meaning of the Greek verb *skeptomai* was to observe or look about oneself carefully, but later, when applied to activity of the mind, it meant to examine or consider. Thus, *skeptikos* meant thoughtful or reflective, and a "skeptic" was simply an inquirer or investigator. The term, however, came to be associated with the intellectual position of questioning or doubting all truth claims. In the post-classical era of ancient Greece, commonly referred to as the "Hellenistic age," Skeptics as a philosophical school clashed in particular with the Stoics, who had a strong set of dogmas regarding the nature of reality. Contrary to the common belief that Skeptics dogmatically denied the possibility of knowledge (which is a self-contradictory claim), they simply held that dogmatic certainty should be avoided. Later Skeptics looked back to Socrates as the original model of questioning and doubting the statements of others, but the actual founder of the tradition was Pyrrho, a contemporary of Alexander the Great. The only ancient Skeptic whose writings are well preserved is Sextus Empiricus, who lived around AD 200. Skepticism as a modern philosophy began with the rediscovery and translation of Sextus' writings, and it has an excellent pedigree with such names as Montaigne, Bayle, Hume, Condorcet, and Wittgenstein.[3]

Leaving aside the rarefied world of theoretical philosophy, what does skepticism mean in an everyday sense? Commonly speaking, a skeptic is one who prides him- or herself on the use of rational thinking, who holds science and the scientific method in high regard, and who readily rejects claims about the world that do not conform to those standards. The Skeptics Society (founded 1992) describes itself as

3. For a brief introduction to ancient Skepticism, see Philip P. Hallie's introduction in Sextus Empiricus, *Selections*. For the revival of Skepticism in early modern Europe, see Popkin, *History of Scepticism*. There is an excellent overview of the history of Skepticism by Popkin in *Britannica.com*.

a nonprofit 501(c)(3) scientific and educational organization whose mission is to engage leading experts in investigating the paranormal, fringe science, pseudoscience, and extraordinary claims of all kinds, promote critical thinking, and serve as an educational tool for those seeking a sound scientific viewpoint.[4]

In describing their intellectual approach, it is clear that the society tries hard, in all good faith, to show that they are not closed-minded against various truth claims, but declares simply that "we must see compelling evidence before we believe." That sounds extremely broad-minded, but it soon becomes clear that the only type of "compelling evidence" they will accept is testing according to the "scientific method," which "involves gathering data to formulate and test naturalistic explanations for natural phenomena." Such an approach by definition excludes from consideration not only all possibility of a transcendent reality beyond the reality of everyday existence; it also excludes any aspect of our day-to-day world which is not readily susceptible to scientific, quantitative analysis—friendship, for example. In spite of the widely held assumption that science is the only field capable of producing hard knowledge, it is still very much open to question whether strict logic, mathematics, and the scientific method are the only valid methods of discovering what is true.

THE LIMITS OF LOGIC

For those of us who are of a rationalist bent of mind, it is easy to deceive ourselves into supposing that we are strictly rational thinkers, that we base virtually all our thinking on evidence, and that we are inherently superior to those who do not. There is nothing wrong, of course, with rational thought. I believe deeply in the importance of rational thinking and do not endorse embracing irrationality in the name of religion. But we have to recognize that while logic is a powerful tool, it has strict limitations when it comes to ferreting out the absolute truth about the real world. Although our logic may be impeccable, the quality of any particular conclusion is directly related to the quality of the knowledge and assumptions with which we began. As the saying goes, garbage in, garbage out.

This is especially clear in the case of deductive reasoning. Deduction begins with certain assumptions, or premises, and moves logically step by step to a conclusion. With deductive reasoning, if your assumptions are true and your reasoning is sound, your conclusions can be accepted as true. The main limitation of deductive reasoning is that the conclusion will only be true if the assumptions are true. Consider the classic three-step syllogism:

> All men are mortal.
> Socrates is a man.

4. Skeptics Society, "Brief Introduction."

Therefore, Socrates is mortal.

Quite obviously, if either of the two premises is false, the conclusion is likewise false. Just how confident can we be in our *assumptions* that all men are mortal and that Socrates is indeed a man? And on what basis is our confidence founded?

Presumably both premises are in fact conclusions based on *inductive* logic; for example, we know from extensive experience that men are mortal—they all die. Inductive reasoning begins with specific facts (data) obtained by experience or observation and attempts to draw logical generalities from them—general principles that explain the data. If we have lived for many years and seen countless men and women, not one of whom has permanently avoided death, it seems perfectly reasonable to conclude that all humans are mortal. One problem with induction, however, is that it only takes one exception to prove the statement false. Consider a second syllogism:

All swans are white.
Your pet bird is a swan.
Therefore, your pet bird is white.

The reasoning is sound, because it is true that *if* all swans are white and *if* the bird in question is indeed a swan, it follows absolutely that the bird is white. Yet here the first premise (assumption) is patently false, and therefore the conclusion cannot be said to be proven. The statement that "all swans are white" might well seem true to many people who *think* (based on their experience—i.e., inductively) that they know a great deal about swans and have never encountered a non-white swan. Yet a complete survey of all swans (particularly in Australia!) will eventually lead to the conclusion that the statement is false. Only one black swan is necessary to falsify our premise and demolish the soundness of our conclusion. Of course, pragmatically, even if we know of the existence of black swans, it is still easy to conclude that your pet swan has a high *probability* of being white, because it is true that a huge majority of swans in the world are white. But such a conclusion takes us outside the realm of strict logic.

There is also a second serious problem with inductive logic. Even if our facts and data are precisely correct, the second step requires that we attempt to *interpret* the data we have collected. Interpretation means that we must infer generalities that make sense of the data. This approach, of course, is at the heart of the scientific method. Yet the quality of our interpretive conclusions, once again, depends on the nature and quality of our prior knowledge and assumptions. We interpret specific evidence by placing it in one or more intellectual *contexts*. But if the contextual environment we use to interpret the evidence is imperfect, our conclusions about the meaning of the evidence may well be skewed, or just plain wrong.

Consider the following real-world example. In 2007–2008, countless real estate investors were financially devastated when the bottom dropped out of the real estate market. It was common wisdom at the time that housing prices generally would never decline. Real estate had never declined significantly since the Great Depression, and it seemed intuitively true that, since the supply of land and property is limited while the population continues to grow, prices naturally face upward pressure. This assumption was supported by statements from experts like Alan Greenspan, the long-time chairman of the Federal Reserve and one of the most respected economic thinkers in the U.S. David Lereah, the chief economist of the National Association of Realtors, even published a book entitled *Why the Real Estate Boom Will Not Bust—and How You Can Profit from It* (2007). As a result, the practice of "flipping" houses became widespread, particularly in the booming real estate markets of places like Las Vegas, Phoenix, and Florida, and millions of people took on mortgages to purchase houses they could not afford.

This behavior was, at least in great part, quite rational. It was based on common sense, substantial evidence, and the authority of experts. Yet it was also based on a faulty assumption: that prices would continue to rise indefinitely. Most people, even those who try to be rational and sensible, do not have time to do massive economic research, and hardly anybody at the time (even the best experts) had pieced together the disparate pieces of evidence to realize that a financial house of cards was being constructed through the simultaneous abuse of real estate, irresponsible lending practices, and the widespread investment in risky securities.[5] We naturally rely on common sense and the opinions of experts. But if our assumptions are faulty, no amount of "evidence" will save us from disaster.

Often the "evidence" that is necessary to make decisions in life is far from adequate if you want to make decisions based purely on reason. Think about the wide range of decisions we must make on a daily basis. What do you do when you want to make a purchase, be it a nice dinner or an automobile? You try to collect the available "evidence" and make a reasoned decision. You may study and make a comparison of various eateries or vehicles, with close attention to online reviews, and at the least attempt to avoid making a complete blunder. But we all know that reviews are notoriously inconsistent. What do you do when you want to buy a new cell phone and half the reviewers say it's the greatest phone they've ever owned and the other half say it's the worst? Ideally you could try out each phone for several days to see which one is superior, but for most of us that option is not available. At some point you have to throw up your hands and go with your instinct.

The narrow limits to our knowledge means that bigger decisions are even more difficult to resolve based purely on evidence and reason. When President Barack Obama in 2011 decided to proceed with the attack on Osama bin Laden's supposed residence in Abottabad, Pakistan, he did not have anywhere near as much information as he would have needed in order to make a purely rational decision, including the key information of whether bin Laden was inside the building—or, indeed, whether he had *ever* been there. Obama gathered as much intelligence from his team

---

5. Of course, Michael Lewis notoriously pointed out the stories of several individuals who assembled many of the pieces and successfully predicted the coming disaster in his *The Big Short*.

as he possibly could and then had to make a decision based in large part on pure intuition—gut feeling.

If it is virtually impossible to acquire enough knowledge to purchase a cell phone on a strictly rational basis, how much of a chance is there that we will ever be able to know for sure whether God exists or whether there is a life after death? We can never know enough to prove the great questions, one way or the other. If we wait for absolute, infallible proof, we will never decide—we will be agnostics our whole lives. Perhaps you may think that that is the best approach. But again, if we did that in all aspects of our lives, we would be completely passive. We would never get married without assurance that our intended was the perfect person for us. We would never have children. We would never take a job without complete assurance that it was the ideal job. We would never even go on a trip—or leave the house! And if we never make a serious attempt to seek out God, we will surely never find him.[6]

THE VASTNESS OF HUMAN IGNORANCE

My favorite parable is the story of the blind men and the elephant. There are numerous versions found in India, China, and throughout the world. The following is one rendition:

> Once upon a time there were six blind men who lived in a village in India. Every day they went to the road nearby begging. They had often heard of elephants, but they had never seen one for the very obvious reason.
>
> One morning, an elephant was led down the road where they stood. When they heard that an elephant was passing by, they asked the elephant

---

6. The famous science popularizer Carl Sagan, when once asked in an interview whether extraterrestrial life existed, refused to commit himself, and when the interviewer asked him for his "gut feeling," responded: "I try not to think with my gut. Really, it's okay to reserve judgment until the evidence is in." Richard Dawkins, in *God Delusion*, 47, quotes this as a healthy example of agnosticism. I am sympathetic toward this view; but again, the problem is that if we truly wait for conclusive proof regarding all the pressing questions in life, we will be forever frozen into inaction. Philosophers sometimes refer to a third type of reasoning known as "abductive." When Sherlock Holmes, for example, in the story "The Red-Headed League," claims to *deduce* that a certain gentleman is a Mason, because he is wearing an "arc-and-compass breastpin," he is actually using abduction rather than deduction, which can be described as "reasoning to the best explanation." Deductive reasoning would have required him to be using as one premise that *all* people who wear an arc-and-compass pin are Masons. While this assumption is not *necessarily* true, it certainly is logical to conclude that the overwhelming majority of such wearers are. Therefore it is a very reasonable conclusion—the "best explanation"—that a man wearing such a pin is indeed a Mason. For a good brief explanation of all three types of reasoning, see Pojman, *Philosophy*, 30–36. Pojman notes that while abductive reasoning is generally neglected by philosophers, it is really a very common type of reasoning. For example, if you happen to believe in God, or in evolutionary theory, or in many other things, your reasoning is most likely abductive—i.e., your belief is based on what seems to you to be the best explanation among all the competing explanations of the evidence known to you. For an in-depth discussion of the role of evidence with respect to religion, see Welch, "Role of Evidence."

driver to stop the beast for a while so that they could take a "look" by feeling it. The favor was granted to them. So they approached the elephant to touch it.

The first blind man happened to place his hand on the elephant's side. "Well," he said, "This elephant is just like a wall." The second blind man happened to touch one of the elephant's tusks. "No. I think you're quite mistaken," he said to the first man. "The elephant is round and smooth and a little sharp on the top. He's more like a spear than a wall."

The third happened to take hold of the elephant's trunk. "You both are completely wrong," he said. "This elephant is obviously like a snake." The fourth opened both his arms then closed them around one of the elephant's legs. "Oh, how blind you are!" he cried. "It's very clear that he's round and tall like a tree."

The fifth was very tall and he caught one of the elephant's ears. "Even the blindest person must see that this elephant isn't like any of the things you mentioned." he said. "He's exactly like a huge fan." The sixth man went forward to feel the elephant. He got hold of the beast's tail and said: "Oh, how silly you all are! The elephant isn't like a wall, or a spear, or a snake, or a tree; neither is it like a fan. Any man with eyes in his head can see that he's exactly like a rope."

Then the driver and the elephant moved on, and the six men sat by the roadside all day, quarrelling about the elephant. They could not agree with one another, because each believed that he knew just what the beast looked like.

The moral here is the importance of intellectual modesty. It is all too common for men and women to assume that their narrow perspective of the world is entirely, or at least mostly, correct. How often do you read a book or hear a speaker acknowledge that his ideas might indeed be wrong, or that they will likely become outdated by future discoveries, or that a specialist from another field might be able to prove his ideas wrong?

If the elephant is taken to stand for the sum total of all knowledge in the cosmos, it quickly becomes obvious that no one, not even the most intelligent person on the face of the earth, has more than a thimbleful of knowledge. Experts may know a considerable amount about one particular piece of the elephant, yet know virtually nothing about the balance. As the saying goes, specialists are those who know more and more about less and less. Yet even within their own specialty, how much do they really know with complete certainty? One of the great virtues of doing post-graduate study is that one discovers just how much even the experts in one's field disagree with each other, even over the most basic matters. And with regard to matters outside their field, their knowledge is likely to be very limited. The most accomplished physicist in the world may be fairly well read, for example, in philosophy or literature, but compared to experts in the field he or she would be strictly an amateur. And then how much would she know of psychology, sociology, history, music, engineering, politics, finance, biology, statistics, economics, etc.? Indeed, she would be, strictly speaking, an expert only in her *sub*specialty. If she is a particle physicist, how much would she know of astrophysics or geophysics or biophysics? There are now hundreds of different specialties in science alone, each with its own journals, conferences, and professional societies.[7] And again, even within an expert's own specialty, how much is there that is still quite unknown or not well understood?

We are all strictly limited in how much of the world we can come to understand in any depth, no matter how intelligent we may be, no matter how retentive our memory. So what do we do? Typically, we *extrapolate* from our limited knowledge to try to make up for our ignorance. That is, we make the common assumption that in light of our knowledge of *part* of reality, the rest of it must be pretty much the same. If we have seen hundreds of swans and they have all been white, it is a reasonable extrapolation that all swans are white. If we have conducted research on real estate prices and seen that prices have not suffered a general decline in over seventy-five years, it seems reasonable to suppose that they will continue to rise (or at least remain stable) for the foreseeable future.

This approach seems to serve generally well in everyday life—meaning life when it is free from the unexpected. But there are dangers in assuming that the unexpected will never happen, as Nassim Taleb pointed out in his surprise bestseller, *The Black Swan*. A turkey, he noted, may live for a thousand days in the firm conviction—supported by copious evidence—that the purpose of life is for him to be generously fed by humans, only to discover on the day before Thanksgiving that he was grossly mistaken! All of us, on a daily basis, make judgments based on our assumptions and presuppositions rather than on firm knowledge. We do this partly because we are lazy, and partly because we have no choice. There is far too much information for any one person to even become *acquainted* with it all, let alone master it.

Just how vast is our ignorance? We need only look at the immense revolutions in science in the last hundred years or so to get an inkling of how little the human race as a whole knows, particularly in contrast to how much we think we know. Men of every historical age have assumed that their own thinking was modern, true, and more or less complete. Yet history teaches that revolutions in knowledge are a constant. Lord Kelvin notoriously stated in 1900 that there was "nothing new to be discovered in physics now. All that remains is more and more precise measurement."[8] Yet that was only a handful of years before Einstein's discoveries regarding relativity, not to mention the later discoveries of quantum mechanics, the big bang, dark matter, dark energy, the Higgs boson, and many other stunning finds, each of which completely revolutionized our understanding of the world in which we live.

Just think: the germ theory of disease was not widely understood or accepted until the late nineteenth century—a little over a century ago! As recently as the 1860s the

---

7. Sheldrake, *Science Set Free*, 322.

8. This quotation may be apocryphal. But the same sentiment about the state of science (not limited to physics) was expressed by others. See Sheldrake, *Science Set Free*, 19.

most widely accepted cause of contagious diseases was *miasma*—a noxious form of air associated with decaying animal remains, rotting vegetation, and stagnant water.[9] And as late as the 1920s some scientists were still skeptical of the existence of atoms. "What couldn't be seen or measured directly in the laboratory, they scoffed, didn't exist."[10]

Are there still profound areas of ignorance akin to the biological basis of disease? Of course. We have come far in the last 150 years, but not all that far in the grand scheme of things. Einstein once said that "all our science, measured against reality, is primitive and childlike—and yet it is the most precious thing we have."[11] Precious indeed—can any of us today imagine what it would have been like to live without antibiotics or to undergo surgery without anesthesia? But despite all our technical and theoretical advances, our overall understanding of things is still perhaps more on the level of children than of adults.

Medicine, for all its progress since the discoveries of Pasteur, is still as much art as science. The medical community "knew" for decades that stomach ulcers were caused by excess stomach acid or by stress, yet in the 1980s it was discovered that their primary cause was an unknown bacterium and that they could be cured with antibiotics. And there are still numerous common diseases of which the cause is unknown: diabetes, rheumatoid arthritis, multiple sclerosis, Parkinson's disease, and schizophrenia.[12] How about cancer? Survival rates for certain cancers have increased considerably, yet no cancer patient can ever properly talk about being completely *cured*. We have made great strides in understanding the brain, yet scientists have no clue about what basic human consciousness is or where it comes from.[13] And of course we have all felt the frustration from the constant variations and reversals in the accepted wisdom regarding good nutrition: in 2014, after fifty years of having fats in our diet vilified, we suddenly learned that the anti-fat campaign was ill thought out and based on superficial evidence; moreover, there is significant evidence showing that even saturated fats are an important part of a good diet.[14] John Ioannidis, a specialist in health research at the Stanford School of Medicine, has calculated that roughly two out of three studies published in the most respected peer-reviewed medical journals are either fully refuted or found to be considerably exaggerated by additional studies within a few years—sometimes within a few months.[15]

9. Porter, *Greatest Benefit*.

10. Kaku, *Hyperspace*, 111.

11. Calaprice, *Ultimate Quotable Einstein*, 404.

12. Sheldrake, *Science Set Free*, 265.

13. Noë, *Out of Our Heads*, xi.

14. Teicholz, *Big Fat Surprise*.

15. Ioannidis's original paper was published in 2005 in PLOS Medicine: "Why Most Published Research Findings Are False." His findings were summarized in Freedman, "Lies, Damned Lies." Freedman has also published a book on the fallibility of experts of all types, including scientists: *Wrong: Why Experts Keep Failing Us*.

Our knowledge of the cosmos in the last century has expanded astronomically (pun fully intended!), but our ignorance has exploded even more dramatically. Consider the following observation from Timothy Ferris:

> We might eventually obtain some sort of bedrock understanding of cosmic structure, but we will never understand the universe in detail; it is just too big and varied for that. If we possessed an atlas of our galaxy that devoted but a single page to each star system in the Milky Way (so that the sun and all its planets were crammed in one page), that atlas would run to more than ten million volumes of ten thousand pages each. It would take a library the size of Harvard's to house the atlas, and merely to flip through it, at the rate of a page per second, would require over ten thousand years. Add the details of planetary cartography, potential extraterrestrial biology, the subtleties of the scientific principles involved, and the historical dimensions of change, and it becomes clear that we are never going to learn more than a tiny fraction of the story of our galaxy alone—and there are a hundred billion more galaxies. As the physician Lewis Thomas writes, "The greatest of all the accomplishments of twentieth-century science has been the discovery of human ignorance."[16]

Freeman Dyson, a leading theoretical physicist who died in 2020, echoed this sentiment, observing that

> science is not a collection of truths. It is a continuing exploration of mysteries. Wherever we go exploring in the world around us, we find mysteries. Our planet is covered by continents and oceans whose origin we cannot explain. Our atmosphere is constantly stirred by poorly understood disturbances that we call weather and climate. The visible matter in the universe is outweighed by a much larger quantity of dark invisible matter that we do not understand at all. The origin of life is a total mystery, and so is the existence of human consciousness. We have no clear idea how the electrical discharges occurring in nerve cells in our brains are connected with our feelings and desires and actions.[17]

Science and its sibling field, technology, have certainly come a long way since the nineteenth century. But how much closer are we to really understanding what makes the universe tick? I think most scientists would concede that their research has raised as least as many new questions as it has answered old ones. Dartmouth physics professor Marcelo Gleiser uses the metaphor of an island to represent our knowledge: as our knowledge (the island) increases in size, the shore or coastline of the island (our ignorance) also grows.[18] According to Robert Lanza, the classic approach to science can tell us a great deal about the "properties and processes *within*

16. Ferris, *Coming of Age*, 383.
17. Dyson, "How We Know," 10.
18. Gleiser, *Island of Knowledge*, xxii.

the cosmos," for example, "how to form metals into bridges, how to build an airplane, how to perform reconstructive surgery." It is effective at providing knowledge dealing with "classifications and subclassifications of all manner of objects, living and non-living, and categorization of their properties, such as the ductility and strength of steel versus copper, and how processes work, such as how stars are born and how viruses replicate." It is much less capable, however, of answering the grander, more basic questions about the nature of fundamental reality:

> How did the Big Bang happen? Unknown. What was the Big Bang? Unknown. What, if anything, existed before the Big Bang? Unknown. What is the nature of dark energy, the dominant entity of the cosmos? Unknown. What is the nature of dark matter, the second most prevalent energy? Unknown. How did life arise? Unknown. How did consciousness arise? Unknown. What is the nature of consciousness? Unknown. What is the fate of the universe; for example, will it keep expanding? Seemingly yes. Why are the constants the way they are? Unknown. Why are there exactly four forces? Unknown. Is life further experienced after one's body dies? Unknown.[19]

THERE ARE MORE THINGS IN HEAVEN AND EARTH, HORATIO . . .

Michio Kaku, an eminent theoretical physicist, relates that as a child he was fascinated by the fish in the pond at the Japanese Tea Garden in San Francisco, and would ask himself some "childish" questions, such as: How did the fish perceive the world around them? What awareness did they have of the greater world outside their pond (i.e., the human world)? When a rainstorm caused the lilies on the pond to move around, how would they explain such an event with no visible cause? And yet the fishes' world and the human world were separated only by inches—and by the surface of the pond. He continues:

> I often think that we are like the carp swimming contentedly in that pond. We live out our lives in our own "pond," confident that our universe consists only of those things we can see or touch. Like the carp, our universe consists only of the familiar and the visible. We smugly refuse to admit that parallel universes or dimensions can exist next to ours, just beyond our grasp. If our scientists invent concepts like forces [e.g., the gravitational and electromagnetic forces], it is only because they cannot visualize the inevitable vibrations that fill the empty space around us. Some scientists sneer at the mention of

---

19. Lanza and Berman, *Biocentrism*, 155–57. Karl Popper also recognized that science alone was not able to solve the "ultimate questions": "It is important to realize that science does not make assertions about ultimate questions—about the riddles of existence, or about man's task in this world" (Popper, "Natural Selection," 141). Of course, individual scientists *do* make such assertions, but their statements fall at least partially under the heading of philosophy, not pure science.

higher dimensions because they cannot be conveniently measured in the laboratory.[20]

He took these same concerns with him to Harvard University, but when he approached his professors with such questions . . .

> I still remember solving a problem in electrodynamics for my instructor, and then asking him what the solution might look like if space were curved in a higher dimension. He looked at me in a strange way, as if I were a bit cracked. Like others before me, I soon learned to put aside my earlier, childish notions about higher-dimensional space. Hyperspace, I was told, was not a suitable subject of serious study.

Later on, as a graduate student, he encountered such groundbreaking theories as *superstring theory*, which "postulates that all matter consists of tiny vibrating strings" and "predicts a precise number of dimensions for space and time: ten." In the last half-century, the notion of higher-dimensional space (that is, more than the traditional three dimensions) has become widely accepted by the scientific community (though there are some who point out that the theories are virtually untestable) and is no longer considered "the last refuge for mystics, cranks, and charlatans."[21] And hyperspace is hardly the only outlandish theory that reputable scientists now take seriously. Consider the following small sampling.[22]

20. Kaku, *Hyperspace*, 3–5.

21. Kaku, *Hyperspace*, 23.

22. I should note here that I make no pretense of being even an amateur scientist. But I am fascinated by the slew of physics books for non-scientists that is flooding the market, each one attempting the remarkable feat of explaining the modern revolutions in physics to the mathematically challenged. In addition, numerous books by skilled scientists have explored parallels and possible connections between the "new physics" and various religious beliefs and traditions. Francis S. Collins, the former director of the National Institutes of Health and former leader of the Human Genome Project, and Karl Giberson, a former professor of physics at Eastern Nazarene College, are evangelical Christians who wrote *The Language of Science and Faith*. They endorse a traditional doctrinal view of Christianity but also insist that Christianity is not at odds with science, including evolution. Paul Davies, a theoretical physicist at Arizona State University, suggests in *The Mind of God* that the best evidence for God is in the deep logical structures that underlie the universe. Howard Smith, an astrophysicist at the Harvard-Smithsonian Center for Astrophysics, finds parallels between modern ideas of cosmology and the traditional texts of the Kabbalah, in *Let There Be Light: Modern Cosmology and Kabbalah*, while *The Quantum and the Lotus* by Matthieu Ricard and Trinh Xuan Thuan is an intriguing dialogue between a Buddhist monk trained as a molecular biologist and an acclaimed astrophysicist who was raised in a Buddhist home. John Polkinghorne, an eminent physicist who played a significant role in the discovery of the quark and later became an Anglican priest, says that he believes in the existence of the quark despite the fact that no one has ever seen one, "because quarks make sense of a lot of direct physical experience." By the same token, he is able to believe in an unseen God, because his existence "makes sense of many aspects of our knowledge and experience [including] the order and fruitfulness of the physical world, the multilayered character of reality, [and] the almost universal human experiences of worship and hope." See his *Quarks, Chaos and Christianity*, 116–18, and also his *Quantum Physics and Theology*, where he outlines a number of comparisons between quantum physics and the traditional Christian understanding of the nature of God. The literature on the subject of "Science and

a) Superstring theory

In physics, Einstein's theory of relativity, which describes the macroworld of cosmic distances, and quantum mechanics, which describes the micro- or subatomic world, appear to conflict in certain ways with each other. The leading contender in the attempt to fuse these two areas of physics is superstring theory, which proposes that the fundamental building blocks of all matter are not atoms made up of little "balls" of protons, neutrons, and electrons, but little loops of strings that vibrate at various frequencies. As we have already noted, superstring theory predicts that there are a total of ten dimensions (or eleven in the case of the related M-theory) rather than just four (three spatial dimensions plus time).

b) Dark matter and dark energy

One of the most surprising discoveries of current physics is that *matter* as we all know it makes up only 4 percent of the universe. Dark matter—that is, matter that is completely invisible and intangible—together with the even stranger dark energy, makes up the remaining 96 percent—96 percent!—of the cosmos. As you might imagine with regard to something that cannot be directly observed or detected in any way, scientists really have no idea what dark matter and dark energy are. But they are quite certain that they exist. Otherwise, it would mean that our best understanding of the nature of the physical universe is entirely wrong.

c) Quantum mechanics

As remarkable as is the existence of dark matter and dark energy, nothing surpasses "quantum weirdness" for utter strangeness. Discovered as long ago as the 1930s, the theory of quantum mechanics asserts that matter at the atomic and subatomic levels behaves in very unexpected ways. In the first place, reality at the quantum level does not conform to the principles of *regularity* and *predictability*, which are supposedly the hallmarks of all physical science. Subatomic particles simply do not behave as they should according to the normal physical principles of everyday life. According to Heisenberg's famous *uncertainty principle*, it is impossible to simultaneously know, or predict, the velocity *and* the position of a subatomic particle. We are limited to calculating probabilities only, not because our instruments of measure are imprecise, but because the behavior of particles is *inherently unpredictable*. Brian Greene summarizes the principle as follows:

> Most physicists agree that probability is deeply woven into the fabric of quantum reality. Whereas human intuition, and its embodiment in classical

Religion" is voluminous.

physics, envision a reality in which things are always definitely one way *or* another, quantum mechanics describes a reality in which things sometimes hover in a haze of being partly one way *and* partly another. Things become definite only when a suitable observation forces them to relinquish quantum possibilities and settle on a specific outcome. The outcome that's realized, though, cannot be predicted—we can predict only the odds that things will turn out one way or another.[23]

However, the strangeness of that principle is outstripped by the quantum principle of *nonlocality*. Brian Greene again:

> [Einstein was] the first to point out that quantum mechanics—if taken at face value—implies that something you do over here can be *instantaneously* linked to something happening over there, regardless of distance. . . Normally, spatial separation implies physical independence. If you want to control what's happening on the other side of a football field, you have to go there, or, at the very least, you have to send someone or something . . . across the field to convey your influence. . . Quantum mechanics challenges this view by revealing, at least in certain circumstances, a capacity to transcend space; long-range quantum connections can bypass spatial separation. Two objects can be far apart in space, but as far as quantum mechanics is concerned, it's as if they were a single entity.[24]

Einstein famously refused to accept the implications of quantum theory, calling the principle of nonlocality "spooky action-at-a-distance" and remarking with respect to the uncertainty principle that "God does not play dice with the universe." Nonetheless, these principles have been confirmed countless times in the laboratory. If you find these concepts hard to conceive of, you can take comfort in the fact that every physicist agrees with you, including Richard Feynman, who declared, "I think I can safely say that nobody understands quantum mechanics. . . Do not keep saying to yourself . . . 'But how can it be like that?' because you will get 'down the drain', into a blind alley from which nobody has escaped. Nobody knows how it can be like that."[25]

d) The multiverse

Scientists have realized since the late 1960s that there are several dozen physical constants in the universe that are exactly right for the existence of life.[26] For example, if the big bang had been more powerful by merely one part in a million, the speed of

---

23. Greene, *Fabric of the Cosmos*, 11.

24. Greene, *Fabric of the Cosmos*, 11–12.

25. Feynman, *Character of Physical Law*, 129.

26. A list of these values can be found in Lanza, *Biocentrism*, 85–86. The most thorough discussion of this principle is by Leslie, *Universes*.

expansion would have been too great to allow for the formation of heavenly bodies. Similarly, the ratio between the electromagnetic force and the so-called strong force (which holds atomic nuclei together) could not differ from its actual value by more than one part in 10^{16} (i.e., ten with sixteen zeroes after it). If any of these quantities had deviated by just a tiny fraction of their actual values, the existence of atoms, planets, water, and life would have been impossible. It thus *appears* that the cosmos has been created just right for life (hence it is sometimes called the "Goldilocks principle"). The eminent physicist Freeman Dyson has written, "it almost seems as if the universe must in some sense have known we were coming."[27]

Many scientists, not surprisingly, resist the conclusion that there is any force or intelligence outside nature—deity, for example—that programmed the universe for our benefit. One theory that has been proposed to avoid the conclusion that the universe was actually designed for the introduction of life (or that, contrary to all probability, it just happened to be that way!) is that there is a grand infinitude of universes—a multiverse—each of which has a different set of constants. Thus, the fact that the universe we live in seems designed for life is pure coincidence—or rather, it is the only one of countless extant universes which happens to have the proper means to support life, and for that very reason we are here and not in some other universe where those constants are different.[28]

The point of this brief discussion of science, however, is neither to claim that any of these theories are necessarily final descriptions of ultimate reality nor to suggest that they lend direct support to the doctrines of Latter-day Saint theology. My only purpose is to show that, indeed, truth is often stranger than fiction, and we need to keep an open mind about the nature of truth and reality. Or as Hamlet averred, "There are more things in heaven and earth, Horatio, than are dreamt of in your philosophy."[29] Reputable scientists are seriously considering theories about the nature of reality that only a few decades ago would have been laughed out of the academy. It seems to me that compared to such implausible notions as hyperspace and quantum weirdness, the claim of angelic visitations seems positively tame. The Mormon view of reality, while

27. Quoted in Lennox, *God's Undertaker*, 59. Even Fred Hoyle, who most of his life was an atheist, was severely shaken in his confidence in his atheistic views by his discovery of one of these constants. He said that it clearly seemed as though "a superintellect has monkeyed with physics as well as with chemistry and biology." Quoted in Lennox, *God's Undertaker*, 70.

28. Another response to the theistic view of the anthropic principle is to argue that because we are here in the universe, all these values must be what they are—otherwise, we would not be here to observe it. John Leslie has countered with the analogy of a firing squad: "A man in front of a firing squad of one hundred riflemen is going to be pretty surprised if every bullet misses him. Sure he could say to himself, 'Of course they all missed; that makes perfect sense, otherwise I wouldn't be here to wonder why they all missed.' But anyone in his or her right mind is going to want to know how such an unlikely event occurred." Quoted in Lennox, *God's Undertaker*, 91. See also Leslie, *Universes*, 13–14. Incidentally, Latter-day Saints are quite open to the theory of multiple universes—that is, multiple universes created by deity, with many planets in existence. They reject the classical Christian doctrine that our earth is the sole special creation of God.

29. *Hamlet*, act 1, scene 4.

it may have seemed absurd, as Dickens contended, in an era of railways, is hardly out of place in an era of hyperdimensionality, superstrings, and dark matter![30]

SCIENCE AS DOGMA

Let me emphasize again that none of this discussion of the limitations of logic and science is intended to suggest that we should give up on science and rationality, throw up our hands, and mindlessly accept religion based purely on the authority of others. Nor should we conclude that, based on humankind's immense ignorance, we should suppose that all truth claims, no matter how preposterous, are equally valid. Science and reason have a very important role in our lives, and it would be wrong to devalue them. At the same time, it is equally wrong to *over*value them.

The renowned philosopher of science Karl Popper noted the limits of science and the scientific method: "I am on the side of science and rationality, but I am against those exaggerated claims for science that have sometimes been, rightly, denounced as 'scientism.'"[31] Scientism has been described as "the exaggerated confidence in the methods of science as the most (or the only) reliable tools of inquiry, and an equally unfounded belief that at least the most well established of its findings are the only objective truths there are."[32] This exaggerated confidence is surprisingly widespread in the modern world, but it is coming under increasing criticism by philosophers of science and even scientists themselves.[33]

Alfred North Whitehead had this to say about such dogmatic skepticism:

> The Universe is vast. Nothing is more curious than the self-satisfied dogmatism with which mankind at each period of its history cherishes the delusion of the finality of its existing modes of knowledge. Skeptics and believers are all alike. *At this moment scientists and skeptics are the leading dogmatists.* Advance in detail is admitted; fundamental novelty is barred. This dogmatic certainty is the death of philosophic adventure. The Universe is vast.[34]

Michael Polanyi has echoed this sentiment:

> In the days when an idea could be silenced by showing that it was contrary to religion, theology was the greatest single source of fallacies. Today, when any human thought can be discredited by branding it as unscientific, the power

---

30. Or, as J. B. S. Haldane said, "'[Nature is] not only queerer than we suppose, it is queerer than we can suppose." Quoted in Kaku, *Hyperspace*, 252.

31. Popper, "Natural Selection," 141.

32. Rosenberg, *Atheist's Guide to Reality*, 6

33. See, for example, Sorell, *Scientism*; Williams and Robinson, *Scientism*; Boudry and Pigliucci, *Science Unlimited?*

34. Quoted in Price, *Dialogues of Alfred North Whitehead*, 5.

previously exercised by theology has passed over to science; hence science has become in its turn the greatest single source of error.[35]

And when it comes to the inability of science to address—let alone resolve!—the truly profound questions of reality, the eminent quantum physicist Erwin Schrödinger put it most bluntly:

> The scientific picture of the real world around me is very deficient. It gives a lot of factual information, puts all our experience in a magnificently consistent order, but it is ghastly silent about all and sundry that is really near to our heart, that really matters to us. It cannot tell us a word about red and blue, bitter and sweet, physical pain and physical delight; it knows nothing of beautiful and ugly, good or bad, God and eternity. Science sometimes pretends to answer questions in these domains, but the answers are very often so silly that we are not inclined to take them seriously.[36]

Skepticism is a highly useful tool to help us avoid being deceived—and heaven knows how much deception is in the world today, from economic frauds to sheer nonsense, whether about politics, religion, or the latest commercial product. But it should not become so ingrained a habit in us that we come to insist that there is *no* truth to be found anywhere. In other words, we should indeed question everything, *including our own questioning.* Skepticism should not be a goal in itself. We should be skeptical *even about our own skepticism.* As Sigmund Freud once declared, "If one regards oneself as a skeptic, it is a good plan to have occasional doubts about one's skepticism."[37]

Many people justify their absolute skepticism toward religion on the basis of history. There has been so much corruption and hypocrisy in religions for thousands of years, they argue, that it seems all but certain that no religion is valid. This attitude may seem reasonable, but it is akin to the investor who examines the history of corruption in the financial markets and concludes that making any type of investment is merely throwing one's money down the drain. Investors in such fraudulent companies as Tyco, WorldCom, and Enron lost billions, as did the victims of Bernie Madoff's massive Ponzi scheme. Even those who made intelligent and judicious investments in the 2000s suffered massive losses from the near collapse of the world economy

---

35. Polanyi, "Scientific Outlook," 480–84. On the dogmatic nature of modern science, see further, Sheldrake, *Science Set Free*; Mary Midgley, *Science as Salvation.*

36. See Wilber, *Quantum Questions*, 81. Elsewhere Schrödinger stated that "No personal god can form part of a world-model that has only become accessible at the cost of removing everything personal from it." Quoted in Wilber, *Quantum Questions*, 89. In other words, the scientific method, developed over many centuries, focuses single-mindedly on the physical world and excludes—or rather, *attempts* to exclude—all subjectivity from its parameters, so as to focus on specific aspects of the world. Subjectivity—one's personal experiences and feelings, including such things as love, hate, duty, obligation, and friendship—has no significance in the physics or chemistry lab. This does not mean that such aspects of our lives don't exist, simply because science has chosen to ignore them in order to focus strictly on the material, objective aspects of the universe.

37. Freud, *New Introductory Lectures*, 48.

in 2008, which was in large part engendered by the greed of bankers and financiers generally.

But is it truly reasonable to conclude that all investment is counterproductive, that one should place one's wealth under the mattress and be done? Or that one should actively preach against investment—to dissuade one's friends and relatives from putting their money into banks and funds? Surely most people would say no. Despite the spectacular fall of certain companies through their own hubris and greed, there are plenty of companies that are at least *reasonably* honest. If one uses due diligence and care, there is still money to be made in the public markets, and to forego such investments is foolish and pigheaded. (Apologies to my mother, who grew up during the Great Depression and was dogmatically opposed to investing in stocks.) Skepticism should prompt one to use caution rather than dissuade one from participating at all.

MORMONS ON RATIONALITY AND EDUCATION

Though it may come as a surprise to some, Latter-day Saints in fact tend to pride themselves on believing in a *rational theology*. Mormons believe that the acquisition of knowledge is a divine mandate, and view their religion as the foundation of all true knowledge, whether spiritual or secular. A well-known maxim from LDS scripture is "The glory of God is intelligence," while Joseph Smith further asserted that "it is impossible for a man to be saved in ignorance" and that "a man is saved no faster than he obtains knowledge."[38] Knowledge in this context is not limited to religious knowledge but includes what might be called "secular" knowledge. For Mormons, knowledge equates with "light and truth," and truth with "knowledge of things as they are, and as they were, and as they are to come"—in other words, total knowledge.[39]

John A. Widtsoe, a former apostle of the LDS church with a PhD in biochemistry from the University of Göttingen, who prior to his apostleship worked as a professor of chemistry and agriculture and as president of the University of Utah, even published a book entitled *A Rational Theology as Taught by the Church of Jesus Christ of Latter-day Saints* (1915). Widtsoe's stated purpose was to show that Mormon theology presented "a philosophy of life which, because of its *complete harmony with all knowledge*, should be the one to which all men might safely give adherence." He did not mean that Mormonism perfectly coincided with all current knowledge in all intellectual fields, but rather that it was coherent, self-consistent, and consistent with all "true knowledge."[40] One could therefore expect that as secular knowledge developed, it would come more and more to support the foundations of the restored gospel.

38. D&C 93:36; 131:6; *HOTC* 4:588.

39. D&C 93:24.

40. He states that the LDS understanding of the gospel, "a rational theology, is founded on truth, on all truth, for 'truth is knowledge of things as they are, and as they were, and as they are to come,' and 'truth has no end.' In building a philosophy of life, a man, therefore, cannot say that some truth

Mormons embrace secular education. Latter-day Saints have been shown to have higher levels of education than the general public, and to a considerable extent they actually view education and learning as a form of worship.[41] Several passages in the Doctrine and Covenants exhort the disciple to seek out broad learning:

> . . . that you may be instructed more perfectly in theory, in principle, in doctrine, in the law of the gospel, in all things that pertain unto the kingdom of God, that are expedient for you to understand; of things both in heaven and in earth, and under the earth; things which have been, things which are, things which must shortly come to pass; things which are at home, things which are abroad; the wars and the perplexities of the nations, and the judgments which are on the land; and a knowledge also of countries and of kingdoms. . .
> And as all have not faith, seek ye diligently and teach one another words of wisdom; yea, seek ye out of the best books words of wisdom; seek learning even by study and also by faith.[42]

Note that there is no appreciable separation between secular and religious knowledge. Both are sacred. This is because, according to Brigham Young, "Every discovery in science and art, that is really true and useful to mankind, has been given by direct revelation from God, though but few acknowledge it."[43] As a result, Latter-day Saints are less likely than others to see a fundamental conflict between what they

---

must be considered and other truth rejected. Only on the basis of all truth, that is, all true knowledge, can his religion be built." However, he contends that "truth" should not be limited to knowledge that can be obtained through the five senses, "which recognize, without help, only a very small part of the universe." He argues that there is a "sixth sense" by which one can, "through proper preparation and exertion . . . intercept messages from out of the directly unknown, as completely as this may be done by man-made instruments. Throughout history this power of man has been recognized and usually respected. The experience or knowledge thus gained, when properly examined by the mind, should be given an equal place beside that gained directly through the commoner senses. Prophets, poets, men of vision and faith, have all built their work largely upon this kind of knowledge or inward feeling." However, all truth claims "should be carefully examined in the light of reason. The only knowledge that will help in the establishment of a satisfactory religion is true knowledge. Truth is the end of the search. False or apparently true knowledge often intrudes itself upon the attention and at times it is so well disguised as to be dangerously deceptive. Man must learn to know the universe precisely as it is, or he cannot successfully find his place in it. A man should therefore use his reasoning faculty in all matters involving truth, and especially as concerning his religion. He must learn to distinguish between truth and error." Widtsoe, *Rational Theology*, 8.

41. See Albrecht and Heaton, "Secularization, Higher Education," 293–314.

Years Completed	Males (% of population)		Females (% of population)	
	U.S.	Mormon	U.S.	Mormon
0–11	30.7	15.3	31.8	16.4
12	32.8	31.2	40.5	39.3
13–15	15.6	25.0	14.1	28.6
16 or more	20.9	28.5	13.6	15.7

42. D&C 88:78–79, 118.

43. Brigham Young, in *Journal of Discourses*, 9:364–70.

are taught in school and what they learn in church. One statistical study dealing with religiousness and education showed a very clear positive correlation between levels of education and outward signs of devotion among Mormons—i.e., Mormons tend to be *more* religious the more education they have, unlike many other Christian groups.[44] Mormons tend to recognize that secular education is true and useful as far as it goes, based on limited human knowledge. But as human knowledge progresses, more of ultimate reality will become accessible to our understanding.

But Latter-day Saints also believe that there is another dimension to the cosmos that transcends the world of everyday experience yet is just as real as the everyday world we see around us. (We will consider the possibility of *spiritual knowledge* and divine revelation in chapter 10.) That spiritual realm, as we will see later, is not fundamentally different from the everyday world, in terms of interpersonal relations and natural and moral laws, and it is possible, up to a point, to reason about the nature of God and heaven based on what we know to be true in our current terrestrial existence. For example, Latter-day Saints do not conceive of heaven as a place in which the souls of the dead will spend eternity playing harps and singing praises to God, but one where everyone will be anxiously engaged in actual work that both suits their abilities and promotes the ongoing work of God.

James E. Talmage, an apostle of the LDS church in the early twentieth century and a trained scientist, opined in a beloved LDS classic text that Jesus' miracles were not suspensions or contraventions of natural law, but exploitation of laws and principles that the human race did not yet comprehend.

> In the contemplation of the miracles wrought by Christ, we must of necessity recognize the operation of a power transcending our present human understanding. In this field, science has not yet advanced far enough to analyze and explain. To deny the actuality of miracles on the ground that, because we cannot comprehend the means, the reported results are fictitious, is to arrogate to the human mind the attribute of omniscience, by implying that what man cannot comprehend cannot be, and that therefore he is able to comprehend all that is.[45]

The airplane can serve as a simple example of this principle. Until the Wright brothers demonstrated it at Kitty Hawk, no one had any real comprehension of the aerodynamic principles that allow heavy machines to fly as smoothly as birds. Yet those laws were always true; if a time traveler happened to show up in first-century Rome in a

44. With respect to regular attendance at church, 43 percent of LDS male high school graduates attended on a weekly basis; 65 percent of males with some college, 71 percent with a college degree, and 80 percent of those who attended graduate school; the corresponding percentages of women are similar, if not quite so consistent: 54, 71, 82, and 76 percent, respectively. Percentages for payment of a full tithe (10 percent of income): 42, 57, 68, and 71 percent for males; 49, 59, 73, and 73 percent for women. Daily prayer: 44, 54, 60, and 68 percent (men); 58, 63, 75, and 62 percent (women). Albrecht and Heaton, "Secularization, Higher Education." See also Stott, "Effects of College Education."

45. Talmage, *Jesus the Christ*, 148–49.

single-engine Cessna, it would have seemed an inexplicable miracle, though it follows quite natural principles. Miracles, in the usual sense of temporary suspensions of natural law, are impossible.[46] Mormons typically view the human power of reasoning as a God-given gift, but believe that it has limitations, which essentially boil down to our own lack of knowledge and wisdom.

It is good to be skeptical of implausible claims, so long as we keep in mind that much of reality is . . . well, implausible. The basic claims of relativity theory and especially quantum mechanics seem not only dubious but downright inconceivable; yet they have been rigorously and repeatedly tested and shown to be true. There is still much that we do not know and do not understand about the world we live in. We can either rest contentedly on the principle of extrapolation and assume that reality, as we seek to plumb its depths, will turn out to be roughly the same as how it currently seems to be, or we can acknowledge as a real possibility that ultimate reality may turn out to be radically different from how we currently conceive of it. There is enough knowledge being accumulated in today's world to suggest that the latter is the more realistic stance.

I am convinced that there is much more to be known than what we encounter every day in the world of common experience, and that some things which may appear irrational at first or second or even third glance may in fact be quite reasonable and, in fact, true—when viewed in the proper context. And I believe that the restored gospel at the very least presents one of the most radical yet simultaneously most plausible challenges to our current assumptions about the nature of God, life, death, and the very purpose and meaning of our being. The rest of this book, in essence, addresses the question of plausibility: not whether the claims of Mormonism are *true*, but whether they are *plausible enough* to be worth the seeker's time in his or her quest to know the truth.

---

46. Talmage also stated: "Miracles are commonly regarded as occurrences in opposition to the laws of nature. Such a conception is plainly erroneous, for the laws of nature are inviolable. However, as human understanding of these laws is at best but imperfect, events strictly in accordance with natural law may appear contrary thereto. The entire constitution of nature is founded on system and order." Talmage, *Articles of Faith*, 220.

3

The Meaning of Life—or, Why Do I Have to Die?

When I die, shall I neither exist, nor shall any one ever have any remembrance of me, while boundless time bears all things of all men into forgetfulness? and shall I then be without being, or acquaintance with those who are; neither knowing nor being known, neither having been nor being? And has the world ever been made? and was there anything before it was made? For if it has been always, it shall also continue to be; but if it has been made, it shall also be dissolved. And after its dissolution, shall there ever be anything again, unless, perhaps, silence and forgetfulness? Or perhaps something shall be which is not possible now to conceive.

—Clementine Homilies (Christian writing, late-second-century Rome)[1]

To-morrow, and to-morrow, and to-morrow,

Creeps in this petty pace from day to day
To the last syllable of recorded time,
And all our yesterdays have lighted fools
The way to dusty death. Out, out, brief candle!
Life's but a walking shadow, a poor player
That struts and frets his hour upon the stage
And then is heard no more: it is a tale
Told by an idiot, full of sound and fury,
Signifying nothing.
—Shakespeare, *Macbeth*, act 5, scene 5

The following list consists of what we might call the "grand questions of human existence," some of the most perennial and baffling questions regarding the human condition:

> ➤ Why is there something rather than nothing?

> ➤ Is there a God?

1. ANF 8:223.

> If so, did he (or she or it) create me?

> If so, why was I created? That is, what was God's *plan* or purpose in creating me?

> What is the nature of God?

> Why didn't I get a chance to agree to come into the world?

> What is the purpose of life?

> What should I be doing with my life?

> Why is there evil and suffering in life?

> Why must I die?

> Is there existence after death? If so, what is it like?

> How do I prepare for death?

> Will I be punished for any evil I have committed and rewarded for the good I have done?

The Danish philosopher Kierkegaard penned a rather more poetic version of the same:

> Where am I? What is the 'world'? What does this word mean? Who has duped me into the whole thing, and now leaves me standing there? Who am I? How did I come into the world; why was I not asked, why was I not informed of the rules and regulations . . . ? How did I come to be involved in this great enterprise called actuality? Why should I be involved in it? Am I not free to decide? Am I to be forced to be a part of it? Where is the manager, I would like to make a complaint![2]

People undoubtedly practice religion for a variety of reasons. But most people, I would venture to guess, join a religion or remain in the religion they were raised in because it helps them feel connected to something that transcends their own narrow lives, something greater than themselves. Religion gives meaning to their lives and thereby helps them cope with the vicissitudes of life, the proverbial "slings and arrows of outrageous fortune."[3]

The queries listed above are at the heart of the human desire for meaning. There are many similar questions that one could ask, but these, I believe, cover the essentials. Such questions have been around since the dawn of human history, and there have been countless attempts to provide meaningful answers. Yet many people in the modern world are convinced that there are no answers, and they feel that life is meaningless and absurd. The most fundamental absurdity about our existence is best

---

2. Kierkegaard, *Repetition and Philosophical Crumbs*, 60.
3. *Hamlet*, act 3, scene 1.

summarized in the words of Joseph Smith: "What is the object of our coming into existence, then dying and falling away, to be here no more?"[4]

For whatever reason, human beings are constituted so as to be nearly incapable of living without some sense of purpose, whether that be to become wealthy and powerful or to become a saint. Meaninglessness and pointlessness are intolerable. I remember reading in my college psychology textbook of an experiment in which prisoners in a penitentiary were assigned the task of moving a huge pile of rocks from one end of the prison yard to another. When that job was completed, they were then ordered to move the same pile of rocks back to the other side of the yard. That done, they were then . . . yes, instructed to move them across the yard once again. The fourth time they were given the same instruction, they flatly refused. Dostoevsky once observed:

> The thought once occurred to me that if one wanted to crush and destroy a man entirely, to mete out to him the most terrible punishment, one at which the most fearsome murderer would tremble, shrinking from it in advance, all one would have to do would be to make him do work that was completely and utterly devoid of usefulness and meaning.[5]

The ancient Greeks captured this idea of utter futility in the myth of Sisyphus, in which the king of Ephyra was condemned to the eternal fate of having to roll a huge bolder up a hill, only to have it roll downhill each time just before he reached the summit. The French philosopher Albert Camus made this myth the principal symbol for his discussion of the absurdity of existence, suggesting that whatever work and effort we may engage in, it ultimately turns into nothingness. Meaninglessness, a general sense of pointlessness and futility in life, is indeed at the foundation of much of our modern malaise.

How often have you felt that your life was about as meaningful as moving a pile of rocks back and forth across a prison yard? Most of us—some more frequently than others—reach a point at which the daily grind of "wake up, eat your breakfast, brush your teeth, go to work, come home, watch TV, go to bed, wake up, eat your breakfast . . ." becomes nearly intolerable, and we want to just . . . *quit*. For some, taking an extended vacation does the trick; for others, finding a new career, such as teaching first grade, is enough. Some join a new club, or a new church. Some begin reading the Bible or some other set of holy writings. Some satisfy themselves with getting married and raising a family; a small number, out of desperation, begin planning their own demise.

Human beings crave meaning in their lives.

Victor Frankl became fully aware of this fact of human existence as a result of his interactions with fellow inmates in the Nazi death camps. He noticed that those inmates who had no reason for living were the most likely to die. The man who had lost all reason to live, who no longer saw any sense in continuing to live, "no aim, no

---

4. *HOTC* 6:50.

5. Fyodor Dostoyevsky, *The House of the Dead*, quoted in Svendsen, *Work*, 35.

purpose, and therefore no point in carrying on . . . was soon lost."[6] He consequently theorized that human beings need "something for the sake of which to live" and that a person's "search for meaning is the primary motivation in his life."[7] Emily Esfahani Smith has noted that modern-day researchers in psychology have confirmed these theories: "Research has shown that having purpose and meaning in life increases overall well-being and life satisfaction, improves mental and physical health, enhances resiliency, enhances self-esteem, and decreases the chances of depression."[8]

Ancient peoples typically viewed their existence as possessing an inherent meaning insofar as their lives conformed to a series of mythical prototypes. They perceived all existence as permeated with divine patterns around which human beings ordered their lives. As Mircea Eliade has written, the life of "archaic man" was in essence "the ceaseless repetition of gestures initiated by others," namely divinities. Human activity such as eating, hunting, city and temple building, marriage, and sex "acquire[d] meaning, reality, solely to the extent to which it repeat[ed] a primordial act" by the gods.[9] Ancient temples, in Mesopotamia and elsewhere, were not considered simple workaday structures erected for the worship of the gods. Rather, they were built according to specific plans revealed by deity to his prophets and rulers, corresponding to models of temples already existing eternally in celestial realms. Transcendent meaning was thereby granted to human activities.

In more recent centuries, history itself imparted meaning to people's lives. In Medieval Europe, for example, history was conceived of in a linear rather than cyclical fashion. History was not only a record of God's intervention in the lives of his people, but could be traced in a direct line stretching from the time of creation to its final culmination in the Second Coming of Christ, the destruction of the wicked, and the final judgement. Because history was perceived as "going somewhere," i.e., as leading to a concrete goal or *telos*, namely the fulfillment of God's purposes for all mankind, it provided a degree of transcendent meaning to everyone's life.

Moreover, even in the more secular worldviews of the nineteenth and early twentieth centuries, historians and philosophers frequently cast their analyses in terms of the ongoing progress and evolution of civilization, leading ultimately to a kind of worldly fulfillment of the Christian millennium. Kant, for example, argued that there was necessarily some type of cosmic *telos* toward which history was moving, even if the individual actors in history were entirely unaware of it. Hegel developed an elaborate theory in which he saw history as a "universal cosmic spirit that works toward the full realization of Absolute Spirit."[10]

6. Frankl, *Man's Search for Meaning*, 76.

7. Frankl, *Man's Search for Meaning*, 99

8. Smith, "There's More to Life." See also her follow-up article, "Meaning Is Healthier," as well as her book *The Power of Meaning*.

9. Eliade, *Eternal Return*, 5.

10. Conkin and Stromberg, *Heritage and Challenge*, 62.

Neither of these broad historical paradigms—the cyclical and the linear—has any real meaning for men and women today. Postmodernist thought has deprived history of any teleological significance, whether based in religion or not. Science has for large numbers of people demolished all belief in any type of metaphysical reality beyond the cold, clinical world of our material existence. And some basic assumptions of existentialist philosophy have become so pervasive that the general public, at least in the Western world, has become convinced that the only meaning available to anyone is what the individual invents for him- or herself.

Various scientists have suggested that we should derive a profound satisfaction from the fact that our bodies are literally composed of cosmic matter. Carl Sagan, in his famous television series *Cosmos*, declared: "The nitrogen in our DNA, the calcium in our teeth, the iron in our blood, the carbon in our apple pies were made in the interiors of collapsing stars. We are made of star stuff."[11] Neil deGrasse Tyson has echoed this observation:

> Recognize that the very molecules that make up your body, the atoms that construct the molecules, are traceable to the crucibles that were once the centers of high mass stars that exploded their chemically rich guts into the galaxy, enriching pristine gas clouds with the chemistry of life. So that we are all connected to each other biologically, to the earth chemically and to the rest of the universe atomically. That's kinda cool! That makes me smile and I actually feel quite large at the end of that. It's not that we are better than the universe, we are part of the universe. We are in the universe and the universe is in us.[12]

That fact is undoubtedly "cool." But its implications for finding overall meaning in the universe are limited, since most people do not find great significance in their teeth, blood, or even DNA, but rather in their actions, their consciousness, and in the less tangible aspects of human life such as love, friendship, and good and evil. Moreover, it is difficult to find any direct guidance from these physical facts on how we should live our lives—i.e., what we are *here for*.

In the absence of any belief in a deity or metaphysical reality, philosophers have tried to reinterpret the question of *meaning*.[13] Julian Baggini, a philosopher who is a self-described humanist and atheist, insists that there is no single transcendent, mysterious answer to the question of the meaning of life.[14] Instead, each person, in accord with his or her unique identity, preferences, and personality, should seek for that which brings him happiness and contentment, whether that be working in the service of others, pursuing one's passion, or merely living for the enjoyment of the day. The

11. Quoted at "As It Turns Out."

12. Quoted in Papadopoulos, "Dear Neil DeGrasse Tyson.".

13. Examples of this approach are numerous. Apart from Baggini, discussed in the text, see Landau, *Finding Meaning*; Kurt Baier, "Meaning of Life."

14. Baggini, *What's It All About?*

word "meaning," he points out, does not merely refer to what something is designed for (your car is *meant* to take you from point A to point B), but also to what is of value to a person (the opportunity to work in a homeless shelter *means* a lot to you). In the latter sense, the "meaning of life" should be taken then to refer to why life is of value to us, why we think it to be important and worth living.

Certainly Baggini's approach to meaning makes a certain amount of sense. As we have already seen, engaging in activities that one finds totally without purpose—like carrying rocks back and forth—quickly becomes intolerable. Adam Grant, a widely respected professor of business and psychology at the Wharton School, has written that if you ask people "what they want in a job . . . meaningfulness looms large. For decades, Americans have ranked purpose as their top priority—above promotions, income, job security, and hours." But it is interesting to note what types of jobs most people find meaningful. Meaningfulness, apparently, excludes occupations that may be quite stimulating personally but which do not have "a significant, lasting impact on other people." For instance, it excludes such jobs as fashion designer and graphics animator, and includes such occupations as adult literacy teacher and addiction counselor.[15] A survey of over two million workers holding more than five hundred different jobs showed that those who found the greatest degree of meaning in their careers held *service* jobs that were felt to help people and make the world a better place: clergy, English teachers, surgeons, school administrators.[16]

So it would appear that, despite Baggini's noble attempt to equate meaningfulness with self-fulfillment, there is much more to people's desire for meaning than that. He admits implicitly that most people, when they speak of meaning in their lives, are referring to the types of questions with which we began this chapter. Are there answers to such questions? Baggini says no:

> The problem [with those who believe that life is meaningless] is that often the thought that 'life is meaningless' is only true if we confine ourselves to one narrow way of considering how life could be meaningful. If we do this, we might agree that life is meaningless in those terms . . . If, for example, we think that for life to have meaning it must have been created with some purpose in mind, then I would agree that life is meaningless *in that sense*.[17]

Unfortunately for Baggini's approach, most people seeking answers about the meaning of life are essentially seeking to discover whether *life was in fact created with some purpose in mind*.[18] If it was, then it is only reasonable that we should live our lives in conformity with the limits and structures of that purpose. If not, then one

---

15. Grant, "Meaningless Job."

16. "Most and Least"; Grant, "Three Lies."

17. Baggini, *What's It All About*, 159.

18. Einstein acknowledged that the very posing of the question of whether there is any meaning of human life, or life in general, implies a religion. Einstein, *World as I See It*, 1.

is philosophically (or metaphysically or spiritually or morally) free to live life willy-nilly—seeking fame, wealth, or physical pleasure, or in any other way one wishes. That is the essence of existentialism, the reigning philosophy of the last sixty years. Many such activities may truly be fulfilling in certain ways, but involvement in meaningful *activities* is *not* the same as finding that there is meaning in life *overall*. For most people, the concept of finding the meaning of life implies that there is some transcendent aspect to our lives that imparts meaning to the overall human situation, something that goes beyond our own narrow outlook.

Life has been described as a three-act play in which we find ourselves on stage for a few bare minutes. In the memorable words of Shakespeare's Macbeth:

> Life's but a walking shadow, a poor player
> That struts and frets his hour upon the stage
> And then is heard no more: it is a tale
> Told by an idiot, full of sound and fury,
> Signifying nothing.[19]

On numerous occasions I have had a nightmare in which I find myself on stage in front of an audience, but I have no idea of what my lines are or even the name of the play I am in. I don't think I'm alone in having such dreams.[20] That can be a frightening dream, but it is also a metaphor for life. We know that life has been going on for many thousands of years, and that it will (hopefully!) continue on many thousands after we are gone. If we don't even know the gist of the plot of the play that we are stuck in, how can we act out our part in any meaningful way? We simply stumble our way through a few lines, and then are "heard no more." The modern solution to this problem is to say either that there is no plot at all, in which case we should simply make up our own plot for our own lives—and to hell with the rest of the cast—or that even if there is a plot, there is no way of discovering with any certainty what it is, and so we might as well act as if there is none. Robert Nozick, for example, proposes that a person has three choices: one can simply *accept* the meaninglessness of life and nevertheless go on with one's life (or alternatively *end* one's life!); one can seek to *discover* meaning; or one can *create* meaning. Since number one is not very appealing and number two is *impossible* (according to Nozick), one is left with the personal creation of meaning in one's own life.[21]

Of course, the assumption that discovering any true meaning in life is impossible is not only pessimistic; it is self-defeating. And for most people the third choice, creating one's own meaning, does not feel very satisfying, at least in the long run. The primary reason for that dissatisfaction is, to put it bluntly, death. The inescapable feeling that life is pointless and absurd is founded in the indisputable fact of our impending

19. *Macbeth*, act 5, scene 5.
20. See Cavett, "Enough with the Agony."
21. Nozick, "Philosophy and the Meaning of Life," 230.

doom. What could possibly be the point of our lives at all if we are on stage for a mere hour or two and then are "heard no more?"[22] To make matters worse, we often feel that our lives are filled with frustration, disappointment, and suffering. Yes, of course, something of us may live on in our children and grandchildren, if we have any, and more tenuously in the lives of others we may have influenced, directly or indirectly. Writers and artists have long sought a kind of immortality through their works, hoping that those will endure at least a few decades after their death. But is that really all there is? Must we be content with such hopes for immortality or is there something more?[23] And if there is, how can we know what it is?

Most religions address the question of what will happen to us after death. Many people if asked about the primary value of religion would most likely respond that it was in providing an explanation regarding the afterlife. Even Peter Berger, a highly regarded sociologist of religion, has declared that "the power of religion depends, in the last resort, upon the credibility of the banners it puts in the hands of men as they stand before death, or more accurately, as they walk, inevitably, toward it."[24] And the eminent literary scholar Harold Bloom has concluded, "Of all religions that I know, the one that most vehemently and persuasively defies and denies the reality of death" is Mormonism. Joseph Smith himself understood the centrality of human suffering and death to our understanding of the meaning and purpose of life:

> All men know that they must die. And it is important that we should *understand* the *reasons and causes of our exposure to the vicissitudes of life and death,* and the *designs and purposes of God in our coming into the world, our sufferings here, and our departure hence.* What is the object of our coming into existence, then dying and falling away, to be here no more? *It is but reasonable to suppose that God would reveal something in reference to the matter,* and it is a subject we ought to study more than any other. We ought to study it day and night, for the world is ignorant in reference to their true condition and relation. *If we have any claim on our Heavenly Father for anything, it is for knowledge on this important subject.*[25]

22. The great Leo Tolstoy put it this way in *My Confession*: "Sooner or later there would come diseases and death (they had come already) to my dear ones and to me; and there would be nothing left but stench and worms. All my affairs, no matter what they might be, would sooner or later be forgotten, and I myself should not exist. So why should I worry about all these things? How could a man fail to see that and live—that was surprising! A person could live only so long as he was drunk; but the moment he sobered up, he could not help seeing that all that was only a deception, and a stupid deception at that! Really, there was nothing funny and ingenious about it, but only something cruel and stupid." As quoted in Klemke, *Meaning of Life*, 11.

23. As the great philosopher Woody Allen has said, "I don't want to achieve immortality through my work; I want to achieve immortality through not dying. I don't want to live on in the hearts of my countrymen; I want to live on in my apartment."

24. Berger, *Sacred Canopy*, 51.

25. *HOTC* 6:50.

This view of life, God, and man was absolutely central to Joseph's understanding of reality, as scholars are coming to recognize. In addition to Bloom just quoted above, Douglas J. Davies has argued that "death was a crucial factor in the emergence of Mormonism and . . . it continues to contribute to the movement's continuing success."[26] Similarly, Samuel Morris Brown, an LDS critical care physician and historian, speaks of the "Mormon Conquest of Death." He quotes Joseph's assertion that "'salvation is nothing more or less than to triumph over all our enemies . . . & the last enemy is death.' [Joseph's] solutions to the problem . . . transformed the enemy death—'annihilation'— into a blessed state of heavenly community he termed 'exaltation.'"[27]

But Mormonism does more than simply defy death; it also illuminates the *purpose of living*. Many religions declare that we will live again following our demise. Mormonism provides a distinct explanation of why we are on this earth, why God placed us here and why we agreed to come, and what we are supposed to be accomplishing during this life in preparation for the eternity which is to follow. One key to the powerful appeal of Mormonism, and why Latter-day Saints find such spiritual power in its theology, is that it provides a fully *three-dimensional system* that imparts greater depth and significance to our lives. It fills in many of the gaps that are present in traditional Christianity and tend to leave one perplexed.

Many other faiths, including traditional Christian belief, provide a two-dimensional system. They explain where we are going after this life, but have little or nothing to say about why we are here in the first place. Why did God put us here? What were his intentions? Why does he demand certain behaviors of us, and why will he condemn us to eternal punishment if we do not obey him? Traditional Christianity declares only that we were created for God's glory or his good pleasure; that he created us for his purposes, which are mostly unknown to us, and that we must follow his commands simply because he is God and they are his commands. The Westminster Catechism declares, "Man's chief end is to glorify God, and to enjoy him forever." A Methodist theologian states that "God's purpose in creation was to make men and women who would glorify and enjoy a holy presence and a personal relationship with God."[28] Another devout Christian writer gives the following description of God's purposes:

> If God is God, and if He made all these things, why did he do it? . . . God created a universe, bounded by the categories of time, space, matter, and causality, because He desired to enjoy forever the society of a fellowship of finite and redeemed spirits, which have made to His love the response of free and voluntary love and service.[29]

---

26. Davies, *Mormon Culture of Salvation*, 1.

27. Brown, *In Heaven*, 15–16.

28. Mickey, *Essentials of Wesleyan Theology*, 81; see also Givens, *Feeding the Flock*, 1.

29. Neill, *Christian Faith*, 240–41.

But why would an infinite God desire the society and fellowship of finite beings? Why would he create us just so that we might love and serve him? To Latter-day Saint ears, this attitude sounds an awful lot like divine vanity, though various Christian thinkers have insisted otherwise.

Fundamental Mormon doctrine, in contrast, declares that we existed *before* we came to this earth; that we are literally the *children* of our divine Father, not merely his *creations*; that during our premortal existence we all consciously accepted God's plan for us, which involved coming to this temporary but crucial plane of existence on the earth; that our earthly lives have been specifically designed for *our* benefit, to permit us to learn certain crucial lessons and to otherwise prepare for living eternally with God; and that the afterlife consists of a *return home* to the presence of God, our Father, where (if we have properly prepared) we will live eternally the kind of life he lives, which includes direct participation in his work.

This teaching is what Latter-day Saints call the "plan of salvation" or "plan of happiness"; in other words, our earthly existence is part of an explicitly designed divine *plan* for the *salvation* of the human family. God did not simply create us out of thin air—or out of the dust of the earth—for his good pleasure. He sent us to this earth to give us an opportunity to progress (if we are willing) to become more like him and ultimately to become as he is.

Thus, salvation is not simply a matter of pleasing God and being rewarded by him. It is, rather, the *fulfillment* of our deepest selves. It is, according to one phrase from LDS scripture, "filling the measure of our creation"—i.e., becoming what we were explicitly designed for. It is attaining the goal to which God has dedicated his entire existence, out of love for each of us as his children. Many Christians declare that the purpose of our lives is simply to *glorify God*. That is fine as far as it goes, but our vision of life should not stop there. One of the most oft-repeated Mormon verses of scripture is a ringing declaration by God to Moses: "This is my *work* and my *glory*, to bring to pass the immortality and eternal life of *man*."[30] In other words, our life should indeed be dedicated to glorifying God—in the full knowledge that he has dedicated himself to glorifying *us* (see also John 17:22).

---

30. Moses 1:39. The Book of Moses can be found in the LDS volume of scripture known as The Pearl of Great Price.

4

Life Before Life—or, How Did I Get Here?

Our birth is but a sleep and a forgetting:
The Soul that rises with us, our life's Star,
Hath had elsewhere its setting,
And cometh from afar:
Not in entire forgetfulness,
And not in utter nakedness,
But trailing clouds of glory do we come
From God, who is our home.

—William Wordsworth, "Ode: Intimations of Immortality from Recollections of Early
Childhood"[1]

However many [people] believe that their soul will survive death, rather few, I imagine, believe
that it also pre-existed their birth. The religions that have shaped Western culture are so
inhospitable to the idea of pre-existence that you probably reject the thought out of hand, for
no good reason.

—Miles Fredric Burnyeat[2]

The LDS notion of human existence begins long before birth. This belief in a preter-restrial existence is one of the most unusual doctrines of Mormonism. It is also one of the fundamental keys to understanding the LDS attitude toward life. It is what pro-vides a crucial *third dimension* to create a fully developed picture of human existence. Most religions have some notions regarding a postmortal existence—an afterlife. Traditional Christianity, of course, asserts that all souls will end up either in heaven or in hell. To Latter-day Saints, however, such a two-dimensional picture of existence is marvelous as far as it goes, but is ultimately as unsatisfying as a photograph of the Taj Mahal when compared to the real thing. The belief in a premortal existence

---

1. Wordsworth, *Complete Poetical Works*, 359.
2. Burnyeat, "Other Lives."

has frequently been described as providing a complete and satisfying human story—a three-act play, as it were, with a beginning, middle, and end. A proper understanding of all three acts in our existence helps us to keep our current mortal existence in proper perspective: we lived long before we were born, and we will live long after we die. According to this perspective, mortality is crucially important but limited in scope. In contrast, most people in today's world are completely unaware of the first act, and doubtful about the third act. From such a unidimensional perspective, the second act (our mortal life) takes on an exaggerated significance.[3]

Consider, for example, the typical modern secular attitude toward life—what we might term a strictly one-dimensional view of life. If we suppose, as many millions of people do, that this current existence is all there is and all there ever will be, we will immediately conclude that the few decades that are our allotment on this earth are of utmost importance. This life *is "our life."* We have a single shot at enjoying ourselves and fulfilling our desires. Whatever we achieve while we are here is all we ever will achieve, and whatever we miss out on or fail to accomplish is lost to us forever. The prospect of an earlier-than-average death is considered an absolute tragedy.

Now consider the attitude of the typical Christian, who believes in an afterlife—a two-dimensional existence, as we can call it. Death is no longer quite as tragic, because our life, at least in some sense, will go on. Christians traditionally have had very diverse ideas about the next life, and we haven't space here to do a thorough survey of even the most common beliefs. But the most common assumption, of course, is that the "wicked" people will go to hell, the "good" to some type of heaven. Those two terms, of course, can be defined in radically different ways, and in recent years there has been a pulling away from traditional notions of the devil and hell. But again, traditionally it has been believed that those going to hell would be at least a significant minority of the human race, if not a majority. For strict Calvinist Christians, only the tiniest fraction of mankind will be saved. It is only natural to ask the question of why God created mankind at all, knowing that a huge percentage of them would suffer eternal condemnation.

In traditional Christian theology, as we have seen, God's purpose in creating us is somewhat vague and non-specific—most Christians would say that he created mankind for his "good pleasure" or his "glory." Of course, Adam messed things up by falling out of God's good grace and becoming mortal. This could not have been a surprise to God, however, who knows all things past, present, and future, so he must have created us in full awareness of what the ultimate result would be. He would certainly have known that he was creating an imperfect race of beings such that the overwhelming majority of them would not qualify for salvation. Many billions of people, as we have

---

3. Maxwell, *Deposition*, 41–42. Compare Packer, "Play and the Plan": "In mortality, we are like one who enters a theater just as the curtain goes up on the second act. We have missed Act I. The production has many plots and sub-plots that interweave, making it difficult to figure out who relates to whom and what relates to what, who are the heroes and who are the villains. It is further complicated because you are not just a spectator; you are a member of the cast, on stage, in the middle of it all!"

already noted, lived long before Jesus' birth, and hence never even had an opportunity to believe. But even for those who have lived in the Western world during the last two thousand years, a large majority have been either non-believers or relatively nominal believers. Why would a loving God create billions of people in full knowledge that a large majority would be condemned to hell?[4]

A closely related question is why God's creations—i.e., us—are imperfect in the first place. If we are wholly creations of a perfect God, where did the imperfections come from? How could he produce anything that was less than perfect? A typical Christian might respond that God is not able to create other perfect beings like himself, because then there would be many gods—a logical impossibility since God, by definition, is one. But mankind, as we are all well aware, is not merely imperfect (i.e., a hair less than perfect) but often downright evil. Why is this? How did it come about? Where did the extreme evil of a Hitler or Stalin or Pol Pot come from? According to the Bible's account (as commonly interpreted), evil entered this world with the fall of Adam. Adam and Eve had been created in a state, presumably, of near perfection, but they were given free will because God wanted them to love him entirely by their own choice. Unfortunately, they chose to reject God and to disobey his commands. When God allowed Satan to tempt them, by means of the forbidden fruit, they succumbed to the temptation. By rejecting God, they placed themselves in the power of Satan, where they and all their descendants would remain for eternity. The only ones who would be saved from this fallen state were those who exercise faith in Christ and accept him as their Savior.

But if belief in God and faith in Christ are so crucial to our eternal salvation, why doesn't God make it a little easier on us all? First of all, as we have already noted, billions of souls have existed without the slightest knowledge of the Christian God or even the Jewish understanding of God. Why wouldn't he have disclosed his reality to them as well as to the Jews and the people of the Roman Empire? Moreover, as countless people have wondered, why doesn't God simply show us who he is? If he really exists, and if it's so crucially important that we believe in him, why doesn't he simply reveal himself in his power and glory so that everyone can readily perceive him?[5] If

---

4. Again, there is great variety of opinion among both past and present Christians regarding the fate of the unevangelized, those who never had the opportunity to accept Christianity. For a convenient summary of the three main views, see Fackre et al., *What About Those*; see also Sanders, *No Other Name*.

5. Norwood Russell Hanson, a philosopher and an atheist, explained in a playful passage just what it would take for him to believe in God: "Suppose . . . that on next Tuesday morning, just after breakfast, all of us in this one world are knocked to our knees by a percussive and ear-shattering thunderclap. Snow swirls; leaves drop from trees; the earth heaves and buckles; buildings topple and towers tumble; the sky is ablaze with an eerie, silvery light. Just then, as all the people of this world look up, the heavens open—the clouds pull apart—revealing an unbelievably immense and radiant Zeus-like figure, towering above us like a hundred Everests. He frowns darkly as lightning plays across the features of his Michelangeloid face. He then points down—*at me!*—and exclaims, for every man, woman and child to hear 'I have had quite enough of your too-clever-logic-chopping and word-watching

his purpose in creating us was so that we can all enjoy eternal communion with him, why does he hide his presence from us? Why does he, as it were, create a *guessing game* so that, whether we believe in him or not, we never know for sure whether we are right or wrong? Why does he make the game seemingly so hard and then punish us if we guess wrong?

From the LDS perspective, all these questions become much easier to comprehend when one obtains an awareness of the crucial *third dimension* of human existence. Mormon teaching posits a God with whom we already lived for an eternity prior to our mortal birth. He knows us better than we know ourselves, just as a parent understands her ten-year-old child better than the child himself. Our coming to earth was for our own benefit, planned out by God and approved by us, to enable us to progress in certain ways that we could not do in any other way. Indeed, our terrestrial lives should be seen as a mere moment, a blip on the timeline of our eternal existence. God's plan for us, outlined long before this earth was created, was to help us to grow and improve ourselves, so that ultimately we could come to be very much like he is—wise, good, pure, holy—and, yes, divine. Our current imperfections are partly inherent in us, due to our spiritual immaturity, and partly given us by God to challenge and test us. This life is indeed designed as a test, but it is not so much a pass/fail, all-or-nothing test from which there is no appeal as it is an aptitude test, a learning experience to show what we are made of. While we are here we will learn many things, but we are also expected to demonstrate the extent to which we are attracted to good or evil. Hence God deliberately allows us to be tempted by Satan, but he also speaks to our minds through his spirit so that we are equally pulled in both directions. God also quite consciously and deliberately hides himself from us so that it is a fair test. We must then make choices throughout our lives based on our own inherent predilection for good or evil. And after this life all of us, with the exception of those few who are utterly incorrigible, will be saved to a greater or lesser degree, even those who during their life didn't believe in God or never heard of Jesus Christ. But the degree of glory to which we are ultimately assigned will be based on our willingness to conform our wills and behavior to the laws and principles that pertain to that level of spiritual development. And the judgment will be based less on our approval or condemnation by God than on our own judgment of where we rightly belong.

Thus our time on this earth is far from being the totality of our existence. Rather, it is much more like a college career, a brief but extremely crucial part of our eternal existence. We leave behind home and parents for a short while with the expectation that we will return considerably matured—more knowledgeable, capable, and independent. It may seem at times like a great trial, at times almost overwhelming, and we may be tempted to quit and go home—indeed, some do quit. Yet later on in life we

---

in matters of theology. Be assured, N.R. Hanson, that I do most certainly exist.'" Quoted in Morris, *Making Sense*, 93. Morris has an excellent, clear discussion of the issue of God's hiddenness in his chapter 6.

will look back on it with a combination of fondness for our memories and gratitude that it is all over and behind us. Most importantly, despite the relative brevity of that episode, our success in later life is determined in large measure by the degree to which we took it seriously and acquired the skills and knowledge we were there to learn. And finally, it is important to keep in mind that even after our return home we do not stop learning and growing, which to some extent continue forever.

The idea of a premortal existence is by no means unique to Mormonism. It can be found, at least in inchoate form, in some of the earliest records of the human race, and it has appeared here and there in the historical and literary record throughout the last two and a half millennia. Yet a recent in-depth survey of the concept in Western literature demonstrates that, while it has appealed to certain thinkers and writers, often because of its great explanatory power regarding the human condition, the idea has never broadly caught on. Versions of the doctrine can be found in certain ancient Jewish and early Christian writings, but long ago it was condemned as heretical by most Christian schools of thought. Plato was one of the earliest and strongest advocates of the notion, and over the centuries one can find both writers who have advocated for it and others who have disdained the idea as absurd and lacking in supporting evidence. In the last century and a half, however, the idea seems to have been either deliberately discarded or simply fallen into disuse, so that few people today are even aware that it was ever a subject of discussion.[6] As a result, as the classical scholar M. F. Burnyeat has pointed out, the very idea of a premortal existence seems so foreign that most people (at least in the West) "reject the thought out of hand, for no good reason."[7]

Yet despite its overall dismissal, the idea possesses an impressive ability to explain the seeming inequities in the circumstances of the individual. For example, why is one woman born with stunning good looks while another must suffer throughout her life the indignities of homeliness? Why does one man enjoy excellent health while another is born crippled in mind or body? Some are born into great wealth and power, while others are consigned to grinding poverty and obscurity. If one believes that humans are created by a good God, the notion that some people are hampered from birth by their circumstances seems unfair and hard to justify.

The value of a belief in an afterlife is a little more obvious. It can provide us with a goal to seek after, and the notion of reward versus punishment supplies a strong motive to behave ourselves in this life. But how important is it to know where we came from? According to the conventional Western understanding of divine creation, God decided at some point in his eternal existence to create a world populated with, among other things, rocks, plants, birds, beasts, and human beings. The heavens, the earth, and everything in the earth were created out of absolutely nothing (*ex nihilo*) except for an idea in God's mind. Adam, as God's crowning creation, was created in God's own image and likeness. This is usually taken to mean that the human *soul*,

6. Givens, *When Souls Had Wings*.

7. Burnyeat, "Other Lives."

in contrast to the body, was patterned after God's own spiritual nature. God created the physical body of the "dust of the ground" and then "breathed into his nostrils the breath of life."[8]

This view of human origins, however, raised a fundamental issue of divine fairness that has never been resolved. If God created man's soul out of nothing, where did sin come from? If God is naturally conceived of as perfect in an absolute sense, then anything he created should naturally be perfect as well. Yet, as the Genesis story relates, Adam and Eve sinned almost immediately, and the world since then has been far from a perfect place. But if human beings were the creation of a perfect God, why were they even capable of sin? Where did the imperfection and the ability to sin come from?

Medieval theologians, in addition to speculating over the origin of Adam's soul, also puzzled over the origin of each individual human spirit. For example, when Adam famously "knew" Eve and they had Cain and Abel, where did the souls of their children come from? The two obvious alternative possibilities are that the parents created the soul at the time of conception along with the body, or that God created for each body a new soul that was "breathed into" the body at the time of birth. But neither of these theories comes without difficulties. On the one hand, if the mortal parents created their child's soul along with its body, how could the soul be inherently immortal while the body decayed and returned to the earth? Yet if each body received a new soul from God, how could it be that this fresh spirit from deity acquired the sinful nature of its parents? How could the sin of Adam and Eve be transmitted to their offspring if the soul of each individual came directly from God? How could the creations of a perfect God be so imperfect?[9] Even more concerning is the manifest unfairness of God's condemnation of a soul for its sinfulness if that very imperfection came from God himself.

Joseph Smith taught that in fact man's spirit is itself, in some sense, as immortal as God. I state "in some sense" because there was some ambiguity in Joseph's teachings, specifically his use of the words "intelligence" and "spirit." He declared in the Doctrine and Covenants that

> Man was also in the beginning with God. Intelligence, or the light of truth, was
> not created or made, neither indeed can be.[10]

Joseph also taught quite specifically that God did not create the world "out of nothing," as most theists believe today, but made use of chaotic preexistent matter, which he organized. He declared in his famous King Follet discourse that the account of the creation in Genesis 1 refers not to an *ex nihilo* creation but to the organization

8. Genesis 2:7.

9. Givens, *When Souls Had Wings*, 2.

10. D&C 93:29

of chaos. Many biblical scholars today generally agree with this interpretation.[11] But in this context the reference above to "intelligence" would seem to refer to some type of fundamental element from which the spirits of men and women were formed. Elsewhere, however, he referred to "intelligences" in the plural, suggesting that there were indeed discrete individual entities known as "intelligences" that have existed eternally.

In his famous dialogue *Republic*, Plato relates the account of Er, a soldier who is killed in battle but revives just before his body is burned on the funeral pyre. The story that Er tells is what today we would call a near-death experience. He witnessed the afterlife and, like many Hebrew prophets, was specifically commissioned to return to life to tell of what he saw. The substance of his narrative, as related by Plato, is that human souls are immortal—they die but are never destroyed—and are judged based on the good or evil deeds done during their life. Following a period of judgment and punishment or reward, they are required to choose another (reincarnated) life. They are given the opportunity to choose among many situations for their next existence:

> Every single kind of human and animal life was included among the samples [from which to choose]. For instance, there were dictatorships (some lifelong, others collapsing before their time and ending in poverty, exile, and begging), and also male and female versions of lives of fame for one's physique, good looks, and general strength and athleticism, or for one's lineage and the excellence of one's ancestors; and there were lives which lacked these distinctions as well . . . [T]here was every possible combination of qualities with one another and with factors like wealth, poverty, sickness, and health, in extreme or moderate amounts.[12]

Naturally, many souls would be inclined to select lives of good fortune—wealth, good looks, health, and power. However, many of those choices might end up being quite foolish. For instance, Plato tells of one soul who, through stupidity and greed, chose the most powerful dictatorship available, without inspecting the life thoroughly enough to discover that it also involved eating his own children, among many other horrendous crimes—for which, naturally, he would suffer severe punishments at the next judgment. It was announced at the start of this process that the chooser bore the responsibility for his or her choice and would be judged for his or her behavior. Thus, while the prenatal choice irrevocably set the *circumstances* of one's existence, one was still free to choose one's moral *behavior* within those circumstances. This was not a

---

11. The eminent scholar E. A. Speiser translates Genesis 1:1 to read: "When God set about to create heaven and earth—the world being then a formless waste, with darkness over the seas and only an awesome wind sweeping over the water—God said, 'Let there be light.' And there was light." See his *Genesis*, 3, 11–13. The NRSV translates: "In the beginning, when God created the heavens and the earth, the earth was a formless void . . ." These translations (along with other modern translations) suggest that already in the beginning, at the time of creation, there existed a "formless void" or "waste," which God then organized in some fashion.

12. Plato, *Republic* (618a–b), 376.

system of unalterable fate. Nonetheless, the future dictator, upon realizing his foolish mistake, "blamed fortune, the gods, and anything rather than himself."

Numerous later thinkers have recognized that basic fairness demands that we have at least an element of choice regarding our life situation if we are going to be judged for our deeds.

Lord Byron placed the following words in the mouth of Cain:

> And this is
> Life!—Toil! and wherefore should I toil?—because
> My father could not keep his place in Eden.
> What had *I* done in this?—I was unborn,
> I sought not to be born; nor love the state
> To which that birth has brought me.[13]

Edward Beecher, brother of the nineteenth-century novelist Harriet Beecher Stowe, and a well-known minister and Christian writer in his own right, struggled mightily for years to understand how a righteous and just God (according to orthodox belief) could impute sinfulness to all men from the very moment of their birth, before they have any opportunity to actually sin. The solution he finally arrived at through rational analysis was that men must have existed prior to their birth.

> If, in a previous state of existence, God created all men with such constitutions, and placed them in such circumstances, as the laws of honor and of right de-manded, - if, then, they revolted and corrupted themselves, and forfeited their rights, . . . then all conflict of the moving powers of Christianity can be at once and entirely removed. [Indeed,] by supposing the pre-existent sin and fall of man, the most radical views of human depravity can be harmonized with the highest views of the justice of God."[14]

Beecher was hardly the first Christian to hold a belief in preexistence of souls. The concept can be traced as far back as the biblical book of Jeremiah and to numerous subsequent Jewish writings, through the New Testament and the early church fathers. In the first chapter of the book of Jeremiah, God declares to the prophet Jeremiah:

> Before I formed you in the womb I knew you; and before you were born I consecrated you; I appointed you a prophet to the nations.[15]

Some commentators argue that this verse merely refers to Jeremiah as a thought in God's mind before he was created. But the Hebrew word translated "knew" (*yada'*) connotes a profound and intimate knowledge, suggesting that God knew him deeply and personally before his birth.

---

13. Lord Byron, *Cain*, act 1, scene 1.
14. Givens, *When Souls Had Wings*, 225.
15. Jeremiah 1:5.

The teaching can be found in many postbiblical Jewish writings. The book of Jubilees, a Jewish text that contains expansions of some of the stories told in the biblical book of Genesis, declares that on the first day of creation God created not only the heavens and the earth and brought forth light, but also created his angels and "all of the *spirits* of his creatures which are in heaven and on earth."[16] In a text that purports to be a revelation given by God to the prophet Enoch, an angel refers to "all the souls of men, whatever of them are not yet born," all of which were "prepared for eternity, before the composition of the earth."[17] In another Jewish text from the same time period, known as the Apocalypse of Abraham, the patriarch Abraham is given a vision of creation, and when he asks the identity of the multitudes he sees, he is told by God, "These are the ones I have prepared to be born of you and to be called my people."[18] A Jewish wisdom text known as the Wisdom of Solomon suggests that premortal spirits did not simply exist in a vacuum but had opportunities to become good or evil: ". . . a good soul fell to my lot; or rather, being good, I entered an undefiled body."[19]

The Talmud and other rabbinic writings contain even more explicit teachings regarding the preexistence of spirits. The Jewish scholar Angelo Rappoport summarized these Jewish teachings as follows:

> In the beginning of things God the All-Father also created a great number of souls destined one day to inhabit a human body. There is a treasure or storehouse in Heaven where these souls are kept until the moment arrives for each of them to descend upon earth and be united to "mortal coil." According to some myths these souls are hidden beneath the throne of All-Father, whilst in other places it is maintained that the souls yet unborn walk freely in the celestial fields in company of the souls of the pious who have already passed through a body. . . Some souls are spirits sent down upon earth and ordered to inhabit a human body as a punishment for faults committed. For others it is a test and an opportunity to show their strength. In the struggle of the soul, the celestial inmate, against the passions and instincts inherent in matter, the soul has an opportunity to show its worth and remain faithful to its celestial origin or to betray it.[20]

Several rabbinical texts even mention that God took counsel with the souls of the righteous prior to the creation of the earth.[21]

The idea of preexistent spirits can also be found in certain early Christian writings, beginning with the New Testament. In the Gospel of John, the story is told of a man who was born blind, whom Christ healed. On first encountering the man, the

16. *Jubilees* 2:2, in OTP 2:55.

17. *2 Enoch* 23, in OTP 1:140.

18. *Apocalypse of Abraham* 21.7–22.5, in OTP 1:699–700.

19. *Wisdom of Solomon* 8:19–21, in NOAB 81 (Apocrypha).

20. Rappoport, *Myth and Legend*, 20–21. See also Schwartz, *Tree of Souls*, 164–67.

21. Schwartz, *Tree of Souls*, 160–62.

disciples asked Jesus, "Master, who did sin, this man or his parents, that he was born blind?"[22] An implicit assumption behind the question is that the man must have had an opportunity to sin prior to his birth. This passage does not present this as a specific doctrine, but makes clear that Jews in the time of Jesus had a clear concept of the pre-existence of souls, and that there was a correspondence between one's righteousness prior to birth and the circumstances of one's birth.

The doctrine is also at home in the earliest post-New Testament writings. In the Clementine Recognitions, a Christian text dating to the late second or early third century, the apostle Peter states, in reference to creation:

> But after all these things He made man, on whose account He had prepared all things, whose internal species is older, and for whose sake all things that are were made.

The editor in the *Ante-Nicene Fathers* series notes that the phrase "internal species" refers to man's "soul, according to the doctrine of the pre-existence of souls."[23]

In the early third century a Greco-Egyptian named Origen, the first Christian writer genuinely deserving of the title of theologian, recognized that certain men

> from the hour of their birth, are reduced to humiliation and subjection, and brought up as slaves . . . Others, again, are brought up in a manner more consonant with freedom and reason: some with sound bodies, some with bodies diseased from their early years . . . And why should I repeat and enumerate all the horrors of human misery, from which some have been free, and in which others have been involved, when each one can weigh and consider them for himself?[24]

Origen did not accept the conclusion of some thinkers that the creator God was not just but, in fact, wicked. Gnostic writers of the time supposed that there were in fact two gods, the perfectly righteous but distant Father, and the wicked or foolish creator god, known variously as Ialdabaoth, Saklas (foolish one), or Samael (blind god), and that the wickedness and injustice in the world was attributable to the latter. Origen, in contrast, concluded that men had existed prior to their birth, had exercised their free will, and that God very justly allotted to men in this world according to the degree of their merits. Origen's theology, however, including his doctrine of preexistence, was viewed with increasing skepticism by the later fathers of the church, and was ultimately condemned by Emperor Justinian in 543.[25]

Many of these writings date from the Hellenistic or early Roman period (roughly 300 BC to AD 250), when there was mingling of Greek culture with native Near

---

22. John 9:1–2.
23. *Clementine Recognitions* 1.28, in ANF 8.84.
24. Origen, *De Principiis* 2.9.3, in ANF 4.290.
25. Givens, *When Souls Had Wings*, 91–98, 123–27.

Eastern cultures. Therefore it is possible to see them as influenced by Platonic doctrine. It makes better sense, however, to see them as reflecting a tradition of thought separate from Plato. In the first place, there is no indication that the descent of a spirit into a body is seen as a "fall" or bad thing, as it was in the Platonic thought of that era; rather, it is cast in an entirely positive light. Secondly, there is no belief in reincarnation or cyclical rebirth—the spirits of mankind enter into a human body only once. Origen himself viewed this doctrine as being of Jewish origin and in fact superior to the similar teaching of Plato.[26]

THE LATTER-DAY SAINT CONCEPT OF PREMORTALITY

Joseph Smith never specifically taught, like Plato, that we were given an opportunity in the spirit world to choose what kind of life we would lead on earth. But he did proclaim that we voluntarily chose to follow God's plan to come to earth life despite our awareness of the potential risks involved. Readers of Milton's *Paradise Lost* are familiar with the story that the devil, Satan, was originally known as Lucifer, an angel who rebelled against God and was expelled from heaven. This story did not originate with Milton, but can be found in various lesser-known predecessors. It ultimately goes back to a few scattered references in the Bible. In the Gospel of Luke, Christ says, "I beheld Satan as lightning fall from heaven," while the book of Revelation refers to a "war in heaven," in which "Michael and his angels fought against the dragon," who was ultimately "cast out, that old serpent, called the Devil, and Satan, which deceiveth the whole world; he was cast out into the earth, and his angels were cast out with him."[27] But the significance of this episode is quite opaque in the Bible. The only hint of its meaning is from a statement from the prophet Isaiah: "Oh Lucifer . . . thou hast said in thine heart, I will ascend into heaven, I will exalt my throne above the stars of God."[28] So the usual conclusion is that Lucifer rebelled against God out of pride and a feeling of superiority.

In Milton's telling of the tale, the war in heaven and the fall of Satan were merely the precursors to the story of the fall of Adam. Milton was interested in man's disobedience and subsequent loss of paradise. Satan's fall explains the origin of evil, specifically how the devil came to be wicked and why he chose to tempt the first humans. Lucifer resented the authority of God, particularly his decision to give all preeminence to Christ and his command that "to him shall bow / All knees in heaven, and shall confess him Lord."[29] Satan's pride and jealousy led him not only to rebel against God but to start a war among the angels. Many of the angels sided with him, but their

26. Givens, *When Souls Had Wings*, 49; Bostock, "Sources of Origen's Doctrine"; Edwards, *Origen Against Plato*.

27. Luke 10:18; Revelation 12:7–9.

28. Isaiah 14:12–13.

29. *Paradise Lost* (V.607–8), 166.

cause was of course hopeless from the start: to try to defeat God the Father was a fool's errand. Then, having been cast out of heaven into a hell created just for that purpose, Satan concocted a plan to cause Adam and Eve to sin, thereby undermining God's purposes for mankind. In this scheme, of course, he partially succeeded, bringing about the fall, but through the grace of God and Christ's willingness to sacrifice himself for mankind, Adam's posterity would ultimately be redeemed.

The stories of the fall of Lucifer and the fall of Adam take on much richer meaning in Mormon doctrine. The LDS version bears some similarity to Milton's but provides additional key details. The most important of these is that the war in heaven was not merely between good and bad angels but included all of us—all the premortal spirits created by God. Lucifer was a "son of the morning," or one of the first born of God's spirit children, while the premortal Christ was the firstborn of all.

According to LDS scripture, God presented to his assembly—i.e., to the premortal spirits of all mankind—his "plan of salvation," whereby an earth would be created and each of us would come to this earth in order to be tested. This gives each of us the satisfaction of knowing not only that we were ourselves present at the foundation of the world, but that we were aware of God's purpose in creating the earth and signed on as a participant.

Joseph Smith taught that the occurrence of a council in heaven prior to the creation of the earth was one of the key events in the history of mankind's salvation:

> God Himself found Himself in the midst of spirits and glory. Because He was greater He saw proper to institute laws whereby the rest [of the spirits], who were less in intelligence, could have a privilege to advance like Himself and be exalted with him.[30]

In other words, God's purpose from the beginning was not to merely create beings to praise his name, as is commonly asserted by Christian theologians, but to give his spirit children the chance to *progress*, to become even as he is. God's plan for mankind's eternal progression involved the creation of the earth, and he presented this plan to all of us in a divine council.

> "We will go down, for there is space there, and we will take of these materials, and we will make an earth whereon these [spirits] may dwell; and we will prove [i.e., test] them herewith, to see if they will do all things whatsoever the Lord their God shall command them . . . And the Lord said: Whom shall I send? And one answered like unto the Son of Man: Here I am, send me. And another answered and said, Here am I, send me. And the Lord said: I will send the first. And the second was angry, and kept not his first estate; and, at that day, many followed after him.[31]

30. Quoted in Givens, *Wrestling the Angel*, 157.

31. Book of Abraham 3:24–28. The Book of Abraham is found in the volume of LDS scripture known as The Pearl of Great Price.

The one to be sent would be the appointed savior of the world, and so Lucifer was passed over for this crucial role in favor of Christ. Not only did he rebel out of jealousy toward Christ (as in Milton), but he actively rejected the Father's plan and proffered his own alternative plan of salvation in lieu of the Father's.

> Satan . . . came before me, saying—Behold, here am I, send me, I will be thy son, and I will redeem all mankind, that one soul shall not be lost, and surely I will do it: wherefore give me thine honor. But, behold, my Beloved Son, which was my Beloved and Chosen from the beginning, said unto me—Father, thy will be done, and the glory be thine forever. Wherefore, because that Satan rebelled against me, and sought to destroy the agency of man, which I, the Lord God, had given him, and also, that I should give unto him mine own power; by the power of mine Only Begotten, I caused that he should be cast down.[32]

It is important to keep in mind that the term "spirit" in this context suggests not some vague, ethereal essence, but rather a concrete being with a fully conscious and intelligent existence. One of the crucial elements of our premortal spirits is that we had free will—the ability to make moral choices and be held responsible for those choices. Lucifer had wanted to negate our free will so that he could take all the credit for the salvation of all God's children. Hence the war in heaven that ensued was not only about whether to choose good or evil, to follow God or Satan, but over the very concept of free agency itself. The Father's plan, indeed, was the riskier of the two. Because it entailed free choice on the part of each spirit, there was a chance that some spirits might not be saved. Each individual had a fundamental choice to make: either to continue to follow the Father or to follow the rebels. The fact that each of us is on the earth is proof that we "kept our first estate"—i.e., that we did not side with the rebels, all of whom were cast out of heaven, together with their ringleader, and became the demons that today afflict and torment mankind under the direction of Satan. Instead, we agreed to exercise faith and follow our Father's plan for us, even with the risk that we might fall away and fail to keep our "second estate"—our current life.

Scholars have uncovered plentiful evidence that the ancient Hebrews believed in a divine council held before the foundation of the world. According to Theodore Mullen, the chief authority on the subject, "The concept of the divine council, or the assembly of the gods, was a common religious motif in the cultures of Egypt, Mesopotamia, Canaan, Phoenicia, and Israel."[33] It is found in numerous passages in the Hebrew Bible, though many translations, concerned about the reference to multiple "gods," obscure the nature of the assembly, and render the phrase instead as "angels" or something similar. For example, in the well-known passage from Psalm 82 referring to mankind as having been made by God on a level "a little lower than the angels" (KJV), the word "angels" is actually *elohim*, and is translated by Mitchell Dahood as

32. Book of Moses 4:1–3.
33. Mullen, *Assembly of the Gods*, 228.

"gods."[34] In Psalm 29:1, the phrase translated as "O ye mighty [ones]" in the King James Version literally means "sons of God."[35] In the majority of cases, this divine council appears to consist of gods and angels, but not the preexistent spirits of men and women. Nevertheless, a passage in the Dead Sea Scrolls refers to a single "council of *gods and men*."[36] Daniel Peterson, a Latter-day Saint scholar, has argued at great length that the confusing passage in Psalm 82 (quoted by Christ in John 10) which begins "Ye are gods" makes the most sense in light of the doctrine of the antemortal existence of humans who possess the ability to become divinized.[37]

BUT IS THERE ANY EVIDENCE?

The skeptical reader will no doubt respond that the whole notion of a premortal existence and a council with God in heaven is an interesting story—an intriguing myth—but one with absolutely no hard evidence. Admittedly, it is difficult to provide concrete, tangible evidence for these ideas. Nevertheless, some proponents of the idea of a premortal existence have pointed to the experience of friends or lovers who form an instant bond as though they had known each other in a prior existence. Others have noted how strange it is that humans have a deep longing for an ideal existence as though they had known one in the distant past. Plato pointed to the fact that people possess an intuitive understanding of ideas that they have never been taught to demonstrate that "our souls also existed apart from the body, before they took on human form, and they had intelligence."[38] One can think of children born with an intuitive and remarkably sophisticated understanding of mathematics, music, or mechanics. Then there are the extreme cases of savant syndrome. Where—and how—did they obtain such understanding and abilities? Is it possible that they acquired their skill before their birth, in some type of prior existence?

These suggestions are all intriguing but obviously fall far short of compelling evidence or proof. Skeptics have pointed out the obvious contrary evidence that no human has ever reported even a single clear memory of such an existence. How could we have completely forgotten about it? Defenders, on the other hand, point out that neither do we have any recollection of our first two or three years after birth, which we obviously lived through.

In chapter 6 I will discuss the phenomenon of *near-death experiences* (NDEs), about which so much has been written. As I discuss there, no one can prove with iron-clad certainty that these are real experiences of a spiritual realm after death. But the

---

34. Dahood, *Psalms*, 48. Similarly, verse 1 of Psalm 82 is translated "congregation of the mighty" but is more properly "assembly of the gods." See also Psalm 8:5.

35. See note in NOAB 798 (Hebrew Bible).

36. This translation is by Florentino García Martinez, as quoted in Peterson, "'Ye Are Gods,'" 486.

37. Peterson, "Ye Are Gods."

38. Plato, *Phaedo* 76c, in Cooper, *Plato*, 67; see also 75b–d.

amount of evidence that has been collected—some of it reasonably scientific in nature, given the practical and ethical constraints of researching death—must at least give the open-minded skeptic pause. For the Latter-day Saint, the number of strong parallels between such mainstream reports and Mormon theology regarding the afterlife is striking, as the appendix will try to show. One of the clear parallels is the number of reports of those who have experienced NDEs who report an awareness that the spiritual realm they experienced was not new to them but was a familiar world where they existed before their life.

One man named Craig, who drowned while rafting on a river and was later resuscitated, stated: "[I had] a sense of travelling a long distance and finally making it home. I sensed that I had been here before, perhaps before being born into the physical world."[39] Another man declared about the realm he found himself in during his experience, "It was eternity. It's like I was always there and I will always be there, and that my existence on earth was just a brief instant."[40] A woman named Marsha referred to an intense awareness that there were "babies yet to be born" as well as "babies that had died" in the realm of light she found herself in during a near-death experience.[41]

One Latter-day Saint reported a lengthy and detailed account of an NDE including, as it were, a vision of his own premortality. This individual suffered throughout his life from cystic fibrosis, but he had been able to live a fairly full life, including a college degree, a church mission, marriage, and children. The following are a few brief excerpts from his story.

> I became aware of a voice talking to me . . . There was no one that I could see—but the voice persisted, not in my ears but in my mind . . . [The voice said]: You chose your disease and the amount of pain you would be willing to suffer before this life—when you were in a premortal state. It was your choice." While I was hearing this voice, I became aware that it was a familiar voice. . . it was a voice that I had not heard during my mortal lifetime [but] there was no question but that I knew who it was. There was enormous love for me in the voice. When he told me that it was my choice, in a premortal environment, to suffer when I came to earth, I was both astonished and incredulous. He must have understood my incredulity, because I was immediately transported to my premortal existence. There was a room that I was viewing from above and to the side, but at the same time I was sitting in it. In a sense I was both an observer and a participant. About thirty people were in the room, both men and women, and we were all dressed in the white jump-suit type of garment. An instructor was in the front of the room, and he was teaching about accountability and responsibility—and about pain. He was instructing us about

39. Ring and Valarino, *Lessons from the Light*, 14.

40. Ring, *Heading toward* Omega, 54.

41. Ring and Cooper, *Mindsight*, 36.

things we had to know in order to come to earth and get our bodies. Then he said, and I'll never forget this: "You can learn lessons one of two ways. You can move through life slowly, and have certain experiences, or there are ways that you can learn the lessons very quickly through pain and disease." He wrote on the board the words: Cystic Fibrosis, and he turned and asked for volunteers. I was a volunteer; I saw me raise my hand and offer to take the challenge.[42]

The story is striking, and one is tempted to take it seriously on the grounds that it would explain so much about our lives. As I have suggested previously, aside from concrete external evidence, perhaps the best support for the validity of an idea is its internal coherence and *explanatory power*. The more light that an idea is able to shed on otherwise obscure subjects, the more it deserves our respect. I would suggest that the belief in a premortal life can help us understand many aspects of our lives that otherwise seem unjust, unfair, and downright inexplicable.

We have already considered how the idea of a preexistence provides an illuminating third dimension to clarify the meaning of our existence. One of the great questions of humanity is how we came to this world, and how God can justify putting us here against our wills. LDS scriptures provide few details of how exactly our spirits ended up on this earth with physical bodies, but Joseph Smith taught that we were all present in the Grand Council. The assumption is that we all agreed—explicitly or implicitly—to come to this earth and suffer its ills, in the faith that in the end it would all be worth it.[43] It is also generally assumed that we were given enough details about those future sufferings, so that we in essence knew what we were getting into. We may or may not have had the chance to pick and choose our destiny as Plato speculated in the *Republic*. But with the belief in a premortal life, we cannot complain, as Byron's Cain, "I sought not to be born," nor with Kierkegaard, "How did I come into the world? Why was I not consulted?"[44]

The doctrine of premortal existence not only provides Latter-day Saints with the satisfaction of knowing that we all agreed to come here to be tested, but it also gives them a powerful sense of identity. As already noted, traditional Christian theology asserts only that men and women are the *creations* of God. LDS theology, on the other hand, teaches that all mankind are a) in some sense eternal and b) literal *offspring* of God. These two observations provide a powerful combination. On the one side, Latter-day Saints believe that there is a part of them (depending on how one interprets the term *intelligence*) that has always existed, that is entirely independent of God. This provides a strong sense of self-identity, a feeling that one is not simply a plaything, as it were, of God—to be controlled, shaped, manipulated.

42. Gibson, *Fingerprints of God*, 176–77.

43. Joseph taught that "the organization of the spiritual and heavenly worlds, and of spiritual and heavenly beings, was . . . voluntarily subscribed to by themselves." Ehat, *Words of Joseph Smith*, 253.

44. Lord Byron, *Cain*, act 1, scene 1; Kierkegaard, *Repetition and Philosophical Crumbs*, 60.

On the other side, Mormons believe that God actually begot the human family (again, the precise details are lacking) as his children, and therefore that we have a literal divine ancestry. What is more, Latter-day Saints believe that they have a Mother in heaven as well as a Father, and that they were raised as spirits as part of a divine Family. This doctrine of a Mother is not well understood, but it provides much of the justification for the religious emphasis on families, since human families have a divine model.[45]

The general notion that we are all children of God often serves as a basis for the idea of the equality of mankind, the assertion that we are all equal, no matter our backgrounds. For Latter-day Saints the doctrine is even more powerful, founded as it is on the conviction that we are all God's *literal* children and share the same divine potential. Most crucially, the knowledge of premortal existence provides a justification for the apparent unfairness of circumstance that many of us are born into. One commentator has summarized the implications of this doctrine thus:

> In such a view there are no enigmas and no baffling problems of providence to puzzle and confuse the mind. It is all clear, and understandable, and absolutely just . . . And what we are today, our circumstances, what befalls us in our present existence, and the like, these are not chance-blown, but are the fruit of what we were and did . . . All the disabilities that beset us arise from our own mistakes and wrongdoings in the past . . . We have no possible grievance against anyone or anything . . . there is something majestic in this conception of a fundamental justice woven into the very web of life, running through all things, and working itself out in everything that happens to us: a conception which leaves no room for whimpering, or whining, or self-pity, or railing against fate.

Oddly enough, this same commentator, after describing this solution to one of the most intractable problems of theology as "majestic," then condemns it as "too crude and easy a solution."[46] Is it possible for a concept to be both majestic and crude? Admittedly, if that were the *sole* explanation for everything that happened to us in this life (as the above paragraph seems to suggest), it could be criticized as simplistic. But nowhere does it say in the New Testament nor in LDS writings that our past behavior is the *only* cause for everything evil that besets us. In the next two chapters we will discuss such matters as the value of suffering in this life. But as we have already seen, Joseph Smith taught that God's whole purpose was to attempt to bring all of us to eternal life. It is easy to suppose that God, as our Father, placed us each in an earthly situation that would be beneficial for us.

Of course, from our limited perspective, we might view the most beneficial circumstance for us as being born into a wealthy family, with lots of opportunities for

---

45. See Givens, *Wrestling the Angel*, 106–111; Paulsen and Pulido, "'Mother There.'"
46. Buttrick, *Interpreter's Bible*, 8:611.

cultural and intellectual stimulation, a top-of-the-line education, and a high-flying career as a lawyer, doctor, or banker. However, the question we then need to address is: just how much happiness would we attain from such a life? Doctors and lawyers typically enjoy high levels of income and prestige. But lawyers, as a class, are an unhappy lot, grossly overworked and bored by their careers, with high rates of depression and suicide.[47] Dentists suffer from an even higher rate of suicide.[48] Doctors not infrequently suffer from burnout while they are still medical residents. Just how desirable are the most desired lives? Remember Plato's account of the foolish soul that chose the life of a powerful tyrant, oblivious to the fact that his fate would include eating his own children!

The point is that God our Father is more intelligent and much wiser than we, and has a much better idea of what will actually be to our benefit—and not for our superficial happiness in this life, but our eternal happiness. We will discuss this in greater detail in the next chapter. But for now it is enough to consider the possibility that even a life of constant challenge and difficulty may in fact help us to become stronger—emotionally, mentally, and spiritually—whereas a life of material success and physical ease may turn us into spoiled weaklings.

So, although we may not know how much actual choice we had over our specific circumstances in this life, faith in Deity implies trusting that he knew what was best for us and, consequently, being willing to accept our situation and try to learn whatever it is that we are supposed to learn from our brief time on this earth. So, however much say we might have had or not had, the notion of the premortal existence provides a potent assurance that the very idea of our existence on earth is not arbitrary, but is the outcome of a thoughtful plan by a loving Parent, and goes a long way toward answering the question of the meaning of our lives.

47. See, for example, "Lawyers and Depression."
48. Lang, "Stress in Dentistry."

5

Life Before Death—a Vale of Tears

Earth is not intended to be an altogether delightful abode any more than it is to be a place of wrath. Since the soil brings forth thistles, and roses have thorns, why should man's life not have its trials? It is not strange, or cruel. It is the urge of God that impels us to enlarge our lives and keep strong for that higher destiny which cannot be accomplished within the limits of earth. Only by striving for what is beyond us do we win expansion and joy.

—Helen Keller[1]

That which does not kill me makes me stronger.

—Friedrich Nietzsche[2]

Mormonism takes the view that humans are *basically* good. We are, after all, the offspring of deity. But we are also born with underdeveloped, immature spirits that often manifest considerable selfishness. To overcome this selfishness is not as impossible as it seems, but it does require a fair amount of desire and effort. It also requires help from God, which we must ask for—in faith. In the final analysis, the whole purpose of the gospel, the church, the scriptures, and the commandments of God are to help us progress toward a higher level of existence, one in which we can *tolerate* being in the presence of God—and he can tolerate being in ours! As noted in the previous chapter, God loves us in a way akin to how any father or mother loves their children, and his entire work is to bring about eternal life for all of us. Note that "eternal life," in LDS-speak, is not merely living forever (i.e., eternal in a *quantitative* sense), but living the very nature and *quality* of life which the eternal God himself lives.

Our mortal lives, of course, are the diametric opposite of eternal, whether considered in a quantitative or qualitative sense. Everything and everybody we encounter seems designed to be temporary. Our lives, above all, are impermanent, but also jobs,

1. Keller, *My Religion*, 148
2. Kaufmann, *Portable Nietzsche*, 467.

friendships, relationships, civilizations, and all the material goods with which we surround ourselves in a desperate attempt to be happy. The throwaway, consumerist society of the modern West is the epitome of impermanence. Happiness seems entirely fleeting: in those rare times when we think of ourselves as truly happy, we know intuitively that it will not last long. Human life has long been described as a "vale of tears."

For many people, one of the greatest obstacles to understanding the purpose of life and believing in a loving deity is the existence of evil and suffering in this life. This is the long-standing question of *theodicy* or the justice of God: if God is indeed all powerful and all-loving, how is it that we all suffer so much—and some, it seems, suffer a great deal? If he truly loves us and seeks for our happiness, why doesn't he just prevent bad things from happening to us?

Each of us—you, I, and everyone we have ever known or will ever know—endures considerable suffering of one sort or another during our mortal sojourn. Some of this suffering is physical; much of it is psychic. Disappointment—whether failure to get the job of our dreams or the man or woman of our dreams—is so common as to be inestimable in extent. Similarly infinite are the cases of limited suffering from common diseases such as migraines, gallstones, influenza, or pneumonia. There are countless instances where families have lost their homes or their lives through natural disasters. Somewhat less common in the modern West are such terrible occurrences as famines or war. Then there are those cases of particularly severe illness. The brilliant physicist Stephen Hawking contracted motor neuron disease at age twenty-one, which progressed to the point of paralyzing nearly every muscle in his body. Peter Kreeft describes a similarly tragic case, a friend of one of his students at Boston University, who came down with multiple sclerosis. She gradually lost her balance, then the strength in her limbs, and eventually became bedridden. By age twenty-seven she had lost the ability to lift her hand to scratch her nose, and could scarcely move any part of her body apart from her eyes, mouth, and head.[3] Then there are the countless victims of deliberate crimes—violent crimes such as terrorist attacks, rapes, assaults, kidnappings, and murders—and perpetrators of financial fraud—Bernie Madoff (2008), the officers of Enron (2001), and WorldCom (2002) cost their investors countless billions.

Cases of severe suffering can be multiplied indefinitely. The grand question is: how can the existence of such ubiquitous evil be reconciled with the belief in a world created by a good God? This is the classic problem of evil, which dates back at least to the Greek philosopher Epicurus in the third century BC: if God a) exists, b) is all good (omnibenevolent), and c) is all-powerful (omnipotent), how can the evil of this world be explained? The question applies not only to extreme evil, but to the existence of evil itself. Why is there evil at all?[4]

---

3. Kreeft, *Making Sense*, 4–5.

4. The church father Lactantius (third–fourth century) quotes Epicurus as follows: "God either wishes to take away evils, and is unable; or he is able and is unwilling; or he is neither willing nor able, or he is both willing and able. If he is willing and is unable, he is feeble, which is not in accordance

The easiest solution to this quandary is to conclude that God must not exist. Evil is ubiquitous, while God is nowhere to be seen. Why, then, should we insist that somewhere there is a God who desires only good for us and is all-powerful? If God does exist, there are two additional possibilities: either he must be a God who wishes evil on his creations, or he lacks the power to prevent evil.

The belief in an evil or non-beneficent God is not common today, but it has existed in times past. The ancient Gnostics, for example, believed that there were in fact two gods. The true Father was all-powerful and good, but he was entirely remote from this world. In contrast, the Creator of this world—that is, the Jewish *Yahweh*, the god of the Old Testament—was an entirely separate and lesser god, and in fact was an evil god, or at least a morally imperfect one. That is why the world, including human beings, is so imperfect and contains great evil.[5] Other historical religions that have encompassed belief in a dualistic, evil god include Manichaeanism, Zoroastrianism, and Albigensianism.

Some people, in attempting to explain the presence of evil, have theorized that God is less than all-powerful. This might seem counterintuitive—how can there be a God who is not omnipotent? But it is the approach taken by a well-read book, *When Bad Things Happen to Good People*, by Harold Kushner.[6] The author, a Jewish rabbi, describes how he had to face this question of suffering when his three-year-old son was diagnosed with a degenerative disease that would eventually take his life at around age fourteen. He says that he received this news with a strong sense of unfairness. Why would God condemn his innocent son to a brief life filled with physical and psychological pain? His ultimate conclusion to the quandary was that life, with all its random suffering, simply *is*. The world is an orderly place that follows natural laws, and God acquiesces in those laws. Life is inherently unfair, but God has nothing to do with the unfairness. God does not send suffering to people for their sins, and he despises all the pain and evil that humans are subject to. But he cannot prevent it, because that's simply the way life is. He will comfort us to help us endure the bad things in life, and he wants all of us to learn to do the same for others.

Kushner's views are designed to give us reassurance that suffering is normal and it is foolish to fight against it or to blame God for our troubles. God, Kushner assures us, wants all of us to get what we deserve in life, but he is not powerful enough to bring it about. We should not turn to God to have evil removed from our lives, and we should not expect him to miraculously give us what we want from life. Instead, we

---

with the character of God; if he is able and unwilling, he is envious, which is equally at variance with God; if he is neither willing nor able, he is both envious and feeble, and therefore not God; if he is both willing and able, which alone is suitable to God, from what source then are evils? or why does he not remove them?" *Treatise on the Anger of God*, ch. 13, in ANF 7:271.

5. Layton, *Gnostic Scriptures*, 12–19.

6. Kushner, *When Bad Things*.

should look to God for strength and comfort *in* our trials. We will still have to face our troubles—but we will not have to face them alone.

Such a view makes several important points—most importantly that God is not just a puppet master manipulating our fates with invisible strings. But Kushner provides no help when it comes to understanding the *meaning* of suffering in our lives. He acknowledges that God created a world in which people have the free will to commit evil. But why? Why create us and then put us in a situation where evil is ubiquitous and often overwhelming? Is there any purpose—any value—in our suffering?

If we turn to the Bible for an answer to this perplexity about evil, what do we find? As the well-published New Testament scholar Bart Ehrman has pointed out in a book entitled *God's Problem: How the Bible Fails to Answer Our Most Important Question—Why We Suffer*, the Bible has no single, clear-cut answer to the fundamental question of human suffering.[7] The various books of the Bible, of course, were written by many authors over many centuries, so we should not expect them to have a single, simple answer to this question.

What Ehrman calls the "classical view" of suffering, which was held by many writers in the Hebrew Bible, or Old Testament, is that suffering is the result of sin. A large part of the national myth of the ancient Israelites, especially as proclaimed by the classical prophets like Isaiah and Jeremiah, was that their suffering as a nation, and especially their defeat and captivity at the hands of their powerful neighbors such as the empires of Assyria, Babylon, and Persia, was the consequence of their sins and their unwillingness to repent. The Lord had chosen the Hebrews as his own people, but as such they were expected to obey the commands of their God. If they refused, or became lax, he would remove from them his special protection and they would be defeated and enslaved. The commands they were expected to follow included not only detailed religious rituals like animal sacrifices, but also a high level of ethics and morality. The prophet Isaiah declared:

> How the faithful city [Jerusalem]
>   has become a whore!
>   She that was full of justice,
> righteousness lodged in her—
>   but now murderers! . . .
> Your princes are rebels
>   and companions of thieves.
> Everyone loves a bribe
>   and runs after gifts.
> They do not defend the orphan,
>   and the widow's cause does not
>   come before them.
> Therefore says the Sovereign, the

7. Ehrman, *God's Problem*.

Lord of hosts, the Mighty
One of Israel:
Ah, I will pour out my wrath on my enemies,
and avenge myself on my foes!
I will turn my hand against you.[8]

Over a century later, at the time of the fall of Jerusalem to the Babylonians, it appears that the moral state of Israel had worsened:

Run to and fro through the streets of Jerusalem,
look around and take note!
Search its squares and see
if you can find one person
who acts justly
and seeks truth—
so that I may pardon Jerusalem.
Although they say, "As the Lord lives,"
yet they swear falsely.
O Lord, do your eyes not look for truth?
You have struck them,
but they felt no anguish;
you have consumed them,
but they refused to take correction.
They have made their faces harder than rock;
They have refused to turn back.[9]

Yet despite their hardness, the Lord always held out the possibility of redemption through repentance:

Zion shall be redeemed by justice,
and those in her who repent, by righteousness.
But rebels and sinners shall be destroyed together,
and those who forsake the Lord shall be consumed.[10]

With this sort of powerful national ideology, it was an easy step to the conclusion that anyone who was failing or suffering was obviously unrighteous. This was the conclusion of Job's friends, who were convinced that when Job lost his health, his property, and even his family, it was due to his own sinfulness. It is also one of the assumptions behind the comment of the apostles that we noted in the last chapter regarding the man who was born blind. Because the man suffered from blindness from birth, they naturally assumed that the cause was either that the man himself had sinned before birth, or that his parents had sinned before they bore him.

8. Isaiah 1:21–25.
9. Jeremiah 5:1–3.
10. Isaiah 1:27–29.

But this is certainly not the only biblical teaching with respect to suffering. Among many relevant passages in the New Testament, the Epistle to the Hebrews contains the most notable ideas regarding suffering—ideas which Bart Ehrman, in his haste to find fault with the Bible, completely ignores.[11] To the author of Hebrews, suffering is redemptive—that is, it actually leads one to salvation. Indeed, suffering is redemptive not only for mankind, but for Christ himself.

> It was fitting that God, for whom and through whom all things exist, in bringing many children to glory, should make the pioneer [or forerunner] of their salvation [i.e., Christ] perfect though sufferings.

> In the days of his flesh, Jesus offered up prayers and supplications, with loud cries and tears, to the one who was able to save him from death, and he was heard because of his reverent submission. Although he was a Son, he learned obedience through what he suffered; and having been made perfect, he became the source of eternal salvation for all who obey him.[12]

Jesus Christ himself, in the sufferings of his life and his death, was brought to perfection through his absolute obedience to the will of the Father, quite against his own personal preferences. Remember that Jesus prayed intensely to his Father in the garden prior to his crucifixion, "if you are willing, remove this cup from me; yet, not my will be done but yours be done." Christ's anguish at that moment was so great, Luke tells us, that "his sweat became like great drops of blood falling down on the ground."[13] This degree of obedience, according to the author of Hebrews, should be the model for the sacrifice of our own will to God's.

> Let us run with perseverance the race that is set before us, looking to Jesus, the pioneer [or forerunner] and perfecter of our faith . . . Consider him who endured such hostility against himself from sinners, so that you may not grow weary or lose heart . . . Endure trials for the sake of discipline. God is treating you as children. [Our earthly parents] disciplined us for a short time as seemed best to them, but he disciplines us *for our good, in order that we may share his holiness.* Now, discipline always seems painful rather than pleasant

---

11. Ehrman is a very capable scholar of early Christianity, but his book on this very important topic is unfortunately quite superficial. He entirely ignores, for example, the Epistle to the Hebrews, which explores in depth the principle of achieving perfection through suffering. One has the impression throughout that he is simply reacting against the "fundamentalist Bible college" training of his youth rather than seriously engaging the wide variety of sophisticated analytical discussion done by Bible scholars, theologians, and philosophers throughout the ages. Disappointingly, he appears to dismiss all of the latter with the summary comment that many such works are "intellectually unsatisfying, morally bankrupt, or practically useless" (*God's Problem*, 18).

12. Hebrews 2:10; 5:7–10.

13. Luke 22:42, 44.

at the time, but later it yields the peaceful fruit of righteousness to those who have been trained by it.[14]

The book of Hebrews is the best foundation for understanding the Mormon attitude toward the meaning of life, including the purpose of suffering. Joseph Smith's own history was filled with considerable pain, including a childhood of poverty; a severe infection in a leg bone, followed by surgery (without anesthetic) and several years of convalescence; the death of his beloved elder brother Alvin when Joseph was seventeen; the loss of five of his own children before the age of two; and intense persecution from his opponents beginning at age fourteen, including tarring and feathering and numerous arrests on concocted charges. In 1839 he was imprisoned with his brother and four other associates in Liberty, Missouri on charges of murder, treason, burglary, arson, and theft. They spent the entire winter without heat in the basement of a jail so cramped that they could not stand upright. During this insufferable confinement he wrote down a revelation he received in response to his own plea to God:

> O God, where art thou? And where is the pavilion that covereth thy hiding place? How long shall thy hand be stayed, and thine eye, yea thy pure eye, behold from the eternal heavens the wrongs of thy people and of thy servants, and thine ear be penetrated with their cries? . . .
>
> My son, peace be unto thy soul; thine adversity and thine afflictions shall be *but a small moment*; and then, *if thou endure it well, God shall exalt thee on high*, thou shalt triumph over thy foes.[15]

Only a few days later, Joseph recorded the following revelation, in which the Lord describes Joseph's sufferings in personal but hypothetical terms:

> If thou art called to pass through tribulation; if thou art in perils among false brethren; if thou art in perils among robbers; if thou art in perils by land or by sea; if thou art accused with all manner of false accusations; if thine enemies fall upon thee; if they tear thee from the society of thy father and mother and brethren and sisters; and if with a drawn sword thine enemies tear thee from the bosom of thy wife, and of thine offspring, and thine elder son, although but six years of age, shall cling to thy garments, and shall say, My father, my father, why can't you stay with us? O, my father, what are the men going to do with you? and if then he shall be thrust from thee by the sword, and thou be dragged to prison, and thine enemies prowl around thee like wolves for the blood of the lamb; and if thou shouldst be cast into the pit, or into the hands of murderers, and the sentence of death passed upon thee; if thou be cast into the deep; if the billowing surge conspire against thee; if fierce winds become thine enemy; if the heavens gather blackness, and all the elements combine to hedge up the way; and above all, if the very jaws of hell shall gape open the

---

14. Hebrews 12:1–2, 7–11.

15. D&C 121:1–2, 7–8.

mouth wide after thee, *know thou, my son, that all these things shall give thee experience, and shall be for thy good.* The Son of Man hath descended below them all. Art thou greater than he?[16]

The clear message from the Lord was that no matter how severe Joseph's trials and sufferings, the Lord was quite aware of them, and Joseph was being deliberately exposed to them for his own good and benefit. They were necessary experiences for him to endure in mortality, and if he endured them well and did not give in, he would be exalted in the kingdom of God. Note also that his sufferings in jail were described by the Lord as brief—"a small moment"—although they lasted some five months in nearly unbearable circumstances. They were brief, that is, in comparison with the eternal glory that he would eventually receive. As discussed from Hebrews above, the trials and difficulties of mortality, no matter how severe, are an important preparation for the future blessings of exaltation.

Thus, Joseph Smith's answer to the philosopher's quandary discussed above is that God is neither evil nor lacking in power to prevent evil, but deliberately allows his children to experience evil in this life as a kind of "discipline" and "training," as it were. But how does that make any sense? How can suffering benefit us? What good can come out of evil? And for what kind of future life is God trying to prepare us?

Of course, there is an infinite variety of personal suffering. Each instance is its own case, and in many cases it may be difficult for us to identify a specific redeeming value. But let us consider a handful of rather extreme challenges faced by certain individuals and their personal triumphs over adversity. Each of them describes a similar attitude, which can be briefly summarized in the familiar phrase, "what doesn't kill you makes you stronger."[17] Bart Ehrman, from his perspective as an agnostic scholar, says that he simply does not believe that statement is true. While he admits that occasionally "something good can come out of suffering," he insists that "the reality is that *most* suffering is not positive . . . A lot of times, what does not kill you, mars you for life, ruins your mental or physical well-being—permanently. We should never, in my view, take a glib view of suffering—our own or that of others."[18] And he is absolutely correct about the glib views of suffering by those who have had relatively easy lives. Instead of engaging in superficial moralizing, let us examine the personal statements of several individuals who have had lives of greater difficulty than most of us can even imagine.

16. D&C 122:5–8.

17. The statement comes from Nietzsche: *Was mich nicht umbringt, macht mich stärker* ("That which does not kill me makes me stronger"). See his *Twilight of the Idols*, "Maxims and Arrows," no. 8. Kaufmann, *Portable Nietzsche*, 467.

18. Ehrman, *God's Problem*, 156.

A LIFE WITHOUT LIGHT OR SOUND

The remarkable life of Helen Keller used to be well known but is probably less so today. She was born with the full use of all five senses, but a severe illness at the age of nineteen months left her both deaf and blind.

> My life is so complicated by a triple handicap of blindness, deafness, and imperfect speech that I cannot do the simplest thing without thought and effort to rationalize my experiences.[19]

It is nearly impossible for most of us to conceive of how, with such limitations, we would be able to cope even with the normal activities of life, let alone excel in life. Yet with the help of Annie Sullivan, her teacher and constant companion, Helen Keller learned not only to make her way in the world but to communicate effectively with the public. She graduated *magna cum laude* from Radcliffe College, read widely throughout her life, and was the author of twelve books and numerous articles. Her writing had a remarkable charm and flow considering that she had never heard the spoken word (except as a tiny baby) and could read only with her fingers.

As the quotation above indicates, even the simplest activity required tremendous effort beyond what the average person must exert. She described in her own words how she first came to grasp the link between the words her teacher was teaching her and the reality of the objects they referred to.

> My teacher, Anne Mansfield Sullivan, had been with me nearly a month, and she had taught me the names of a number of objects. She put them into my hand, spelled their names on her fingers and helped me to form the letters; but I had not the faintest idea what I was doing. I do not know what I thought. I have only a tactual memory of my fingers going through those motions, and changing from one position to another. One day she handed me a cup and spelled the word. Then she poured some liquid into the cup and formed the letters w-a-t-e-r. She says I looked puzzled, and persisted in confusing the two words, spelling cup for water and water for cup. Finally I became angry because Miss Sullivan kept repeating the words over and over again. In despair she led me out to the ivy-covered pump-house and made me hold the cup under the spout while she pumped. With her other hand she spelled w-a-t-e-r emphatically. I stood still, my whole body's attention fixed on the motions of her fingers as the cool stream flowed over my hand. All at once there was a strange stir within me—a misty consciousness, a sense of something remembered. It was as if I had come back to life after being dead! I understood that what my teacher was doing with her fingers meant that the cold something that was rushing over my hand was water, and that it was possible for me to communicate with other people by these hand signs. It was a wonderful day never to be forgotten!

19. This and all the following excerpts come from Keller, *My Religion*, 142–54.

It is impossible for anyone to imagine what a life of complete darkness and silence might be like, but it is easy to imagine that someone so cursed might become angry, bitter, and frustrated, and avoid most human interaction. Helen Keller, while acknowledging her condition as a superhuman challenge, saw such difficulties as a positive in her life and challenges in general as a necessary component of all human life. She was devoutly religious—not an orthodox Christian but a devoted follower of Emmanuel Swedenborg, a man from the eighteenth century who was both a scientist and a mystic. She is best represented by her own words, so I quote her at length, with certain phrases rendered in italics for emphasis.

> Once affliction was looked upon as a punishment from God—a burden to be borne passively and piously. The only idea of helping the victims of misfortune was to shelter them and leave them to meditate and live as contentedly as possible in the valley of the shadow. But now we understand that a sequestered life without aspiration enfeebles the spirit. It is exactly the same as with the body. The muscles must be used, or they lose their strength. If we do not go out of our limited experience somehow and use our memory, understanding, and sympathy, they become inactive. *It is by fighting the limitations, temptations, and failures of the world that we reach our highest possibilities.* That is what Swedenborg calls renouncing the world and worshipping God.
>
> Sick or well, blind or seeing, bond or free, we are here for a purpose and however we are situated, we please God better with useful deeds than with many prayers or pious resignation. The temple or church is empty unless the good of life fills it. It is not the stone walls that make it small or large, but the brave soul's light shining round about. The altar is holy if only it represents the altar of our heart upon which we offer the only sacrifices ever commanded— the love that is stronger than hate and the faith that overcometh doubt.
>
> A simple, childlike faith in a Divine Friend solves all the problems that come to us by land or sea. *Difficulties meet us at every turn. They are the accompaniment of life.* They result from combinations of character and individual idiosyncrasies. The surest way to meet them is to assume that we are immortal and that we have a Friend who "slumbers not, nor sleeps," and who watches over us and guides us—if we but let Him. With this thought strongly entrenched in our inmost being, we can do almost anything we wish and need not limit the things we think. We may help ourselves to all the beauty of the universe that we can hold. For every hurt there is recompense of tender sympathy. *Out of pain grow the violets of patience and sweetness*, the vision of the Holy Fire that touched the lips of Isaiah and kindled his life into spirit, and the contentment that comes with the evening star. *The marvelous richness of human experience would lose something of rewarding joy if there were no limitations to overcome. The hilltop hour would not be half so wonderful if there were no dark valley to traverse.*

I have never believed that my limitations were in any sense punishments or accidents. If I had held such a view, I could never have exerted the strength to overcome them. It has always seemed to me that there is a very special significance in the words of "the Epistle of Paul to the Hebrews": "If we are chastened, God dealeth with us as with sons." Swedenborg's teachings bear me out in this view. He defines the greatly misunderstood word chastening or chastisement, not as punishment, but as training, discipline, refinement of the soul.

Now, *limitations of all kinds are forms of chastening to encourage self-development and true freedom. They are tools put into our hands to hew away the stone and flint which keep the higher gifts hidden away in our being.* They tear away the bandage of indifference from our eyes, and we behold the burdens others are carrying, and we learn to help them by yielding to the dictates of a pitying heart.

The example of a newly blinded man is so concrete, I wish to use it as a type for all life-training. When he first loses his sight, he thinks there is nothing left for him but heartache and despair. He feels shut out from all that is human. Life to him is like the ashes on a cold hearth. The fire of ambition is quenched. The light of hope is gone out. The objects in which he once took delight seem to thrust out sharp edges at him as he gropes his way about. Even those who love him act unwittingly as an irritant to his feelings because he can no longer give them the support of his labor. Then comes some wise teacher and friend and assures him he can work with his hands and to a considerable degree train his hearing to take the place of sight. Often the stricken man does not believe it, and in his despair he interprets it as a mockery. Like a drowning person he strikes blindly at anyone that tries to save him. Nevertheless, the sufferer must be urged onward in spite of himself, and when he once realizes that he can put himself again in connection with the world, and fulfill the tasks worthy of a man, a being he did not dream of before unfolds itself within him. If he is wise, he discovers at last that happiness has very little to do with outward circumstances, and he treads his dark way with a firmer will than he ever felt in the light . . .

We need limitations and temptations to open our inner selves, dispel our ignorance, tear off disguises, throw down old idols, and destroy false standards. Only by such rude awakenings can we be led to dwell in a place where we are less cramped, less hindered by the ever-insistent External. *Only then do we discover a new capacity and appreciation of goodness and beauty and truth . . .* We may know that in every limitation we overcome and in the higher ideals we thus attain the whole kingdom of Love and Wisdom is present. In this way we learn that the real way to grow is by aspiring beyond our limitations, by wishing sublimely for great things and striving to achieve them. We grow in our increasing consciousness of the deeper meaning of the outer life in which we have always lived . . .

We can decide to let our trials crush us, or we can convert them to new forces of good. We can drift along with general opinion and tradition, or we can throw ourselves upon the guidance of the soul within and steer courageously toward truth. We cannot tell from the outside whether our experiences are really blessings or not. They are cups of poison, or cups of healthful life, according to what we ourselves put into them. The choices offered us are never so much between what we may or may not do, as between the principles from which we act when we are thwarted and limited. *Earth is not intended to be an altogether delightful abode any more than it is to be a place of wrath. Since the soil brings forth thistles, and roses have thorns, why should man's life not have its trials? It is not strange, or cruel. It is the urge of God that impels us to enlarge our lives and keep strong for that higher destiny which cannot be accomplished within the limits of earth. Only by striving for what is beyond us do we win expansion and joy.* Let us, then, take up that limitation which each one has, and follow the example of Him who bore upon his frail human shoulders the cross of the world, that He might become a luminous and inspiring influence, communicating life-giving thoughts and desires to the weak, the tempted, and the despondent.

A LIFE WITHOUT LIMBS

As difficult as Helen Keller's life must have been, it could hardly have been as challenging as Nick Vujicic's. Vujicic (pronounced voy-i-chich) is an inspirational speaker who was born without any limbs whatsoever. He has no arms or legs, although he has a small foot attached to the bottom of his torso. Yet despite his severe handicap, he graduated from high school, earned a college degree in finance and real estate, and has learned to swim, to surf, and to play football and golf.[20]

He describes how depressed his parents were at his birth, and how certain they were that his disabilities would be so completely overwhelming that he could live nothing like a normal or productive life. He also tells of his own despair, particularly as an adolescent, when he prayed for limbs and seriously contemplated suicide. Yet as an adult, and a devout evangelical Christian, he now travels worldwide to give inspirational talks, and he describes his life as "ridiculously good." He is married to a good-looking, physically "normal" woman, and has a general optimism toward life that is as captivating as it is remarkable.

Here are a few excerpts from his own writings regarding his views about his own life and life in general:

> Most of my parents' worst fears never materialized. Raising me was certainly not easy, but I think they'll tell you that for all the challenges, we had plenty of

20. Wardrop, "Man with No Arms."

laughter and joy. All things considered, I had an amazingly normal childhood in which I enjoyed tormenting my siblings.

What my family and I could not foresee was that my disability—my "burden"—could also be a blessing, offering me unique opportunities for reaching out to others, empathizing with them, understanding their pain, and offering them comfort. Yes, I do have distinct challenges, but I am blessed with a loving family, with a keen enough mind, and with a deep and abiding faith.

People often expect someone with a severe disability to be inactive, maybe even angry and withdrawn. I like to surprise them by showing that I lead a very adventurous and fulfilling existence.

As a child . . . I didn't know that I was different or that many challenges awaited me . . . I don't think we are ever given more than we can handle. I promise you that for every *disability* you have, you are blessed with more than enough *abilities* to overcome your challenges. God equipped me with an amazing amount of determination and other gifts too. I soon proved that even without limbs I was athletic and well coordinated.

As a boy, I spent many nights praying for limbs. I'd go to sleep crying and dream that I'd wake up to find they had miraculously appeared. It never happened, of course.

Sometimes, you see, God expects you to help out with the heavy lifting. You can wish. You can dream. You can hope. But you must also act upon those wishes, those dreams, and those hopes. You have to stretch beyond where you are to reach where you want to be.

It's . . . my pleasure to tell [others] how very precious they are. . . [and] to assure them that He does have a plan for their lives. God took my unusual body and invested me with the ability to uplift hearts and encourage spirits.

Too often bad stuff happens to people no matter how good they are. It may not be fair that you weren't born into a life of ease, but if that is your reality, you have to work with it.[21]

SURVIVING HELL

It is hard to think a more extreme case of unmitigated evil and suffering than the Nazi prison camps. Yet Viktor Frankl survived Auschwitz both physically and spiritually, and, surprisingly, was able to view his own sufferings as no different in kind from the sufferings of daily life. In his words,

A man's suffering is similar to the behavior of gas. If a certain quantity of gas is pumped into an empty chamber, it will fill the chamber completely and evenly, no matter how big the chamber. Thus suffering completely fills the human

---

21. Quotations are all from Vujicic, *Life without Limits*.

soul and conscious mind, no matter whether the suffering is great or little. Therefore the "size" of human suffering is absolutely relative.[22]

Even in a world where the individual had no autonomy whatsoever, he relates that it was still possible for persons to change their attitude toward their circumstances and preserve their moral foundations.

> Does man have no choice of action in the face of such circumstances? We can answer these questions from experience as well as on principle. The experience of camp life shows that man does have a choice of action. There were enough examples, often of a heroic nature, which proved that apathy could be overcome, irritability suppressed. Man *can* preserve a vestige of spiritual freedom, of independence of mind, even in such terrible conditions of psychic and physical stress.
>
> We who lived in concentration camps can remember the men who walked through the huts comforting others, giving away their last piece of bread. They may have been few in number, but they offer sufficient proof that everything can be taken from a man but one thing: the last of the human freedoms—to choose one's attitude in any given set of circumstances, to choose one's own way.

Bart Ehrman may refuse to believe Nietzsche's remark that whatever does not kill you makes you stronger. Frankl, on the other hand, not only believed the statement but, remarkably, quoted it to his fellow inmates when he was trying to keep them from losing hope. He believed deeply that each individual must find the meaning of his or her own life, and that suffering itself has a meaning, although that meaning cannot be told you by anyone else. He quoted the further statement from Nietzsche, "He who has a *why* to live can bear with almost any *how*."

No matter how much one might lament the existence of suffering in this life, there is no arguing that it does not, at least in many instances, bring about remarkable good. Of course, as Frankl and the others point out, it can cause one to despair if one allows it to do so. Although it may sound trite, it depends upon one's attitude. It also depends on what one understands life to be. Those who have a deep faith in a loving deity may have greater motivation to seek for a meaning to their suffering.

THE FUNDAMENTAL IMPORTANCE OF FREE WILL

We discussed in the previous chapter how crucial the concept of free agency is in Latter-day Saint thought. It is also of fundamental importance in the LDS understanding of the value of evil. Recall that it was actually Satan's counterproposition to the Father's plan that he would somehow destroy our free agency and thereby take all the credit for our salvation. This does not necessarily mean, as many Latter-day Saints today

22. All quotations are from Frankl, *Man's Search for Meaning*.

assume, that the devil would somehow compel all mankind to be good—the ultimate totalitarian dictatorship, as it were. Many early Latter-day Saints taught, in contrast, that Satan would have circumvented the need for us to choose between good and evil by promising salvation to all—from the most wholesome and virtuous to the most blackhearted villains. If we were all to be saved no matter what we thought or did, there would be no need to choose at all. A life of pure hedonism—or worse—would be just as good as a life of self-denial. And "if choice doesn't matter, then moral agency is an empty cliché."[23]

In the last chapter we posed the question of why God doesn't simply reveal himself to everyone on earth, tell us in a booming voice what he wants us to do, and make it clear that those who do good will be rewarded while those who do evil will be punished, thereby taking all the guessing out of the game. Let's now pursue that idea a little further. What would be the practical effect of such an approach? Suppose that every time you did something good you received an immediate reward, while every evil act resulted in immediate and indisputable punishment. How much room would that leave for meaningful choice? What if, for example, every time you struck someone in anger, your arm seized up with severe pain? Or every time you told a lie, your jaw froze up in lockjaw (or your nose grew an inch)? Or what if every time you stole a dollar, your own bank account shrank by two dollars, while each time you helped an elderly lady cross the street, your account increased by five dollars? If this were the type of world we lived in, only fools would ever do anything wrong. What if earthquakes killed only the wicked, while tornadoes miraculously spared the homes of the righteous? In such a moral environment, evil acts would disappear, but it would hardly be due to people's good hearts, nor would it have anything to do with making free moral choices. Instead of preparing us to be good moral actors, as an ancient Christian document tells us, God would be training us to be good investors:

> Don't be disturbed by the fact that we see the unrighteous enjoying wealth and those who serve God suffering in difficulties. We must have faith, brothers and sisters, for we are all competing in a trial being conducted by the living God. We are being trained [Gr. *gymnazometha*] by this present life, that we may gain a crown in the life which is to come. The righteous man never receives the fruit of his labor promptly, but must wait for it patiently. For *if God were to pay the righteous their reward quickly, we would immediately be training ourselves in commerce and not in godliness; and we would only seem to be righteous when in fact we were pursuing not piety but gain.*[24]

This is what I imagine Satan's plan to have been. If Satan had been put in charge of the world, as he wanted, he would have been the ideal deity—the god that everyone thinks they want. He would have made everything perfectly clear, blessing us

---

23. Givens, *Wrestling the Angel*, 132–34; see also Top, *Life Before*, 122–24.

24. 2 Clement 20, my translation.

whenever we did what he wanted and punishing us whenever we did wrong. He would have been a magnificent god, and he would have reveled in the glory that it brought him. The world would have been a much happier place—on the surface, anyway. The only problem would have been that when our lives were over, we would have learned nothing. It would be tantamount to an instructor handing out the answer book with the test—everybody gets an A! But what would be the point? We would go out of this world the same moral weaklings we were when we entered it. God's purpose of helping us progress in order to become more like him would be completely frustrated.

Instead of a world in which no one would be tempted to do anything wrong, God created a world in which each of us must struggle to make ethical and moral decisions. These decisions are not generally the type of ethical puzzles that philosophers like to invent, such as the famous trolley problem. We are rarely faced with impossible choices like whether to kill one person in order to save five others. Most of the time we struggle over much more mundane questions such as whether to punch someone in the face who just insulted us, whether to lash out angrily at a spouse or child when they irritate us, whether to proposition the young and attractive (but married) woman in the office down the hall who's been giving us flirtatious glances, or whether to return to the store when we realize that the checkout clerk undercharged us by twenty dollars. These types of problems have nothing to do with solving ethical quandaries, but rather with deciding whether we are willing to give up potential pleasures in order to do what we *already know* is right.

Again, if we knew for a certainty that we would be immediately discovered and punished for doing the *wrong* thing, there would be little temptation. It is because we think that we might be able to enjoy the sexual encounter, or the extra twenty dollars, without being found out that we engage in a personal struggle with our conscience.

Let's examine the example of the flirtatious office mate a little more closely. When the man realizes that an opportunity has presented itself, what is likely to go through his head? As a human being he naturally engages in the kind of self-debate that is often portrayed in cartoons with an angel and a demon on either shoulder. (I won't attempt to keep this scenario gender neutral by trying to project what might go through a woman's mind in a similar situation.)

> –Yes, one voice insists, *the woman is ravishingly beautiful and clearly shows an interest in me. Why should I forgo the pleasure of an evening with her? What harm could it do?* –Well (says his alter ego), you might be found out. Someone might see you—another colleague who knows that both of you are married. Gossip might start in the office, and word might even leak out and get back to one or both of the spouses. –Yes, but *think of the sex! Sure I love my wife. But this woman is so incredible! I just need to know what it would be like—just once. It might even help spice up my relationship with my wife!* –Oh, sure—what an excuse! Do you really want to be unfaithful to her? What would she say if she found out? Would she divorce you? –*I don't really know. I know it would break*

her heart. But she doesn't need to find out! As long as we're discreet. –But what if she does find out and she refuses to forgive you? What about the children? –Yeah, I know, but . . . this is an incredible opportunity—how can I just let it go? That woman is so hot! And what if she keeps flirting with me every time I pass by her office? What do I do then? –You could always walk down a different hallway. –Sure, but what if . . . what if . . .?

And so it goes. The controlling question is, of course: what harm would it do? Our hapless husband has already realized that his self-indulgence would *break his wife's heart.* Shouldn't that be enough? Shouldn't he put an end to the inner debate right there? And yet the voice of temptation refuses to go away. The appeal of the alternative is just too strong.

What then might happen to our protagonist in this little morality tale? Let's say that he tries to compromise with his conscience and he decides to have dinner with the woman—just dinner. But she comes on to him so strongly that the evening goes well beyond dinner. And of course the mutual enjoyment is too great to stop at one evening, so he begins to make excuses to his wife about having to work late at the office. And on it goes, until his wife eventually finds out and confronts him with the affair, and after much prevaricating he finally confesses and tells her that he wants a divorce. Or perhaps he swears that he will end the romance if she can forgive him, and she tries to forgive him but can't, and they eventually divorce and have a major custody battle over the children, who are emotionally destroyed over the conflict.

In the alternative, let's consider a slightly different scenario. On the day that he goes to office with the intention of inviting his alluring colleague to dinner, she is not in the office. Oh, of course!—he remembers. Thursday is the day she works from home . . . well, tomorrow then. But that evening he goes home at the usual time and after dinner turns on the television and starts watching a movie based on Tolstoy's *Anna Karenina.* As he becomes caught up in the story of Anna's affair with Vronsky, the dashing army officer, and the resulting downward spiral of her family life and personal happiness, he can't help but reflect on his own life, realizes what a risk he would be taking, and decides to forget about the woman altogether. And as he goes to bed he suddenly thinks of a friend of his who cheated on his wife several years ago, divorced his wife, and married his paramour and has regretted it ever since. Or perhaps the next day, while sitting at his desk, lost in a reverie about the young woman instead of doing his work, he overhears another middle-aged married man in his office hitting on one of the young secretaries and feels a certain disgust at the man's behavior. Reflecting on his own intentions, he suddenly feels a sense of shame and so changes his mind about the dinner invitation.

So what does our little imaginary story demonstrate? Among other things, it shows that one of the most important ways in which we learn to control our impulses and develop moral maturity is by reflecting on the potential results of our actions. And one way in which we learn to project possible evil results of our actions is by observing the world around us. We suffer from the effects of evil ourselves and then see others experience the same, and by means of our inborn sense of empathy we learn to combine those two observations and to recognize that our evil acts can bring about suffering in other people. It is by observing evil in the world and the effects of that evil that we come to understand just how *evil* evil really is.

To make this point clear, let's try to think of what would happen in such a scenario if it took place in a world in which there were no evil or suffering. If by that we refer to a world in which free choice did not exist—that is, the satanic despotism referred to above—it simply would not be possible for the man to choose to commit adultery. He would be literally compelled to do the right thing. If, on the other hand, we mean a world in which evil actions were instantly punished, it again seems unlikely that our man would dare to commit the sin. If it were a foregone conclusion that his momentary enjoyment would result in severe physical pain and immediate tragedy and the destruction of his family, he would probably not proceed with his fantasy.

But what if, on the other hand, by a "world without suffering" we mean a world in which the natural results of one's actions *did not cause any suffering*? What if we were free to act as we wished, but the natural consequences of our evil acts were somehow divorced from the acts themselves? Suppose that the man committed adultery, but somehow magically the effects of that transgression were immediately nullified. That would allow the husband to have his enjoyment without causing any heartache in his wife, without the risk of divorce and child custody battles. We would all be free to commit all kinds of evil without causing any suffering. We would get to eat our cake and still have it. A pretty marvelous world, yes? Maybe not.

Can you imagine a world in which Hitler could commit all his atrocities and nevertheless cause no suffering? No, neither can I, but let's try anyway, because *that seems to be the kind of world that most people think they want*. They want a world in which *they* at least are free to do what they want when they feel like it (as in the scenario outlined above), yet they also want to live in a world without suffering! I think it should be fairly clear that if such a world were possible, it would be the worst of all possible worlds. If the negative results of wrong actions were divorced from the acts themselves, people could violate all kinds of moral principles without causing any harm. Of course such a world is impossible, which is precisely the point. Our actions carry natural consequences, and until people are willing to *do good all the time*, the real world will be one in which evil and suffering play a major part.

To recap, when we dream about a world where there is no evil and no suffering, there are only four (theoretical) possibilities: a world in which a) evil does not exist because we are all automatons, without free will or the ability to do evil; b) evil does not exist because we have no *effective* free will, because the cause and effect nature of our actions are utterly obvious; c) evil exists but it (somehow!) does not result in any suffering whatsoever; or d) evil does not exist because everyone chooses willingly to do good continually. The fourth alternative is the only one that is compatible with real people with real desires *and* free will. Perhaps you think that the fourth alternative is just as unrealistic as the first three? I grant that it does seem too good to be true. Yet that is the one that God is seeking to bring about.

How will he accomplish that? Not by miraculously and instantaneously transforming us after death into creatures that have no desire to do evil. No, he expects us to *learn* to be good by viewing and experiencing evil ourselves. He has placed us in a world in which evil is rampant, and in which we can see the effects of wrong behavior, if we look for it. The real world is one in which we observe the realistic *fruits* of our actions and the actions of others. Those fruits, however, are not always obvious. If a man robs a bank, or a woman has her husband killed after taking out a huge life insurance policy, the perpetrator may seem to be happier as a result of his or her crime. Crooks may often seem to be among the most prosperous people in a society. Yet each of us has been given an inner light—what we typically call a "conscience," and what Mormons often refer to as the "light of Christ." That light tells us—when we listen to it!—that killing our spouse or committing adultery or robbing a bank is wrong. Not wrong simply because sooner or later we will suffer God's wrath, but wrong because of the harm it causes the victim and the victim's loved ones.

The good skeptic will immediately interject: Aren't moral codes just man-made institutions, not God-given? If morality were really given by God, why would moral codes differ so much from one culture to another? Values are inculcated in children almost from birth, and consequently people grow up with a deep-seated assumption that the values of their own cultural traditions are universal, when they clearly are not.

In fact, moral values may not differ as much as we often suppose. Psychologists Christopher Peterson and Martin Seligman, in conducting a cross-cultural study of values and character traits, found "a surprising amount of similarity across cultures" and pointed to "a historical and cross-cultural convergence of six core virtues: courage, justice, humanity, temperance, transcendence and wisdom."[25] Of course those values do not manifest themselves in the same way in every culture. And one can always point to individual cases in which cannibalism or some other seemingly horrendous practice is accepted. But in the larger picture, basic human morality has not changed much since the days of earliest antiquity.

But more important than the precise details of one's moral code is the fact that we *have* a deep-felt sense of right and wrong and whether we adhere to that moral sense or whether we routinely violate it. Do we regularly ignore our conscience when it's inconvenient and act contrary to our inner conviction? Do we occasionally steal money from others when we have the opportunity and feel that no one will find out, and then justify it by telling ourselves that we need the money for something important? Do we routinely justify behavior in ourselves that we condemn in others? To what extent are we even aware of how our actions affect others?

25. Peterson and Seligman, *Character Strengths*, 36.

Since we are here in great part to learn to distinguish good from evil, we must be directly exposed to evil. Whether we experience the Nazi camp in Dachau firsthand or merely read about it, we can see the vivid reality of evil. Those who experience it themselves learn the lesson much more vividly than those who only read about it. But the unfortunate reality is that *evil must actually happen and have actual consequences* before the rest of us can observe it. Hypothetical evil teaches us very little.

Most importantly, as we observe and experience evil, we can come to perceive evil *in ourselves*—hopefully on a much smaller scale than crimes against humanity. Indeed, it is historically quite plausible that the revelation of the Holocaust after World War II played a direct role in leading to the worldwide recognition of the evils of racism. When the world perceived the unmitigated evil resulting from hatred of the Jews, people began to perceive that all anti-Semitism was evil, even the mild, generic type that was quite common in the West in the decades prior to the war. What is more, as a result many people in the United States in particular came to the conclusion that racism and racial prejudice in all its guises was wrong and unjustifiable. This realization was soon expanded to include the repression of women and others.

When we come to a conviction of our own evil, we must repent—in the biblical usage, to "repent" means to lament, to regret, to have remorse, or to change one's path, to turn away and start a new life, as it were. Repentance sets us on a new path, one on which we examine our own behaviors and strive to do what is right, to the best of our ability and understanding.

Why must there be so much evil in the world in order for us to learn to be good? Couldn't we just learn how to be good by observing *goodness*? Unfortunately, it seems that human nature is such that we typically pay more attention to negative experiences than to positive ones—hence we learn more from the bad than from the good, and so suffering must be a significant part of our lives. The psychologists and philosophers confirm that discomfort—pain, suffering, intense challenges—is the best way for us to learn.[26] If we are too comfortable in our lives, it is all too easy to become complacent. Schopenhauer said it best, using the metaphor of shoes:

> We tend not to notice when things go well. Only when things go against our will does it really impress itself on our mind. Just as we are conscious not of the healthiness of our whole body but only of the little place where the shoe pinches, so we think not of the totality of our successful activities but of some insignificant trifle or other which continues to vex us . . . And yet, just as our body would burst asunder if the pressure of the atmosphere were removed from it, so would the arrogance of men expand, if not to the point of bursting then to that of the most unbridled folly, indeed madness, if the pressure of want, toil, calamity and frustration were removed from their life. One can even say that we *require* at all times a certain quantity of care of sorrow or

26. For a discussion of this topic from a psychological perspective, see Tedeschi and Calhoun, *Trauma and Transformation*; Southwick and Charney, *Resilience*.

want, as a ship requires ballast, in order to keep a straight course. Work, worry, toil and trouble are indeed the lot of almost all men their whole life long. And yet if every desire were satisfied as soon as it arose how would men occupy their lives, how would they pass the time? Imagine this race transported to a Utopia where everything grows of its own accord and turkeys fly around ready-roasted, where lovers find one another without any delay and keep one another without any difficulty: in such a place some men would die of boredom or hang themselves, some would fight and kill one another, and thus they would create for themselves more suffering than nature inflicts on them as it is.[27]

The key is that we must experience *both* good and evil, and it is from the contrast that we learn the most. One of the best-known passages from the Book of Mormon says:

> For it must needs be, that there is an opposition in all things. If not so . . . righteousness could not be brought to pass, neither wickedness, neither holiness nor misery, neither good nor bad . . . And to bring about [God's] eternal purposes in the end of man, it must needs be that there was an opposition; even the forbidden fruit in opposition to the tree of life; the one being sweet and the other bitter.[28]

Nobody questions the necessity of *opposition*—challenge, obstacles, and even physical suffering—when it comes to learning physical or mental skills. If we are trying to develop expertise in running, or in playing basketball or tennis, or in ballet, or playing the violin, we must suffer—we must submit to the discipline of the teacher along with countless hours of endurance and even physical pain. And when one is asked to describe the experience of medical school or law school, the word "grueling" is more likely to spring to one's mind than, say, "fun." Why then do we question the need for moral suffering as part of gaining moral strength? *Moral skill* is fundamentally no different from any other skill, though it is much harder to acquire than learning how to hit or throw a ball—and of course it is of infinitely greater importance. Moreover, we have no personal teacher, no coach to guide us step by step along a well-established path toward excellence. Rather, it is up to us to seek understanding by studying the words of the prophets and other great thinkers, based on our *desire* to understand what we are here on this earth to learn.

Thus, we might make a (partial) list of the positive qualities that suffering in all its manifestations can help us develop:

1. *Humility before God.* We learn to accept God's will, just as a child submits to its parents and ultimately comes to the realization that most of the parents' decisions that has it chafed against are in fact beneficial.

27. Schopenhauer, "On the Suffering."
28. 2 Nephi 2:11, 15.

2. *Compassion for others.* When we endure considerable suffering, we can empathize with others who are also suffering.

3. *Self-control, self-discipline, patience, endurance.* In the course of the struggle to become a better person, we are forced to school our appetites, our body, our will. And as we accomplish these things, we feel stronger and more confident in ourselves and our ability to cope with circumstance.[29]

4. *The ability to distinguish between good and evil.* This is one of the most important goals in this life—to learn to *recognize* or *discern* evil in all its guises, in great part through observing the *effects* of evil, both for ourselves and for others, and to use our *free agency* to choose the good.

5. *The ability to appreciate good things.* If everything we ate were sweet and we never experienced any bitterness to contrast with it, we could never really appreciate sweetness at all.

But let us return to a question we posed earlier: What kind of future is God preparing us for by requiring us to suffer through all this adversity? Of what ultimate value are compassion, self-control, and patience? In other words, how does evil in this life prepare us for *heaven*? Isn't heaven supposed to be a place of sheer goodness, peace, and tranquility? Why is it so important for us to become so well acquainted with evil and suffering, if heaven is to be a happy place free of evil? In the next chapter we will discuss in greater depth the LDS notion of heaven (aka the "celestial kingdom"). But for the moment, consider the following.

One easy answer to the question is that in order for heaven to be free of evil, everyone who dwells there must be fundamentally good and free of evil desires. A single particle of evil could eventually corrupt the whole. "The slightest taint of corruption means that the other world would be neither incorruptible nor eternal. The tiniest flaw in a building, institution, code, or character will inevitably prove fatal in the long run of eternity."[30]

But there is more to it than that. The conventional notion of heaven is that it will be simply a place of rest or a place to passively enjoy ourselves for eternity. If that

---

29. This notion of how suffering can help us build up our inner strength is now a trope in common discourse. For example, when the tennis player Caroline Wozniacki reflected back on the painful breakup with her fiancé (the golfer Rory McIlroy) just shortly before the wedding, she described the experience in the following news story (see Hood, "Caroline"):

> While it took some time to regain her footing, she now views the pain she went through as a necessary evil, something that has made her stronger than before. "You have to go through all of that. I think that taught me so much," she said. "I think I grew up so much in that short amount of time. I also realized who is always there for me and who is just there when things are good. And you learn just about life. You have to enjoy it while it's there. You have to enjoy all the great moments. I think now when I look back, I wouldn't have been without it. Because now I really know that I'm strong, I know what I want, I know what I can accept, what I can't accept, what I need, what I don't need."

30. Nibley, "Return to the Temple," 61.

were the case, there would perhaps be little need for us to experience a large degree of suffering. But for Mormons heaven is a place of activity and *engagement*. That is, they do not conceive of heaven as an eternity of worshipping God by singing hymns or playing harps. As many commentators have suggested, such a life would quickly become a hellish boredom. Nor is it an eternity of contemplating God, as the philosophers and mystics assert. Rather, it is an eternity of doing good works—of assisting God in his all-consuming labors on behalf of our fellow men and women (i.e., God's future children). The Bible tells us we are to be coheirs with Christ, and to rule in the universe along with him. This suggests, among other things, that we will possess considerable *power*, far beyond anything we can conceive of in this life. If we are to follow in Christ's footsteps and develop the abilities necessary to wield *responsibly* the kind of power that Christ has, we must learn to become like him—essentially, to develop all the classic virtues, such as self-control, patience, justice, courage, and love.

To sum up, then: for Latter-day Saints, trials and suffering are in fact a kind of blessing—though of course, by definition, they do not seem that way at the time we are experiencing them. It is only with spiritual insight, and *post factum* reflection, that we can perceive how our challenges have shaped us for the better and have taught us things that we could have learned in no other way. Of course, they can also, as Helen Keller pointed out, make us cynical and bitter, if we let them. But an understanding of the divinely ordained purpose of life brings with it at least a partial comprehension of the meaning of our sufferings.

Joseph Smith, who, as we have seen, had no easy life, described his life in the following colorful terms:

> I am like a huge, rough stone rolling down from a high mountain; and the only polishing I get is when some corner gets rubbed off by coming in contact with something else, striking with accelerated force against religious bigotry, priest-craft, lawyer-craft, doctor-craft, lying editors, suborned judges and jurors, and the authority of perjured executives, backed by mobs, blasphemers, licentious and corrupt men and women—all hell knocking off a corner here and a corner there. Thus I will become a smooth and polished shaft in the quiver of the Almighty.[31]

And of course, of all the forms of evil in this life, the greatest, and the most pointless and useless of all, it seems, is death.

---

31. *HOTC* 5:401.

6

Life after Life—Death as a Transition

Religion rises inevitably from our apprehension of our own death. To give meaning to meaninglessness is the endless quest of all religion. When death becomes the center of our consciousness, then religion authentically begins. Of all religions that I know, the one that most vehemently and persuasively defies and denies the reality of death is the original Mormonism of the prophet, seer and revelator Joseph Smith.

—Harold Bloom, Yale University[1]

All men know that they must die. And it is important that we should understand the reasons and causes of our exposure to the vicissitudes of life and death, and the designs and purposes of God in our coming into the world, our sufferings here, and our departure hence. What is the object of our coming into existence, then dying and falling away, to be here no more? It is but reasonable to suppose that God would reveal something in reference to the matter, and it is a subject we ought to study more than any other. We ought to study it day and night, for the world is ignorant in reference to their true condition and relation. If we have any claim on our Heavenly Father for anything, it is for knowledge on this important subject.

—Joseph Smith[2]

Death is the one indisputably *real* thing about our world. One can argue about so many other things—whether God exists, whether we have immortal spirits—but the reality of death is certain and incontrovertible for all of us. Nothing hits home the way death does, whether our own or that of a loved one. Hence, the question of whether there is any type of existence after this life, or whether all is darkness and oblivion, is perhaps the most pressing of all the great questions.

Human reflection on the mystery of death has been with us since the beginning of recorded history. Perhaps the earliest known literary work is the Epic of Gilgamesh, a work from ancient Sumer which dates to before 2000 BC. At the heart of this work

1. Quoted in Haws, *Mormon Image*, 278.
2. *TPJS* 324.

is the desire of the protagonist, Gilgamesh, to transcend his own mortality. When his bosom companion, Enkidu, is taken from him by the goddess Ishtar, he is at first inconsolable at his loss, and then he becomes highly distraught over his own mortality. He sets out on a quest to find the secret of immortality, and travels to a distant land where he meets Utnapishtim, a man who had obtained the gift of immortality from the gods. But it turns out that this gift was given on a one-time basis to Utnapishtim. Before sending Gilgamesh away, the old man tells him (as a kind of consolation) that if he seeks out a special plant at the bottom of the sea and eats the plant, he will regain his youth. Gilgamesh immediately swims down to the sea floor, where he finds the plant, only to lose it to a snake which swallows it first. The snake immediately demonstrates the power of the plant by sloughing off its skin. But Gilgamesh has once again found that, alas, immortality is out of his reach.

The anxious grief that accompanies death, either our imminent demise or the loss of a loved one, is a universal part of the human condition. As Harold Bloom notes, it can be considered at the root of the religious impulse. Our lives may be unpleasant in great part, even distressing, yet for most people, most of the time, the desire to continue living is constant, and the thought of our lives ending—i.e., our absolute extinction—causes acute psychic distress. And yet, apart from religious teachings, there is very little that anyone can point to as hard evidence that we do, indeed, exist after death.

EXPERIENCES NEAR DEATH

Or at least that was true prior to 1975. In that year Dr. Raymond Moody, a young medical student with a PhD in philosophy and an interest in psychiatry, published a best-selling book entitled *Life after Life*. Moody discussed what he called "near-death experiences," or NDEs, in which individuals reported experiences they had after they were declared clinically dead and before they were subsequently revived. He had become aware of such experiences almost by accident while in graduate school and quickly began noticing that many of these accounts contained notable similarities and common elements. He began collecting accounts of such experiences and published *Life after Life* to point out the remarkable ways in which these NDEs resembled each other and fell into patterns. He emphasized that while each subject's experiences were unique and personal, and they described them in somewhat different terms, there were enough striking similarities among them that one could draw up an ideal composite account from the common repeated elements from a survey of approximately 150 such accounts.[3]

3. Moody's first two books, *Life after Life* and *Reflections on Life after Life*, are still the best introduction to the serious study of NDEs, although many later studies have been conducted which have refined, or corrected, some of his statements. Moody's composite consisted of fifteen elements: 1) ineffability of the experience; 2) hearing the news of one's death; 3) feelings of peace and quiet;

Since the appearance of Moody's first book, a veritable industry of book publishing has sprung up around the subject of NDEs. As writers and researchers have sought out a broader sampling of such experiences, many thousands of people have come forward to share their own accounts—in many cases grateful that anyone has taken them seriously, since previously most doctors and nurses and even husbands and wives wanted nothing to do with such bizarre experiences.[4] As the number of accounts has multiplied, Moody's analysis of the core NDE has been generally confirmed, although the wide variety in individual experience has also become clearer. Following are some of the most prominent elements:

---

4) a loud buzzing or other noise; 5) passage through a dark tunnel; 6) an out-of-body experience; 7) meeting other spirits; 8) encountering a great being of light; 9) A review of one's entire life; 10) reaching a border, limit, or point of no return; 11) return to one's body; 12) attempting to tell others of one's experience; 13) profound effects on one's life thereafter, including 14) a dramatic change in one's attitude toward death; and 15) corroboration of certain details of one's experience by others. This model has some obvious limitations, in particular that the last four elements take place *after* the NDE per se has ended. Other researchers have attempted to refine the model. Kenneth Ring, a well-known student of the subject who wrote the first systematic study after *Life after Life*, offers an alternative model with five general elements: 1) peace and a sense of well-being; 2) separation from the body; 3) entering the darkness; 4) seeing the light; and 5) entering the light. See Ring, *Life at Death*.

I am fully aware of the complexities of the study of this subject and the limitations of the evidence available to researchers, but the numerous relevant issues cannot be discussed here in detail. Naturally one cannot conduct controlled experiments when the matter involves death or virtual death. Researchers must therefore rely on personal accounts, or testimonies, of what individuals experienced. These accounts may be presented as connected narratives or as responses to an interviewer's questions (or both). Many times (but certainly not always) the accounts are written down or told years or decades after the experience, although many subjects insist that they can recall the details of the NDE as if it happened yesterday because the experience was so vivid, real, and unforgettable. It is nearly impossible to know the extent to which apparent differences among individual accounts are due to a) actual differences in the original experience; b) differing emphasis on various details; c) varying degrees of recollection; or d) different levels of ability to accurately describe what was a highly unusual experience. With respect to d), it is important to keep in mind that one of the most fundamental and frequently stated aspects of such experiences is that they are *ineffable*. "Ineffable" means that something is impossible to adequately describe in words. One experiencer states that words are "three-dimensional." While the world of normal experience (and the language we use to discuss it!) is limited to three dimensions, the other world is not. "And that's why it's so hard to tell you this. I have to describe it in words that are three-dimensional. That's as close as I can get to it, but it's not really adequate. I can't really give you a complete picture." Moody, *Life after Life*, 19. But despite the otherworldliness of these experiences, they nonetheless seem real and include numerous concrete details.

4. In one case, a woman recounted that while she had an out-of-body experience after her heart stopped during surgery in a severe allergic reaction to the anesthetic, her "spirit" had travelled through the nurses' station. When she returned to the hospital following her eventual recovery, she revisited the same nursing station. "I finally worked up the courage to share what I saw with one of the nurses. The nurse responded with a look of shock and fright. This was a Catholic hospital. Not surprisingly, a nun was sent to talk with me. I patiently explained all that I had experienced. The nun listened carefully and then declared my experience to be the 'work of the devil.' You can understand my enormous reluctance to share my NDE with anyone after this." Long and Perry, *Evidence*, 28. Unfortunately, this type of reaction, while perhaps more dramatic than most, was quite typical for experiencers who attempted to share their experiences with medical professionals or loved ones. Today, now that the widespread phenomenon of NDEs is much better known, they presumably receive a more sympathetic hearing.

1) *An out-of-body experience*

It is quite common for near-death experiencers to suddenly find "themselves" outside their physical bodies. This "self" typically, but not always, has essentially the same shape as the physical body, with head, legs and arms, a mouth, and so on. They can frequently see their own physical bodies, for example, on the operating table, and can witness from a separate vantage point—say, from above, near the ceiling—the frantic attempts by medical personnel to revive them. The spirit-body has enhanced abilities beyond those of their physical bodies. That is, they still have their sense of hearing and sight and can perceive everything that is going on around them, but these senses are enhanced. For example, many people describe their power of vision as encompassing 360 degrees—they can see behind them as well as in front. On the other hand, they are unable to grasp anything physical (their hands pass right through objects) and when they speak, they are unable to make anyone in the normal world hear them. They can easily move through the air, and often witness what is going on, for example, in other parts of the hospital. Blind people report having the power of sight during this experience and deaf people the ability to hear. In numerous cases experiencers have been able to describe very specifically what certain people were doing or saying, which could later be verified with the people they saw and heard.[5]

A woman who had been admitted to the hospital with heart trouble was in her bed when she suddenly had severe chest pains and summoned the nurses.

> Just then, I heard the nurses shout, "Code pink! Code pink!" As they were say-
> ing this, I could feel myself moving out of my body and sliding down between
> the mattress and the rail on the side of the bed—actually it seemed as if I went
> *through* the rail—on down to the floor. Then, I started rising upward, slowly.
> On my way up, I saw more nurses come running into the room—there must
> have been a dozen of them. My doctor happened to be making his rounds
> in the hospital so they called him and I saw him come in, too. I thought, "I
> wonder what he's doing here." I drifted up past the light fixture—I saw it from
> the side and very distinctly—and then I stopped, floating right past below the
> ceiling, looking down . . . I watched them reviving me from up there! My body

5. The blind having sight during NDEs and the deaf being able to hear have been reported in many cases. See, for example, van Lommel, *Consciousness Beyond Life*, 24–26; Miller, *Near-Death Experiences*, 70–73. There are numerous cases of experiencers observing things while their body was unconscious, which could be verified later. Van Lommel, *Consciousness Beyond Life*, 20–21 relates an account told him directly by a nurse in a coronary unit who had to remove the dentures of an entirely comatose man who had suffered a heart attack, in order to intubate him. After more than a week in a coma, he was brought back to the coronary unit, and the patient immediately identified the nurse who, he said, knew where his dentures were. He was able to give a detailed description of the room where he had been resuscitated and of the appearance of those present in the room at the time. There are also reported cases of people who have seen things in the spirit world that they could not have possibly known. One four-year-old boy reported meeting his little brother on the "other side." The only problem was, he didn't have a little brother—that is, until his mother admitted, red-faced, that she had had an abortion at age thirteen. P. M. H. Atwater, in Bailey and Yates, *Near-Death Experience*, 242–43.

was lying down there stretched out on the bed, in plain view, and they were all standing around it. I heard one nurse say, "Oh, my God! She's gone!", while another one leaned down to give me mouth-to-mouth resuscitation. I'll never forget the way her hair looked; it was cut kind of short.[6]

A person who suffered complications during surgery related the following:

What happened was that I suddenly became aware of hovering over the foot of the operating table and watching the activity down below around the body of a human being. Soon it dawned on me that this was my own body. So I was hovering over it, above the lamp, which I could see through. I also heard everything that was said: "Hurry up, you bloody bastard" was one of the things I remember them shouting. And even weirder: I didn't just hear them talk, but could also read the minds of everybody in the room, or so it seemed to me. It was all quite close, I later learned, because it took four and a half minutes to get to my heart, which had stopped, going again. As a rule, oxygen deprivation causes brain damage after three or three and a half minutes. I also heard the doctor say that he thought I was dead. Later he confirmed saying this, and he was astonished to learn that I'd heard it. I also told them that they should mind their language during surgery.[7]

It is notable that during these out-of-body experiences, the person's conscious mind continues seamlessly with their previous consciousness. That is to say, mentally they are still the *same person*, even though they are now missing their physical body.

George Ritchie was a twenty-year-old in the U.S. Army in 1943 when he came down with a severe case of pneumonia only days before he was scheduled to complete basic training and go on to begin medical school. At one point, when he had a temperature of 106 degrees Fahrenheit, too weak to stand, the medical staff took him to have a chest X-ray. Suddenly he lost consciousness and then awoke in a strange room. He found himself "flying" at high speed over varied terrain, but finally decided he had to go back to the hospital to find his "body" which he vaguely understood he had somehow become "separated" from. Following a frantic search—still "flying"—through the various hospital wards, he finally found the room he had previously been in, and saw a body in the bed, with his own ring on the left hand. The hand, however, was entirely motionless, deathly pale. Finally, the reality of his situation began to dawn on him.

I backed toward the doorway. The man in that bed was dead! I felt the same reluctance I had the previous time at being in a room with a dead person. But, if that was my ring, then—then it was me, the separated part of me, lying under that sheet. Did that mean that I was . . . ? It was the first time in this entire experience that the word *death* occurred to me in connection with what was happening. But I was not dead! How could I be dead and still be awake?

6. Moody, *Life after Life*, 26–27.

7. Van Lommel, *Consciousness Beyond Life*, 21–22.

Thinking. Experiencing. Death was different. Death was . . . I didn't know. Blanking out. Nothingness. I was me, wide awake, only without a physical body to function in.[8]

2) A world of beauty, peace, and light

A large percentage of experiencers find themselves in a remarkable, unworldly environment, including such elements as landscapes, flowers, blue sky, and a city.

> The landscape was beautiful, blue skies, rolling hills, flowers. All was full of light, as if lit from within itself and emitting light, not reflecting it.

> There was such beauty, beautiful beyond expression. There was also a bright city or something like a city in the distance. The colors and structures of everything [were] beautiful . . . awesome.[9]

3) An encounter with other beings

It is quite common for an experiencer to see and interact with other spiritual beings, most frequently his or her own deceased relatives. A forty-three-year-old man who suffered cardiac arrest reported:

> I came to some place and there were all my relatives, my grandmother, my grandfather, my father, my uncle who had recently committed suicide. They all came towards me and greeted me. . . My grandparents were dressed . . . all in white and they had a hood over their heads. . . They looked better than the last time I saw them . . . very, very happy . . . I held hands with my grandmother. . . It seems like I had just come up on them and they raised their heads up and they were all happy . . . And all of a sudden they turned their back on me and walked away and my grandmother looked over her shoulder and she said, "We'll see you later, but not this time."[10]

Another heart attack victim encountered an individual whom he didn't recognize at the time, but who turned out to be a close relative:

> During my NDE following a cardiac arrest, I saw both my dead grandmother and a man who looked at me lovingly but whom I didn't know. Over ten years later my mother confided on her deathbed that I'd been born from an extramarital affair; my biological father was a Jewish man who'd been deported and killed in World War II. My mother showed me a photograph. The unfamiliar

---

8. Ritchie, *Return from Tomorrow*, 56–57.

9. Long and Perry, *Evidence of the Afterlife*, 14.

10. Sabom, *Recollections of Death*, 48.

man I'd seen more than ten years earlier during my NDE turned out to be my biological father.[11]

4) *An encounter with a being of light*

Sometimes, but by no means in all cases, the person finds himself drawn through a long dark tunnel at the end of which is a bright light. Even if the tunnel itself is absent, the bright light is typical, and it grows brighter as one approaches it. The light is frequently described as being unusually brilliant, even brighter than the sun, yet at the same time gentle enough to look at without discomfort. It is also described as radiating love. Many people describe the entire environment in this other world as full of love. But the most powerful source of this love seems to be this light, which is not merely a light but an actual being. Sometimes people describe this being as having actual shape or a specific identity, such as God or Jesus. Others refer only to the light, but it is clear that the light has a discrete presence and personality. Several accounts even describe the being as having a marvelous sense of humor.[12]

> Just as clear and plain the Lord came and stood and held his hands out for me. Well, he stood there and looked down at me and it was all bright then. . . He was tall with his hands out and he had all white on, like he had a white robe on . . . It [the face] was more beautiful than anything you've ever seen. His face was beautiful, really and truly beautiful. His skin was almost like it was glowing and it was flawless, absolutely flawless . . . He just looked down at me and kind of smiled . . .[13]

5) *A review of one's life*

In the so-called life review, the person experiences a movie-like panorama of his entire life.

> The flashback was in the form of mental pictures, I would say, but they were much more vivid than normal ones. I saw only the high points, but it was so rapid it was like looking through a volume of my entire life and being able to do it within a few seconds. It just flashed before me like a motion picture that

---

11. Van Lommel, *Consciousness Beyond Life*, 33

12. One woman reports arguing with the being that she was too young to die. The being would not change his mind until she said, "But I'm young, I haven't danced enough yet." At that point the Being gave out a hearty laugh and allowed her to live." Moody, *Light Beyond*, 17. See further Top and Top, *Glimpses Beyond*, 113–14.

13. Sabom, *Recollections of Death*, 49.

goes tremendously fast, yet I was fully able to see it, and able to comprehend it.[14]

The being of light knew everything about me. It knew all I had ever thought, said, or done, and it showed me my whole life in a flash of an instant. I was shown all of the details in my life, the one I'd already lived, and all that was to come if I returned to earth. It was all there at the same time, all the details of all the cause-and-effect relations in my life, all that was good or negative, all of the effects my life on earth had had on others, and all of the effects the lives of others that had touched me had had on me.[15]

This review of one's behavior throughout one's earthly life does not consist of a judgment by the being of light, but the person herself often views certain aspects of her life with considerable remorse.

I proceeded to other situations that had raised question marks in my own life. The how and why of my actions became clear to me because I saw, sensed, and knew how people had felt during (and frequently also after) contact with me. I viewed several episodes from my life. I recognized and felt everything as though I had gone back in time and completely in the actual moment.

What had I done with my life? My God, I was my own judge and executioner at the same time. When I realized that I had done something wrong, I wanted to go back to make amends . . . I hadn't really done anything wrong, but I felt the pain, the misgivings, the anger, the powerlessness, and the sadness of all the people who felt upset by my words and actions.[16]

6) *The choice to return*

Following the life review, the person often perceives a boundary or limit beyond which they cannot go and still return to normal life. They are often given a specific choice of whether to return to their physical bodies, and it is not uncommon for the person to be reluctant to return, as the experience they are having is so blissful. Nonetheless, frequently they decide to return when they reflect on the pain that their death would cause loved ones. In some cases they are instructed by the being of light or another being that their mission in life has not been completed and that they should choose to return to complete it. In certain cases they seemed to be required to return to their body even when they chose to remain.

I wondered whether I should stay there, but as I did I remembered my family, my three children and my husband. Now, this is the part that is hard to get

14. Moody, *Life after Life*, 52.

15. Long and Perry, *Evidence of the Afterlife*, 116.

16. Van Lommel, *Consciousness Beyond Life*, 206.

across: When I had this wonderful feeling, there in the presence of that light, I really didn't want to come back. but I take my responsibilities very seriously, and I knew that I had a duty to my family. So I decided to try to come back.[17]

He showed me a gate behind which I saw the same landscape. But now, with this gate in front, it suddenly looked extremely familiar. I came to the startling conclusion: I've been here before. It felt like a homecoming after an arduous journey. A state that led to complete peace of mind, a peace of mind I hadn't known for a long time. For me this was the highlight of the experience. Without a word the figure encouraged me to decide whether I wanted to remain in this state or whether I wanted to return to earthly life. I could either enter the gate or return to the lifeless body, which I immediately sensed below me. I had the impression that entry through this gate meant definitive physical death. Aware that this was my chance to go back knowing that this state of being is a reality that feels more real than what we call reality and thinking of my young wife and our three small children, I opted to return . . .[18]

7) *A profound change*

Perhaps the most significant and concrete aspect of these experiences is the dramatic effect they have on the individuals who have experienced them. The overwhelming majority of NDE experiencers are absolutely certain that the other world they experienced was real—that they have a spiritual existence that transcends the death of the body, that God is real, and that they returned from that world to this one for a specific reason. That reason might be, as already mentioned, to raise their children or to comfort their loved ones. But often they feel a deep commitment to live their lives in a more spiritual way. Many people do not feel any great desire to go to church (though some do), but they feel that it is deeply important to show love to the people they encounter in life. Many people also feel a deep need to gain additional knowledge in this life. Above all, they typically feel a greater sense of meaning and purpose in their own lives and in the world in general. One man said:

Whatever we go through individually—or collectively as a nation and a world—it is all for a common . . . goal. That goal is to learn and improve so as to move closer to the source of the light of love. . . It's like a preschool preparing you for another school—and that's what life is. I don't know when those schools end, maybe never. And that's exciting to me. . . the experience of life is so profound and has so much more to offer than we normally think. Pain and suffering for example are an important part of life. One day of life is worth all the pain and suffering that we might have to go through. My death

17. Moody, *Life after Life*, 58.
18. Van Lommel, *Consciousness Beyond Life*, 39–40.

experience—if that's what it was—doesn't hold a candle to how I now value and get joy from each day.[19]

A woman named Sylvia, who had her NDE while a rebellious teenager, following a motorcycle accident, had always considered herself an atheist. Following the experience, she said that she considered herself

> a very spiritual person, however I am not associated with any denominational creed. My spirituality did not unfold overnight after my NDE, but it developed—slowly but surely—and is still expanding today. . . I came back feeling that I had to learn, that I had to absorb like a sponge as much as I could. It was as though I was charged with a duty to learn. . . when I was floating through the tunnel, I understood that it was important and dutiful that I learn all that I could. I no longer could afford to be a superficial teenager. . . before my NDE I was not all that excited about school. Within a few years of my NDE, I became, and remained, a 4.0 student. From that point on, I have been thirsty to read and learn about a variety of subjects.

When one first hears of such accounts, it is quite reasonable to be skeptical. After all, how could anything so bizarre be real? The person must have simply imagined the experience, or must have been dreaming. Perhaps the experiences are hallucinations caused by shock or drugs administered to the victim. Yet the commonalities in these accounts seem to belie the possibility that they are mere dreams or imaginings. What are the chances that any two individuals, let alone hundreds or thousands, could have *dreams* or hallucinations with such a high degree of correlation? Even more significantly, there are large number of cases in which the NDE was experienced by individuals whose heart and brain had completely ceased functioning. According to all medical understanding, the brain shuts down within seconds after it stops receiving blood from the heart, and there is no explanation for a non-functioning brain to have any thoughts at all, let alone experiences as powerful, vivid, and spiritually moving as NDEs typically are.[20]

The following excerpt suggests just how lucid and vivid an NDE can be. In response to the question of whether her experience could have been a dream or hallucination, one woman stated:

> No [it was not]. There is no doubt in my mind that my NDE was a real event, and that I was experiencing it while it happened. I heard the sounds, felt the

---

19. Gibson, *Fingerprints of God*, 66–67. The effects of NDEs on those who experience them has been discussed at length in Morse, *Transformed by the Light*. See also, Ring, *Heading toward Omega*.

20. Dr. van Lommel, a cardiac surgeon, points out that upon cessation of blood flow to the brain in cardiac arrest, and the consequent loss of oxygen to the brain tissue, there is a total loss of electrical activity in the cerebral cortex, resulting in a flat EEG after an average of fifteen seconds. Tests suggest that the brain stem also ceases functioning, although van Lommel points out that the bare possibility that there is still some basic functioning in the lower brain cannot explain how there could be *any* type of consciousness with a non-functioning cortex. Van Lommel, *Consciousness Beyond Life*, 161–65.

coolish temperature, saw the surprising colors. It was a harmonious, consistent and coherent development of a very complex set of elements which I could have never thought of, or made up myself. Nothing which I had experienced up to that moment in my life would have led me to even come close to being able to invent such dynamics or coherence. It was as real as when I drive to school from home, or when I shop at a supermarket. I'm sure that it was not a hallucination, a dream, or any other type of fantasy.[21]

Naturally, many attempts have been made to find a purely rational and naturalistic explanation for these experiences. Yet so far, none of these attempts has been at all successful in discovering adequate causation for the complexities and vividness of NDEs or the variety of circumstances under which they occur. A wide variety of physical causes have been discussed as possible triggers, including hypoxia (low oxygen levels in the brain), hypercarbia (elevated carbon dioxide level), and various drugs and chemicals, including endorphins, ketamine, and DMT. Some of these factors produce elements that bear similarity to certain elements of the NDE, yet none of them have reproduced anything even closely resembling a full-blown near-death experience. One sometimes encounters the claim that all the *elements* of NDEs have been reproduced scientifically. Even if that statement is true in a strictly literal sense—though I find it questionable—it is highly misleading. Just because other causes have been found that occasionally cause, for example, feelings of euphoria, visions of tunnels or bright lights, or glimpses of the faces of deceased loved ones, one should not equate those individual elements with, as the quotation above states, "a harmonious, consistent and coherent development of a very complex set of elements." To my knowledge, no one has ever recorded an instance of any naturally explicable experience that can compare with, for example, George Ritchie's highly complex account of travelling in the air over hundreds of miles of recognizable terrain (i.e., he recognized the details of the terrain when he travelled through it by car *after* his experience) and meeting with a being and taking a tour with him of several different levels of postmortal existence.[22]

While those who find in NDEs clear evidence of a real afterlife are sometimes criticized as being biased, or engaging in wishful thinking, or going beyond where the evidence takes us, the accusation of bias cuts both ways. It is not only the proponents of NDEs as proof of life after death that have found the so-called scientific approach guilty of reductionism. There is a strong tendency of reductionism among scientific and academic types to declare that a certain phenomenon is "nothing but X"—e.g., the NDE is "nothing but a hallucination" or "merely the effect of one's cultural expectations." Allan Kellehear, a sociologist who cannot be accused of trying to prove the reality of NDEs, maintains that the cloak of value neutrality with which the scientists

---

21. Gibson, *Fingerprints of God*, 65.

22. For a discussion of more naturalistic explanations of these experiences, see Greyson, *After*, 98–111. For more detailed discussions, along with extensive bibliography of such claims, see Greyson et al., "Explanatory Models."

clothe themselves does not completely hide their partisanship. He argues at length that despite the claim of value neutrality, "more than a few current neuroscience explanations are partisan ones." They often "appeal in loaded terms to fellow believers" of the theory that NDEs are essentially hallucinations, and subtly "question the rationality and credibility of other views and their advocates."[23]

Michael Sabom tells of a skeptic's article that appeared in the *Journal of the American Medical Association* in the early years following the publication of *Life after Life* (before Sabom himself, I should note, became a believer in NDEs). Dr. Richard Blacher, the author of that article, insisted that "death experiences" were caused by hypoxia and "the fantasy of death," establishing "the certainty of heaven" and answering "so many puzzles of mankind" that it is a "tempting conceit for speculation." For this reason, Blacher said, "the physician must be especially wary of accepting religious belief as scientific data." Sabom replied in the same journal that NDEs were "not by themselves prima facie evidence of life after death," but that the appearance of "sensational after-life proclamations by prophets in the lay media" should not be "countered with scientific assertions based on anecdotal evidence . . . Dr. Blacher points out that 'the physician must be especially wary of accepting religious belief as scientific data.' I might add that equal caution should be exercised in accepting scientific belief as scientific data."[24]

As there isn't room here to do a fair summary of the evidence and arguments pro and con, I will merely refer the interested reader to the publications mentioned in the footnote attached here.[25]

23. Kellehear, *Experiences Near Death*, 119–39.

24. Sabom, *Recollections of Death*, 152.

25. The fact that the phenomenon of NDEs has been the subject of extensive scholarly study has unfortunately been obscured by a seemingly unending stream of popular books and movies. Most people are familiar with the bestsellers that narrate the individual author's experience with death. But the topic has been studied in considerable depth from scholarly perspectives, including studies published in top medical journals. The best in-depth discussions are Van Lommel, *Consciousness Beyond Life* and Sabom, *Recollections of Death*. Van Lommel and Sabom are both cardiologists who were at first skeptical about the reports they heard from patients about their experiences. Sabom writes from the position of a highly skeptical physician initially certain that all consciousness was a product of the brain and could not exist apart from the brain. His investigations, however, convinced him that NDEs provided clear evidence that the soul departed from the body at death, but not necessarily that there was a full-fledged afterlife. ("I must admit that when I first read *Life After Life*, I felt these experiences were either fabrications by persons who had taken advantage of the author, Dr. Raymond Moody, or were embellishments by Moody himself to produce a best-selling book. Five years and 116 interviews later [with experiencers], I am convinced that my original suspicions were wrong" [p. 156]). Alexander, *Proof of Heaven*, relates that his personal NDE caused him to completely abandon his scientific conviction that consciousness is entirely brain-based. Morse, *Closer to the Light*, focused on NDEs of children, on the grounds that they would be less likely "contaminated" by religious and other backgrounds typical of adults. The fact that many experiencers are non-religious, or even atheists, goes a long way to making the same point.

Difficulties with such studies from a scientific point of view have been pointed out—for example, that the evidence is anecdotal and often the accounts are retold many years after the fact. But given the practical constraints of death research, the evidence is now quite copious . . . and the parallels

NDEs AND MORMONISM

My father happened to buy a copy of Dr. Moody's *Life after Life* at about the same time I joined the LDS church. He told me briefly about the book and I was intrigued, but I never got around to reading it until several years later, after I returned home from my two-year stint as a missionary. I was immediately struck by the parallels with Mormon teachings about the afterlife. My further research has strengthened that reaction, though I have become much more aware of the complexities and nuances of the matter. There isn't space in this chapter to do a detailed comparison of LDS beliefs regarding death with the elements of the NDEs we have considered, but I have included a detailed discussion of such parallels in the appendix.

For present purposes, I will merely point out that for many decades—and long before publication of *Life after Life* (1975)—Latter-day Saints passed down a variety of stories about visits to the spirit world. Mostly these accounts were buried in sources that were not readily available either inside or outside the Mormon community, such as transcripts of sermons and personal diaries, until they were compiled and analyzed by Duane Crowther in his book *Life Everlasting*, published in 1967. Numerous themes and details found in the experiences he recorded in that book anticipated specific aspects of Moody's and his successors' findings.

One of the most familiar of such accounts to Latter-day Saints is that of Jedediah M. Grant, an associate of Brigham Young's, who, while on his deathbed, related to his colleague Heber C. Kimball an account of two visits he had recently made to the spirit world. At the funeral, Kimball related to the mourners what Grant had told him. Grant said that he had visited the spirit world two nights in succession, and that he had "felt extremely sorrowful at having to leave so beautiful a place and come back to

among accounts go a long way to supporting the contention that they are in general fairly accurate. See Morse, *Transformed by the Light*. Susan Blackmore, *Dying to Live*, is a strong attempt to make a sustained argument in favor of a strictly naturalistic view of NDEs. She goes to great lengths to make her discussion "fair," in the sense that she takes counter-arguments seriously and is willing to take a critical attitude toward some of the well-known scientific theories that she finds unconvincing. But her conclusion that NDEs have nothing to do with a real afterlife is clearly based at least as much on her *a priori* philosophy as on the evidence she examines. In her preface she states her major assumption: "There is no future heaven toward which evolution progresses. And no ultimate purpose . . . Yet our minds have evolved to create purposefulness and cling to the idea of a self because that will more efficiently keep alive the body and perpetuate its genes. In other words, our evolution makes it very hard for us to accept the idea of . . . our own individual pointlessness." Blackmore, *Dying to Live*, xii. In her conclusion, she insists that the evidence in favor of her "dying brain hypothesis," which she discussed throughout the book, is overwhelming, but she then goes far beyond the evidence to claim: "We are biological organisms, evolved in fascinating ways for no purpose at all and with no end in mind. We are simply here and this is how it is" (263–64).

There is also the additional complexity of so-called hellish NDEs, which have not been very widely studied, in part because those who have experienced them may be highly reluctant to talk about them. It is nearly impossible to find a strictly neutral examination of the evidence regarding NDEs, but the closest thing is Mark Fox, who maintains a balanced tone in *Religion, Spirituality*. Fox is an academic in philosophy and religious studies. A good encyclopedic survey of the field is Holden et al., *Handbook of Near-Death Experiences*.

earth," which is precisely the sentiment expressed by many experiencers when faced with the choice of whether to stay in the other world or to return to their families.[26] He encountered there many people he had known, and he conversed with his deceased wife, who was holding their small daughter who had died during the migration to Utah. He described the buildings he saw as surpassing the beauty of the temple of Solomon, and spoke of exquisite flowers and other vegetation.[27]

In 1898 a certain Latter-day Saint named Peter Johnson related:

> my spirit left the body; just how I cannot tell. But I perceived myself standing some four or five feet in the air, and saw my body lying on the bed. I felt perfectly natural, but as this was a new condition, I began to make observations. I turned my head, shrugged my shoulders, felt with my hands, and realized that it was myself. I also knew that my body was lying, lifeless, on the bed. While I was in a new environment, it did not seem strange, for I realized everything that was going on, and perceived that I was the same in the spirit as I had been in the body. While contemplating this new condition, something attracted my attention, and on turning around I beheld a personage, who said: 'You did not know that I was here.' I replied: 'No, but I see you are. Who are you?' 'I am your guardian angel; I have been following you constantly while on earth.' I asked: 'What will you do now?' He replied: 'I am to report your presence, and you will remain here until I return.'[28]

Many years later, Heber Q. Hale, an LDS stake president in Boise, Idaho, related that he had been allowed to "visit" the spirit world, and said that the things he saw and experienced were "as real to me as any experience of my life." He told of meeting his

> beloved mother. She greeted me most affectionately and expressed surprise at seeing me there and reminded me that I had not completed my allotted mission on earth. She seemed to be going somewhere and was in a hurry and accordingly took her leave, saying that she would see me again soon. I moved forward, traversing an appreciable distance and consuming considerable time, viewing the wonderful sights of landscapes, parks, trees, and flowers, and meeting people, some of whom I knew, but many thousands of whom I did not recognize as acquaintances. . . I moved forward feasting my eyes upon the beauty of everything about me and glorifying in the indescribable peace and happiness that abound in everybody and through everything. The further I went the more glorious things appeared.

Among the things that emerge most clearly from these accounts, as from the modern NDEs, are the perception that there is complete continuity between one's consciousness in this life and the next; that spirit beings appear much like they do in

26. Crowther, *Life Everlasting*, 9.

27. Crowther, *Life Everlasting*, 76–77.

28. Crowther, *Life Everlasting*, 4–5.

this life—i.e., they are easily recognizable; that there is full sociability between spirits; that the experiencer is often highly reluctant to return to his or her body; that he or she comes away from the experience with no doubt that it was as real as (or more real than!) anything experienced in this life.

Experiencers also report, as we have seen, the presence of a being of light. According to Moody, many people report that this light, though "of an indescribable brilliance . . . does not in any way hurt their eyes, or dazzle them . . . Despite the light's unusual manifestation . . . not one person has expressed any doubt whatsoever that it was a being, a being of light. Not only that, it is a personal being. It has a very definite personality."[29]

But it is not only this one being that is made of light. The experiencer himself sometimes describes his own spirit body as glowing. One man told Dr. Moody that "his hands were composed of light with tiny structures in them. He could even see the delicate whorls of his fingerprints." Another man reported:

> Looking at my hands I could see that they were white and they glowed—and I was dressed in a glowing white garment. I could feel the energy coming from me. It was coming from every part of my body.[30]

This description bears considerable similarity to that of Joseph Smith regarding the appearance of the angel Moroni.

> While I was thus in the act of calling upon God, I discovered a light appearing in my room, which continued to increase until the room was lighter than at noonday, when immediately a personage appeared at my bedside, standing in the air, for his feet did not touch the floor. He had on a loose robe of most exquisite whiteness. It was a whiteness beyond anything earthly I had ever seen; nor do I believe that any earthly thing could be made to appear so exceedingly white and brilliant. His hands were naked, and his arms also, a little above the wrist; so also were his feet naked, as were his legs, a little above the ankles. His head and neck were also bare. I could discover that he had no other clothing on but this robe, as it was open, so that I could see into his bosom.[31]

Brigham Young similarly explained about the next world:

> The brightness and glory of the next apartment is inexpressible. It is not encumbered with this clog of dirt we are carrying around here so when we advance in years we have to be stubbing along and to be careful lest we fall down. We see our youth, even, frequently stubbing their toes and falling down. But yonder, how different! They move with ease and like lightning. If we want to visit Jerusalem, or this, that, or the other place—and I presume we will be

29. Moody, *Life after Life*, 43.
30. Lundahl and Widdison, *Eternal Journey*, 108.
31. *HOTC* 1:11.

permitted if we desire—there we are, looking at its streets. . . If we wish to understand how they are living here on these western islands, or in China, we are there; in fact, we are like the light of the morning, or, I will not say the electric fluid, but its operations on the wires.[32]

The reader who desires a more thorough discussion of these parallels can refer to the appendix. But this brief discussion should be sufficient to show a significant degree of similarity between modern accounts of NDEs and earlier accounts of Latter-day Saints regarding the afterlife.

THE POWER OF GOD

Latter-day Saint theology declares that this life is only a small part of an eternal existence. Latter-day Saints believe that our life stretches eternally in both directions, and that this life is a crucial but relatively brief segment that will seem in retrospect like a mere moment, much as an eighty-year-old man can reflect on the four years he spent in college. While he is in college, it may seem like the most significant stage of life, full of profound learning and excitement, suffering and terror, but sixty years later it will seem instead that it was an important *formative* stage in his life but on the whole not that big a deal. Similarly, a law student may feel that she is learning the law during three grueling years of instruction, yet a year or two later, after engaging in professional practice, she will realize how little law she actually knew upon graduation.

In addition to the belief that death is only a (relatively) minor change in the venue of one's existence, Mormons have a vastly different idea regarding the nature of the afterlife in comparison with the usual Christian beliefs. To begin with, they have nothing like the conventional belief of a stark division in the afterlife between the wicked, who will dwell in hell, and the blessed dead, who will dwell forever in heaven. Instead, Joseph Smith taught that there are three degrees of glory, to one of which virtually everyone will go. (The one small exception consists of those few souls who absolutely reject God in full knowledge of what they are doing and are consigned to "outer darkness" as "sons of perdition.")

Thus, from one perspective, it seems as though everyone will be allotted some level of heaven, although there is a great divide between the various degrees. The highest degree of divine glory is referred to as the "celestial kingdom," which is where Latter-day Saints expect and hope to go, so long as they are "true and faithful" to the covenants they make with God in baptism and elsewhere. The celestial kingdom is considered the holiest place, in the presence of God himself. It is populated by the "just," who have been "made perfect" through Jesus Christ. The second level of heaven, the "terrestrial kingdom," is for those who lived "honorable" lives but who were "blinded by the craftiness of men," and as a result will "receive of [God's] glory,

32. *Journal of Discourses*, 14:231.

but not of his fulness" and will live in the presence of the Son but not God the Father. Finally, the "telestial kingdom" will be filled with those who were "liars, and sorcerers, and adulterers, and whoremongers, and whosoever loves and makes a lie." Thus, the telestial world is made up of what we would commonly call the "wicked," who will "suffer the wrath of Almighty God" until the completion of all things, at which point they will be "redeemed from the devil" into this lowest kingdom.[33] Note that the lowest kingdom is not a place of suffering but a place of *glory*, though far below the other two. The term "glory" is frequently associated in LDS Scripture with the concept of light, and the differences among the three kingdoms, or degrees of glory, are often compared to the differences among the sun, the moon, and the stars.[34]

Christian theologians, of course, have argued for centuries over who will be saved and who will be damned. Reformed Christians follow the teachings of Calvin, who notoriously taught absolute predestination—that all men and women were allotted, before their birth, to either salvation in heaven or damnation in hell, and that nothing that one does in this life could alter that destiny. Universalists, in the opposite extreme, believe that all mankind will ultimately be saved into heaven. While they may first experience a long period of punishment, at long last they will be reconciled with God.

Mormons are closer to the universalist belief, in that no one, except the sons of perdition, will be condemned to eternal suffering. Everyone else will live in glory, although the nature of that glory may differ greatly. God our Father has absolutely no desire to condemn anyone to eternal suffering. At the same time, the celestial kingdom is intended to be a place of complete purity and joy, free from any taint of evil or ungodliness. As a consequence, only those who have proven that they are willing to follow the path of godliness can be allowed to enter.

This point merits considerable emphasis. Heaven, as it is popularly conceived, is a kind of reward for good behavior, like an eternal Christmas ("He knows if you've been bad or good, so be good for goodness' sake!"). It is a marvelous place where everyone will be happy forever. Perhaps we will dwell in green meadows and spend all the rest of our existence glorifying God and playing harps. The LDS conception of the celestial kingdom, however, is quite different. It is not so much an everlasting reward as it is a place of great glory where great *work* is done—God's work. To dwell there, to be sure, implies eternal joy and happiness, but it also means to become a coparticipant with God in his future works. Remember the scripture that states that God's "work and glory" is to bring about the immortality and eternal life of man—not only on this earth but on many, many other worlds that exist throughout the cosmos. Exaltation means not only to live in God's presence, but to participate in God's life.

33. All these phrases are found in section 76 of D&C.

34. On glory and light, see 2 Corinthians 3:7; 4:6; Alma 19:6; D&C 65:5; 76:19; 93:36. On three degrees of glory, see 1 Corinthians 15:40–42; D&C 76:70–71, 78, 81.

Some reflection on the implications of this idea are in order. What would it actually mean to be participants in God's work? We discussed in chapter 3 the human need for fulfilling work, activity with real meaning and purpose. Have you ever reflected on the question of what would really bring you happiness for eternity? No, perhaps not. But consider it now: if you could create your own designer heaven, how would you do it? What kind of life would bring you optimum satisfaction—*forever*? Once you got past the flippant suggestions (eternal mind-blowing sex, a self-replenishing refrigerator full of beer, an endless marathon of episodes of *Cheers* or *Friends* or *The Twilight Zone*), what would be your considered answer? An open-ended opportunity to develop all those hobbies you never had time for? An infinite library of good books? Endless opportunities for stimulating companionship, perhaps?[35] The assumption that our basic desire for meaningful work will suddenly disappear in the next life is not realistic. Thus, despite the reassurances of the theologians and mystics, mere contemplation of God for eternity will not fit the bill. Nor will a heaven that is merely a rest from all labor—frolicking among the clouds, etc. Who would really find an eternal picnic attractive?

The only realistic view of heaven, it seems, is one in which there is great potential for significant, meaningful labor and accomplishment. But what kind of labor?

According to the distinguished Hungarian psychologist Mihaly Csikszentmihalyi, what really brings us happiness is involvement in an activity in which we are completely absorbed—so absorbed that we are scarcely aware of the passage of time. It must be an activity that fully engages one's abilities—if it is too easy, it results in boredom; too hard, and the result is frustration. The state known as "flow" is "being completely involved in an activity for its own sake. The ego falls away. Time flies. Every

35. *Heaven: A History*, by McDannell and Lang, is an excellent scholarly overview of the varying perspectives of what a Christian heaven would be like, drawing on popular art and literature as well as theology. There is a wide range of views, as one would expect over a two-thousand year history. Yet the macro-perspective, as the authors portray it, reveals an alternation between a "God-oriented heaven" and a "people-oriented heaven." The former, in its most extreme formulation, is a heaven in which deity is the sole focus of attention. There are no meaningful relationships between individuals, only with God. As Augustine opined, "He [God] shall be the end of our desires who shall be seen without end, loved without cloy, praised without weariness." The people-centered view of heaven, in contrast, is one where opportunities exist to interact with one's loved ones and perhaps great figures of the past whom one has always been dying to meet (pun intended). Some nineteenth-century authors took this to an extreme, imagining a world in which God took a clear backseat to one's own beloved, and "souls actively pursue their enlightenment without the direct intervention of God" (p. 301). Twentieth-century Mormonism, in this view, is a peculiar carryover of nineteenth-century domestic views of heaven, as mainstream views in the modern era have mostly reverted to an extreme minimalism. Paul Tillich, for example, considered one of the most influential theologian/philosophers of the twentieth century, contended that the individual soul itself is not immortal, but rather "the spirit or the essence of being: not the essence of the *human* being but the essence of all being." Fundamentalist preachers insisted, meanwhile, that the Bible tells us next to nothing about the nature of heaven or eternal life, and that our concern should be with how to get there rather than with what it will be like once we do. Randy Alcorn, on the other hand, a current popular Christian author, makes a rather convincing claim that the Bible tells us much more about heaven than most serious theologians are willing to admit, in *Heaven*.

action, movement, and thought follows inevitably from the previous one, like playing jazz. Your whole being is involved, and you're using your skills to the utmost."[36] It is an "optimal experience" that involves "deep concentration, high and balanced challenges and skills," as well as "a sense of control and satisfaction."[37]

But there is one further element that he ignores, which I believe is of fundamental importance for long-term satisfaction and contentment with one's life, namely, that one's activities must be *other-directed*. As we discussed in chapter 3, jobs that are merely quite interesting and self-rewarding are not considered truly meaningful. It must be something that has a significant and lasting impact on others—an adult literacy teacher, as one example.

So we return to the question: what would it mean to become a participant in God's work? If we believe, along with much of Christianity, that God is on an entirely different level of being from us (or, as the theologian Karl Barth put it, God is not *a being* at all but instead is *Being itself*), the question scarcely makes any sense. If God merely speaks and it is done, he has no need whatsoever of help from us. There is nothing left for us to do but praise his incomprehensible power and glory. If, however, God is an *actual* being of tremendous power and glory but one who makes use of countless messengers—angels—to carry out his work, then there is much for us to do.

The LDS God is both less and more than the conventional God. He does not create a universe merely by uttering a word, but neither does he limit himself to creating a single world. His creations are many—in fact, they are virtually infinite:

> And worlds without number have I created; and I also created them for mine own purpose . . . For behold, there are many worlds that have passed away by the word of my power. And there are many that now stand, and innumerable are they unto man; but all things are numbered unto me, for they are mine and I know them. . . And as one earth shall pass away, and the heavens thereof even so shall another come; and there is no end to my works, neither to my words. For behold, this is my work and my glory—to bring to pass the immortality and eternal life of man.[38]

These words of God, according to LDS scripture, preceded the revelation to Moses which we call the Genesis creation account in the Bible. Moses had asked God to tell him in detail about all his creations, but God refused; it was enough to tell him about the world on which he lived. But Latter-day Saints believe that it would be odd for an infinite God to create only one world, especially when the astronomers today inform us that there are over one hundred *billion* galaxies in the universe, each of which contains billions of stars. Scientists are aware of thousands of exoplanets, at least a few of which are potentially habitable, and there are surely countless more.

---

36. Geirland, "Go with The Flow."
37. Csikszentmihalyi, *Flow*, 83.
38. Moses 1:33, 38–39.

However many worlds may exist in such near-infinity, the key point is that those other worlds are populated not with bug-eyed aliens but with humans, all of whom, like us, were literally created in the image of God. And God of course is not merely their creator but is intimately involved in bringing to pass their immortality and eternal life. As God's children, we will be privileged to participate in that work.

Of what will this work consist? That question goes well beyond what has been revealed to us. But if we are trying to imagine a work that will be interesting, complex, multilayered, compelling, and infinite in extent, the LDS image of the eternities is hard to beat. Doubtless it will involve such activities as teaching, exhorting, administering, managing, building, and creating. Perhaps even researching and writing books!

One thing seems certain, however: the heirs of the celestial kingdom will be granted considerable power as corulers with Christ. This doctrine is found not only in Mormon scripture but in the New Testament as well:

> If we have died with him [Christ] we will also live with him; if we endure, we will also *reign* with him.[39]

> What are human beings that you [i.e., God] are mindful of them, or mortals, that you care for them? You have made them for a little while lower than the angels; you have *crowned* them with *glory* and *honor, subjecting all things under their feet.* Now in subjecting all things to them, God left nothing outside *their control.*[40]

> To everyone who conquers and continues to do my works to the end, I will give *authority* [Greek: *exousia*, meaning *power* as well as authority] over the nations; to *rule* them with an iron rod . . . even as I also received authority from my Father.[41]

LDS scripture states clearly the importance of learning to live the law of God before one can be trusted with power:

> Then shall they be gods, because they have no end; therefore shall they be from everlasting to everlasting, because they continue; then shall they be above all, because all things are subject to them. *Then shall they be gods, because they have all power, and the angels are subject to them.* Verily, verily, I say unto you, *except ye abide my law, ye cannot attain to this glory.*[42]

As we all know, power corrupts, and absolute power corrupts absolutely.[43] So the question becomes: how can God entrust others with even a small degree of the

---

39. 2 Timothy 2:12.

40. Hebrews 2:5–8.

41. Revelation 2:26–28.

42. D&C 132:20–21.

43. This is a common misquote of a statement by Lord Acton, who actually wrote: "Power tends to corrupt and absolute power corrupts absolutely. Great men are almost always bad men, even when

power he possesses? Clearly only those who have a high degree of goodness can be so entrusted. And what is goodness? Put simply, it is freedom from corrupt influences. Put even more simply, it is freedom from selfish desires.

Why is it that power typically leads to corruption in the one who possesses it? It is because with the acquisition of power comes the overwhelming temptation to use it for one's own selfish purposes. A ready example of this is King David. David, as the Old Testament tells the story, was a remarkably humble young man of great purity and devotion to God, who, among many other remarkable accomplishments, repeatedly resisted the temptation to kill King Saul when it was within his power to do so, even though he knew that Saul was trying to kill him. He was eventually rewarded by God with the kingship itself. However, one day he saw Bathsheba bathing on a rooftop near the palace, and conceived an overwhelming desire to bed her. When she became pregnant with his son, he determined to marry her, but he first had to get rid of her husband, Uriah. He did not have Uriah killed outright, but he ordered his general Joab to place Uriah "in the forefront of the hardest fighting, and then draw back from him, so that he may be struck down and die."[44] The plan worked like a charm, and David was able to wed Bathsheba.

The prophet Nathan afterwards confronted David with his sin by the use of a parable. There were two men, Nathan told him, in one city. The one man was wealthy and had many flocks and herds. The other was poor and had only a single lamb, which he cherished almost as if it were his own child. When the rich man had a visitor, instead of killing one of his own flock for dinner, he seized the poor man's lamb and slaughtered it for the meal. When David heard this story, he was incensed and said,

> As the Lord lives, the man who has done this deserves to die; he shall restore the lamb fourfold, because he did this thing, and because he had no pity.

Then Nathan issued his stinging rebuke:

> *You are the man!* Thus says the Lord, the God of Israel: I anointed you king over Israel, and I rescued you from the hand of Saul. . . Why have you despised the word of the Lord, to do what is evil in his sight? You have struck down Uriah the Hittite with the sword and have taken his wife to be your wife.[45]

It is hard to imagine a clearer example of the misuse of power for selfish ends. Did David commit this wickedness because he was a thoroughly evil man? Clearly not. He was, in general, a very good man, but a man with all-too-human weaknesses. The Lord entrusted him with power as the king of Israel, but when David betrayed that trust, the Lord cursed him. What would be the result if God gave cosmic power

---

they exercise influence and not authority; still more when you superadd the tendency of the certainty of corruption by authority."

44. 2 Samuel 11:15.

45. See 2 Samuel 12:1–10.

to those who could not wield it responsibly? The answer is obvious: if there is any risk that we will misuse that power, he cannot give it to us.

How, then, can we qualify for such blessings? Clearly, none of us is perfect and even the best among us are cursed with a greater or lesser degree of selfishness. Most people essentially assume that if and when we get to heaven, our natures will suddenly be transformed, "in the twinkling of an eye,"[46] from so-so or pretty good to perfect. But that is not the LDS view. In the Book of Mormon it is stated that "the same spirit which doth possess your bodies at the time that ye go out of this life . . . will have power to possess your body in that eternal world."[47] The implication of this is that we cannot be satisfied in this life with being more-or-less good, clinging to certain sins and assuming that everything wrong with us will somehow be fixed after we die. We cannot plan to come before God and plead that we really didn't mean it, that we really meant to be a better person, but the temptations were just too strong for us. Remember Huck Finn's experience:

> And I about made up my mind to pray, and see if I couldn't try to quit being the kind of a boy I was and be better. So I kneeled down. But the words wouldn't come. Why wouldn't they? It warn't no use to try and hide it from Him. Nor from ME, neither. I knowed very well why they wouldn't come. It was because my heart warn't right; it was because I warn't square; it was because I was playing double. I was letting ON to give up sin, but away inside of me I was holding on to the biggest one of all. I was trying to make my mouth SAY I would do the right thing and the clean thing . . . but deep down in me I knowed it was a lie, and He knowed it. You can't pray a lie—I found that out.[48]

Thus, *repentance* from our sins is not merely an attempt to show God that we can be good little boys and girls so that he will give us nice presents and not condemn us to hellfire. Rather, it is an ongoing attempt to struggle against one's imperfections, both large and small. This life, we are told in the Book of Mormon, is the time to *prepare* to meet and to live with God—i.e., to prepare as well as we can for life in a perfect, eternal society. Latter-day Saints have no false expectations that they will achieve perfection in this life. They do, however, believe that one must continue genuinely to struggle to get as close to that goal as is humanly possible. Another way of putting it is that we must demonstrate full commitment to the work of our own salvation. A half-hearted attempt will not be enough.

To those who come from a Christian Reformed or evangelical background, this may sound as though Mormons believe in working their way to heaven. Martin Luther, John Calvin, and all who followed in those traditions taught and believed that faith alone—without good works—is necessary for salvation, and that belief in the

---

46. 1 Corinthians 15:52.

47. Alma 34:34.

48. Twain, *Adventures of Huckleberry Finn* (ch. 31), 208–9.

essentiality of works is a kind of heresy, because it denies the salvific power of Christ. Christ's death on the cross, for them, is a free gift, one that comes from the pure good-ness of God without any effort on our part.[49]

This is not the place to discuss the grand controversy over faith versus works, on which huge amounts of ink (and now gigabytes) have been consumed.[50] My only point here is that LDS doctrine does *not* teach that we can somehow pull ourselves up into heaven by our bootstraps, as it were—by our own efforts. We cannot even pull ourselves up part way. Mormons believe without reserve in the salvific power of Christ's atonement. Instead, LDS theology asserts that God wishes to give his richest blessings to *all* his children, but that many will not be willing or able to *accept* them. Why not?

As an analogy, think of a teenager who is eager to get his or her first car. If he is a typical teenager, he may want this more than he can possibly express. His father, a generous man, is eager to buy it for him. In fact, it turns out that his father has a huge fleet of cars and is ready to give one of them to each of his children entirely *gratis*. But the father does have one qualification that each child must accept: *they must learn to drive safely and obtain their driver's license.* Does this mean that the car is not a free gift? Not at all; the stipulation is merely a reasonable requirement for anyone who is to be granted the privilege of driving a motor vehicle. If the son or daughter is willing to make the effort to learn to drive responsibly, they will receive that gift; if not, they will lose it.

Like the car, the blessings of exaltation include great power, as we have just seen. And with great power naturally comes great responsibility. Again, God is willing and eager to give us as great a gift as we are willing to accept. But accepting this gift means that we must prepare for it. We cannot assume, as we have already said, that God will miraculously transform us into a perfect being simply because of our superficial

---

49. Timothy Keller, in *The Reason for God*, oddly contrasts the "Christian gospel" with what he calls "religion." "Religion" he defines as belief in salvation through *moral effort*, while he equates the "gospel" with salvation through *grace*. The attitude of the former is that you must live your life by "avoiding sin and living morally so that God will have to bless you . . . You are trusting in your own goodness rather than in Jesus for your standing with God. You are trying to save yourself by following Jesus." It is "self-salvation through good works" (p. 177). For the Latter-day Saint (as for many other Christians throughout history), this is a false dichotomy. As the Epistle of James points out, while we are saved by faith in Christ, and not through our works per se, good works are still *necessary* for salvation, because there is no such thing as true faith without them. Martin Luther famously criticized James as "an epistle of straw, compared to the others, for it has nothing of the nature of the gospel about it." See Luther, *Word and Sacrament I*, 395–97. This of course sidesteps the awkward fact that Paul himself, the great apostle of grace, repeatedly emphasized that God "will repay according to each one's deeds: to those who by patiently doing good seek for glory and honor and immortality, he will give eternal life; while for those who are self-seeking and who obey not the truth but wickedness, there will be wrath and fury. There will be anguish and distress for everyone who does evil . . . but glory and honor and peace for everyone who does good." Romans 2:6–10; see also Galatians 5:21; 1 Corinthians 6:9; 2 Corinthians 5:9; Ephesians 5:5; 1 John 2:3–5.

50. For a brief discussion of this issue in LDS thought, see Givens, *Wrestling the Angel*, 236–40.

desire. We must be willing in this life to allow ourselves to be transformed, which means that we must submit to God's will. That, of course, requires *faith*—but, as it says in the Epistle of James, "faith without works is dead"[51]; that is, it is without power to save. The truth is that a person who is not willing to live by the laws of the celestial kingdom would not even want to be there. They would feel as out of place there as a casual violin player would feel onstage with the New York Philharmonic.

To understand this, let's suppose for a moment that this violinist had always dreamed of playing for a great symphony orchestra but never really devoted herself to learning to play her instrument at the highest level. She practiced a few hours a week—whenever it was convenient—and played well enough to get some genuine praise from her non-musician friends and pleasant smiles from her musician friends. But now suppose that she had a friend who played cello in the Philharmonic who felt sorry for her. This friend knew how much she wanted to play in a professional orchestra, but she was also fully aware that the woman was nowhere near skilled enough. Nevertheless, because of her feelings of pity for the woman, she managed to wangle an audition for her, naïvely hoping for a miracle. When the woman began to play in the audition, she would know instantly from the frowns of the judges that she simply didn't belong there. She would no doubt slink away from that audition in embarrassment, and then she would go home and stew in her regrets for not having made the necessary effort.

Nevertheless, despite her embarrassment and regrets, and her greatly dashed dreams, she would know in her heart that she would be much happier somewhere else—perhaps in the local community orchestra. She simply was not prepared to devote the time and effort to playing at a professional level. If the judges had been merciful and admitted her into the orchestra despite her lack of skill, it would have been a nightmarish experience. By the same token, admitting souls into the celestial kingdom who had not prepared adequately would be a travesty. Not only would they be unprepared for the experience and a danger to all if they were given power, but they themselves would be utterly miserable.

As it states in the Doctrine and Covenants, those who are assigned to the telestial kingdom shall "enjoy that which they are willing to receive, because they were not willing to enjoy that which they might have received."[52]

Ye Are Gods

Doubtless one of the most perplexing—and seemingly outrageous—claims of Mormon theology is the doctrine that those who are admitted to the celestial kingdom will be gods. According to traditional Christian theology, there can only be one God, and the idea that a human being should ever strive to become like God is not only

51. James 2:20 (KJV).
52. D&C 88:32.

heretical but blasphemous. The teaching, however, is not as unbiblical as many Christians assume.

The Second Epistle of Peter declares that there have been given to the followers of Christ "his precious and very great promises, so that through them you may . . . become *participants of the divine nature.*"[53] The apostle Paul taught that we would receive the same inheritance as Christ himself:[54]

> The Spirit itself beareth witness with our spirit, that we are the children of God; and if children, then heirs; *heirs of God, and joint-heirs with Christ*; if so be that we suffer with him, that *we may also be glorified together.*[55]
> He that spared not his own Son, but delivered him up for us all, how shall he not *with him* also freely give us *all things*?[56]

"All things" included the power and authority to rule with Christ, as we have just seen above.

Beyond the writings of the New Testament itself, we can find the doctrine of becoming like God—and even becoming gods ourselves—in many early Christian writings. Justin Martyr, one of the earliest post-New Testament writers, said:

> All men are deemed worthy of becoming gods and of having power to become the sons of the highest.[57]

Irenaeus, a bishop of Lyon in Gaul in the second century, declared:

> We have not been made gods from the beginning, but at first merely men, then at length gods.[58]

Clement of Alexandria, a theologian who also lived near the end of the 2nd century, wrote:

> The Word of God [i.e., Christ] became man, that thou mayest learn from man how man may become God.[59]

Hippolytus, a third-century bishop and theologian, stated:

> But if thou art desirous of also becoming a god, obey him that has created thee, and resist not now, in order that, being found faithful in that which is small you may be able to have entrusted to you also that which is great.[60]

53. 2 Peter 1:4.

54. See the analysis of Paul's writings in Litwa, *Becoming Divine*, 58–68, esp. 64–66. An exhaustive discussion is available in Litwa's *We Are Being Transformed*.

55. Romans 8:16–17.

56. Romans 8:32.

57. *Dialogue with Trypho* 124, in ANF 1:262.

58. *Against Heresies* 4.38.4, in ANF 1:522.

59. *Exhortation to the Greeks* 1, in ANF 2:174.

60. *Refutation of All Heresies*, in ANF 5:151.

The ultra-orthodox theologian of the fourth century, Athanasius, bishop of Alexandria, declared the same:

> The Son of God became man so that we might be made God.[61]

The notion of deification (also referred to as *theosis*) can be found here and there throughout the history of Christianity. But in general it was discarded as a doctrine, though it was never denounced as a heresy.[62] The best-known modern proponent of the idea was C. S. Lewis, who said:

> If we let Him—for we can prevent Him, if we choose—He will make the feeblest and filthiest of us into a god or goddess, a dazzling, radiant immortal creature, pulsating all through with energy and joy and wisdom and love as we cannot now imagine . . .[63]

What does it mean for a human being to become a god? For many modern Christians, such an idea is at best an absurdity, at worst blasphemy. Why an absurdity? Because the conventional notion of God is a being who not only possesses great power and knowledge but is *ontologically* different from humans.

Medieval thinkers theorized that there were many levels of *being* in the cosmos. Indeed, they conceived of a great chain of being, extending from inanimate objects—rocks and basic elements—up through plants, lesser animals, greater animals, mankind, then angels, and, at the very summit, God. The fundamental criteria for determining where something fell in this hierarchy was the amount of *spirit* it possessed. Rocks were pure matter and possessed no spirit. Plants were mostly matter but had a spiritual component. Humans, of course, were more spiritual than either plants or animals, while angels were highly spiritual creatures. God himself was pure spirit. Each level on this chain was proper to itself, and it was the height of absurdity to believe that somehow a being on one level could ever rise to a level above it. Thus, the idea of a man aspiring to godhood would be akin to a dog or an ant—or a tree—aspiring to become human—a sheer impossibility.[64]

Today we realize, of course, that the distinction between animals and mankind is mostly one of intelligence. Biologically—genetically—we are roughly 96 percent identical to chimpanzees and 80 percent identical to the mouse. Our brains, however, are much larger and we have correspondingly greater mental abilities. The notion of

61. Athanasius, *On the Incarnation* 54.3.

62. Much scholarly attention has been paid in recent years to the doctrine of deification. See, for example, Russell, *Doctrine of Deification*. The Greek Orthodox Church continues to regard deification, or *theosis*, as a legitimate doctrine and as central to their theology. Surprisingly, both the Roman Catholic and Protestant schools of thought are coming to recognize it as well. For the Catholics, see Keating, *Deification and Grace*. For an evangelical discussion, see Rakestraw, "Becoming Like God."

63. Lewis, *Mere Christianity*, 176. For a discussion, see Jensen, "Shine as the Sun." Jensen notes that Lewis believed, despite his conviction that Christians were all potential gods and goddesses, in an "irreducible ontological distinction" between creature and Creator.

64. The classic study of this concept is Lovejoy, *Great Chain of Being*.

different levels of being is not only archaic scientifically but philosophically meaning-less. It may be an interesting abstraction that helps us to think about the nature of living things, but it has no direct correspondence to the real world. Similarly, God is not "wholly other" in any *real* sense. He is not utterly incomprehensible, nor is he so different from us that we could never dream of becoming assimilated to him.[65]

THE BODY OF GOD

I'll never forget the feeling of disappointment I had as a sixteen-year-old when I first cracked open the Mormon classic *A Marvelous Work and a Wonder*, sitting on the bus on the way home from high school. My LDS friends had given me the book, and I was quite excited to find out what the Mormons actually believed. Everything seemed to make relatively good sense . . . until I got to chapter 3, entitled "Personality of the Father and the Son," when I suddenly got this terrible sinking feeling: did Mormons actually believe that God had a physical body? *You have got to be kidding!*

Traditional Christian theology, of course, asserts that God is pure spirit, formless and invisible, purely immaterial, and incomprehensible. The Westminster Confession of Faith, which is the official creed of Reformed or Calvinist churches, declares,

> There is but one only living and true God, who is infinite in being and per-fections, a completely pure spirit, invisible, without body, parts, or passions; immutable, immense, eternal, incomprehensible, almighty, most wise, most holy, most free, most absolute.[66]

In contrast, Joseph Smith declared,

> It is the first principle of the Gospel to know for a certainty the Character of God, and to know that we may converse with him as one man converses with another . . . and . . . if you were to see him today, you would see him like a man in form—like yourselves in all the person, image, and very form as a man.[67]

I readily confess that when I first encountered it, this doctrine threw me for a loop and was almost a deal-breaker in my nascent exploration of the LDS religion. In my family, whenever we had one of our Profound Discussions about Reality, it was almost a running joke—*of course* no intelligent person actually believed that God was an old man with a beard and a robe sitting up in the sky. And yet the Mormons apparently did!

Despite my misgivings, I persevered in my investigations of the restored gospel, and eventually I began questioning my own skepticism. Why does the idea of God

65. Note that in the Gospel of John (17:20–23) Jesus, in his great prayer to God prior to his arrest and crucifixion, prays that all his disciples and followers "may all be one . . . [a]s you, Father, are in me and I am in you, may they also be in us . . . that they may be one, as we are one."

66. Quoted in Allison, *Historical Theology*, 219.

67. *TPJS* 345.

having a body seem so absurd? Where did the assumption come from that he is pure immaterial spirit, intangible, and literally *omnipresent* throughout all creation? Many of the ideas we hold in life, including some of our most deeply held assumptions, are based entirely on what we were taught (and accepted unquestioningly) as a child. Often when we begin to question those deep-seated assumptions, they may not hold up quite as well as we had thought they would.[68]

The story is told of a housewife who always cut the ends off the ham before she served it. When one of her guests asked her why she did this, she shrugged and said, "That's just how my mother taught me." Curious, the guest went into the next room and asked the mother the reason for the practice. She replied that she had just followed the example of her mother. Now more intrigued than ever, the guest got in touch with the ninety-year-old grandmother, who was too ill to come to the dinner. When asked the same question, she replied with a sheepish laugh. "Oh," she said, "that was just because the plate was too small for the whole ham and I was too cheap to buy a larger platter!"

So too, many of our deep-seated presuppositions have a great deal to do with how we were raised, rather than the correctness or sensibleness of those assumptions.

A discussion of historical theology and philosophy is unavoidable here. One of the peculiar things about the doctrine of the immateriality of God is that it fits so poorly with the Bible. When one reads the Bible objectively, God appears throughout as a real, personal, even physical entity, and not as an abstract, intangible spirit. Christopher Stead of Cambridge University notes that the Hebrews "pictured the God whom they worshipped as having a body and mind like our own, though transcending humanity in the splendour of his appearance, in his power, his wisdom, and the constancy of his care for his creatures."[69]

68. Evangelical theologian Clark H. Pinnock wrote: ". . . is God in some way bodied? . . . I do not believe that the idea is as foreign to the Bible's view of God as we have assumed. *In tradition,* God is thought to function primarily as a disembodied spirit but this is scarcely a biblical idea . . . It seems to me that the Bible does not think of God as formless" (*Most Moved Mover,* 33–34).

69. Stead, *Philosophy in Christian Antiquity,* 120. Gerhard von Rad, an eminent Old Testament scholar, wrote: "Actually, Israel conceived even Jahweh himself as having human form . . . But the way of putting it which we use runs in precisely the wrong direction according to Old Testament ideas, for, according to the ideas of Jahwism, it cannot be said that Israel regarded God anthropomorphically, but the reverse, that she considered man as theomorphic . . . Jahweh himself was conceived as a man" (Von Rad, *Old Testament Theology,* 1:145–46). A great deal of bibliography on this topic, including anthropomorphism in early Christianity and early Islam, can be found in Williams, "Body Unlike Bodies, 19–44. See also Sommer, *Bodies of God;* Webb, *Jesus Christ, Eternal God;* Markschies, *God's Body.* Sommer's opening statement reads: "The God of the Hebrews has a body." He then goes on to acknowledge the reader's likely skepticism: "The formidable authority of childhood teachers and the less robust influence of theologians have embedded the notion of the noncorporeal Hebrew deity so deeply into Western thought that some readers may be skeptical of my starting point" (Sommer, *Bodies of God,* 1). H. Wheeler Robinson states: "Yahweh's body is shaped like a man's but its substance is not flesh but "spirit," and spirit seen as a blaze of light" (Robinson, "Hebrew Psychology," 367). There is an obvious parallel between these descriptions of the Hebrew God and the being of light in a typical NDE.

In the Genesis creation story, God interacts with Adam and Eve on a very personal basis:

> They heard the sound of the Lord God walking in the garden at the time of the evening breeze, and the man and his wife hid themselves from the presence of the Lord God among the trees of the garden. But the Lord God called to the man, and said to him, "Where are you?" He said, "I heard the sound of you in the garden, and I was afraid, because I was naked; and I hid myself." He said, "Who told you that you were naked? Have you eaten from the tree of which I commanded you not to eat?" The man said, "The woman whom you gave to be with me, she gave me of the fruit from the tree, and I ate."[70]

Of course, there is also a talking snake in the garden of Eden story, so how seriously are we to take it? Yet we find the same relationship between God and his prophets throughout the Hebrew Bible (Old Testament). In the story of Moses, there is comparable direct interaction between Moses and the Lord.

> Thus the Lord used to speak to Moses face to face, as one speaks to a friend.[71]

The seventh-century BC prophet Isaiah saw God in glorious vision when he received his prophetic call directly from God:

> In the year that King Uzziah died, I saw the Lord sitting on a throne, high and lofty; and the hem of his robe filled the temple. . . And I said, "Woe is me! I am lost, for I am a man of unclean lips . . . yet my eyes have seen the King, the Lord of hosts! . . . Then I heard the voice of the Lord saying, "Whom shall I send, and who will go for us?" And I said, "Here am I, send me!"[72]

When we look at how God is portrayed in the New Testament, the picture changes very little. According to the Gospel of Matthew, when the apostles Peter, James, and John found themselves on the Mount of Transfiguration with Jesus, they heard the direct voice of God:

> And [Jesus] was transfigured before them, and his face shone like the sun, and his clothes became dazzling white. . . While [Peter] was still speaking, suddenly a bright cloud overshadowed them, and from the cloud a voice said, "This is my Son, the Beloved; with him I am well pleased; listen to him!" When the disciples heard this, they fell to the ground and were overcome by fear.[73]

In the Acts of the Apostles, when Stephen is about to be stoned, he declares:

70. Genesis 3:8–12.
71. Exodus 33:11.
72. Isaiah 6:1–8.
73. Matthew 17:1–6.

Look . . . I see the heavens opened and the Son of Man standing at the right hand of God![74]

And shortly thereafter Saul (later known as the apostle Paul) has a direct confrontation with the resurrected Jesus:

Now as he was going along and approaching Damascus, suddenly a light from heaven flashed around him. He fell to the ground and heard a voice saying to him, "Saul, Saul, why do you persecute me?" He asked, "Who are you, Lord?" The reply came, "I am Jesus, whom you are persecuting."[75]

In the book of Revelation, John is addressed by a divine figure:

I saw one like the Son of Man, clothed with a long robe and with a golden sash across his chest. His head and his hair were white as white wool, white as snow; his eyes were like a flame of fire, his feet were like burnished bronze, refined as in a furnace, and his voice was like the sound of many waters . . . When I saw him, I fell at his feet as though dead. But he placed his right hand on me, saying, "Do not be afraid . . ."[76]

In none of these accounts do God's followers seem to be dealing with a God who is incomprehensible or "wholly other." Rather, although he is clearly a being of great power and glory, and exists perhaps in a different dimension, he is still entirely personal, with an actual voice, a real presence, and even an actual body, and humans are quite able to speak with him "as one man converses with another." The theological term for this view of God is that he is "anthropomorphic," meaning that he has a human form or human traits. (Of course, technically speaking, the proper usage would actually be to state that humans are "theomorphic"—since in Genesis God creates *man* in *his* image, not the other way around!)

When we look at the earliest postbiblical texts, we find descriptions of God that differ little from those in the Bible, emphasizing his greatness and power but strictly in concrete, anthropomorphic terms:

Even the Architect and Lord of the universe Himself takes a delight in working. In His supreme power He has established the heavens, and in His unsearchable wisdom set them in order. He divided the earth from the waters around it, and settled it securely on the firm foundation of His will . . . Above all, with His own sacred and immaculate hands he fashioned man, who in virtue of his intelligence is the chiefest and greatest of all of His works and the very likeness of His own image."[77]

74. Acts 7:56.

75. Acts 9:3–5.

76. Revelation 1:12–15, 17.

77. *1 Clement* 33, in Staniforth, *Early Christian Writings*, 40.

The Almighty Himself, the Creator of the universe, the God whom no eye can discern, has sent down His very own Truth from heaven, His own Holy and incomprehensible Word, to plant it in their hearts. To this end He has not, as one might imagine, sent to mankind some servant of His, some angel or prince; it is none of the great ones of the earth, nor even one of the vice-gerents of heaven. It is no other than the universal Artificer and Constructor Himself, by whose agency God made the heavens and set their bounds . . .[78]

Note that while there is much emphasis on God's greatness, the writers primarily focus on God's *works*—how he has blessed us through the creation, through his Son—rather than trying to discuss God's actual nature. And while his *wisdom* is described as unsearchable and his words as incomprehensible (i.e., beyond human wisdom), God himself is not portrayed as incomprehensible or unknowable, nor is he described with the kind of abstract and paradoxical language that quickly began to penetrate Christian discourse.

Contrast this view of deity with a statement from an apocryphal Christian work from the second century, known as the Preaching of Peter. Peter describes God as

the invisible who sees all, the uncontained who contains all, the one without needs whom all need and for whom they exist; incomprehensible, eternal, imperishable, unmade, who made all by the word of his power.[79]

This language sounds partly biblical, but also bears signs of philosophical language—especially the negative words—"uncontained," "incomprehensible," and "unmade"—along with the "paradoxical" language—"the uncontained who contains all." Rather quickly in second-century writings, descriptions of God take on a strong philosophical (mostly Platonic) cast. Albinus, a Platonist philosopher (non-Christian) in the mid-second century, stated in an introductory philosophical text that gods are entirely removed from the world of sense perception, relating only to the mental world. And the First God is

eternal, ineffable, self-sufficient—that is, without needs, ever-sufficient—that is, always perfect, all-sufficient—that is, completely perfect; Deity, Substantiality, Truth, Symmetry, Good. I mention these aspects not as providing definitions but as naming aspects in every respect characteristic of the one under consideration. And he is Good because he benefits all things as he is able, being the cause of every good thing; beautiful, because his form is by nature perfect and symmetrical; Truth, because he is the source of all truth, as the sun is of all light; he is Father because he is the cause of all and sets in order the heavenly Mind and the soul of the universe toward himself and toward his own thoughts.[80]

78. *Diognetus 7*, in Staniforth, *Early Christian Writings*, 178.

79. Clement of Alexandria, *Stromata* 6.39.2–3, quoted in Grant, *Gods and the One God*, 51–52.

80. Quoted in Grant, *Gods and the One God*, 80.

The best example of a description of this Platonic, abstract deity is, ironically, from Philo Judaeus, a *Jewish* theologian who made a valiant attempt to create an amalgam of Judaism and Platonism. In one text he describes God as a being who

> transcends all quality, being better than virtue, better than knowledge, and better even than good itself and the beautiful itself. He is not in space, but beyond it; for He contains it. He is not in time, for He is the Father of the universe. . . He is without body, parts or passions; without feet, for whither should He walk who fills all things; without hands, for from whom should he receive anything who possesses all things; without eyes, for how should he need eyes who made the light. He is invisible, for how can eyes that are too weak to gaze upon the sun be strong enough to gaze upon its Maker. He is incomprehensible; not even the whole universe, much less the human mind, can contain the conception of him.[81]

One popular mode of discussing God was the so-called *via negativa*. This entailed an acknowledgement that *nothing* could actually be said about God, so far is he above all of us—and so abstract. Clement of Alexandria described God as incorporeal, formless, and possessing no attributes. According to Robert M. Grant, Clement viewed God as transcending "the world of sense perception" and being "above space and time." Further, "as One, he is even above the monad. He is also above virtue; that is, beyond goodness. He cannot be comprehended by the human mind and thus he is 'unknown' and he is 'ineffable.'"[82] Thus, God could not even be described as "good," since he was far beyond what humans call "goodness." Later theologians took this approach even further. Cyril of Jerusalem, in his *Catechetical Homilies*, says: "For we explain not what God is but candidly confess that we have not exact knowledge concerning Him. For in what concerns God to confess our ignorance is the best knowledge."[83]

Beginning in the later second century, there arose a notable conflict between those Christians who viewed God in simpler, biblical terms and those who preferred the more abstract, philosophical, intellectually respectable deity. Origen, like most of the theological writers whose works were preserved through the Middle Ages, fit squarely in the latter category, yet he acknowledged the struggle with those of anthropomorphic views.

> How God himself is to be understood—whether as corporeal, and formed according to some shape, or of a different nature from bodies—[is] a point which is not clearly indicated in our teaching.[84]

He acknowledged that "the Jews indeed, but also some of our people supposed that God should be understood as a man, that is, adorned with human members and

---

81. Quoted in Hatch, *Influence of Greek Ideas*, 244–45.

82. Grant, *Gods and the One God*, 90–91.

83. Cyril of Jerusalem, Lecture VI, *Concerning the Unity of God*, in NPNF 7:33.

84. Origen, *De Principiis* pref. 9, in ANF 4:241.

human appearance."[85] Sometimes he argued that only the unsophisticates in the church held to such beliefs, but he also noted that Melito, an early bishop of Sardis, taught that God was corporeal. Indeed, even Tertullian, the first Latin-speaking Christian theologian, insisted that the Son was a corporeal being prior to his birth, though of a more subtle type of matter than human bodies. For how could it be, he declared, that

> He Himself is nothing, without whom nothing was made? how could he who is empty have made things which are solid, and He who is void have made things which are full, and He who is incorporeal have made things which have body? For although a thing may sometimes be made different from him by whom it is made, yet nothing can be made by that which is a void and empty thing.[86]

As Origen acknowledged, it was not only the earliest Christians who held the clear view that God was embodied and appeared like man, but many of the Jews from the same period held the same. The rabbinic writings testify to this clearly.[87]

So where did the notion of an immaterial God come from? We will look more closely in a later chapter at exactly how early Christian doctrines were transformed in the centuries after Christ. But generally, in the Mormon view, Christianity went astray in great part because of the need felt by many early Christians to hitch their theological wagon to Greek philosophy. In ancient times philosophy was not the specialized subject that it is today, but instead served as the foundation for all intellectual learning. By the second century, Platonism had become one of the principal foundations of nearly all speculation in the fields of cosmology and theology. This was not the original Platonism of classical Athens, but a slowly developing school of thought which came to focus increasingly on such matters as the nature of God, the relationship between the earth and heaven, and between man and God. In other words, late-antique Platonism was a principal basis for all attempts at intellectualizing religion.

Thus the Christians, when they wanted to argue their faith to the educated classes in the Roman Empire, had no choice but to make some use of Greek philosophical ideas and categories.[88] This would have been fine up to a point, but the obvious danger was that the very teachings could become corrupted by this attempt at translating them into a foreign intellectual idiom. One of the most commonly held assumptions of this period was that God could in no wise be bounded physically by any type of body. Physical bodies belonged strictly to this world, the world of *becoming*—the messy world of change that we all belong to—in contrast to the permanent, unchanging, immaterial world of *being*.

85. Origen, *Homilies on Genesis* 3.12, in Origen, *Homilies*, 89.
86. Tertullian, *Against Praxeas* 1.7, in ANF 3:602.
87. Gottstein, "Body as Image of God," 172. See also Bar-Ilan, "Hand of God."
88. Hatch, *Influence of Greek Ideas*, see 25–49 on Greek education.

Before Plato and his successors, the concept of *immateriality* did not exist. The idea that something could exist that was completely free of material substance was not exactly rejected—it simply had never occurred to anyone because it made no sense. Plato invented the concept along with his doctrine of Forms, and despite its lack of intuitiveness, it became one of the most successful ideas in the history of the world.

> The notion of God's incorporeality . . . was first attained by the Greek philosophers . . . Hebraic antiquity always imagined Yahweh as humanlike. The notion of the deity as a fully spiritual being, without body, would have been totally incomprehensible to the ancient Hebrew.[89]

Augustine, considered the greatest of the Latin-speaking theologians, became so attached to the thought world of Plato that he was unable to accept Christianity until he discovered how to view the God of the Bible through a Platonic lens. He had been raised a Christian by his mother, Monica, but as a young man preferred philosophy and rhetoric (and women!) to Christianity. He stated quite clearly that one of the reasons he could not take the Christian belief seriously was the contention that God had a "bodily shape," and "hair and nails."[90] As a teacher of rhetoric, Augustine eventually came to the city of Milan, where he encountered bishop Ambrose, who was himself an eminent Platonist and rhetorician. Ambrose was apparently the first to introduce him to the possibility that the Christian God was not "limited . . . by the outlines of a human body." With help from Ambrose, he eventually came to the conclusion that

> O God, you who are so high above us and yet so close, hidden and yet always present, you have not parts, some greater and some smaller. You are everywhere, and everywhere you are entire. Nowhere are you limited by space. You have not the shape of a body like ours . . .[91]

Thus reassured, Augustine became a devout Christian, and soon thereafter a highly influential bishop and theologian, profoundly shaping Christian views of God.

HOW TO CREATE A UNIVERSE

Of what importance, you might ask, is all this theology? So what if later Christians altered the original teaching about the nature of God? Does it really matter so much how we picture God in our heads, whether with a body or as an immaterial spirit? One could make a plausible argument that many theological controversies in history, particularly those debated at greatest length, were of relatively minor importance in the grand scheme of things. That may be true in part, but it is also true that if you are going to worship God (and worship means in part to *imitate*—like the rock star groupie

89. Von Rad, *Old Testament Theology*, 1:145–46. See also R. Renehan, "On the Greek Origins."
90. Augustine, *Confessions* 3.7, 62.
91. Augustine, *Confessions* 6.3–4, 114–15.

who wants to wear the same clothes and use the same toothpaste as her idol), it only makes sense to have a good idea who and what God is. "I give unto you these sayings that you may understand and know how to worship and know what you worship, that you may come unto the Father in my name and in due time receive of his fulness."[92]

In one of the most poignant passages of the Gospel of John, Jesus declares that "eternal life" is to gain a true knowledge of God: "And this is eternal life, that they might *know* you, the only true God, and Jesus Christ whom you have sent."[93] But how does one come to know an unknowable God? Augustine preferred to believe that God, by definition, could not be understood: "A God understood is no God at all."[94] Of course, no one is suggesting that achieving knowledge of God is easy or simple. It requires considerable effort and sacrifice. In fact, we shall not truly know God until—someday—we become like him.

> The day shall come when you shall comprehend even God, being quickened in him and by him.[95]

The main point to this discussion about the nature of God is that in the traditional Christian view of God, the distance between God and mankind is so great that it can never be transcended. The Mormon view is that God is far above earthly man, but since we were created specifically in the likeness and image of God, we are much more like him than appears at first glance.

Latter-day Saints are sometimes accused of believing in a *limited* God, a God who is neither omniscient nor omnipotent nor omnipresent. This accusation is quite true if we take the absolutist perspective of Greek philosophy—that is, for example, if by "omniscient" we mean that God knows everything abstractly conceivable. But I suggest that the Mormon perspective, like the Old Testament, depicts a God who possesses all *possible* and *necessary* power rather than all *conceivable* power. What is the difference? Latter-day Saints believe that there are simply certain things that are not possible in the real world, not even for God. It is impossible to achieve certainty about the details, but it is likely that certain basic principles of physics are eternal. In any case, it is certain that God could not have created a world in which robbing banks and molesting children is moral and good, nor one in which all circles are square. Nor could he have created light and all creation out of nothing (*ex nihilo*) by just uttering a few phrases. Real effort is required. Those actions, while quite conceivable theoretically, are simply not within the realm of actual possibility. As the saying goes, "nothing comes from nothing." (Or, if we prefer our philosophy in Latin, *ex nihilo nihil fit*.)

According to the traditional Christian view of the creation, God merely conceived of an idea, and spoke, and *voilà!* it came into being: "'Let there be light!' And

---

92. D&C 93:19.
93. John 17:3.
94. Quoted in Cherbonnier, "Logic of Biblical Anthropomorphism," 195.
95. D&C 88:49; see also 1 John 3:2–3.

there was light." God himself exists eternally—he is *being itself*, while everything else was *brought into being* by him. Thus, God is self-existent, while the universe has only conditional existence.

LDS theology rejects this notion of creation. We have already discussed the belief that human beings (and animals!) had a spiritual existence eternally with God. "Man was also in the beginning with God," taught Joseph Smith. "Intelligence, or the light of truth, was not created or made, neither indeed can be."[96] When Mormons say that God did not create the world *ex nihilo*, they are saying that some form of matter or energy was already extant when God set his hand to create the universe. He took of this preexistent matter and *organized* it in some fashion, not miraculously but in accord with the most fundamental principles of physics.

Just how hard would it be to create a universe? It sounds like something only an infinite and incomprehensible God could do, yet scientists today are suggesting that it may not be quite the superhuman achievement that it seems. Andrei Linde, a Stanford University physicist, has proposed only half-jokingly that our universe could have been created not by a god, but by a physicist hacker in a laboratory. He theorizes that a scientist in a slightly more advanced civilization than ours could create an entire universe from just a milligram of matter. It would require very high temperatures and extreme compression of that matter. But it would not require supernatural powers.[97] And Linde is not alone in these speculations. His fellow cosmologist Alan Guth at MIT

> shocked many physicists a few years ago when he claimed that the physics of wormholes may make it possible to create a baby universe of our own in the laboratory. By concentrating intense heat and energy in a chamber, a wormhole may eventually open up, serving as an umbilical cord connecting our universe to another, much smaller universe.[98]

The Harvard physicist Michio Kaku cautions that only a much more advanced civilization than ours would have such a technological capacity, because, among other things, it would require the ability to generate enormous amounts of energy, far beyond what we are currently capable of. But he does consider it well within the realm of possibility. Our modern civilization he describes as currently being at Level 0 technologically. We are just beginning, he says, to make use of our planet's resources of power. We use primarily fossil fuels such as oil and coal, and we are able to control atomic fission in nuclear reactors, but our understanding regarding atomic fusion is limited to the uncontrolled reaction in a hydrogen bomb. By contrast, a Type I

96. D&C 93:29.

97. Rucker, "Big Bang Bust." Linde adds: "I don't entirely think of this possibility as a joke. Even if something seems counterintuitive, you must be honest and follow the thought line and not be influenced by the common point of view. If you agree with everything everybody else thinks, you never move." See also Carroll, "How did the Universe Start?"

98. Kaku, *Hyperspace*, 20. See also Guth, *Inflationary Universe*.

civilization would be capable of harnessing the power of an entire planet. A Type II civilization would be able to use the power of a star—our sun, for example. This does not refer to the passive use of solar energy, as we do in a limited fashion today, but rather the direct "mining" of the sun—direct consumption of the power of the sun to power machines. Kaku describes a Type III civilization as having the capacity to harness the power of an entire galaxy. The development of a Type III civilization would take thousands of years, not, as one might suppose, millions of years. It would have mastered the ability to warp space-time by means of wormholes (as in *Star Trek*), thereby having the ability to explore galaxies. It might even have the knowledge to harness the power of a supernova or a black hole.

For most of us, this all sounds like wild speculation—and speculation it is, but these are the intelligent musings of a top-flight theoretical physicist. The point here is that Kaku conceives of the harnessing of sufficient power to create universes as well within the capacity of human beings, if not for several millennia.

I don't presume to know exactly where God lives or where the world of spirits exists in relation to this world. But the easiest way that I can conceive of it is that they live in the fourth dimension. From there they can observe us and interact with *us*, although it is difficult for us to interact directly with *them*. If we accept this hypothesis as true for the sake of discussion, we can try to think of what the implications of such a world might be.

Kaku tells us that it is impossible to visualize the fourth dimension. To help us imagine such a world, he proposes the following exercise of imagination. Imagine what it would be like for a being from our three-dimensional world interacting with a world of only two dimensions. In this Flatland, for example, a two-dimensional human could be imprisoned merely by a circle being drawn around him—without the third dimension of height and depth, he would be trapped. We, however, from our three-dimensional world, could easily spring him from his jail by peeling him off his flat world, thereby removing him from his prison, and placing him back inside his two-dimensional world outside the circle. To all his fellow Flatlanders, he would seem to have disappeared when we peeled him up into the third dimension (which they could not visualize or conceive of) and then suddenly have reappeared when we put him back into his world.[99]

In a similar way, says Kaku, a being from the fourth dimension, when interacting with us, would seem utterly superhuman.

> You wouldn't have to bother with opening doors; you could pass right through them. You wouldn't have to go around buildings; you could enter them through their walls and pillars and out through the back wall. You wouldn't

---

99. Lisa Randall echoes this idea: "We are in this three-dimensional flatland . . . Our world is stuck in this three-dimensional universe, although extra dimensions exist. So we live on a three-dimensional slice of a higher-dimensional world" (Randall, "New Dimensions," 301). See also the very interesting discussion from the perspective of a historian of religion of I. P. Couliano, *Out of This World*, 12–32.

have to detour around mountains; you could step right into them. When hungry, you could simply reach through the refrigerator door without opening it . . . Imagine being able to disappear or reappear at will. Instead of driving to school or work, you would just vanish and rematerialize in your classroom or office. You wouldn't need an airplane to visit far-away places, you could just vanish and rematerialize where you wanted. You would never be stuck in city traffic during rush hours; you and your car would simply disappear and rematerialize at your destination. Imagine having x-ray eyes. You would be able to see accidents happening from a distance. After vanishing and rematerializing at the site of any accident, you could see exactly where the victims were, even if they were buried under debris . . . Imagine what a criminal could do with these powers. He could enter the most heavily guarded bank. He could see through the massive doors of the vault for the valuables and cash and reach inside and pull them out. He could then stroll outside as the bullets from the guards passed right through him. With these powers, no prison could hold a criminal. No secrets could be kept from us. No treasures could be hidden from us. No obstructions could stop us. We would truly be miracle workers, performing feats beyond the comprehension of mortals. We would also be omnipotent.[100]

A moment's thought is sufficient to realize that it would be the height of insanity for God to grant even such limited powers to a being who was morally imperfect.[101] For a being who was even partially in thrall to his or her selfish desires, the ability to wield such power could easily result in havoc. Thus, the most important characteristic for a being of great power to have would be pure, unselfish desires—moral purity. Of equal importance, undoubtedly, would be tremendous knowledge and wisdom—so that no matter how pure one's desires, one did not make a mess of things through ignorance.

Latter-day Saints are sometimes mocked for believing that when they die they will be given their own planet to rule. The reality is much more complex. Mormons have no delusions that they will automatically upon their death be given tremendous power and authority. That is something that one will have to prepare to receive over much time—eons perhaps. But acquiring knowledge and even wisdom is of an entirely different order from gaining moral purity. Refusing to accede to one's selfish desires is ultimately a matter of *will*. Developing the ability to control one's own will

100. Kaku, *Hyperspace*, 45–46.

101. I call these powers "limited" in contrast to what Paul Davies conceives of as "superforce" —the unity of all forces, which is "responsible for generating all forces and physical structures" and is "the fountain-head of all existence." By achieving control over this superforce, Davies tells us, "we could change the structure of space and time, tie our own knots in nothingness, and build matter to order. Controlling the superforce would enable us to construct and transmute particles at will, thus generating exotic forms of matter. We might even be able to manipulate the dimensionality of space itself, creating bizarre artificial worlds with unimaginable properties. Truly we should be lords of the universe." Davies, *Superforce*, 168.

is ultimately much more difficult than learning to harness the power of the atom. The ability to *be good*—at all times and in all places—is doubtless the most difficult as well as the most important thing we could ever learn. Most of us *want* to be good. In difficult moral situations most people desire to do the right thing. But often enough we fail—not only through ignorance or foolishness, but through lack of self-control. The desire to satisfy our personal needs and desires (for sleep, food, wealth, prestige, sex, etc.) is simply too great and wins out over our desire to be a good person.

God is perfectly aware of how difficult this task is, and he doesn't expect us to completely master our wills in this life. But for some reason this life of mortality is the best environment in which to learn key lessons. I believe there are two reasons. First, our minds are restricted to thinking of one thing at a time. That forces us to make choices. Secondly, we come to know who we really are, what we really desire—i.e., what our *fundamental values* really are. This life is less about proving our mettle to God than proving it to ourselves. I believe that the main thing we are to acquire in this life is the knowledge of who we really are—and what we really care about.

THE PLAN OF SALVATION—SUMMED UP

For Mormons, then, our earthly lives must be seen in light of what came before and what will come after. Our existence stretches from eternity to eternity—i.e., from pre-eternity to posteternity. The few decades we spend in this current stage of existence are but a brief time—a mere moment—on the scale of eternity, and must be seen in that perspective. Thus, both the pleasures and the suffering we experience while we are here, no matter how blissful or how severe they may seem at the moment, are really very minor blips on the timeline of eternity.

With the insight that comes from that three-dimensional perspective, we can see that this life is not reality in the ultimate sense, but a temporary voyage into a strange world. If my analogy is correct that the divine realm is akin to a world of four dimensions, it means that this life is a brief trip to a three-dimensional world. To make ultimate judgments about the meaning of our lives on the basis of only three dimensions is foolish. It is when we believe that three dimensions and the seventy-five years or so that we spend here are all there is to our existence that we come to view suffering and death as the ultimate tragedy.

Thus, an awareness of preexistence is an important prerequisite for realizing that suffering and death are the not the tragedy we typically believe them to be. A belief in an *afterlife* allows one to assume that justice will be meted out, and compensation received for the suffering one has experienced. But knowledge of preexistence *plus* an afterlife helps us to realize that the other world is our *true home*, and that this life is merely an interim between two eternities of existence. Our beforelife and our afterlife are our true life—where we really belong. An early death no longer seems like a tragic occurrence, but merely an early return home. And suffering is not something that stifles our pursuit of happiness, but rather an experience that trains us for the glories that lie ahead.

Moreover, we not only existed eternally before this life, but we actually were aware of God's plan to lead us to exaltation and agreed to accept this plan. God's purpose in sending us to this world was so that we could have experiences, both good and bad, which would teach us much in preparation for the next stage of our existence. It is akin to parents who send their teenage children away to college not only to get an academic degree but to develop into mature, self-reliant adults. It is quite possible that many of our experiences have been specifically prepared for us as individuals, since each of us has different strengths and weaknesses and we each need to learn different lessons.

Ultimately, then, mortality is a *test*—to see if we will do all that God commands us. This test, it should be clear by now, is not merely a random test to see if we will submit to arbitrary orders, but a carefully laid-out plan to help us to develop the qualities that we will need before we can be given great power—the power of godhood. If we prove ourselves capable of this high achievement, we will be allowed to continue on toward godhood. If not, we will be *damned*—literally, dammed or stopped—on the path of progression and be allowed to accept only as much glory as we are willing to. In the words of the Doctrine and Covenants, we must be willing to "abide the law" of the celestial kingdom if we expect to be permitted to dwell there.[102]

Of primary importance in all this is the fundamental fact that God loves us. We are literally his spirit children. He wants us to have the opportunity to become like him—to grow up and mature into the divine beings that we have the right and ability to become.

This doctrine of the three-dimensional life is the basis for the statement of Harold Bloom quoted above that Mormonism completely denies the reality or significance of death. Death really is just a passage—back to where we came from. For Latter-day Saints, death, like birth, is merely a transition from one state of existence to another. Naturally, like all people, Mormons are reluctant to face death and are saddened by the loss of a loved one. But LDS funerals are typified by "a spirit of joyfulness" and "an atmosphere of optimism and friendliness."[103] Wilford Woodruff, a president of the church in the later nineteenth century, once said about his own funeral:

> I wish my body washed clean and clothed in white linen . . . and put into a plain, decent coffin, made of native wood, with plenty of room. I do not wish any black made use of about my coffin, or about the vehicle that conveys my body to the grave. I do not wish my family or friends to wear any badge of mourning for me at my funeral or afterwards, for, if I am true and faithful unto death, there will be no necessity for anyone to mourn for me. . . There speech will be to the living. *If the laws and customs of the spirit world will permit, I*

102. D&C 88:22–24.

103. Palmer, *Deity and Death*, xv.

should wish to attend my funeral but I shall be governed by the counsel I receive in the spirit world.[104]

What I find striking in this passage is not only the optimism it demonstrates toward death, but the assumption in the final sentence that life in the spirit world will be little different from life as we know it, *although they may have different laws and customs*! The afterlife truly is, in many ways, a mere continuation of the life we currently lead, though on a different, and much richer, plane of existence.

104. Quoted in Palmer, *Deity and Death*, 71–72.

7

Living the Mormon Lifestyle—on Smoking, Sex, Service, and Sacrifice

A religion that does not require the sacrifice of all things never has power sufficient to produce the faith necessary [to lead] unto life and salvation.

—Joseph Smith[1]

The mad bad talk rambled on. "I want to know what passion is," she heard him saying. "I want to feel something strongly." . . .
"I don't understand." Lenina's tone was firm.
"I know you don't. And that's why we went to bed together yesterday—like infants—instead of being adults and waiting."
"But it was fun," Lenina insisted. "Wasn't it?"

—Aldous Huxley, *Brave New World*, chapter 5

When you come out here [to Utah] and talk to people, you look in their eyes, they're so damned happy. Everyone looks so innocent. Maybe there's something we've been missing.

—Mike Wallace[2]

The word "repent" has a highly archaic feel today: repentance is something that people did in ancient times or perhaps in the Victorian Age, but not in the twenty-first century! For most people the word calls to mind a cartoon of a scruffy little man wearing a robe and carrying a sign announcing the end of the world. Even mainstream Christians rarely speak in terms of repentance anymore. One would be hard-pressed to find a mainstream book on Christianity published in the last fifty years that emphasizes the term or even the concept of repenting of one's sins. Even the term "sin" gets

---

1. *Lectures on Faith*, 6:5.
2. Quoted in Haws, *Mormon Image*, 167–68.

very little screen time today. It seems too negative, too depressing, too focused on the past rather than the future.[3]

Modern-style preachers like Rick Warren, Kenneth Copeland, and Joel Osteen preach a gospel of positive thinking and rarely refer to repenting from sin. But even more traditional evangelicals are uncomfortable with the concept of repentance because it smacks too much of works—in their view, salvation does not *require* any change in behavior, although they do stress that a Christian who has been saved by turning to Christ should naturally want to live according to Christian principles.[4]

Latter-day Saints, in contrast, believe that repentance is a fundamental principle of the Christian gospel. They do not overemphasize it, because the focus should indeed be on the future rather than the past. But they do believe, as I have already discussed in the last chapter, that turning to Christ is a matter of *changing one's behavior* and not merely professing belief.

The English word "repent" derives from the Latin *paenitere*, which means to regret or feel sorry for something. That definition captures the LDS attitude quite well. To repent means to feel sorrow for one's past behavior. Of course, there are different types of sorrow. Feeling regret for yelling at your wife because she is now sleeping in the guest bedroom is not enough. True sorrow—"sorrow unto repentance"—is genuine regret for doing harm to another person—which includes hurting their feelings—and a resolution not to do it again. Even more, it is sorrow that comes from the awareness that your past action displeases God—not because he is some arbitrary tyrant who becomes angry whenever you transgress one of his laws, but because you know that he is a loving and wise father who wants the best for you and desires your eternal happiness.

The Greek word used in the New Testament is *metanoia*, which means a change of mind or heart, or regret or remorse. No one can be sure of the Hebrew word that lies behind that Greek usage, but the common words (roots) used in the Hebrew Bible (Old Testament) are *shuv* and *nhm*. The root meaning of *shuv* is to turn, specifically to turn away, to turn back, to return, while *nhm* means to be sorry. When read in context, repentance in both Greek and Hebrew involves a change of mind as well as

---

3. As Billy Graham observed, "The word repentance is sadly missing today from the average pulpit. It is a very unpopular word." Quoted in Graham, *Billy Graham in Quotes*, 295.

4. The following statement by Hank Hanegraaff is representative: "[W]e must repent of our sins . . . Repentance is an old English word that describes a willingness to turn from sin toward Jesus Christ. It literally means a complete U-turn on the road of life—a change of heart and a change of mind. It means a willingness to follow Jesus and receive Him as Savior and Lord." Note that Hanegraaff emphasizes a change of *heart* and a change of *mind*, but says nothing about a change in one's *behavior*. That is because in the evangelical view, "the requirements for eternal life are based not on what *we can do* but on what *Jesus Christ has done*" (Hanegraaff, *Christianity in Crisis*, 314). Good behavior is presumed to be implicit in the "change of heart," but receives little stress. As one Christian website puts it, "To repent, in relation to salvation, is [simply] to change your mind in regard to Jesus Christ." That is, repentance means merely to change one's mind "from rejection of Christ as the Messiah to faith in Him as both Messiah and Savior" ("What Is Repentance?").

a change of behavior—turning away from one's sins and turning towards God and righteousness. Neither by itself is sufficient.

And what is sin? Sin is typically defined as a violation of the law of God. Again, this definition tends to call to mind an image of arbitrary dictator or judge who is just waiting for the chance to condemn those who violate even the smallest rule. In LDS theology, it cannot be stressed enough that the commandments of God are viewed as great blessings. They act as a pathway along which one may find both happiness in this life and preparation for a much more glorious life afterwards.

The commandments are not random orders to keep the faithful busy and out of trouble. Even when the object is not obvious or explicit, Latter-day Saints assume that the commandments are for our benefit. Why are we willing to do things for which we don't know the purpose? Because of faith—faith, but not blind faith. What is the difference? Blind faith is, for example, when you decide to buy a half-million shares in Harry's Blank-Check Company based on the prediction of a junk mass email that the shares will quadruple in price from ten to forty cents in the next week. On the other hand, we all exercise a *reasonable* faith on a regular basis. If you hire an expert in order to learn tennis, basketball, piano, singing, or basket weaving, you can't expect your teacher to explain the value of every exercise you do. Sometimes you just need to do what the teacher tells you, and eventually the value of it will become evident. Much of the time you simply must take it on faith that the teacher knows what he or she is talking about.[5]

This is what might be called the "wax on, wax off" principle. In the 1984 movie *The Karate Kid*, when the aging Japanese gentleman Mr. Miyagi agrees to teach karate to the young man he calls Daniel-san, he begins by instructing Daniel to wax his cars. To Daniel this seems like just a ploy to get free labor. He agrees to do it, though under protest. But eventually it becomes clear that by doing the waxing he has been strengthening and training his arm and shoulder muscles for the movements that karate requires. Daniel was willing—though just barely—to exercise faith in Miyagi to go through the exercises even though he saw no connection between waxing cars and karate. Was this blind faith? No, because he had some basis for his confidence—or faith—in Miyagi's karate skills. He had seen him defeat several much younger men in live combat. He also felt that Miyagi was a good man and had his interests at heart, because of the relationship they had previously established. If Miyagi had been a complete stranger who out of the blue asked him to start washing cars as a means of learning karate, he probably would have refused.

All of this is applicable to faith in God. Once we have reason not only to believe in but to trust God, we should be willing to exercise a degree of faith in him and do what he asks of us. As we see the results of following those rules, our faith increases and we are more willing (less reluctant) to follow his rules.

5. See Polanyi, *Personal Knowledge*, 53.

THE WORD OF WISDOM

Take, as an example, the LDS health code known colloquially as the "Word of Wisdom." The name comes from the part of the Doctrine & Covenants (section 89) that presents the code:

> A word of wisdom, for the benefit of . . . the saints in Zion.

The code was originally voluntary, not given "by commandment or constraint," though from the beginning most Saints followed its teachings and many felt that it should be considered binding on the church as a whole.[6] But by the early twentieth century it became a basic requirement for all Latter-day Saints. It was designed as an easy set of commandments, "adapted to the capacity of . . . the weakest of all saints." It instructs that wine, strong drink, tobacco, and hot drinks (interpreted to mean coffee and tea) "are not for the body" and should be refrained from. (All illicit drugs, by extension, are also considered prohibited.) In contrast, "wholesome herbs" and fruit and the flesh of beasts are appropriate and good for humans, although meat should be used "sparingly." All grains, but particularly wheat, are highly encouraged. These principles come with a promise—a promise not only of good physical health, but of mental and spiritual health as well.

> And all saints who remember to keep and do these sayings, walking in obedience to the commandments, shall receive health in their navel and marrow to their bones; and shall find wisdom and great treasures of knowledge, even hidden treasures; and shall run and not be weary, and shall walk and not faint.

Mormons love to point out how prescient much of this advice sounds today, as it has been confirmed by extensive current scientific research. They mention that, for example, the physical harm caused by alcohol, caffeine, and tobacco was little understood in 1833, the date of the revelation. While this is literally true—e.g., the link between smoking and lung cancer was not understood until the 1950s and 60s—it is also true that most of this advice was hardly brand new. Many other figures of the nineteenth century, including many doctors and a number of public crusaders—most famously Sylvester Graham (the father of the graham cracker)—proclaimed that alcohol, coffee, tea, and tobacco should be abstained from or used in great moderation.[7] A more subtle and interesting point is that while the advice given in the Word of Wisdom is generally sound in the eyes of modern science, it does not contain much of the other health advice current in the nineteenth century that today appears, well, odd. Graham, for example, preached against "excessive" marital intercourse, which he defined as more than once a month.[8]

6. Arrington, "Economic Interpretation."
7. Bush Jr., "Word of Wisdom."
8. Hoskisson, "Different and Unique."

In any case, Mormons can quite legitimately point to a high success rate for their lifestyle. Numerous scientific studies have shown that Latter-day Saints as a group live significantly longer than non-Latter-day Saints, which is primarily attributed to their health practices. A twenty-five-year study of Latter-day Saints in California found that the life expectancy of married LDS men and women who had never smoked, had attended church weekly, and had at least twelve years of education was remarkably greater than the average. The men had a life expectancy of 9.8 years above that of white American males in general, while the women's life expectancy was 5.6 years greater than that of American women.[9]

In another study, middle-aged Mormon men had dramatically lower rates of cancer and cardiovascular diseases than the general male population.[10] And in a wide-ranging study on the health of Latter-day Saints in Utah, researchers found a high degree of correlation between the Mormon lifestyle and a low incidence of many types of cancer, compared to the general Utah population. In the case of certain cancers, Seventh-Day Adventists in California had an even lower incidence, but the authors note that the Seventh-Day Adventists are much stricter than the LDS church in expelling those who violate their respective health codes.[11]

One interesting practice of Latter-day Saints is the monthly fast. The standard practice is to fast for two meals, or twenty-four hours, on the first Sunday of the month, and to donate at a minimum the amount saved in food costs to a fund that supports the poor and needy of the church. Fasting is not directly related to the Word of Wisdom, and it is rarely discussed as a health practice. Yet several studies have found that those who practice a monthly fast have a significantly lower risk of diabetes and heart disease.[12]

One of the most intriguing phrases found in the Word of Wisdom is the declaration that it was specifically given to the Saints in modern times "in consequence of evils and designs which do and will exist in the hearts of conspiring men in the last days." Although no official interpretation of that statement has ever been given, it is hard not to link it with the pattern of aggressive marketing for which tobacco and alcohol manufacturers have become notorious. The American Public Health Association in 1992 published an official statement noting that "the aggressive marketing and promotion tactics of both the alcohol and tobacco industries heavily target the youth market. Both industries use similar strategies to appeal to youth and increase market share." It notes specifically that

> alcohol and tobacco use are two of the most common risk factors for pre-ventable diseases, injuries, and premature death. Alcohol use by youth is also

9. Enstrom and Breslow, "Lifestyle and Reduced Mortality."
10. Enstrom, "Health Practices."
11. Lyon and Nelson, "Mormon Health."
12. "Routine Daily Fasting."

associated with motor vehicle injuries, suicide, and homicide, all of which are major causes of adolescent mortality. Although it is illegal to sell alcoholic beverages to youths under 21 and, in most states, to sell tobacco products to teenagers under 18, the alcohol and tobacco industries actively target young people with advertising and promotions. Through youth-oriented campaigns, the alcohol and tobacco industries create an environment in which the consumption of these dangerous products is acceptable and, within some teenage peer groups, even expected.[13]

Although the Word of Wisdom is primarily considered a health code, Mormons stress that it is not aimed narrowly at achieving good physical health. In the final promise quoted above, the obedient are promised that they will receive not only "health" and the ability "to walk and not faint," but also "treasures of knowledge, even hidden treasures." In fact, all the instructions and commandments given by the Lord are considered to be primarily for spiritual purposes. As the Lord himself declares in one verse of the Doctrine & Covenants, "Not at any time have I given unto you a law which was temporal . . . for my commandments are spiritual."[14]

Latter-day Saints will say that they follow the Word of Wisdom because it is a divine commandment—i.e., out of faith—but that the rewards of keeping the commandment are obvious. This is not only because science accords with its principles, but because one's life is happier and more fulfilling when one is not a slave to one's appetites. Following the word of God is its own reward.

THE LAW OF CHASTITY

A policy of abstaining from cigarettes, cigars, coffee, alcohol, and illicit drugs is hardly controversial in today's world. It is entirely otherwise with the Mormon approach toward sexuality. The church teaches that sex is a gift from God designed not only for propagation of the human race, but also as a means for seeking love and intimacy between married partners. Outside of marriage, however, all sexual contact is forbidden. Even for affianced couples, physical affection should be restricted to such things as handholding and light kissing. These views are clearly in conflict with modern-day, post-1960s assumptions about sex. Why do Mormons insist on adhering to such old-fashioned attitudes to something as innocuous as sex?

The question is a deliberately loaded one, because even today only a moment's reflection should be sufficient to realize that sex is *anything* but innocuous. Our modern sex-saturated society tries hard to transform sex into a fun, harmless distraction, without any connection to the deeper aspects of our humanity. We have attempted to sanitize sexuality and turn it into a mere physical appetite, like eating, or even like

---

13. "Advertising and Promotion of Alcohol."

14. D&C 29:34.

scratching an itch. Sexual activity is often described as "hot," but this heat is superficial, temporary, nearly meaningless. Previous ages and societies understood sex quite differently, particularly its *heat*.

Catullus, an ancient Roman poet, tries to convey the fire he feels toward his lover, Lesbia:

> Godlike he seems—
> Or even superior to the gods—
> who, sitting near you,
> gazes at you again and again,
> and hears your sweet laughter
> that wrests all my senses.
> For whenever I see you
> my tongue fails
> and a delicate flame
> courses through my limbs,
> my ears filled with an inner humming,
> even my eyes go blind.[15]

Consider the Song of Solomon:

> Set me as a seal upon your heart,
> as a seal upon your arm;
> for love is strong as death,
> passion fierce as the grave.
> Its flashes are flashes of fire,
> a raging flame.[16]

And Philodemos, a Greek poet, puts it most bluntly:

> Her strumming, her talk,
> her expressive eyes and song
> and the fire just lit makes my soul
> burn.
> I do not know the why or the how—
> unlucky!—
> I know only that my heart is on fire.[17]

Are these examples of human passion from classic literature just another misguided mirage of ignorant ages? A mere literary conceit? Hardly. Consider the following real-life attempt by the actor Richard Burton to describe his initial reaction upon meeting Elizabeth Taylor:

15. Catullus, *Poems* 51 (my translation).

16. Song of Solomon 8:6.

17. *Greek Anthology*, 5.131 (my translation). See Paton and Tueller, *Greek Anthology*, 288.

> She was so extraordinarily beautiful that I nearly laughed out loud. She [was] famine, fire, destruction and plague . . . the only true begetter. Her breasts were apocalyptic, they would topple empires before they withered . . . her body was a miracle of construction . . . she was unquestionably gorgeous.[18]

The infinite renditions of passion—spiritual and physical, requited and unrequited—in literature, music, and art are an indelible testament to the real power of love, romantic passion, and physical desire, which are all inextricably linked to each other. Indeed, they are testimony of the dangerous power of such passions. In contrast, the focus in the last sixty years has been on *isolating* sex from any deep emotions—on controlling, or ignoring, the passions of human interaction, on making sex into a prosaic, commonplace, almost trivial activity. The primary method for doing this is to focus narrowly on the physical experience of sex, divorcing it from our emotions, from our inner being. Sex should be "satisfying," we are implicitly told—a bloodless description if there ever was one. Note that such an approach focuses on the lover's *own* fulfillment, while a person who is "in love" is typically obsessed with the *other* person—the beloved—and has an intense desire to please *them*.

Gina Ogden, in *The Heart and Soul of Sex*, argues that our personal relationships have been robbed by an overemphasis on the physical aspects of sex. Especially since the Kinsey Reports on sexual behaviors, which appeared around 1950, we have thought about sex in terms of orgasm and body parts rather than in the context of whole people with complex needs, thoughts, and emotions or of real, multifaceted human relationships.[19]

We have become so obsessed in the last fifty years with overturning thousands of years of tradition regarding physical and social relations between the sexes that our view of sex has become impoverished, trivialized. And of course something that is trivial requires no rules, no limits, and can simply be enjoyed, like your favorite TV show or a chocolate éclair. The focus can be entirely on one's level of satisfaction with the experience—how to make an éclair that best fits your tastes.

Yet no matter how convinced we are that we have become emancipated from the shackles of the past, is it possible for us to liberate ourselves from the human passions associated with love and sex? Have we truly outgrown the human verity that sex and love are dangerous? Although that seems to be the assumption our modern culture has adopted, reality all too often teaches another lesson. Sadly, the number of murders of passion is astounding. According to FBI statistics, 45 percent of the women killed in 2007 in the United States were victims of a husband or boyfriend, or an ex-husband or ex-boyfriend.[20] Some experts believe the true percentage may be much higher, possibly as high as 70 percent. Murderers from passion tend to choose particularly

---

18. Quoted in Rodgers, *Sex*, 161.
19. Ogden, *Heart and Soul of Sex*, 11.
20. Catalano, "Female Victims."

violent—and intimate—means of killing: stabbing, slashing, or strangulation rather than shooting. According to Dr. Donald Dutton, a psychologist at the University of British Columbia, many such killers cannot bear being abandoned. "What's going on deep down is that they believe the woman is leaving them and they can't live without her."[21] And of course the perpetrators are not always men, as the infamous case of Jodi Arias shows: she killed her boyfriend by stabbing him twenty-seven times, slitting his throat from ear to ear, and then shooting him in the head.

The most extreme version of modern sexuality is the so-called hookup culture of the modern American university. While some accounts of this culture have exaggerated it, it is nonetheless a real, pervasive phenomenon.[22] Contrary to the popular image, the principal aspect of hookup culture is not to have sex with as many people as possible, but to *divorce sex—including kissing—from all desire, passion, or commitment.* Consider the following definition of a hookup:

> A hookup is a quick, ostensibly meaningless sexual intimacy, so there's no muss and no fuss. Each person enters into the encounter with the expectation that there will be no expectations. Both know why they are there, and it's not for conversation, caring, or hope for a future. *Emotional entanglement is not only not part of the deal, it is verboten, going against the very nature of a hookup.*[23]

What kind of personal fulfillment does this approach to sex offer? By definition, none—outside of a brief physical stimulation. Despite the deliberately drama-free nature of hooking up, participants sometimes admit that they went into it looking for something more. Many people reach a point at which it begins to dawn on them that this approach is personally emptying rather than satisfying. "After a few hookups (and morning afters)," said one female student, "I realized that it doesn't feel as good if you don't care about the person and don't think he cares about you. It can be fun, but hooking up is sex without the intimacy, which I think is more important."[24]

Nowadays dating apps like Tinder provide a way of extending the hookup lifestyle well past college. Even more convenient is the ubiquitous phenomenon of hardcore pornography.[25] Wendy and Larry Maltz, in *The Porn Trap*, state that in the

21. Goode, "When Women Find Love."
22. See Bogle, *Hooking Up.*
23. Freitas, *End of Sex*, 30.
24. Freitas, *End of Sex*, 36.
25. Dines, in *Pornland*, 114–19, discusses how our modern porn/sex culture and hookup culture are interrelated. She goes on to describe how a convicted child rapist talked about "grooming" his ten-year-old stepdaughter into consenting to his sexual advances. By progressively responding to her questions of childish curiosity about sex, he introduced her to porn and deliberately desensitized her to sexual experiences. In a similar way, pop culture, "by inundating girls and women with the message that their most worthy attribute is their sexual hotness and crowding out other messages . . . [it grooms] them just like an individual perpetrator would. It is slowly chipping away at their self-esteem, stripping them of a sense of themselves as whole human beings, and providing them with an identity

1980s they had no particular problem with the existence of porn and were not above recommending it to their clients as a way of spicing up their romantic lives. Beginning in the 1990s, however, porn became transformed into something else. Not only was it infinitely more available on the internet, but the substance of it had changed. Instead of providing a visual stimulus to couples, it "began to offer *itself* as the object of desire." It was designed to arouse the user "to have a sexual relationship *with it*." "Today's porn teaches users to think only about body parts and specific sexual actions, robbing them of the ability to experience romance, passion, and emotional and physical closeness with a real partner." As one user observed, "Why bother with setting the mood, meeting the needs of another person, or even taking off your clothes, when sex can be just a mouse or remote control click away?"[26] Porn has become the drug of choice for many people who would never smoke, swallow, or inject other types of drugs.

How is it like a drug? Porn use stimulates the production of feel-good chemicals such as dopamine, adrenaline, endorphins, and serotonin. And with the artificial stimulation of such chemicals, the user's mind becomes desensitized to *normal* types of stimulation and it becomes harder for the body to effectively release them in everyday activities, such as sex with a real person. Consider the following statements by porn users: "Doing porn felt like an incredible rush of life blowing through my veins and the good part was I could always go back for more." "No matter how much porn I looked at, my mind was always ready for more."[27] Like other drug use, porn has frequently been the cause of lost jobs, wrecked marriages, and shattered families.[28]

To reiterate, the common thread between hooking up and porn is the utter divorce between sex and real passion, between sex and love, between sex and human relationships. This divorce of sex from reality is such a vicious perversion of our humanity that the most appropriate word I can find to describe it is "satanic." It is anti-love. Love in all its guises (e.g., romantic love, friendship, compassion, empathy, and altruism) is truly what "makes the world go round." It is absolutely necessary for human life to flourish. Without it, life quickly becomes cold, sterile, and intolerable.

In contrast to the superficial connection of a hookup or the satisfaction a man receives from making love to his porn, consider the nature of true love—not the type found in fairy tales but the kind that takes place between two people in real life. Helen Fisher, an anthropologist, observes that among the most typical characteristics of a person in love are a desire for: a) a sexual connection, b) sexual exclusivity, and c) emotional union. Of the three, the last is by far the most important: the "yearning for emotional togetherness far surpasses the desire for mere sexual release." Fisher notes

---

that emphasizes sex and de-emphasizes every other human attribute." It is remarkable that the child rapist observed that grooming his stepdaughter was made much easier because "the culture did a lot of the grooming for me."

26. Maltz and Maltz, *Porn Trap*, 15.

27. Maltz and Maltz, *Porn Trap*, 19.

28. "How Porn Can Change the Brain"; see also Wilson, *Your Brain on Porn*.

that in a survey 75 percent of men and 83 percent of women agreed with the statement that knowing that their lover was in love with them was more important to them than having sex with them.[29]

The link among these three elements is a desire for unity with the beloved—complete physical *and* emotional union. The feeling that the other person desires you and you alone is heady stuff. But this desire for emotional unity cannot be divorced from the desire for physical oneness. They are inextricably interlinked. Sexual desire is much more than a desire for physical pleasure. It is a desire for union—complete oneness—with the other person. A Latin poet from the sixth century, Paulus Silentiarius, wrote: "And there lay the lovers, lip-locked / delirious, infinitely thirsting / wanting to go completely inside the other."[30]

In a more comic vein, the ancient Greek playwright Aristophanes (as portrayed in Plato's *Symposium)* declared that every human was originally a "whole" body with two heads, four arms, and four legs, like two people attached back to back. As a punishment for their arrogance, Zeus split them all into halves, so that they would have to walk upright with only two legs. But because they now were all merely one-half of a true human,

> each half yearned for the half from which it had been severed. When they met they threw their arms round one another and embraced, in their longing to grow together again, and they perished of hunger and general neglect of their concerns, because they would not do anything apart . . . Each of us then is the mere broken tally of a man . . . and each of us is perpetually in search of his corresponding tally.[31]

Under this concept, once this feeling of union and completion has been achieved, the experience of being torn apart from one's "other half" by infidelity drives lovers to insanity—even the insanity of murder.

In dramatic contrast with this picture of sex as a passionate longing for union with another, consider the following "post-modernist" description of sex in society:

> Almost all of us hope for good, healthy sex lives—sex that leaves us feeling ecstatic, satisfied, fulfilled; sex that is free from risk or guilt and that doesn't harm us in any way, mentally or physically, that even does us good; sex that is convenient, accessible, and within the budgets of most households.[32]

This is a purely utopian view of sex that completely ignores human nature. It naïvely supposes that sex that is free from any risk or inconvenience can somehow also be

29. Fisher, *Why We Love,* 21–22.
30. Quoted in Fisher, *Why We Love,* 14.
31. Plato, *Symposium,* 59–63.
32. Moloney, "Euphoric, Harmless."

personally fulfilling![33] It is reminiscent of the culture portrayed in Aldous Huxley's famous dystopian novel *Brave New World*, in which the key to society is the abolition of any strong ideas or strong feelings. When strong feelings begin to well up in one's heart or mind, the drug soma is available to quell them. The purpose of sex is recreation—and promiscuity is encouraged to prevent any strong personal attachments. Even a bond with one's parents is *verboten*. When the protagonist, John ("The Savage"), rushes to the bedside of his ill mother and then bewails her death, he is sharply criticized. In fact, the very concept of having an identifiable mother is considered revolting. The natural process of child-bearing and -rearing within families has been abolished and replaced with a Directorate of Hatcheries and Conditioning.[34]

The bottom line of all our discussion to this point is that sex is a *big deal*. Believe it or not, even that innocuous idea is being seriously questioned by the young generation. Having grown up in an environment in which sex is the ubiquitous object of sitcom humor and is treated as (at most) a titillating form of recreation, it is hardly surprising that, as Donna Freitas relates:

> Recently at a university lecture, a young woman in the audience asked me—in all sincerity—why sex was such a big deal. "Why does sex have to be any different than, say, taking a walk by myself?" she wondered. "What distinguishes sex from all other things we do that *aren't* such a big deal?" A number of students began to speculate in answer. They definitely thought that sex was a big deal, though no one could articulate why they felt this way.[35]

Freitas then goes on to identify with pinpoint accuracy the hidden but very real irony embedded in modern sexual attitudes.

> The great irony of hookup culture—whether pre-, during, or post-college—is that it's ultimately a culture of repression. If the Victorian era represents the repression of sexual desire, then the era of the hookup is about the repression of romantic feeling, love, and sexual desire, too, in favor of greater access to sex—sex for the sake of sex. Women and men both learn to shove their desires deep down into a dark place, to be revealed to no one. They learn to be ashamed if they long for love, and embarrassed if they fail to uphold the social

---

33. See also E. Smith, "Is Sex Still Sexy?"

34. Compare the following statement by writer Alana Massey regarding what she calls "the tyranny of chill" in our society ("chill" meaning acting cool, blasé, sophisticated): "Chill has now slithered into our romantic lives and forced those among us who would like to exchange feelings and accountability to compete in the Blasé Olympics with whomever we are dating . . . Chill asks us to remove the language of courtship and desire lest we appear invested somehow in other human beings. It is a game of chicken where the first person to confess their frustration or confusion loses . . . Chill presides over the funeral of reasonable expectations. Chill takes and never gives. Chill is pathologically unfeeling but not even interesting enough to kill anyone." Quoted in Emba, *Rethinking Sex*, 60–61.

35. Freitas, *End of Sex*, 181.

contract of hookup culture and do not happen to enjoy no-strings-attached sex that much.[36]

My contention is that modern-day sexual mores in general are only a step or two removed from the ultra-casual college hookup culture. For all the appearance of liberation from repression, a lax approach toward sex—i.e., sex without love and commitment—destroys the whole purpose of sexuality. That purpose is to create deep and lasting—ideally permanent—bonds between two people, which can then provide a foundation for the fundamentally important job of bearing and raising children.

Consider the curious modern phenomenon of living together, or cohabiting, with one's "significant other." (I suppose it's comforting to know that you are at least considered *significant* by the person you sleep with.) What exactly is the purpose of lovers living together without benefit of marriage? Some people may think of it as a trial marriage in which the couple can find out how compatible they are without going through the expense of marriage—or the drama of divorce if they decide to split up. But consider what effect this cautious approach to interpersonal relations can have on two people in love with each other. If you are truly, passionately in love and have the kind of yearning for absolute union with your beloved that we have just described as typical of lovers, what happens when your significant other proposes—with all the scientific reasonableness of a liberated modern man or woman—that you should live together for a while, "just to see how things go." It immediately, though subtly, puts the lie to the assumption of oneness. After all, if the other person is assuming that things may in fact not work out, it is hard to suppose that he/she really believes in the relationship. While neither person may realize it consciously, such an attitude results, much like a hookup, in a loss of intimacy and passion. The refusal of one partner to *commit* to a permanent relationship is surely a sign of their lack of true love. Do they really love you at all? Are they secretly in love with someone else? Still longing for their ex? Or are they just trying to keep their options open?

When this attitude becomes the social norm, of course, one may not have these conscious thoughts at all, but this unspoken tentativeness of romantic entanglements creates a hardened shell around people's feelings. It creates a huge barrier from the outset of any relationship. Again, as in hookup culture, each person comes to a romance with emotional reservations—knowing that it may not last, and that the other person may not even want it to last very long. In such a context—love and sex without commitment—what happens when one partner hooks up with someone else? Does the other *significant other* have the right to feel betrayed? How can there be betrayal

36. Freitas, *End of Sex*, 182. Christine Emba remarks that women seeking sexual freedom have in essence obtained "the freedom to be people open to anything except connection" (Emba, *Rethinking Sex*, 46). Her book is loaded with statements by (mostly) women who don't even find enjoyable much of the sex they participate in: "*I didn't really want it, but I did it; it wasn't rape, but it feels bad*" (p. 4, emphasis original). Many women feel compelled by modern culture to consent to sex, even when they would prefer not to, e.g.: "I don't want to have sex with you, but I'm doing it because, like, I have to be . . . polite" (p. 106).

when there was never any commitment? Presumably there was an unspoken *expectation* of sexual exclusivity for so long as they were living together, yet they deliberately avoided making any formal promises to each other.[37]

Despite the modern urge to reduce sexual desire to the level of a mere itch that frequently needs attention, I think that everyone still recognizes implicitly that it is much more than this. Our modern culture has removed most, but definitely not all, of the constrictions on sexual behavior. Sex between brothers and sisters, parents and children, or adults and minors is not only forbidden legally but is still considered highly immoral by almost everyone. Even sex between cousins is generally frowned upon in most cultures, and the prohibitions against sexual relations are not limited to sexual intercourse that could result in children but includes other types of sexual contact as well, such as sexual touching. Why is this? If the reason for the universal societal prohibition against incest is the objective risk of inbreeding, why do we still frown on *non-coital* sex between siblings or between parent and child? If sex is really no big deal, why do we object so fiercely to *any* type of physical intimacy between adults and children? What if an adult woman has a fully consensual relationship with her father?

The "sordid psychodrama" of Woody Allen with his now-wife, Soon-Yi, who is the adoptive daughter of his then-partner Mia Farrow, is an interesting case in societal views.[38] Previously Farrow and her then-husband, Andre Previn, had adopted Soon-Yi at age eight from a dismal life in South Korea. Allen never married Farrow, and so never became Soon-Yi's stepfather. In fact, he never even lived in the same house with Farrow or Soon-Yi. In 1992, Farrow discovered nude pictures of the girl, now twenty-one, taken by Allen, and the story of their sexual relationship exploded onto the Hollywood/New York scene, threatening to destroy Allen's career. That did not happen, and he and Soon-Yi later married and have remained married despite the scandal and the thirty-five-year age gap.

My question is: What was the basis for the scandal? What was it precisely that disturbed people about this relationship? There was no evidence that he had done anything wrong while she was a minor. Was it just distaste over a middle-aged man's libido for a sweet young woman? Was it simply an example of lingering traditional, Puritan morality, even among the glitterati? Or were there more concrete concerns? The fact that he had never really been in a position of parental authority over her deflected the argument of abuse of power.

---

37. Sociologist Mark Regnerus, quoting Anthony Giddens, refers to the modern ideal of the "pure relationship": "where a social relation is entered into for its own sake, for what can be derived by each person from a sustained association with another; and which is continued only insofar as it is thought by both parties to deliver enough satisfactions for each individual to stay within it" (Regnerus, *Cheap Sex*, 9). Such an attitude of course reduces the idea of personal commitment to something resembling a joke.

38. The phrase comes from Edelstein, "Mamma Mia!"

Why did the judge in the suit against him by Farrow deny him all custody and even visitation rights of his own children with Farrow? Why did he ultimately deny Allen visitation rights with his son Dylan and permit him to see Satchel only under supervision? Moses, an older child, was given a choice and declined to see his father. The judge accused Allen of being "self-absorbed"—hardly a crime—and "decried what he saw as Allen's inability to comprehend the negative impact on his children of his and Soon-Yi's relationship."[39] Allen himself has stated consistently that he never did anything wrong, and declares himself at a loss to understand the basis of the controversy. As Woody himself has put it, "the heart wants what the heart wants."

The point here is that everybody still recognizes—more subconsciously than consciously—that sex is much more than just a physical experience. Woody Allen could have had an emotionally intimate but non-physical relationship with Soon-Yi and nobody would have cared. Yet the moment it became known as a sexual one, the world blew up. Why? And why is sexual assault, for example, considered much more grievous than simple physical assault? It is not simply a matter of invading someone's body through penetration, because sexual assault does not necessarily involve physical penetration, while other types of penetration—forcing one's fingers into another's mouth, say, or nose—might be offensive but would carry none of the baggage that sexual penetration does.

If sex were merely a matter of flesh rubbing against flesh for physical pleasure, it would not be the highly charged subject it is.[40] Clearly, sex is something that touches us in our deepest wellsprings of mind, emotion, and spirit. Why is this? I believe it is reasonable to say that sex *and* love—sex *with* love—are deliberately designed to provide a highly pleasurable means of helping to bind two people together for the long-term—i.e., to provide one, but certainly not the only, motive to strengthen two people's personal—and permanent—commitment. And when a married couple remains together, the family as a whole (assuming there are children) remains together. Thus, love, sex, marriage, reproduction, and family are inherently related—and not only related but intimately connected.

Sexual stimulation of *any* kind is inherently loaded and not just a normal kind of physical contact. Sex is not just about physical gratification, recreation, or having fun. It has a very powerful effect on people, whether we want it to or not. It is not an expression of mere affection or friendship (the phrase "friends with benefits" being the ultimate euphemism). It is not even just about child-bearing. A sexual relationship amounts to the deepest sort of connection between people and has long-lasting, even permanent effects on the psyche, or the soul, of men and women. It has a powerful

---

39. Biskind, "Reconstructing Woody."

40. Or, as the Roman emperor and Stoic philosopher Marcus Aurelius so delicately put it, "As for sexual intercourse, it is the rubbing of a piece of intestine, then a convulsion, and the spurting of some mucus" (Aurelius, *Meditations* [6:13], 47).

effect on how we view both ourselves and other people. It is not something to be treated casually under any circumstances.

It is for this reason that I feel justified in describing sex as *spiritual*—not in some vague, new-agey sense, but because it reaches down into the most intimate (the Latin *intimus* means deepest, innermost) part of our souls. Its effect is not limited to the body or even the mind or emotions, but has a very deep resonance with people, which the modern world tries hard to ignore.[41]

MORMONS ON SEX

What has all this to do with the LDS church's law of chastity? From the beginning the Latter-day Saints rejected the old traditional Christian belief regarding the evils of the flesh. Parley P. Pratt in 1840 noted:

> Some persons have supposed that our natural affections were the results of a fallen and corrupt nature, and that they are carnal, sensual, and devilish, and therefore ought to be resisted, subdued, or overcome as so many evils which prevent our perfection, or progress in the spiritual life…. Our natural affections are planted in us by the Spirit of God, for a wise purpose; and they are the very main-springs of life and happiness—they are the cement of all virtuous and heavenly society—they are the essence of charity, or love . . . There is not a more pure and holy principle in existence than the affection which glows in the bosom of a virtuous man for his companion . . .[42]

Note that Pratt does not limit the virtue of sexual desire to child-bearing but describes it as "the very main-springs of life and happiness." But despite the highly positive attitude toward *marital* relations, there is zero acceptance in the church of non-marital relations. Why is this? What is wrong, for example, with an engaged couple who are preparing for marriage and are sure that their love will last for an eternity enjoying each other physically before the wedding? What is wrong with testing their sexual compatibility before they make a permanent commitment?

Latter-day Saints view the traditional prohibition of premarital sex as a commandment without exception. The first and most basic reason for this is because sexual intercourse is directly linked to procreation. Modern technology has done its best to sever that link, but no contraceptive is 100 percent effective: the pill on average allows eight pregnancies out of one hundred, and even an IUD is only 99 percent effective.[43] It is even possible for a man to father a child after a vasectomy. Although technology is improving, there is *no* way of having intercourse that is 100 percent certain not to

---

41. See Emba, *Rethinking Sex*, 95–110.

42. Crawley, *Essential Parley*, 124.

43. Christine Emba notes that 45 percent of the six million pregnancies each year in the U.S. are unintended. Emba, *Rethinking Sex*, 74.

result in conception. Even a hysterectomy is not a perfect solution, although a woman without a uterus who became pregnant would not be able to bring the fetus to term.

Mormons view sex as a divinely bestowed means of propagation for God's children—us—to bear and raise their own children. For Latter-day Saints, child-bearing and -raising is among the most profound and sacred activities of our lives. Boyd K. Packer, a recently deceased apostle of the church known for his strict and conservative views, declared: "This power [of creation] is good . . . It is a sacred and significant power, and I repeat . . . that this power is good . . . It is a gift from God our Father. In the righteous exercise of it, as in nothing else, we may come close to Him." On another occasion he described the power of procreation as "the very key to happiness. Hold this gift as sacred and pure."[44] While the church has no prohibition against family planning or the use of contraceptives (except for abortion, and even there the proscription is not absolute), church members are encouraged to have children and not to avoid having children for selfish reasons. The opportunity to effectively *create* a new life is indeed the closest that we can come to acting like God in this life—and hence is a most sacred gift.

From a Mormon perspective, it seems odd that modern society has built up countless hedges against *taking* another person's life, yet has virtually abandoned all restrictions on activities that lead to the *creation* of new life. Both should be done only with the most careful considerations. There are few things more tragic than an unwanted child or a child born to parents who are still children themselves. As we all know, this happens regularly to young people who do not understand the importance or proper use of contraception, but it also happens to older couples who let their guard down or whose contraceptive methods have simply failed.

But even if there were a foolproof contraceptive, would the church then countenance premarital sex? The answer must be a definite no. Why not? This brings us back to the discussion above regarding sex as much more than a physical act—sexual activity as a deeply emotional and spiritual activity. To understand the LDS attitude toward sex, we need to back up and reconsider the plan of salvation and the role that families play in it.

As we discussed in a previous chapter, God's entire purpose is to bring to pass immortality and eternal life for all his children. The church has declared that "the family is ordained of God" and is "central to the Creator's plan for the eternal destiny of His children." There are several bases for such a statement, but the most fundamental is that "children are entitled to birth within the bonds of matrimony, and to be reared by a father and a mother who honor marital vows with complete fidelity. Happiness in family life is most likely to be achieved when founded upon the teachings of the Lord Jesus Christ," including the importance of stable families bound by ties of love and commitment.[45]

44. Packer, *Teach Ye Diligently*, 259–61; Packer, "Why Stay Morally Clean?," 113.

45. The quotations are from "The Family—a Proclamation," issued by the top councils of the

The importance of strong, stable families for the well-being of children is common sense but is also supported by social science research. According to sociologists Sara McLanahan and Gary Sandefur, the evidence strongly points to the conclusion that "children who grow up in a household with only one biological parent are worse off, on average, than children who grow up in a household with both of their biological parents." Statistically, "compared with teenagers of similar background who grow up with both parents at home, adolescents who have lived apart from their parents for some period of childhood are twice as likely to drop out of high school, twice as likely to have a child before age 20, and one and a half times as like to be 'idle'—out of school and out of work—in their late teens and early twenties."[46] Single parents (typically mothers), for all the love they may give their children and the effort they may put forth on their children's behalf, cannot provide the same level of financial, physical, or emotional support that two parents can.[47]

To put it simply, the sex drive is one of the major forces that helps bind a family together—particularly for the benefit of children, but also for the individuals and the family itself. To repeat, the LDS church does not teach, as many churches have done and some still do, that sex is only for the purpose of having children. That is too limited a perspective. Rather, as I suggested above, sex is first and foremost designed to bind *a couple* together. That purpose presupposes marriage, in the first instance, because it is self-contradictory to suppose that two people who are not ready for marriage are ready to be bound together in any meaningful way. Sexual relations are a way of signaling one's commitment to the other person, and expressing one's love in a way that deeply affects them on all levels—physically, emotionally, and spiritually. Sex is designed to make *two* people as *one*—one flesh, but also one spirit, the ultimate kind of unity. Cohabitation, in direct contrast to marriage, is designed to keep two people as *two*.[48]

LDS Church in 1995. Church leaders have always preached the importance of families, but they apparently concluded in the 1990s that the institution of the family (in the traditional sense) had so deteriorated that it was necessary to make a formal declaration of its paramount importance in human society. Available at https://www.churchofjesuschrist.org/bc/content/shared/content/english/pdf/36035_000_24_family.pdf.

46. McLanahan and Sandefur, *Growing Up*, 1–2. They point out that single parent families are not the only, nor even the primary, reason for these negative outcomes in individual cases, but *statistically* they are a major contributor. Just as failure to exercise is only one among several significant risk factors for heart disease, "many people who don't exercise never suffer a heart attack, and many children raised by single mothers grow up to be quite successful." Yet regular exercise makes it statistically much less likely that a heart attack will occur.

47. Waite and Gallagher, *Case for Marriage*, 110–23.

48. Consider the extensive comparison of "The Marriage Contract" versus "The Cohabitation Deal" in chapters 2 and 3 of Waite and Gallagher, *Case for Marriage*. Married couples are much more inclined to share their financial assets and to consider those assets as belonging to both partners mutually, while cohabiting couples nearly always keep their money separate. Similarly, unmarried couples are much more likely to see their time as basically their own, to spend as they wish, than those who are married.

Once the sex drive has fulfilled its principal purpose, so to speak, of binding two adults together, the couple is then ready to commit to having children. If sex is had outside the realm of a permanent commitment, it risks bringing children into an unstable and unpredictable environment that provides a less-than-ideal foundation for them to grow into mature and well-adjusted adults. Of course no family is entirely stable—there are always stressors that can cause breakage, including death. And one-parent families are in no way *evil*. But they are less than ideal and cannot be eternal.

For the marriage bond in LDS theology is not merely for this life ("until death do you part") but is potentially eternal. Likewise, families also are intended by God to be eternal, which is why the family is considered the fundamental unit not only of the church, but of eternity. Specifically, in order for their marriage to endure into the afterlife, a couple must be *sealed* together in an LDS temple "for time and all eternity" and both partners must remain faithful to their marriage vows and keep the commandments generally. Latter-day Saints believe that their faith in the eternal nature of their marriage vows and of the family as a whole provides a strong motive to help them resist temptations, whether of infidelity or of other types of selfishness that can lead to divorce. It provides them with added strength to devote themselves to the needs of their spouse and their children—i.e., to create a *unity* that can transcend time.

The perceptive reader will have realized by now that I have avoided the topical controversy of same-sex marriage. I don't intend to go into this issue in depth, but it should be reasonably clear from the above discussion why the idea of marriage between same-sex partners is problematic in LDS beliefs. It is not simply that Mormons are narrow-minded traditionalists, nor that homosexuality is viewed in Mormonism as evil or non-Christian—the subject of an arbitrary prohibition by an authoritarian deity. Rather, Mormonism rejects gay marriage because the very concept is utterly incompatible with its theology of eternal families. If the entire purpose of marriage and sexuality is to create an unbreakable bond between two people that can lead to the eternal propagation of children, a same-sex marriage, which is inherently barren, can seem almost like a mockery. At the same time, although the concept of gay marriage is incompatible with traditional LDS theology, church leaders in recent years have tried increasingly to be sensitive to the feelings of LGBT individuals, particularly those who belong to the church. The church has in recent years softened its stance on the issue of same-sex *attraction* (in contrast to *behavior*) in church members.

The *extraordinarily* perceptive reader will have realized that I have also side-stepped another major controversy in Mormonism—polygamy, or what is known in the church as "plural marriage." It is no secret that Mormons were once extreme advocates of plural marriages—of a man having two or more wives (properly known as polygyny). That practice was discontinued in 1890, but the extent of the controversy it created for the church for decades is hard to comprehend today. As I noted in chapter 1, it resulted in the imprisonment of hundreds of LDS men, as well as a congressional act, a major Supreme Court decision, and the legal confiscation of nearly all the church's property. The identification of Mormons with polygamy is still pervasive, even today. According to a recent survey, a mere 15 percent of Americans feel certain that Mormons do *not* practice polygamy. An equal percentage are certain that Mormons *are* polygamists, while the majority (70 percent) are uncertain one way or the other.[49] Doubtless part of the confusion is due to the amount of attention which the small apostate groups of Mormons that continue to embrace plural marriage (e.g., the FLDS—Fundamentalist Church of Jesus Christ of Latter-day Saints) receive in the media.

Plural marriage is an extremely complex subject in the context of Mormon studies, and I don't intend to break open that can of worms apart from a few general remarks about Mormon theological views. From the perspective of Mormon doctrine, polygamy was a decisive commandment from God. The text of that commandment is found in section 132 of the *Doctrine & Covenants*, where the Lord declares that, like Abraham, Moses, David, and Solomon, his followers may enter into marriages with more than one wife, so long as the first wife gives her consent and the second wife is sealed to the husband through the temple ritual of celestial marriage. Any other approach to multiple marriages or relationships is forbidden.

The primary purpose of this practice was to raise up seed—i.e., to have numerous offspring and thereby strengthen the church. The Book of Mormon states clearly that men are to have one wife only, unless the Lord specifically commands them otherwise. "For if I will, saith the Lord of Hosts, raise up seed unto me, I will command my people; otherwise they shall hearken to these things."[50] Similarly, Hagar was given to Abraham as a second wife, and from her "sprang many people."[51] David, on the other hand, sinned only in the case of Bathsheba, when he took her without the Lord's permission and without marriage, and subsequently had Uriah killed in order to have her for himself.

Despite the notoriety of the practice of plural marriage among the Latter-day Saints, the practice was far from universal throughout the church. Although complete statistics are lacking, roughly between 25 and 50 percent of families in Utah between 1860 and 1880 were polygamous. In the large majority of cases men had only two wives or occasionally three. A few principal church leaders, most notoriously Brigham Young, had several dozen wives, but we have no way of knowing how many of them were sexually consummated. In numerous instances such marriages were arranged either to provide economically for an older unmarried woman or were sealings "for eternity only"—i.e., the marriage was not considered valid until the afterlife.[52]

---

49. Lawrence, *How Americans View Mormonism*, 45.

50. Jacob 2:30.

51. D&C 132:34.

52. *The Encyclopedia of Mormonism* has an excellent summary of the practice under "Plural Marriage." Beyond that, the scholarly literature on polygamy is voluminous. One excellent volume is Daynes, *More Wives than One*. For the voices of the actual women who lived the practice, see Harline,

THE PRINCIPLE OF SERVICE

Hopefully it is clear by this point that the emphasis on family values in the church is much more than just belief in a conservative lifestyle. Families are a fundamental aspect of LDS theology. Although it may appear to outsiders that the church is simply trying to turn the clock back to the 1940s, there is clearly much more going on. But beyond the conviction that members of a family should try to forge a unity that can overcome death, families are also seen as a microcosm of life that provide an excellent, ongoing environment in which to learn the principle of *service*.

As I have already emphasized, Latter-day Saints are striving, ideally, to embody the teachings of Jesus. One of the most important of these, clearly, is the command to serve one's fellow man. For Mormons, religion is much more than a part of life that occupies an hour or two on Sunday and perhaps another hour or two of Bible study during the week. Indeed, Mormonism is much more than a system of belief; it is a way of life.

The church worldwide is divided into *stakes* and *wards*. A stake of Zion is the larger geographical entity, corresponding closely to the Roman Catholic term "diocese," and harks back to the Old Testament imagery of the portable tabernacle/temple built by Moses, surrounded by curtains held in place by stakes or pegs.[53] Each stake is divided into a number of wards, which correspond to parishes or individual congregations. Mormons often refer to their ward as a secondary "family," because ward members tend to interact on a number of levels.

Each ward member typically holds a specific assignment, or "calling," from the bishop (i.e., pastor) of the ward. This calling can range anywhere from being a Sunday greeter to being president of the Relief Society, the principle women's group in each ward. Many callings can require a commitment of several hours during the week, while certain callings can demand up to twenty hours in a week or even more. All these assignments, including that of the bishop himself, are strictly volunteer. The priesthood is held by all male members of the church, each of whom has his own job or career outside the church. No one receives pay for ecclesiastical assignments except for a small number of men and women who are the full-time administrators of the church.

These callings are viewed as opportunities to provide service to others. Many ward members are assigned as instructors of the various classes taught on Sunday. A large ward, for example, would have a nursery for very small children, Primary classes for each age group of children from three to twelve, classes for the youth, and a class for adults. Sunday services, including all these classes and a general sacrament meeting, last two hours. Other individuals will be assigned to work specifically with

---

Polygamous Wives; for a simple introduction to the subject written for Latter-day Saint readers, see Nash, *Let's Talk about Polygamy*; for the political aspects, see Talbot, *Foreign Kingdom*.

53. See Isaiah 54:2–3.

the youth, who typically meet for less structured activities one evening a week. In addition, most men and women in a ward are assigned as "ministering brothers and sisters" who are responsible for establishing friendships with several individuals or families in the ward and generally paying attention to any special needs they may have. The purpose of this program is to watch over the members and give each member at least one person whom they can specifically rely on when special needs arise, as well as to help the bishop and Relief Society president keep track of the status and necessities of ward members.

The bishop is the chief administrator and pastor of the entire ward. With the help of two counselors and a couple of clerks, he organizes and runs the weekly sacrament meeting, interviews ward members and assigns them to do the work of the ward, interviews those who come to him with particular concerns or needs, including those seeking welfare assistance from the church, interacts directly with the youth of the ward, and keeps track of the finances and membership records of the ward, along with various and sundry other activities. Similarly, the Relief Society president watches over the needs specifically of the women, in particular those who are needy, elderly, disabled, or have other special needs.[54]

All of this activity is clearly time-consuming, and Latter-day Saints, like most people in today's world, have plenty of other activities to keep them busy, such as careers, helping children with homework and driving them to music and sports activities, preparing meals, doing housework, yardwork, etc. The church also encourages parents to engage in various types of family-oriented and spiritually uplifting activities with their children. Naturally, not all Latter-day Saints are equally diligent in fulfilling their callings and duties, but many are committed to doing their level best to carry out all these responsibilities.

One frequently cited passage of scripture relates to the importance of serving others:

> "Then the king will say to those at his right hand, 'Come, you that are blessed by my Father, inherit the kingdom prepared for you from the foundation of the world; for I was hungry and you gave me food, I was thirsty and you gave me something to drink, I was a stranger and you welcomed me, I was naked and you gave me clothing, I was sick and you took care of me, I was in prison and you visited me.' Then the righteous will answer him, 'Lord, when was it that we saw you hungry and gave you food, or thirsty and gave you something to drink? And when was it that we saw you a stranger and welcomed you, or naked and gave you clothing? And when was it that we saw you sick or in prison and visited you?' And the king will answer them, 'Truly I tell you, just as you did it to one of the least of these who are members of my family, you did it to me.'"[55]

54. See further, Bushman, *Contemporary Mormonism*, 27–35.
55. Matthew 25:34–45.

Just as wards are considered locales where individuals are regularly given opportunities to serve others, the family is regarded as the optimal place where one can learn to interact with others on a daily, intimate basis, to learn to tolerate each other's foibles and flaws, and to learn such basic principles as honesty, commitment, and love. Nowhere else do we interact with such frequency and intensity as in the family, and Latter-day Saints believe that the family is an actual gift of God's grace that helps us learn those very qualities I discussed in chapter 5—the qualities that lead us to godhood.

SACRIFICE AND OBEDIENCE

One of the chief principles underlying the Latter-day Saint approach to life is *sacrifice*. Joseph Smith declared:

> A religion that does not require the sacrifice of all things never has power sufficient to produce the faith necessary [to lead] unto life and salvation; for, from the first existence of man, the faith necessary unto the enjoyment of life and salvation never could be obtained without the sacrifice of all earthly things. It was through this sacrifice, and this only, that God has ordained that men should enjoy eternal life.[56]

What did Joseph Smith mean with this striking statement? Why does salvation "require the sacrifice of all things"? He certainly did not mean that it was necessarily to live an extreme life of self-denial. True asceticism has never been a part of Mormonism; there are no Latter-day Saint monks. Nevertheless, there is a mild but serious strain of self-abnegation that permeates Mormon thinking. Once-a-month fasting is a perfect example of this. Church leaders have actually discouraged members from engaging in "heroic" or long-term fasting. Yet they consistently teach that moderate fasting is a divinely ordained method of learning to abstract oneself from the incessant demands of the body and of acquiring self-discipline. Tithing is another example: church members are encouraged to pay a full tenth of their income, not only for the financial benefit of the church, but for their own spiritual benefit. Learning to live on nine-tenths of one's income requires considerable commitment as well as self-discipline. Yet the true blessings, Mormons believe, that come from this practice are spiritual. There is nothing that proves where one's heart truly lies than parting with money. Even attending meetings is viewed in this light. Most people have other things they could be doing on a Sunday morning than attending church meetings for two hours. But sacrificing one's time and personal preferences are believed to be worthwhile in the long run.

The spiritual purpose underlying all such practices is not abstract but concrete. As I discussed in a prior chapter, the most important thing we can learn in this life is

56. *Lectures on Faith*, 6.7.

to overcome our own self-centered will. The commandments are not meant to make us miserable but to make us holy. If we are unwilling to part with a segment of our time and wealth—and food—in this life, how will we ever be capable of managing the power and glory of God? Think about the example of King David. There was nothing shameful *per se* about his suddenly desiring Bathsheba when he glimpsed her bathing from the rooftop. It was a perfectly natural reaction. The sin was in indulging in his selfish impulses, which led not only to adultery but to murder.

The intent behind Joseph Smith's statement above is not that a follower of Christ must actually sacrifice everything he or she possesses and embrace a life of self-denial, but that one must be genuinely *willing* to sacrifice everything—up to and including one's own life, if necessary. And the principle behind what I am calling "mild self-denial" is that most of us need to practice giving up what we want. If we are in the habit, for example, of going without food and drink for twenty-four hours on a monthly basis, it would be at least somewhat easier, for example, if we found ourselves in a Nazi prison camp, to give up our crust of bread to someone else who needed it more than us.

Closely associated with the concept of sacrifice is that of obedience. The word "obedience" has a very negative connotation in today's individualistic world. Like faith, it is often associated with the word "blind." But Latter-day Saints do not consider the command of obedience to be to blind obedience. Rather, it springs from the faith and confidence that the teachings of the prophets will lead, in the short term, to greater happiness and, ultimately, to unimaginable blessings. Joseph Smith was once asked how he managed to keep his people so orderly, and his reply was, "I teach them correct principles and they govern themselves."[57]

A final note. Why are Latter-day Saints so happy and upbeat? Mike Wallace, the former host of *60 Minutes,* a self-described "dyed-in-the-wool, jaded, New York-based reportorial cynic," once quipped, "When you come out here [i.e., Utah] and talk to people, you look in their eyes, they're so damned happy. Everyone looks so innocent. Maybe there's something we've been missing."[58] If you were to visit a typical LDS

---

57. There are at least two accounts of this story. John Taylor, the third president of the church, reported: "Some years ago, in Nauvoo, a gentleman in my hearing, a member of the Legislature, asked Joseph Smith how it was that he was enabled to govern so many people, and to preserve such perfect order; remarking at the same time that it was impossible for them to do it anywhere else. Mr. Smith remarked that it was very easy to do that. 'How?' responded the gentleman; 'to us it is very difficult.' Mr. Smith replied, 'I teach them correct principles, and they govern themselves.'" Brigham Young, the second president of the church, related it as follows: "The question was asked a great many times of Joseph Smith, by gentlemen who came to see him and his people, 'How is it that you can control your people so easily? It appears that they do nothing but what you say; how is it that you can govern them so easily?' Said he, 'I do not govern them at all. The Lord has revealed certain principles from the heavens by which we are to live in these latter days. The time is drawing near when the Lord is going to gather out His people from the wicked, and He is going to cut short His work in righteousness, and the principles which He has revealed I have taught to the people and they are trying to live according to them, and they control themselves.'" *Teachings of Presidents: Joseph Smith,* 284.

58. Haws, *Mormon Image,* 167–68.

temple visitors center, and an enthusiastic young female missionary (in the jargon, a "sister missionary") approached you with a huge smile and gave your hand a vigorous shake and said with as much eagerness as she could muster, "I'm so glad you came today!," you might take a step backwards. You might even be inclined to assume that her whole demeanor was a put-on, that she was merely using the time-honored selling technique of the upbeat and friendly salesman to try to persuade you to listen to the message. But it is much more than that. The reality is, whether anyone else finds it plausible or not, that Latter-day Saints genuinely believe that they have been blessed with an understanding of the true principles of happiness (see chapter 10 below). As a result, they have a genuine desire to share it with others. The feelings underlying such behavior are quite genuine.

THE PUDDING IS THE PROOF

Latter-day Saints believe that one can discover the truth of the commandments simply by living them. Missionaries point out to their investigators that they will be happier if they start living a new kind of lifestyle. Living by the law of chastity frees one from the fear of AIDS and other diseases, as well as from the emotional trauma of infidelities and adulteries. Living the Word of Wisdom brings remarkable health benefits. Learning to sacrifice one's money and time brings, among other things, a sense of focus and dedication to one's life. Despite the challenge and sacrifice they may require, the commandments are their own reward. Jesus once said, "If you continue in my word, you are truly my disciples; and you will know the truth, and the truth will make you free."[59] Knowing the truth—and living it!—brings freedom from the constraints of sin (i.e., disease, insecurities, confusion). Put simply, clean living is its own reward.

59. John 8:31–32.

8

Old Things Become New—the Restoration of the Ancient Church

LATTER-DAY SAINTS FREQUENTLY DECLARE, with seeming conceit, that they belong to "the only true church." While I must admit that this attitude may at times be tinged with unrighteous pride, the doctrine, at heart, is a valid theological position. The phrase comes from the preface to the Doctrine and Covenants, where the Lord explains why he called Joseph Smith as a prophet and commanded him to establish another church on the earth. He describes this church as "the only true and living church upon the face of the whole earth, with which I, the Lord, am well pleased, speaking unto the church collectively and not individually."[1] Here God is not praising Latter-day Saints as perfect or as the only righteous people in the world, nor is he condemning all other Christians as wicked people. Neither is he declaring that no other church possesses any truth. Instead, he is proclaiming that this is the only church that *as an institution* is pleasing to him, because it has the proper organization and the correct doctrines. Other churches had some true doctrines, but their creeds had become corrupted over time and diverged from the pure teachings of Christ and the original apostles. Elsewhere God had told Joseph that the teachings of the established churches taught "the commandments of men, having a form of godliness but they deny the power thereof."[2] In other words, he did not condemn the pious Christians who were attempting to follow God's teachings as best they knew how, but he declared that the institutional churches had drifted so far from the true understanding that their teachings reflected only a shadow of the true divine reality. Of course, correct doctrine itself has never been God's ultimate concern; rather, it is how people conduct themselves. But there is a direct correlation between how they think of God—his purposes for creating them, etc.—and how they conduct themselves in this life.

1. D&C 1:30.
2. *HOTC*, 6.

Note that God does not state simply that the LDS Church is the only true church, but that it is the only true *and living* church. Virtually all other churches had abandoned the idea of *living revelation* and based their beliefs entirely on the Bible. The LDS teaching that God was again *revealing* his will through a prophet and that those revelations were equal with the Bible was anathema to Christians who believed that the Bible contained the sum total of everything that God wanted his children to know of divine things. The Mormons proclaimed, however, that while the Bible was certainly true, its meaning was not always clear, and incorrect interpretations had accreted to it over the centuries, obscuring the original message.

So how had this turn of events come about? How had Christendom strayed so far from the original teachings of Jesus that God himself felt the need to restore them? Is there any real historical evidence for this, or is it just the Mormons' perverse interpretation of history? In an attempt to answer those questions, this chapter will focus on the history of Christian thought. It should go without saying that this is a highly complex subject, which we will only be able to touch on very superficially. I will attempt to paint a picture with a very broad brush, focusing on only two or three fundamental issues.

In the study of history, it is a truism that attitudes change over time. No matter how thoroughly we might peruse the historical records, there is no way that we can enter into the minds, say, of Henry VIII of England and his contemporaries and truly understand how they thought. Even the Victorian Age, which was only a bit over a century ago, is mostly a closed book to us in terms of understanding exactly what made them tick. We may have read historical novels such as Wharton's *The Age of Innocence*. We may even have read the diaries of Queen Victoria herself and numerous other figures of the age. Yet there is no way we can truly understand what it was like to live in a prior age. As the opening line in L.P. Hartley's classic novel *The Go-Between* states, "The past is a foreign country; they do things differently there."[3] I would add that they also *think* differently. In other words, even though we do many of the same things as our ancestors, our way of thinking about what we do—our attitudes and assumptions—is quite different.

At the same time, we have to be aware that many of the unspoken assumptions which we cling to unquestioningly—our mental furniture, as it were—were formed long ago. And like the story of the housewife who cut the ends off the ham before serving it, it is very easy to carry on the attitudes and practices of the past for many generations, without ever questioning them or subjecting them to close scrutiny.

Most Christians assume without giving it much thought that modern Christianity is essentially the same as the religion founded by Jesus and his disciples two millennia ago. They take it for granted that there is a direct line of transmission of the Bible from ancient times to the contemporary world, and that the traditional doctrines

---

3. Hartley, *Go-Between*, 17.

have been preserved in a more-or-less linear progression, so that at least the essential teachings have been preserved into the modern world in their original form.

Of course, many Christians accept it as an article of religious faith that God preserved the Bible in more-or-less pristine form. They believe that God has been at work throughout the history of the world to ensure that his word has been transmitted properly and exactly, thereby ensuring that his followers of all ages can rely on holy writ. As an article of faith, that is perfectly acceptable—but the historical record presents a much more ambiguous picture.

As should be clear by now, Latter-day Saints reject this view of historical continuity. Instead, they assert that there was a "Great Apostasy," beginning as early as the end of the first century, with the death of the original apostles, and progressing through the medieval and into the modern age. This apostasy was in part conscious, carried out by men who rejected certain aspects of Christ's teachings and attempted to alter them, and partly unconscious, driven by what we might call "historical drift"—changes that subtly creep in over time as people interact with the world around them. The result of these historical processes was a transmuted Christianity that would scarcely have been recognizable by Jesus himself.

This tendency toward corruption is visible from the very beginning of the Christian movement. Paul, in what was probably his earliest epistle, declared to the Christians in Galatia:

> I am astonished that you are so quickly deserting the one who called you in the grace of Christ and are turning to a different gospel—not that there is another gospel, but there are some who are confusing you and want to pervert the gospel of Christ.[4]

Indeed, many of Paul's writings are his attempts at correcting the beliefs and practices of the churches that were scattered throughout the wide Roman world and had only limited contact with each other. In many cases he argued against the so-called Judaizers, who taught that Jesus had never meant for the Mosaic law to be superseded and insisted that all Christians should keep the traditional rules of circumcision, of kosher, and so on. In a well-known passage from the same epistle, Paul speaks of publicly reprimanding the apostle Peter for caving in to the demands of the circumcision faction.

> I said to Cephas [Peter] before them all, "If you, though a Jew, live like a Gentile and not like a Jew, how can you compel the Gentiles to live like Jews? We ourselves are Jews by birth and not Gentile sinners; yet we know that a person is justified not by the works of the law but through faith in Jesus Christ.[5]

---

4. Galatians 1:6–7.
5. Galatians 14–16.

The Mormon doctrine of apostasy is sometimes criticized because of the difficulty of pointing to a single moment in history when the church apostatized. But that is neither the way history works nor an accurate understanding of Mormon doctrine. The apostasy was not a single event but a long process of change that culminated in a need not only for ecclesiastical *reform* but for an actual *restoration* of the original teachings.

It is easy to imagine the early days of Christianity as a kind of golden age, in which the believers were pious, devout, and humble, devotedly loyal to the common cause, and unified against the persecutions from without. *The Robe*, a classic biblical epic movie, depicts the early Christians as almost angelic in their purity. In fact, however, the picture we get from our historical sources is just the opposite. Consider the following sampling of passages from the New Testament:

> I know that after I have gone, savage wolves will come in among you, not sparing the flock. Some even from your own group will come distorting the truth in order to entice the disciples to follow them.[6]

> "Beware that no one leads you astray. For many will come in my name, saying 'I am the Messiah!' and they will lead many astray . . . Then many will fall away, and they will betray one another and hate one another. And many false prophets will arise and lead many astray."[7]

> Now I appeal to you, brothers and sisters, by the name of our Lord Jesus Christ, that all of you be in agreement and that there be no divisions among you, but that you be united in the same mind and the same purpose. For it has been reported to me that there are quarrels among you, my brothers and sisters. What I mean is that each of you says, "I belong to Paul," or "I belong to Apollos," or "I belong to Cephas," or "I belong to Christ." Was Paul crucified for you? Or were you baptized in the name of Paul?[8]

> Let no one deceive you in any way; for that day [i.e., the day of the Lord] will not come unless the rebellion comes first. ["Rebellion" is a translation of the Greek word *apostasia*, i.e., "apostasy." It could also be translated "revolt" or even "mutiny" and suggests a powerful *internal* contention.][9]

> But false prophets also arose among the people, just as there will be false teachers among you, who will secretly bring in destructive opinions. They will even deny the Master who bought them—bringing swift destruction on themselves. Even so, many will follow their licentious ways, and because of these

---

6. Acts 20:29–30.

7. Matthew 24:4–5, 10–11.

8. 1 Corinthians 1:10–13.

9. 2 Thessalonians 2:3.

teachers the way of truth will be maligned. And in their greed they will exploit you with deceptive words.[10]

I find it necessary to write and appeal to you to contend for the faith that was once for all entrusted to the saints. For certain intruders have stolen in among you, people who long ago were designated for this condemnation as ungodly, who pervert the grace of our God into licentiousness and deny our only Master and Lord, Jesus Christ.[11]

In other words, the earliest records we have for the Christian churches scattered around the Roman Empire show these groups full of disunity and discord. The apostles accused a wide variety of individuals and groups of deliberately perverting the teachings they had given, of teaching corrupt doctrines, even of denying Christ. There seems clearly to have been a steady barrage of attacks on the teachings of the apostles *from inside the church*. One passage even declares that there are many "antichrists"—again, not critics from outside the church, but men who "went out from us." An antichrist is "one who denies the Father and the Son."[12]

Were these assertions just overheated complaints from a few crabby reactionaries who were opposed to change? Were the doctrinal conflicts just the growing pains of the early decades of a new teaching, or was it something more insidious? Later documents show the same pattern continuing well into the second century.

But when good repute and rising numbers were granted to you in full measure, the saying of Scripture came to pass: my beloved did eat and drink, he grew and waxed fat and kicked. Envy and jealousy sprang up, strife and dissension, aggressions and rioting, scuffles and kidnappings. men of the baser sort rose up against their betters; the rabble against the respectable, folly against wisdom, youth against its elders. And now all righteousness and peace among you is at an end.[13]

Your disunity . . . has led many astray; and yet, in spite of the discouragement and doubt it has sown in many minds and the distress it has brought upon us all, you still persist in your disaffection.[14]

And so I entreat you . . . not to nourish yourselves on anything but Christian fare, and have no truck with the alien herbs of heresy. There are men who in the very act of assuring you of their good faith will mingle poison with Jesus Christ; which is like offering a lethal drug in a cup of honeyed wine, so that the unwitting victim blissfully accepts his own destruction with a fatal relish.[15]

10. 2 Peter 2:1–3.

11. Jude 3–4.

12. See 1 John 2:18–26.

13. *1 Clement* 3, in Staniforth, *Early Christian Writings*, 24.

14. *1 Clement* 46, in Staniforth, *Early Christian Writings*, 47–48.

15. Ignatius, *To the Trallians* 6, in Staniforth, *Early Christian Writings*, 96.

To deny that Jesus Christ has come in the flesh is to be Antichrist. To contradict the evidence of the Cross is to be of the devil. And to pervert the Lord's words to suit our own wishes, by asserting that there are no such things as resurrection or judgment, is to be a first-begotten son of Satan.[16]

They were even aware that if the corruption progressed far enough, the entire project could run aground, just as had happened centuries before when the children of Israel rejected the teachings of Moses:

No assumption that we are among the called must ever tempt us to relax our efforts, or fall asleep in our sins; otherwise the Prince of Evil will obtain control over us, and oust us from the kingdom of the Lord. Moreover, there is this to bear in mind, my brothers: when you see that even after such great signs and wonders had been wrought in Israel, they were nonetheless rejected, let us be very careful not to be found among those of whom it is written that *many are called but few are chosen.*[17]

A lesser-known document, The Martyrdom and Ascension of Isaiah, dates from roughly the same era and contains a striking prophecy of total corruption in the church.

And afterwards, at his [Christ's] approach, *his disciples will abandon the teaching of the twelve apostles, and their faith, and their love, and their purity.* And there will be *much contention* at his coming and at his approach. And in those days there will be many who will love office, although lacking wisdom. And there will be *many wicked elders and shepherds* who wrong their sheep. And many will exchange the glory of the robes of the saints for the robes of those who love money; and there will be much respect of person {i.e., favoritism} in those days, and lovers of the glory of this world. And there will be many slanderers and much vainglory at the approach of the Lord, and the Holy Spirit will withdraw from many. And in those days there will not be many prophets, nor those who speak reliable words, except one here and there in different places, because of the spirit of error and of fornication, and of vainglory, and of the love of money, which there will be among those who are said to be servants of that One, and among those who receive that One. And *among the shepherds and the elders there will be great hatred towards one another.* For there will be *great jealousy* in the last days, for *everyone will speak whatever pleases him in his own eyes.*[18]

This prediction was only too accurate, as witness the testimony of Eusebius, the great fourth-century historian of the Christian church, describing the state of leadership in the church in the later third century:

16. *Polycarp* 7, in Staniforth, *Early Christian Writings*, 129–30.
17. *Barnabas* 4, in Staniforth, *Early Christian Writings*, 197–98.
18. *Martyrdom and Ascension of Isaiah* 3.21–31, in OTP 2:161.

But increasing freedom transformed our character to arrogance and sloth; we began envying and abusing each other, cutting our own throats, as occasion offered, with weapons of sharp-edged words; rulers hurled themselves at rulers and laymen waged party fights against laymen, and unspeakable hypocrisy and dissimulation were carried to the limit of wickedness. . . Those of us who were supposed to be pastors cast off the restraining influence of the fear of God and quarreled heatedly with each other, engaged solely in swelling the disputes, threats, envy, and mutual hostility and hate, frantically demanding the despotic power they coveted.[19]

Shockingly, for those of us accustomed to the picture of the pious Christians being unjustly persecuted by the Romans, Eusebius contends that the great persecution under Emperor Diocletian was actually God's retribution against the Christians for their arrogance and wickedness! Nor did such intense competition and jockeying for power and influence diminish after Emperor Constantine legalized Christianity and offered greater prestige, influence, and power to Christian bishops. As one might expect, the intense doctrinal disputes among Christians were driven at least as much by competition in the quest for power as they were by genuine intellectual or spiritual disagreements. Constantine loudly lamented the tendency of Christians to create divisions among themselves, declaring that "it has come about that the very persons who ought to display brotherly unity and concord are estranged from each other in a way that is disgraceful if not positively sickening."[20] The Council of Nicaea itself was called by the emperor in an attempt to reunify the church—and the empire—by resolving some of the most violent doctrinal disputes.

Unfortunately, it is extremely difficult to reconstruct historically the evolving doctrines of the early church. Scholars cannot determine with much precision exactly when any of the writings of the New Testament or the early Christian writings were composed, and without reliable dates for these sources it is impossible to describe very precisely who said what and when, and exactly how doctrine changed.[21] What is quite clear from the historical record is that by the later second century there was a surprising number of strikingly different interpretations of basic Christian doctrine. In fact, the diverse variety of beliefs among the Christians for the first two centuries and more was much greater than anything one finds today, for example, among groups as varied as Catholics, Baptists, Latter-day Saints, and Jehovah's Witnesses. To take a simple example, all Christians in the modern world accept the Bible, comprising the Old and New Testaments, as divinely inspired. By contrast, Marcion, a well-known Christian leader in the mid-second century, rejected the entire Old Testament on the grounds that it was incompatible with the New Testament. He also rejected many

19. Eusebius, *History of the Church* (8.1), 328.

20. Eusebius, *History of the Church* (9.5), 406.

21. Many of the accepted dates assigned to the Christian documents of the second century have been established based on extremely weak grounds.

of the New Testament writings (note that the canon of New Testament books had yet to be formed!), retaining only one of the four Gospels—Luke—and that only in modified form. He also rejected the Pastoral Epistles (1 and 2 Timothy and Titus), Hebrews, and Revelation.[22] Valentinus, another "heretic," had been a candidate for the bishopric in Rome around the same time, before he began his own school of thought, which came to be known as Valentinianism. Yet despite his strong Gnostic leanings, he still considered himself a Christian, though a Christian who preached the "higher," esoteric truths that were ignored by or unknown to most believers.

Throughout this period there flew numerous accusations of apostasy and even alterations of Christian writings to conform to certain viewpoints. Hegesippus, the first known Christian historian, whose writings have been entirely lost except for a handful of fragments, declared that up to the time of the death of the original twelve apostles,

> the church continued . . . as a pure and uncorrupt virgin. If there were any who tried to corrupt the sound doctrine of the preaching of salvation, they still hid in a dark hiding place. But when the sacred chorus of the apostles in various ways departed from life, as well as the generation of those who were deemed worthy to hear their inspired wisdom, then also the faction of godless error arose by the deceit of teachers of another doctrine. These, since none of the apostles survived, henceforth attempted shamelessly to preach their "knowledge [*gnosis*] falsely so-called" against the preaching of the truth.[23]

A bishop in the Greek city of Corinth named Dionysius accused his opponents of modifying his own writings and even sacred writ:

> When my fellow-Christians invited me to write letters to them I did so. These the devil's apostles have filled with tares, taking away some things and adding others. For them the woe is reserved. Small wonder then if some have dared to tamper even with the word of the Lord himself, when they have conspired to mutilate my own humble efforts.[24]

This was not a short-lived problem. Origen, a third-century theologian writing more than fifty years later, complained about the differences among the Greek manuscripts of the Gospels:

> The differences among the manuscripts have become great, *either through the negligence of some copyists or through the perverse audacity of others; they either*

---

22. Many scholars now see Marcion as instrumental, in an ironic kind of way, in the formation of the Christian canon of books. As he was the first to specify exactly which books should be accepted (excluding a large number of books that were generally considered acceptable), he pushed the more orthodox leaders into specifying which books they accepted. See the discussion in Kruger, *Christianity at the Crossroads*, 216–18.

23. Eusebius 3.32.7, as translated in Grant, *Second Century Christianity*, 61.

24. Quoted in Ehrman, *Misquoting Jesus*, 53.

neglect to check over what they have transcribed, or, in the process of checking, they make additions or deletions as they please.[25]

Given the dramatic differences among believers, each of whom claimed that their own doctrines went back to Christ himself, it must have been an irresistible temptation to occasionally alter a manuscript that didn't quite agree with one's views. In any case, the doctrines about which Christians disagreed were not minor. Origen again:

> [M]any . . . of those who profess to believe in Christ differ from each other, not only in small and trifling matters, but also on the subjects of the highest importance, as, e.g., regarding God, or the Lord Jesus Christ, or the Holy Spirit; and not only regarding these, but also regarding others which are created existences, viz., the powers and the holy virtues.[26]

Why were there such widely differing views about some of the most fundamental aspects of Christian theology? How had these discrepancies come about? There are, naturally, differing views. The traditional Christian viewpoint declares that the orthodox teachings of Christ and the early Christians have come down to us in a straight line. This view maintains that while there were many groups, especially prior to Constantine, which broke away from the orthodox church and created their own schismatic groups, the orthodox tradition was there from the first and was never in danger of being lost. In other words, there was always a clear line between orthodoxy and heterodoxy, and any departure from the former was willful heresy. True Christianity was always a powerful lion, while the other groups were merely dogs nipping at its heels.

Another approach, which might be labeled evolutionary, maintains that the issues that were fought over, such as the true position of Christ vis-à-vis God, no matter how seemingly fundamental to the Christian message, had never been made explicit either by Jesus or his disciples. Christian theology in the second and third centuries was still in its infancy and needed time to ripen into maturity. This is why many Christian scholars assert (or at least imply) that the earliest Christian thought was "primitive." Thus, the widespread divergences between early Christian writings and "mature" theology of the fourth century and later simply indicates that many of the kinks had not been worked out.[27] It was the job of later theologians of the second and

---

25. Ehrman, *Misquoting Jesus*, 52.

26. Origen, *De Principiis* pref. 2, in ANF 4:239.

27. Jean Daniélou, a Roman Catholic cardinal and eminent scholar of early Christianity, wrote two volumes outlining the dramatic differences between earliest Christianity, which was primarily Jewish in its ideas and thought patterns, and later Gentile (i.e., Greco-Roman) Christianity, which replaced it. The core of the former was "the affirmation that Christ alone has penetrated beyond the veil, and opened the seals of the heavenly scroll, achieving Paradise for those who bear the Name of the Son of God." However, he adds, "this theology suffered from *serious limitations* in its terminology and in some of its conclusions; and these *defects* exposed it to heresies and misinterpretations which *vitiated its usefulness* as a vehicle of salvation, and led to its supersession by *a more adequate instrument*" (Daniélou, *Theology of Jewish Christianity*, 4). A typical Mormon reaction to such a statement would

third centuries and beyond to illuminate and clarify those doctrines that remained obscure at the end of the New Testament period.

A third view, which has been championed in recent decades by many secular scholars of early Christianity, is that from the very beginning of Christianity there were many different schools of thought, many different approaches to Christ's teachings, each of them equally legitimate. This happy state of diversity was brought to an end by the late second century and beyond, when the church had become solidified into

> an institution headed by a three-rank hierarchy of bishops, priests, and deacons, who understood themselves to be the guardians of the only "true faith." The majority of churches, among which the church of Rome took a leading role, rejected all other viewpoints as heresy. Deploring the diversity of the earlier movement, Bishop Irenaeus and his followers insisted that there could only be one church, and outside of that church, he declared, "there is no salvation."[28]

Church authorities and, ultimately, imperial authority in the form of Constantine declared that there was only one valid interpretation. Through the use of soft and sometimes hard political power, Rome championed the school of thought that eventually came to be regarded as orthodox and suppressed and ultimately destroyed all the others.

The modern Latter-day Saint approach bears a slight resemblance to each of these approaches but is fundamentally different from all of them. In the LDS view, Christ taught his disciples, particularly the twelve apostles, many doctrines apart from those found in the current New Testament writings. The Bible by no means presents the totality of the early Christian message, for much of it was taught orally (the Roman Empire was still very much an oral society compared to the modern world). The impression we have from reading Paul's letters, for example, that he was expounding a formal, fully developed theology is quite misleading. Instead, he was for the most part dashing off messages to groups of Christians whom he and others had already taught previously (orally) at great length. Thus the Epistles do *not* attempt to provide a primer of Christian teachings but rather *assume* a broad common understanding on the part of its readers, an understanding that we have no way to recreate.

Similarly, the four Gospels make no pretense of describing the entire life of Jesus or the entire gamut of his teachings, but merely furnish a brief outline of his ministry during the last three years of his life. In particular, we know nothing of what Christ taught during the forty days he spent with the Twelve between his resurrection and

---

be: The earlier Jewish Christianity was surely closer to the original teachings of Christ and the apostles. Why would it need to be superseded by "more adequate" teachings created by later theologians? Indeed, much of what is today called by scholars "Jewish Christianity" bears a striking resemblance to Mormonism in many particulars. See Bickmore, "Early Jewish Christian Milieu."

28. Pagels, *Gnostic Gospels*, xxiii.

his final ascension, during which we are told merely that he spoke of "the things pertaining to the kingdom of God."[29] Thus, many of the earliest writings, including the New Testament Epistles, drew on or alluded to those additional teachings, but did not lay them out clearly for later readers to understand. An example of this would be the doctrine of deification, which we discussed in a previous chapter. Jesus (i.e., the resurrected Christ) likely taught that principle to his closest followers. They, in their writings, did not explain the doctrine at length but merely alluded to it, for example in 2 Peter 1:5, which reads: "Thus [Jesus Christ] has given us . . . his great precious and very great promises, so that through them you may . . . become participants of the divine nature."

Thus the purest doctrine would have been the earliest, as taught from the mouth of Christ himself and his immediate followers. Whereas certain later adherents began to depart from the original path, either because they did not fully understand the correct teachings (and communications in the ancient world were of course quite limited) or because they found certain teachings displeasing or even offensive, and preferred their own interpretations. They then tried to substitute their modified teachings, claiming that they were privy to the secret teachings of the Lord. The Gnostics are the best example of this, since we have access through the Nag Hammadi discovery to original Gnostic texts. Many of those texts claim, for example, that they were drawing upon the teachings of the forty-day period noted above. As early as the mid-first century, we see Paul racing from one town to another in the Mediterranean, attempting to shore up his original missionary teachings and to correct the errors that had crept into people's understanding.

Over time, matters did not improve but grew worse, ultimately resulting in a smorgasbord of teachings that bore little resemblance to each other. Early Christian writings testify of numerous groups such as Montanists, Marcionites, Elchasaites, Valentinians, and many others. It is important to note, however, that many, if not most, of these alternative doctrines, including many that seem very bizarre to us today, must have drawn in part on genuine, authentic Christian traditions. By this I am suggesting that even the most peculiar teachings most likely had *some* legitimate grounds for claiming that their views went back to actual teachings of Christ and the apostles, however much they had been corrupted in the intervening years.

This is important to keep in mind, because in contrast to the traditional Protestant view of *sola scriptura*—that all the word of God can be found in the Bible—the Mormon view is that the Bible, while inspired, was subject to the vagaries of history, and contains only a part of God's word and must therefore be supplemented with additional prophetic (i.e., inspired) teachings, whether oral or written, in order to receive a more complete understanding.

---

29. Acts 1:3.

DEUS IMPASSIBILIS—GOD WITHOUT FEELING

In an earlier chapter I discussed how the Christian understanding of the nature of God changed. I contrasted the biblical and very early Christian picture of God with the conception of God after the inroads of Greek philosophy, which came to be perceived as the traditional view of deity. I will now return to that subject to provide a little more historical light on how such changes took place. I will then move on to two related topics: Christology, meaning the status of Jesus Christ as both man and God, and the Trinity. Although I am quite aware of how taxing such theological discussions may be on the reader's mental health, I am emphasizing these subjects a) because they are fundamental to understanding how Mormonism differs from traditional Christianity, and b) because LDS doctrines on these subjects are generally at the core of traditionalists' rejection of Mormons as Christians. In particular, the refusal by Latter-day Saints to accept the Nicene Creed with its triune "one in three and three in one" approach to the Trinity is probably the most common reason given by other Christians for excluding the LDS church from the "club" of true Christianity.

Scholars of early Christianity have been aware for decades that Christian thinkers in the first centuries of this era slowly adopted ideas from the world around them—i.e., the Roman Empire—and adapted them to Christian theology. Adolf von Harnack, a prominent historian and theologian in the decades around the turn of the twentieth century, insisted that Christianity from the second century to the fifth century was heavily influenced by Platonism, or better said, Neoplatonism, the teachings of Plato's followers in the later Roman Empire.[30] More modern scholars have provided a more nuanced view of this historical process, but the overall judgment of the Hellenization of Christianity remains a historical certainty. For example Jürgen Moltmann, a major theologian at the world-famous University of Tübingen, has stated:

> Christian theology acquired Greek philosophy's ways of thinking in the Hellenistic world; and since that time most theologians have simultaneously maintained the passion of Christ, God's son, and the deity's essential incapacity for suffering—even though it was at the price of having to talk paradoxically about "the sufferings of God who cannot suffer." But in doing this they have simply added together Greek philosophy's "apathy" axiom and the central statements of the gospel. The contradiction remains—and remains unsatisfactory.[31]

30. "Middle Platonism" is the scholarly term for the followers of Plato during the first two and half centuries of the modern era, while the "Neoplatonists" are those who essentially took Platonic thought in the direction of mysticism in the two centuries thereafter. Harnack declared that "the influx of Hellenism, of the Greek spirit, and the union of the Gospel with it, form the greatest fact in the history of the Church in the second century, and when the fact was once established as a foundation it continued through the following centuries." Harnack, *What Is Christianity?*, 214.

31. Moltmann, *Trinity*, 22. See also the remarks by Pelikan, *Jesus Through the Centuries*, 39–40, 123–24. Even Millard J. Erickson, an eminent conservative evangelical theologian, acknowledges that there is "a considerable substance to the charges" of Hellenistic influence in the traditional Christian understanding of God: "It appears that much of what has been regarded as the classic view derives

The odd self-contradiction that Moltmann describes of a suffering God who is impervious to suffering is typical of many historical Christian dogmas. They are the awkward result of an ongoing attempt to combine incompatible doctrines. Theologians, never satisfied with the doctrines of the Bible (either because they are unclear or because they seem too crude and primitive), have repeatedly attempted to blend the more sophisticated doctrines of philosophy with the simpler biblical statements. The seams still show.[32]

Ancient Greek philosophy, from its very beginnings in the sixth century BC, distanced itself from the mythological conceptions of the Homeric gods, who were all too human in nature, who feuded and thieved, lied and lusted. In their place they developed more abstract forms of deity. Xenophanes of Colophon (c. 570–c. 475), a city in modern-day western Turkey, insisted: "One god is the greatest among gods and men; in neither form nor thought is he like mortals." This supreme god "ever abides in the selfsame place without moving; nor is it fitting for him to move hither and thither, changing his place." Indeed, there is no need for him to move even slightly, because he is able to accomplish all his acts without the tiniest effort: "But effortlessly he sets all things astir by the power of his mind alone."[33]

At first glance, this description may seem highly compatible with the biblical God. Like the philosophical God, the God of the Old and New Testaments is all-powerful, and he effects the creation of the world seemingly without any effort apart from speech alone. But in fact the differences are at least as great as the similarities. After Xenophanes, Plato taught that God amounted to the abstract, disembodied Idea of *the Good*. The Good, for Plato, consisted in absolute perfection, so that God was utterly unlike anything else, independent and alone.

> The good differs in its nature from everything else in that the being who possesses it always and in all respects has the most perfect sufficiency and is never in need of any other thing.[34]

Aristotle later made explicit the following implication:

> One who is self-sufficient can have no need of the service of others, nor of their affection, nor of social life, since he is capable of living alone. This is

---

from Thomas Aquinas's adoption of Aristotle's view of God as the Unmoved Mover" (Erickson, *Christian Theology*, 235).

32. Bruce Metzger, one of the great scholars of textual studies of the Bible, refers to Catholicism as an "amalgam" of "primitive Christianity" with Greek philosophy and Roman methods of government (Metzger, *Canon of the New Testament*, 113). Werner Jaeger, a renowned expert on Greek culture, declared: "Through the door that [the early Christian apologists] opened, Greek culture and tradition streamed into the church and became amalgamated with its life and its doctrine"(Jaeger, *Early Christianity*, 35).

33. See Grant, *Gods and the One God*, 76.

34. Plato, *Philebus* 60c, as quoted in Lovejoy, *Great Chain of Being*, 42.

especially evident in the case of God. Clearly, since he is in need of nothing, God cannot have need of friends, nor will he have any.[35]

On the other hand, the God of the Bible, as we have seen, was conceived of by the Hebrews as possessing a glorious physical body, and he was intimately involved in the all the goings-on on the earth, and especially among his people. The Greek deity, by contrast, was entirely passive—or to use the technical term, "impassible." Impassibility meant that God was entirely self-sufficient, to the degree that nothing outside of him could have any effect on him. The Latin root of the word, *passio*, means not only passion, but suffering. *Passio* in turn is derived from the verb *patior*, which not only means to suffer in the sense of affliction, but also to suffer in the older sense of to bear, allow, permit, and by extension to undergo or experience, or to acquiesce in something. Thus, God was considered impassible because he was entirely self-sustaining, independent of everything and everyone, and could not be *affected* by anything outside of him. Aristotle took this concept to its logical conclusion, in that his god merely existed as the Unmoved Mover: he did not actually *do* anything, but was the impassible, immovable center of existence toward which everything else strove. That is, the lesser beings of the cosmos inevitably moved toward him; he made no motion toward them—or, indeed, any motion whatsoever.

It is difficult, to say the least, to combine this view of deity with one that is as intimately involved with his creation as the Jewish and Christian God. The Bible refers to God not only as actively creating the world, but constantly intervening in the affairs of men, defending the Hebrews against their enemies, punishing them, rewarding them, and responding in countless ways to the acts of men (and occasionally women). These types of activities are the diametric opposite of impassibility. Aristotle's Unmoved Mover did not even have feelings of love toward his creation. Yet feelings of love and anger were quite typical of *Yahweh*. And the supreme act of God sending his Son to die for men, as well as Christ's sacrifice itself, were the result of indescribable *love*. Consider the classic verse from the Gospel of John:

> For God *so loved* the world that *he gave* his only Son, so that everyone who believes in him may not perish but may have everlasting life.[36]

This verse describes a very specific act of God toward his children. Indeed it first states that God *loved* the world, and second that on account of that he *acted* in history to send Jesus Christ to save them. How, then, could the early theologians describe their God as *impassible*? That is one of the great mysteries of the history of Christian thought (though only one of many!).[37]

35. Aristotle, *Eudemian Ethics* vii, 1244b–1245b, as quoted in Lovejoy, *Great Chain of Being*, 44.

36. John 3:16.

37. Stephen T. Davis poses the question: How can a Being that is timeless and immutable do such things as plan, respond, anticipate, remember, punish, warn or forgive? All such activities involve time and changeableness. Such a God could not even *respond* to our prayers, which also requires God to act

The belief in the impassibility of God had already become widely accepted by the early third century, and a young Origen insisted on it. God was unchanging, he declared, and likewise lacked all emotions. He even used this as a basis for arguing against the appropriateness of sexual passion within marriage. Later in life, however, he came to the realization of the incompatibility of the doctrine of impassibility with the Christian God.

> [Jesus] came down to earth in pity for human kind, he endured our passions and sufferings before he suffered the cross, and he deigned to assume our flesh . . . What is that passion which he suffered for us? It is the passion of love. The Father himself and the God of the whole universe is "longsuffering, full of mercy and pity" [Ps. 86:15]. Must he not then, in some sense, be exposed to suffering? . . . the Father himself is not impassible. If he is besought he shows pity and compassion; he feels, in some sort, the passion of love.[38]

This odd conflict was preserved for centuries in Christian thought, occasionally recognized but never adequately resolved. It can be seen in the conflicting depictions of God found in the work of Jonathan Edwards, the best-known theologian of eighteenth-century New England. In one place Edwards describes God as perfectly unchangeable and independent:

> No notion of God's last end in creation of the world is agreeable to reason which would truly imply or infer any indigence, insufficiency and mutability in God; or any dependence of the Creator on the creature, for any part of his perfection or happiness. Because it is evident, by both Scripture and reason, that God is infinitely, eternally, unchangeably and independently glorious and perfect; that he stands in no need of, cannot be profited by, or receive anything from the creature, or be truly hurt, or be the subject of any suffering or impair of his glory and felicity from any other being.[39]

This picture of the utter independence of Deity stands in dramatic contrast to Edwards's most famous piece, *Sinners in the Hands of an Angry God*:

> They [sinners] are now the objects of that very same anger and wrath of God, that is expressed in the torments of hell; and the reason why they do not go down to hell at each moment, is not because God, in whose power they are, is not at present very angry with them; as he is with many miserable creatures now tormented in hell, who there feel and bear the fierceness of his wrath. Yea, God is a great deal more angry with great numbers that are now on earth, yea doubtless with some who may read this book, who, it may be are at ease, than he is with many of those who are now in the flames of hell.[40]

---

in time and react to what humans do. Davis, *Logic and the Nature*, 14.

38. Origen, *Homily on Ezekiel*, quoted in Bettenson, *Early Christian Fathers*, 186–87.

39. Edwards, *Dissertation*, ch. 1.

40. Edwards, *Sinners in the Hand*, 4.

Here God is depicted, much as in the Old Testament, as a being deeply involved with his creatures, not only observing but responding to their every mistake, and preparing to cast them into an eternal hell at his good pleasure. Is it possible for the same being, one the one hand, to be loving and to suffer, and, on the other hand, to be unaffected by anything outside himself? Many Christian theologians are coming to reject the doctrine of impassibility, recognizing that it is a contradiction to speak of God's love for us and still claim that he is impassible. Love involves vulnerability, even for God. The theologian Charles Hartshorne has stated:

> What it comes to is that in retreating from popular anthropomorphism clas-sical theology fell backward into an opposite error. Intent on not exaggerating the likeness of the divine and the human, they did away with it altogether, if one takes their statements literally. Using the word "love," they emptied it of its most essential kernel, the element of sympathy, of the feeling of others' feelings. It became mere beneficence, totally unmoved (to use their own word) by the sufferings or joys of the creatures. Who wants a friend who loves only in that sense?[41]

The gravest difficulty, as already noted, is with the most fundamental doctrine of Christianity, that God's love resulted in the death of Jesus Christ for the sake of sin-ners. Mormonism rejects the notion of an impassible God in a quite stunning passage of the Book of Moses, where it is revealed that God *weeps* over the wickedness he sees in his children and the suffering it causes:

> And it came to pass that the God of heaven looked upon the residue of the people, and he wept; and Enoch bore record of it, saying: How is it that the heavens weep, and shed forth their tears as the rain upon the mountains? And Enoch said unto the Lord: How is it that thou canst weep, seeing thou art holy, and from all eternity to all eternity? And were it possible that man could num-ber the particles of the earth, yea, millions of earths like this, it would not be a beginning to the number of thy creations; and thy curtains are stretched out still; and yet thou art there, and thy bosom is there; and also thou art just; thou art merciful and kind forever; And thou hast taken Zion to thine own bosom, from all thy creations, from all eternity to all eternity; and naught but peace, justice, and truth is the habitation of thy throne; and mercy shall go before thy face and have no end; how is it thou canst weep?
>
> The Lord said unto Enoch: Behold these thy brethren; they are the work-manship of mine own hands, and I gave unto them their knowledge, in the day I created them; and in the Garden of Eden, gave I unto man his agency; and unto thy brethren have I said, and also given commandment, that they should love one another, and that they should choose me, their Father; but behold, they are without affection, and they hate their own blood . . . [A]mong all the workmanship of mine hands there has not been so great wickedness as among

41. Hartshorne, *Omnipotence*, 29.

thy brethren. But behold, their sins shall be upon the heads of their fathers; Satan shall be their father, and misery shall be their doom; and the whole heavens shall weep over them, even all the workmanship of mine hands; wherefore should not the heavens weep, seeing these shall suffer?[42]

I have focused on this rather arcane doctrine of impassibility because it is probably the easiest to demonstrate one of the fundamental difficulties that Mormonism has with traditional Christianity. As Terryl and Fiona Givens have written, "That God has a heart that beats in sympathy with ours is *the* reality that draws us to Him. That He feels real sorrow, rejoices with real gladness, and weeps real tears with us. This, as the prophet Enoch learned, is an awful, terrible, yet infinitely comforting truth."[43]

THE MYSTERY OF THE HOLY TRINITY

Ronald H. Nash, a conservative Protestant theologian and philosopher, holds that "if a particular concept of God is logically contradictory, then it is impossible for such a God to exist."[44] Yet it is widely admitted that the notion of the Trinity is, at heart, a mystery and must be accepted on faith.[45] The historian Robert M. Grant, who has been described as "the most prolific and influential American historian of ancient Christianity of his generation," states that the doctrines of Father, Son, and Trinity were attempts at rational discussion, but ultimately could not "be resolved without recourse to paradox."[46]

To be sure, the doctrine of the Holy Trinity cannot be easily explained. According to the modern *Catechism of the Catholic Church*, "We do not confess three Gods, but one God in three persons, the 'consubstantial Trinity.' The divine persons do not share the one divinity among themselves but each of them is God whole and entire: "The Father is that which the Son is, the Son that which the Father is, the Father and Son that which the Holy Spirit is, i.e., by nature one God." In the words of the Fourth

---

42. See Book of Moses 7:28–44.

43. Givens and Givens, *God Who Weeps*, 6.

44. Nash, *Concept of God*, 13.

45. According to *The Catholic Encyclopedia*'s entry on "The Blessed Trinity," "All theologians admit that the doctrine of the Trinity is [one of the mysteries strictly so-called]. Indeed, of all revealed truths this is the most impenetrable to reason. Hence, to declare this to be no mystery would be a virtual denial of the canon in question. Moreover, our Lord's words, Matthew 11:27, 'No one knoweth the Son, but the Father,' seem to declare expressly that the plurality of Persons in the Godhead is a truth entirely beyond the scope of any created intellect. The Fathers [of the Church] supply many passages in which the incomprehensibility of the Divine Nature is affirmed. St. Jerome says, in a well-known phrase: 'The true profession of the mystery of the Trinity is to own that we do not comprehend it.'" The same article on the Trinity defines a mystery as "a truth which we are not merely incapable of discovering apart from Divine Revelation, but which, even when revealed, remains 'hidden by the veil of faith and enveloped, so to speak, by a kind of darkness.'"

46. Grant, *Early Christian Doctrine*, 1–36.

Lateran Council (1215): "Each of the persons is that supreme reality, viz., the divine substance, essence or nature."[47]

The classic definition of the Trinity in the so-called Athanasian Creed brings out the almost defiantly paradoxical nature of the doctrine:

> And the catholic faith is this: That we worship one God in Trinity, and Trinity in Unity; Neither confounding the persons nor dividing the substance. For there is one person of the Father, another of the Son, and another of the Holy Spirit. But the Godhead of the Father, of the Son, and of the Holy Spirit is all one, the glory equal, the majesty coeternal. Such as the Father is, such is the Son, and such is the Holy Spirit. The Father uncreated, the Son uncreated, and the Holy Spirit uncreated. The Father incomprehensible, the Son incomprehensible, and the Holy Spirit incomprehensible. The Father eternal, the Son eternal, and the Holy Spirit eternal. And yet they are not three eternals but one eternal. As also there are not three uncreated nor three incomprehensible, but one uncreated and one incomprehensible. So likewise the Father is almighty, the Son almighty, and the Holy Spirit almighty. And yet they are not three almighties, but one almighty. So the Father is God, the Son is God, and the Holy Spirit is God; And yet they are not three Gods, but one God. So likewise the Father is Lord, the Son Lord, and the Holy Spirit Lord; And yet they are not three Lords but one Lord. For like as we are compelled by the Christian verity to acknowledge every Person by himself to be God and Lord; So are we forbidden by the catholic religion to say; There are three Gods or three Lords. The Father is made of none, neither created nor begotten. The Son is of the Father alone; not made nor created, but begotten. The Holy Spirit is of the Father and of the Son; neither made, nor created, nor begotten, but proceeding. So there is one Father, not three Fathers; one Son, not three Sons; one Holy Spirit, not three Holy Spirits. And in this Trinity none is afore or after another; none is greater or less than another. But the whole three persons are coeternal, and coequal. So that in all things, as aforesaid, the Unity in Trinity and the Trinity in Unity is to be worshipped. He therefore that will be saved must thus think of the Trinity.

Even the most ardent Trinitarians admit that the doctrine, strictly speaking, cannot be found in the Bible. That is to say, while the New Testament explicitly mentions the three persons of the Trinity and refers several times to their unity, nowhere is the doctrine of three persons in one God expressly described or asserted.[48] Indeed, a clear declaration of the three-in-oneness of God cannot be found anywhere earlier than the third century, and it was not clearly set forth until at least the fourth century. Yet today it is perhaps the most widely accepted doctrine in mainstream Christianity, and the touchstone of orthodoxy, in the Protestant world as well as in Catholicism. How

47. *Catechism of the Catholic Church* §253, p. 75.
48. Erickson, *Christian Theology*, 297–302.

did the teaching of the incomprehensible Trinity become so fundamental to Christian belief?

Although the Trinity naturally consists of three members, the fundamental issue has always been the relationship between the Father and the Son. The third member of the Trinity, the Holy Spirit, though hardly ignored, has been generally given short shrift in the discussions. So the question we will focus on is: if the Father is God, and the Son is also God, how were the Christians able to claim that they believed in *one God*?

The following excerpt from a third-century dialogue between Origen and Bishop Heraclides illuminates the problem:

> [Origen]: "I ask you, Father Heraclides. God is the almighty, the uncreated, the supreme one who made all things. Do you agree?"
>
> Heraclides said: "I agree; for thus I too believe."
>
> Origen said: "Christ Jesus, who exists in the form of God, though he is distinct from God in the form in which he existed, was he God before he entered a body or not?"
>
> Heraclides said: "He was God before."
>
> Origen said: "He was God before he entered a body, or not?
>
> Heraclides said: "Yes."
>
> Origen said: "God distinct from this god in whose form he existed?"
>
> Heraclides said: "Obviously distinct from any other, since he is in the form of that one who created everything."
>
> Origen said: "Was there not a God, Son of God, the only-begotten of God, the first-born of all creation, and do we not devoutly say that in one sense there are two Gods and, in another, one God?"
>
> Heraclides said: "What you say is clear; but we say that there is God, the almighty, without beginning and without end, containing all things but not contained, and there is his Word, Son of the living God, God and man, through whom all things came into existence, God in relation to the Spirit and man in that he was born of Mary."
>
> Origen said: "You do not seem to have answered my question. Make it clear; perhaps I did not follow you. Is the Father God?"
>
> Heraclides said: "Certainly."
>
> Origen said: "Is the Son distinct from the Father?"
>
> Heraclides said: "How can he be Son if he is also Father?"
>
> Origen said: "While distinct from the Father, is the Son also God?"
>
> Heraclides said: "He himself is also God."
>
> Origen said: "And the two Gods become one?"
>
> Heraclides said: "Yes."

Origen said: "Do we acknowledge two Gods?"

Heraclides said: "Yes; the power is one."

Origen said: "But since our brethren are shocked by the affirmation that there are two Gods, the subject must be examined with care in order to show in what respect they are two and in what respect the two are one God."[49]

The debate continues beyond this point, but in all candor it does not become any clearer. At least as early as the mid-second century, the Christians had the burden of trying to explain how they were monotheists, although they seemingly believed in two gods. In essence, they were caught between a rock and a hard place. On the one hand, as the successors to the Jews, they were absolutely committed to the doctrine of monotheism. Yet the Christian tradition, and the early writings, insisted that Jesus Christ was also God in some sense. He was the "Son of God"—what exactly did that mean? He also referred to himself as the "Son of Man." What did that title mean? The opening line of the Gospel of John declared him to be the *Logos* or "Word" from the beginning of the world: "In the beginning was the Logos (or Word) and the Logos was with God and the Logos was God."[50] How could he be "with" God and *be* God at the same time, unless there were in fact two gods? Yet if they were monotheists, there could be only one.

This quandary was the basis of much discussion and argumentation among Christian partisans for several centuries, until the question was officially resolved at the Councils of Nicaea (AD 313) and Chalcedon (451). Yet one of the astonishing aspects of this issue historically is that no one seemed to notice the problem prior to Justin Martyr in the mid-second century. For well over a century Christians were perfectly content to believe in God the Father, Jesus Christ as the Son of God, and the Holy Spirit without worrying about precisely what the nature of their relationship was. By the fourth century it had become a burning question that split Christendom in two for centuries. What brought about the change?

The question is a simple one; the answer, however, would require hundreds of pages to analyze thoroughly, while we have only a few. In the New Testament Gospels, Jesus presents himself as a kind of semi-divine figure, the Son of Man, without in any way equating himself with God. Indeed, he repeatedly stressed the separateness and superiority of the Father:

I have come down from heaven, not to do my own will, but the will of him who sent me.[51]

49. Quoted in Grant, *Early Christian Doctrine*, 69–70.
50. John 1:1 (author's paraphrase)
51. John 6:38.

I have not spoken on my own, but the Father who sent me has himself given me a commandment about what to say and what to speak . . . What I speak, therefore, I speak just as the Father has told me.[52]

The word which ye hear is not mine, but the Father's which sent me. . . I go unto the Father, for my Father is greater than I.[53]

I am the true vine, and my Father is the vinegrower. He removes every branch in me that bears no fruit.[54]

Father, if you are willing, remove this cup from me; yet, not my will but yours be done.[55]

He did claim a deeply close relationship with the Father, a special kind of oneness—but it was not a kind of unity that others could not ultimately come to share:

"I ask not only on behalf of these [his apostles], but also on behalf of those who will believe in me through their word, that they may all be one. As you, Father, are in me and I am in you, may they also be in us . . . The glory that you have given me I have given them, *so that they may be one, as we are one*, I in them and you in me, that *they may become completely one* . . ."[56]

Bible scholars have demonstrated in recent years that many ancient Hebrew texts, both within the Bible and without, contemplate a wide variety of celestial beings who were subordinate to God, but who held divine or near-divine status. Psalm 82, for example, refers to the "council of God," where he judges "in the midst of the gods," suggesting that God took advice from an assembly of (semi-)divine beings. In the famous story of Moses and the burning bush, the being who appears to him is described as "the angel of the Lord," yet he speaks to Moses as though he were God himself.[57] In the extra-biblical book known as the Book of Enoch, the antediluvian patriarch Enoch is raised up to heaven and transformed into a glorified being, whom all the earth will fall down and worship, and who will sit on God's throne and "judge all the works of the holy ones in heaven above."[58] Certain texts even refer to Moses as not only a prophet, but as an angel and even a god.[59]

In the earliest Christian texts, the picture one gets of Christ is of a being that was already deity *in some sense* prior to his incarnation on this earth, but who nevertheless was exalted to an even higher station following his death and resurrection. The Epistle

52. John 12:49–50.
53. John 14:28.
54. John 15:1–2.
55. Luke 22:42.
56. John 17:20–23.
57. Exodus 3:2–6.
58. *1 Enoch* 61:8, in OTP, 42.
59. Ehrman, *How Jesus Became God*, 61.

to the Hebrews refers to him as "the reflection of God's glory," and declares that he was "made perfect" through his sufferings.[60] The writer later adds that "though he was a Son, he learned obedience through what he suffered; and having been made perfect, he became the source of eternal salvation for all who obey him."[61]

Thus, in one sense, it should have been relatively easy for believers with a Jewish background to accommodate the resurrected Christ "next to God without having to depart from their monotheistic tradition."[62] Instead, this question became a Gordian knot whose solution defied resolution for over two centuries. Why?

The simple answer is that Christian apologists (i.e., defenders) became enamored of Greek philosophical method, namely, an approach to knowledge through the use of speculation, definition, and disputation. As we have seen, scholars have long understood that Christianity absorbed Greek philosophical *doctrine*, in particular the teachings of the later Platonists. What is less commonly recognized is that the entire approach to knowledge shifted by the middle of the second century from a Hebrew mode to a Greek mode.

The early Christians were criticized and persecuted in the Roman Empire by many different people and for different reasons. Best known are the official persecutions by the government, under the emperors Nero and Domitian in the first century, and under Marcus Aurelius, Diocletian, and Galerius in later years. Many of these official actions resulted from the refusal by the Christian believers to sacrifice to the gods of the state and thereby demonstrate their loyalty. There was also popular violence against Christians, driven by reports of obscene practices. Christians were widely rumored to be highly antisocial—"haters of the human race"—and to engage in such unspeakable practices as ritual murder of babies, promiscuous sexual intercourse, incest, and even cannibalism.

As Christians became more visible in the Roman Empire, a few pagan intellectuals made an effort to become acquainted with their actual teachings rather than rely on rumors. Celsus, for example, who wrote a long, in-depth anti-Christian work in the later second century, criticized them for teaching the preeminence of faith over knowledge—that one should simply have faith in Christ and not ask questions.

But the strongest criticisms of Christianity had to do with the place of Jesus Christ with respect to God. On the one hand was Christianity's mythological character. The new religion spoke of a god coming to earth, being born of a woman, and living among men with a physical body, eating and drinking. This god was then nailed to a cross like a common criminal, where he suffered an exceedingly painful and ignominious death. All of this was considered too *undignified* for a deity—any deity, let alone the grand Creator of the universe as conceived of by the philosophers. Celsus wrote that this doctrine was "most shameful."

60. Hebrews 1:3, 2:10.
61. Hebrews 5:8–9.
62. Hurtado, *One God*, 84.

God is good and beautiful and happy, and exists in a most beautiful state. If then he comes down to men, he must undergo a change, a change from good to bad, from beautiful to shameful, from happiness to misfortune, and from what is best to what is most wicked. . . It is the nature only of a mortal being to under-go change and remolding, whereas it is the nature of an immortal being to remain the same without alteration. Accordingly, God could not be capable of undergoing this change.[63]

On the flip side of this coin, the story of Christ was of a man, recently executed, whom his followers now worshiped as though he were coequal with God, claiming at the same time that they were worshipping the only true God, and that pagans who worshipped multiple deities were in fact worshipping demons. To quote Celsus again, if the Christians

worshipped no other God but one, perhaps they would have had a valid argument against others. But in fact they worship to an extravagant degree this man who appeared recently, and yet think it does not offend God if they also worship his servant.[64]

To counter these arguments, the early apologists began discussing the nature of God and Christ in terms of Greek philosophical concepts. Justin Martyr, commonly viewed as the first philosophically trained Christian writer, attempted to create a coherent system of thought for Christianity. He told the story of how he spent his younger years exploring various schools of Greek philosophy, but rejected them all on the grounds that they did not give him what he was seeking—greater knowledge of God. Of all the major philosophical schools, he found the Platonists by far the most attractive, but ultimately concluded that they too were unable to give him what he was looking for. Finally he encountered Christianity by way of an old man who explained to him the need for divine revelation, that the human intellect was too darkened to be able to come to an understanding of God on its own. Such knowledge required enlightenment by the Holy Spirit.

Yet, although Justin rejected the principal doctrines of Greek philosophy and acknowledged the need for superhuman revelation, he nonetheless set himself up as a *philosopher*, albeit one who taught the revealed truth of Jesus Christ. As a defense against the intellectuals who mocked Christians for their inability to provide a reasoned defense of their teachings, Justin began to discuss the doctrines of Christianity from a Greek perspective. Naturally he tried to point out similarities between the Christian and pagan philosophical understanding of God, though he did not shy away

---

63. Origen, *Contra Celsum* 4.14, as quoted in Wilken, *Christians as the Romans*, 102. The Roman satirist Lucian referred to the Christians as worshippers of a "crucified sophist." Quoted in Drake, *Constantine and the Bishops*, 133. In other words, he accused Jesus of being both a criminal and a fraud.

64. Wilken, *Christians as the Romans*, 104–5.

from indicating major areas of disagreement. Yet, despite his protestation against the speculative and argumentative methods of philosophy, Justin took a major step towards turning Christianity into a religious philosophy. From this point on, it became implicitly understood that intelligent discussion of the doctrines of Christianity had to at least *sound* and *look* like philosophical arguments.

And the foundation of Greek philosophical method, dating back to Socrates, was to *define* terms and then use the power of human logic to draw inferences—to speculate—based on those definitions. Yet the distinction between such a speculative and dialectical approach to knowledge and that of divine revelation through prophets could not have been greater. Justin tried to paper over this gap by arguing that the Greek philosophers had partial understanding of the truth—i.e., that their perception of divine knowledge was real but limited and imprecise, compared to the full light of understanding provided by Christ.[65] Furthermore, Plato and others had borrowed some of their ideas from Moses, who predated them by many centuries! Philosophy, according to Justin and many of his later followers, could still be of value to the Christian, once his mind had been enlightened by the Holy Spirit.

This turn toward combining philosophy with Christianity did not go unremarked or unopposed. An unknown writer from about the turn of the third century objected to the habits of the philosophical Christian schools:

> They have not hesitated to corrupt the word of God; they have treated the standard of the primitive faith with contempt; they have not known Christ. Instead of asking what Holy Scripture says, they strain every nerve to find a syllogistic figure to bolster up their godlessness. If anyone challenges them with a text from Divine Scripture, they examine it to see whether it can be turned into a conjunctive or disjunctive syllogistic figure . . . so it was that they laid hands unblushingly on the Holy Scriptures, claiming to have corrected them.[66]

Tertullian, a resident of Carthage in North Africa, who may have been a trained lawyer and rhetorician, complained that the mainstream church had lost sight of the need for ongoing revelation from the Holy Spirit. As a result, later in life he joined a group of Christians known as Montanists because of their faith in the teachings of Montanus and his two female companions, who claimed the divine gift of prophecy. Along with such luminaries as Tatian and Hipppolytus, he lamented and even ridiculed the tendency of Christians to embrace pagan philosophy—all the while borrowing philosophy's logic, terminology, and overall mode of argumentation.

With respect to the place of Christ in the divine economy, Justin did not flinch from the declaration that Jesus is a "second god," numerically separate from and fully subordinate to God the Father, since only the latter could be thought of as "ungenerate,"

65. Norris, *God and World*, 39–42.
66. Eusebius, *History of the Church* (5.28), 237.

or without a beginning. Christ, in contrast, was the *Logos*, or Word, of God—divine, yet still derivative from God himself. He was "God generate"—God who had been generated ("born") at a certain point in time.[67]

Tertullian was the first to use the Latin term *trinitas* as well as the formulation, *tres personae, una substantia* (three persons, one substance). Yet he went one step further than Justin in describing the Son as not only *generate* but *created* by the Father, "for the especial reason that we should not suppose that there is any other being than God alone who is ingenerate and uncreated."[68]

Virtually all the writers of the second and third centuries viewed Christ as inherently inferior or subordinate to the Father. Origen stated:

> The God and Father, who holds the universe together, is superior to every being that exists, for he imparts to each one from his own existence that which each one is; the Son, being less than the Father, is superior to rational creatures alone (for he is second to the Father); the Holy Spirit is still less, and dwells within the saints alone. So that in this way the power of the Father is greater than that of the Son and of the Holy Spirit, and that of the Son is more than that of the Holy Spirit.[69]

Even Novatian, who wrote the earliest formal treatise on the Trinity, insisted that the Son, who was "begotten" of the Father, had therefore a "beginning," whereas the Father himself was "unborn"—i.e., without beginning.[70]

Yet in the early fourth century, a priest in Alexandria, Arius, entered into a dispute with his bishop over the very question of whether Christ had ever *not* existed—i.e., whether he had a beginning to his existence or was eternal like the Father. Arius championed the view that had previously been quite common, that if Christ was *begotten* of God, there must have been a time when he did not exist. Bishop Alexander, however, viewed this as a heretical teaching, on the ground that Christ was as divine and as eternal as the Father. (Alexander was not the first to hold this view—I am greatly simplifying the story.) Alexander deposed and excommunicated him, which (through a complex series of events) resulted in a fierce and bitter debate between the two schools of thought. In 325 a council was held in Nicaea, in modern-day Turkey, to consider the issue.

The detailed story of how the Christian bishops there assembled arrived at the definition of the Trinity is far too complicated to relate here. Suffice it to say that although the basic concept of Arianism—the idea of the (slight) inferiority of Christ—had been accepted as orthodox for over two centuries, it was declared to be heretical—*anathema*—in the Nicene Council. What had changed between the time of Novatian

---

67. Norris, *God and World*, 45–56.

68. Norris, *God and World*, 114.

69. Origen, *On First Principles* (1.3.5), 33–34.

70. Ehrman, *How Jesus Became God*, 336–37.

(middle of the third century) and that of Arius, approximately fifty years later? The most notable development, of course, was that in the year 312 Emperor Constantine legalized Christianity. Although Christianity was not made the official religion of the empire until the year 386 under Theodosius the Great, Constantine began to treat it as a favored religion. He allied himself with Christian bishops, bestowing highly desirable privileges on them, such as freedom from the payment of taxes and other civic obligations. It was a pivotal step that accelerated the ongoing process of "the conversion of Christianity to the culture and ideals of the Roman world."[71]

One of Constantine's main goals in taking such a step was to create a new environment that would help unify the empire under one God and one emperor. He soon discovered, much to his exasperation, that the Christians themselves were anything but unified, being instead riven with divisions and controversies of all kinds. The famous Council of Nicaea in 325 was a meeting of bishops ordered by Constantine intended to result in a meeting of minds on such issues as the relationship of the Son to the Father and several other issues that divided Christians. The outcome of the principal issue hung on the use of the word *homoousios*, a philosophical term not found in the Bible, meaning that Christ, the Son, was "of the same being or nature" as the Father. It was determined that the Son was as eternal as the Father.

What is most notable, however, is not the precise definition of God but rather the felt *need to define God in the first place.* Earliest Christianity had been content to posit the reality of an eternal God and his Son, Jesus Christ, and to focus on the *moral implications* of their existence. It has been described as a "philosophy of proverbs," i.e., a philosophy that declared the importance of loving one's neighbor, etc. To the degree that they were interested in the relationship of Christ to his Father, the important thing was that Jesus was strictly obedient to the wishes of the Father—in other words, *qualitative* unity was much more crucial than *quantitative* unity.

Beginning in the later second century, however, and increasingly through the following centuries, Christians became obsessed with defining, in the subtlest terms, the nature of God, the nature of Christ, and so on. (The concern with human questions of how one should live one's life became secondary at best to these philosophical issues.) This approach was purely that of Greek metaphysics. Moreover, these ideas were clearly speculations. They had no precise scriptural authority behind them, nor any claims of direct divine revelation. All they had was the authority of a majority vote of a certain group of bishops, essentially a consensus of opinion.

Finally, these speculations became *dogma.* That is, after Emperor Constantine lent, as it were, his absolute power to the church, it became increasingly the case that the churches enforced doctrinal orthodoxy. As Hatch has described it, the holding of "approved opinions was elevated to a position at first co-ordinate with, and at last superior to, trust in God and the effort to live a holy life."[72]

71. Brown, *World of Late Antiquity*, 82.
72. Hatch, *Influence of Greek Ideas*, 137.

The theologian Millard Erickson acknowledges that "in practice, even orthodox Christians have difficulty clinging simultaneously to the several components" of the doctrine of the Trinity "and tend to alternate between tendencies toward tritheism, a belief in three equal, closely-related Gods, and modalism, a belief in one God who plays three different roles or reveals himself in three different fashions" (both of which views were condemned long ago as heresies).[73] To justify such an "incomprehensible" doctrine at the heart of traditional Christianity, he makes a fascinating analogy with the modern scientific understanding of light, according to quantum mechanics, as both waves and quanta, or particles. Logically, it cannot be both, yet the experimental evidence is incontrovertible. Thus the nature of light remains a scientific mystery, and perhaps the nature of God is equally complex.

Yet of course, as we have seen, it is hardly the only mystery at the heart of normative Christianity. Consider also the following sample of questions, most of which we have already examined: How could Jesus be fully God and fully human at the same time, especially given the fundamental metaphysical gulf between man and God? How could "Being Itself"—an essence that is nonspatial, infinite, omnipotent and omniscient—transform itself into a spatial, finite, weak, and imperfect physical creation?[74] How could an impassible God—one that cannot be affected in any way by anything outside itself—both love and respond to the needs of human beings and suffer through the crucifixion? (Note that it was a heretical doctrine known as Docetism that said that Christ did *not* suffer at all—that his suffering was just apparent, not real.) How and why did a perfect and infinite God create finite and sin-prone creatures in the first place? What is God's purpose in allowing his creatures to suffer so greatly?

Catholics and Protestant theologians have written innumerable treatises in an attempt to explain these mysteries, and of course each interpreter has had his own particular understanding of the nature of God, the purpose of life, and so on. No point of view can be proven to be definitive, yet neither can they all be correct. For me, the greatest mystery of them all is why God would condition our eternal salvation on the willing acceptance of doctrines that are admittedly beyond the capacity of mankind to comprehend.

Latter-day Saints, in turn, proclaim that their system of belief contains sophisticated, coherent answers to all the questions posed in the paragraph above, and many others besides. Mormon doctrines may frequently be labeled "mysterious" by the general public, but that is mostly because they are unfamiliar, not because they are inherently any stranger or harder to comprehend than the more traditional but radically paradoxical interpretations of Christianity just discussed. Indeed, I think it must

73. Erickson, *Christian Theology*, 311.

74. This challenge was posed by the eminent theologian John Hick in *The Myth of God Incarnate*, 178: "[The claim that] the historical Jesus of Nazareth was also God is as devoid of meaning as to say that this circle drawn with a pencil on paper is also a square." The traditionalist response came by way of Morris, *Logic of God*; see esp. 102.

be acknowledged by the objective observer that they are much *more* comprehensible when they are examined seriously and in their totality. They may not have the authority that comes from many centuries of repetition. But Mormonism is, by any fair account, a more complete and coherent account of God's dealing with mankind than anything else known today.

REMONSTRANCE, REFORM, AND RESTORATION

Joseph Smith was scarcely the first person in history to contend that Christendom had fallen away from true Christianity or that the clergy had become corrupt. (Note that the word "corrupt" does not necessarily refer to moral depravity or dishonesty; it can also mean changed, debased, or watered down.) One of the main culprits was money: the church was frequently criticized for its wealth, and calls for reform were pervasive throughout the medieval age. Several waves of monastic reform led to the creation of new orders of monks, such as the Cluniacs in the ninth century, the Cistercians in the twelfth, and the Franciscans in the thirteenth. As one order became too successful and wealthy, another sprang up attempting to return to the principles of poverty and rigor in the lives of the monks, only to eventually suffer the same fate.

Nor were doctrinal disputes uncommon. Heterodox teachings were frequently condemned as heresy. In eighth-century Spain, a bishop was denounced for preaching that Christ was the adopted rather than the natural Son of God.[75] A man known as Henry the Monk in the early twelfth century declared that baptizing infants was wrong, that children who die before reaching the age of understanding would attain salvation without baptism.[76] The Waldensians rejected the authority of the pope, along with the doctrine of purgatory and the seven sacraments. The Cathars, probably the most successful heterodox sect in the medieval period, taught that marriage and marital intercourse were sinful.

Growing antipathy toward the clergy occasionally resulted in violence—vandalizing churches and even murdering priests.[77] With increasing frequency the pope was denounced as a wicked man. Wyclif, who translated the Bible into English to make it accessible to more people, called the pope "Antichrist," the minion of Satan. His ideas were picked up and transmitted by Jan Hus of Bohemia, who was burned for heresy in 1415. A century later, even a man so eminent as the scholar Erasmus, who always recognized the authority of the pope, was nonetheless willing to publish (anonymously!) a satire in which St. Peter confronts Pope Julius II at the gates of heaven and refuses him entrance:

---

75. Peters, *Heresy and Authority*, 52–53.

76. Peters, *Heresy and Authority*, 76

77. Wallace, *Long European Reformation*, 56.

Peter: With your treaties and your protocols, your armies and your victories, you had no time to read the Gospels . . . You pretend to be a Christian, you are no better than a Turk; you think like a Turk, you are as licentious as a Turk. If there is any difference, you are worse . . .

Julius: Then you won't open the gates?

P: Sooner to anyone else than to such as you . . .

J: If you don't give in I will take your place by storm. They are making fine havoc below just now; I shall soon have 60,000 ghosts behind me.

P: O wretched man! O miserable Church! . . . I am not surprised that so few apply here for admission, when the Church has such rulers. Yet there must be good in the world, too, when such a sink of iniquity can be honored merely because he bears the name of pope.[78]

Modern-day historians of the Reformation period stress that the anticlerical sources frequently exaggerated the extent of the corruption in the church, and that the clergy was not as wicked as is commonly conceived. Of course, rhetorical exaggeration and hyperbole were not uncommon. But even Pope Pius II acknowledged the general validity of the criticisms:

People say that we live for pleasure, accumulate wealth, bear ourselves arrogantly, ride on fat mules and handsome palfreys, . . . keep our hounds for the chase, spend much on actors and parasites and nothing in defense of the faith. And there is some truth in their words: many among the cardinals and other officials of our court do lead this kind of life. If the truth be confessed, the luxury and pomp of our court is too great. And this is why we are so detested by the people that they will not listen to us, even when we say what is just and reasonable. What do you think is to be done in such a shameful state of things? . . . We must inquire by what means our predecessors won authority and consideration for the Church. . . We must maintain that authority by the same means. Temperance, chastity, innocence, zeal for the faith . . . contempt of the earth, the desire for martyrdom exalted the Roman Church, and made her the mistress of the world.[79]

There was a growing tendency among reformers to look back to the early Christian church of New Testament times as a pristine ideal which all Christian churches should attempt to emulate. The Waldenses claimed that they were the true apostolic church, while the papacy ruled the church of the wicked.[80] Martin Luther, of course,

78. Durant, *Reformation*, 281.

79. Durant, *Reformation*, 13. Calls for "reform" of the church had been around for centuries, but were now even more common: "The whole world, the clergy, all Christian people, know that a reform of the Church militant is both necessary and expedient. Heaven and the elements demand it. It is called for by the Sacrifice of the Precious Blood mounting up to heaven. The very stones will soon be constrained to join in the cry." Quoted in George, *Theology of the Reformers*, 32.

80. Leff, "Making of the Myth," 13.

had not intended at first to found another church. He, like nearly everyone in Europe for many centuries, did not view the Roman Catholic church as an individual Christian sect, but as *the* church of Christ—the only church. Even if one criticized the clergy or certain of the church's teachings, there was no question of setting up a rival to the church. Luther, like his numerous predecessors, was at first only intent on *reforming* the church. His revolt against the church was on behalf of the "true, ancient church, one body and one communion of saints with the holy, universal, Christian church."[81]

Along with the emphasis on attaining greater purity in the church came a renewed interest in the Bible. Wyclif, as already mentioned, translated the Bible to enable common men to see for themselves what it said rather than rely on the clergy, and although there was much official resistance (especially in England), others followed in his footsteps, such as Luther and Tyndale, defying church and state to take the Scriptures to the people. (Tyndale was executed, by strangulation and burning, in great part because of his illegal translation of the Bible into English.) Focus on the New Testament led to the widespread conviction that the original church of the Lord's apostles was the purest form of the church and their teachings were the purest form of Christianity. For anyone striving to purify the medieval church from all its historical accretions, the New Testament was the model to follow.

This was a general attitude held by many reformers, including the Puritans, but it emerges mostly clearly from the writings of the most radical reformers. Sebastian Franck, a radical German reformer contemporary with Martin Luther, declared:

> I believe that the outward Church of Christ, including all its gifts and sacraments, because of the breaking in and laying waste by Antichrist right after the death of the apostles, went up into heaven, and lies concealed in the Spirit and in truth. I am thus quite certain that for fourteen hundred years now there has existed no gathered Church nor any sacrament.[82]

This movement to recover New Testament Christianity, sometimes referred to as "Christian primitivism," became almost an obsession with certain early American churches. Roger Williams, who is best known for his powerful insistence on the need to separate church and state, was a true religious radical. Much like Franck, he believed devoutly not only that the true Christian church did not exist on the earth, but also that it could not be restored by men—only by God. Williams came to believe that the only true and properly constituted church was one that had been established by *apostolic ministers* commissioned by Christ, who preached the gospel and brought the converted into church fellowship. Since this was how all the churches in New Testament times had come about, it was absolutely necessary for modern churches to fit the same pattern. The massive problem with this approach, of course, was that there had been no apostles of Christ on the earth for over 1,500 years. And since apostles could

---

81. *Luther's Works* 41:119, quoted in George, *Theology of the Reformers*, 87.

82. Quoted in McGrath, *Reformation Thought*, 191.

only be authorized and appointed by Christ himself, there was no way to create any new ones until Christ himself returned to the earth, at his millennial advent. This total rejection of all contemporary churches, including the Puritan Congregationalists that he lived among, led to his banishment first from Boston and then from Plymouth, and then to the foundation of the state of Rhode Island.[83]

The best-known group of American restorationists was the so-called Stone-Campbell Movement, whose watchwords were the "restoration of the ancient gospel" and the "restoration of the ancient order of things." Thomas Campbell, along with his son Alexander, was an ordained Presbyterian minister who in the process of time became disenchanted with that church and began to establish the Restoration Movement in the area of Pennsylvania and West Virginia.

At approximately the same time, Barton W. Stone, also a Presbyterian clergyman, had begun a similar movement in Kentucky, and within a few years had joined together with the Campbells. They were convinced that the only proper church was one based on the rules set forth in the New Testament.

> Thomas Campbell wrote in the *Declaration and Address*, the keystone of the Campbell movement, that "the New Testament is as perfect a constitution for the worship, discipline, and government of the New Testament church, and as perfect a rule for the particular duties of its members, as the Old Testament was for the worship, discipline, and government of the Old Testament Church, and the particular duties of its members."[84]

Of course, there was a fundamental difficulty with attempting to turn the New Testament into an ecclesiastical constitution: it was nowhere near an adequate record of the early Christian church to serve as a complete blueprint for any modern church. It was a well-meaning but quite hopeless task. This was not only because the texts could be interpreted in any number of ways, nor simply because the New Testament texts originated in the radically different cultural and political context of Judea in the Roman Empire. Rather it was because, despite the optimistic statement of Thomas Campbell quoted above, there was nothing in the writings of the New Testament that even vaguely resembled a constitutional or governance document. The Gospels were written to show the deeds of Christ, and the Epistles were written on an *ad hoc* basis to help individual churches with their problems. They contain very little that is openly organizational in nature. So it was necessary for them to parse the verses of the book of Acts and other books very carefully and try to reconstruct the practices of the first church. And notably, the Campbellites chose not to even embrace all the institutions

---

83. Two excellent sources on this aspect of Roger Williams's thought are Gaustad, *Liberty of Conscience*, 90–98; and Gilpin, *Millenarian Piety*, esp. ch. 5.

84. Hughes and Allen, *Illusions of Innocence*, 116–17.

that *are* mentioned in the New Testament—most notably the practice of having all goods in common.[85]

The younger Campbell was a rough contemporary of Joseph Smith, and many of the first converts to Mormonism had spent some time as Campbellites. Parley P. Pratt, one of the great early missionaries and defenders of the Mormon faith, had become a follower of Campbell but defected soon afterwards, after hearing of the Book of Mormon and Joseph Smith. The following passage summarizes Pratt's opinion regarding the shortcomings of his former faith:

> [In Parley Pratt's view,] the central defect of Protestant restorers such as Campbell was a narrow fixation on the Bible. For Pratt and his Mormon colleagues, the Bible was not the ultimate authority in religion, nor was it the final source of power or knowledge. Rather the Bible simply pointed beyond itself to the God who was the final arbiter of ultimate things. While the scriptures are good and true and useful, Pratt argued, "they are not the fountain of knowledge, nor do they contain all knowledge, yet they point to the fountain, and are every way calculated to encourage men to come to the fountain and seek to obtain the knowledge and gifts of God." The chief function of the Bible, Pratt argued, was not to provide guidelines or blueprints for forms, structures, or static institutions, but rather to demonstrate the divine power behind all forms, structures and institutions. By this power, Pratt contended, Enoch was translated, Moses freed a nation, Joshua conquered the Canaanites, David excelled the wisdom of the East, and Jesus Christ himself conquered death and hell. And by this same divine power, "a Joseph in modern times has restored the fullness of the gospel; raised the church out of the wilderness; restored to them the faith once delivered to the saints."[86]

Thus ultimately, despite many parallels between the so-called primitivists and Joseph Smith, the differences are even more striking. Joseph was not trying to *seek after* the primitive church, but simply claimed that the same order and system had been *revealed* to him *by God*. He was not trying to simplify the existing church, but to simply follow the mandates of God. And although Roger Williams had declared that the world would have to await the return of Christ himself for the church to be restored to the earth, Joseph declared that God and Christ and other beings had appeared to him and given him authority to found the church anew and revealed to him additional knowledge about the church and the gospel beyond what could be recovered from the New Testament.[87]

85. For example, while they accepted baptism by immersion as essential, along with weekly Communion, congregational autonomy, and a plurality of elders, they rejected the following New Testament practices as non-essential: deaconesses, the holy kiss, foot-washing, fasting, and communal living. See Foster et al., *Stone-Campbell Movement*, 636.

86. Hughes and Allen, *Illusions of Innocence*, 140.

87. As merely one example, Joseph Smith, unlike Alexander Campbell, did attempt to institute a communal system among a certain portion of the Saints, known as the United Order, which he

9

The Book of Mormon, the Gold Plates, and the Angel

[N]o man could have dictated the writing of the manuscripts unless he was inspired. For when [I was]acting as [Joseph's] scribe, he would dictate to me hour after hour; and when returning after meals, or after interruptions, he would at once begin where he had left off, without either seeing the manuscript or having any portion of it read to him. This was a usual thing for him to do. It would have been improbable that a learned man could do this; and for one so ignorant and unlearned as he was, it was simply impossible.

—Emma Smith[1]

With my point of view on God, I am incapable of accepting the claims of Joseph Smith and the Mormons, be they however so convincing. If God does not exist, how can Joseph Smith's story have any possible validity? I will look everywhere for explanations except in the ONE explanation that is the position of the Church.

—Dale Morgan[2]

I STRONGLY SUSPECT—THOUGH I have no proof—that most skeptics find the story of the gold plates that led to the Book of Mormon one of the hardest aspects of Mormonism to swallow. Even for many people who consider themselves open-minded, the notion that an angel not only appeared to the young man Joseph Smith but told him where to find a set of gold plates buried in the ground, and that Joseph translated the contents of the plates, which were written in "Reformed Egyptian"—well, that's just

---

claimed to have been revealed by God. Although this attempt was ultimately a failure, it was a much more elaborate system than one could find in the brief New Testament statement that "all who believed were together and had all things in common; they would sell their possessions and goods and distribute the proceeds to all, as any had need" (Acts 2:44–45).

1. "Last Testimony of Sister Emma," *Saints Herald* 26, October 1, 1879, quoted in Vogel, *Early Mormon Documents*, 1:542.

2. Saunders, *Dale Morgan*, 26.

going a bit too far. How could an intelligent, self-respecting skeptic ever buy into such a cockamamie story?

The simplest answer to that question is: by *reading* the book itself—and reading it with a genuine desire to know whether there is any validity to it, or whether, as many good skeptics believe, it is either a bunch of bunkum cooked up by Joseph to impress his fellow country farmers or a terribly screwy story he somehow imagined. It is remarkable how many people dismiss the book on the basis of the story of its origins without reading it at all. However, when they do read it—much like those outsiders who personally visited the prophet Joseph—they are often surprised by what they find.

It is an easy book to dismiss in the abstract. It is much harder to write it off after serious examination. As Jan Shipps has said, ". . . the tale of an unsophisticated farm boy who found some engraved metal plates and used 'magic spectacles' to translate therefrom a thousand years of pre-Columbian American history appears so incredible to many non-Mormons that they simply dismiss the prophet's visions as hallucinations, regard his 'golden bible' as a worthless document, and wonder how any intelligent person could ever accept it as true."[3] Yet if one rejects Joseph's own story of how the book came to be, how does one explain it? Critics since 1829 have tried mightily to find an alternative explanation, yet none has succeeded. The notion that a farmer in his early twenties in rural New York could have written a book of over five hundred pages with the complexity and inner consistency of the Book of Mormon is pretty hard to swallow as well. As Terryl Givens has observed:

> The naked implausibility of gold plates, seer stones, and warrior-angels find little by way of scientific corroboration, but attributing to a young farm boy the 90-day dictated and unrevised production of a 500-page narrative that incorporates sophisticated literary structures, remarkable Old World parallels, and some 300 references to chronology and 700 to geography with virtually perfect self-consistency is problematic as well.[4]

Many skeptics, of course, begin from a position of atheism, like Dale Morgan in the quotation at the head of this chapter. If God does not exist, the official story of the book's origin is simply and unequivocally *impossible*. Such a person is then willing to consider virtually *any* scenario, no matter how unlikely, as at least *more* plausible than the tale told by Joseph Smith.[5] For one who is not a convinced atheist, however, who is willing to concede at least the possibility of God and angels, is there any rational justification for remaining open-minded? Any basis for being skeptical about one's own skepticism?

3. Quoted in Givens, *By the Hand of Mormon*, 4.

4. Givens, *By the Hand of Mormon*, 156.

5. As Sherlock Holmes once said, "When you have eliminated the impossible, whatever remains, *however improbable*, must be the truth." Doyle, "Sign of Four," 160, emphasis original.

I have read the Book of Mormon a number of times and studied it in some depth. And I must acknowledge, in all honesty, that I have not always had a full-throated conviction of its historicity. Yet over the years my studies have consistently strengthened rather than weakened my sense of certainty about the truth of the book.[6] In the final chapter I will touch on the *spiritual* basis of my confidence in the book. For now, I will stick to the reason-based elements of my convictions. Indeed, they are far too numerous and complex to discuss in detail here. The interested reader can refer to the more in-depth discussions in the books and articles found in the notes.

I will not pretend to have found compelling answers for all of my questions regarding the Book of Mormon. But after all, it is rare that a lawyer can hope to build an absolutely airtight case. There are almost always unanswered questions—at least a few loose ends. But I do claim that a compelling overall *case* can be made that Joseph Smith's story of the book's origin—no matter how implausible it may seem at first blush—is in fact the *most plausible* account.[7]

Indeed, I view the very concreteness of the Book of Mormon as the most solid piece of physical evidence for the reality of Mormonism. If it were not for the Book of Mormon, it would be easy to conclude that Joseph Smith was merely another religious visionary who experienced some type of mystical encounters with angels, but which have no connection with reality. But the Book of Mormon takes the story out of the realm of the vague and mystical and places it dead square in the real world.

It is a little bit like the situation described in a poem frequently attributed to Coleridge:

> What if you slept, and what if in your sleep you dreamed,
> and what if in your dream you went to heaven
> and there plucked a strange and beautiful flower,
> and what if when you awoke you had the flower in your hand?
> Ah, what then?[8]

6. See the comments in Welch, "Role of Evidence," esp. 269.

7. Former U.S. Senator Bob Bennett wrote a surprisingly good book, *Leap of Faith*, in which he analyzes at length the question whether the Book of Mormon is genuine or a forgery. Bennett was working for the famously reclusive billionaire Howard Hughes when a Hughes biographer attempted (falsely) to present his work as having been authorized by Hughes himself. Later on, following Hughes's death, a fake will was presented as authentic. Bennett was directly involved in exposing both works as frauds. Based on that experience, he outlines the criteria used to detect forgeries and applies those same criteria to the Book of Mormon. Although he never presents his work as bias free (he was a lifelong member of the LDS Church), he does present a fair, even-handed analysis of the evidence on both sides, not shying away from admitting that a few questions require church members to take a "leap of faith." Nonetheless, he concludes that, on balance, the case in favor of the book's genuineness is fairly compelling. One of his main claims echoes my argument that it's hard to understand why any forger would ever produce a work that is so long and so complex and detailed that it would not only require years of effort to produce but would expose him again and again to the risk of having his fraud revealed. Even master forgers (e.g., Mark Hoffmann) generally attempt to avoid detection by keeping their work short and simple. See Bennett, *Leap of Faith*, 31.

8. The poem is widely attributed on the internet to Samuel Taylor Coleridge, but is not included

Without the flower, the dream of heaven is like any other dream—moving, perhaps, even profound, yet ultimately having nothing to do with real life. The flower, however, places it in a wholly other category. The Book of Mormon, in particular the story of the gold plates, is the flower for Joseph Smith's story.

WHERE DID THE BOOK COME FROM?

In considering the fundamental question of where the book came from, there are, at bottom, only three real possibilities. Either Joseph somehow imagined the appearance of the angel, or he made it up as a conscious deception—or his story is for real. There really is no fourth possibility. However, as we shall shortly see, the notion that Joseph Smith was simply a well-meaning visionary is not tenable. So in the end, then, we are faced with the dual possibilities that Joseph was either a conscious fraud or a true prophet.

Let's examine each of those possibilities carefully. We can first consider the possibility that the angel, the plates, and all the supernatural experiences that Joseph reported were merely a psychological creation of his own mind—in essence, a figment of his imagination. This is the easiest explanation to accept for those who are not believers yet try to approach the subject with fairness and objectivity. Of course, they are unwilling even to begin to consider the possibility that the accounts might be genuine, yet they don't want to presume that Joseph was a complete fraud, a con artist, and that the whole story of visions and mysterious plates was a deliberate hoax. This approach is the usual recourse of many religion scholars when dealing with any account of spiritual or mystical experiences. As religious skeptics, they don't believe that the subject experienced an actual communication with deity, but they opine that he or she *sincerely believed* that his experience was real. It is not uncommon for scholars to try to reduce causation of religious experience to psychology and environmental influences. Yet in the case of Joseph Smith, it is the gold plates that make this explanation, for all its fair-mindedness and reasonableness, virtually untenable.

It is quite plausible *a priori* that Joseph, as an impressionable and emotional young man, might have been caught up in the religious fervor of his time and had an intense desire to know if God really existed and which church to join. We know from his own written account that he had a strong conviction of his sinfulness and desired to know that he had received God's forgiveness. It is certainly conceivable that such a young man might have undergone a subjective experience of God or an angel appearing to him and giving him a message. We also know that Joseph was believed by some of his neighbors to have a gift for finding buried treasure and such, and was occasionally hired by men seeking wealth. Given that history, it is scarcely unreasonable

in any collection of his poems that I have seen. Apparently it is a completely garbled (or deliberately rewritten) version of a comment Coleridge made in his notebooks. See "If He Found That Flower."

to suppose that he might have dreamed that an angel told him about anciently buried gold plates and instructed him where he could find them.

But what would happen the next morning when he went to fetch the plates? He could have dug up the entire hill and never would have found anything. At that point he might have had second thoughts about his dream and decided that it was a mere dream after all and dropped the whole matter. Or, if he had a particularly strong conviction that the dream was truly from God, he might have reimagined it in his own mind, concluding that perhaps God would reveal the content of the plates to him if he were able to return to his trance. He might then have been able to draft a few pages of some type of divine message and then present it to others as a divine revelation to the world.[9]

But Joseph Smith did nothing of the kind. Instead, he claimed that he went to the hill and actually *found* the plates, but that the angel forbade him from taking them out for several years. That might sound at first like a clever ploy on Joseph's part to avoid having to produce the goods, yet at the culmination of the four years he went with his wife, Emma, to the hill and retrieved the plates. The translation process initially went very slowly. Joseph spent most of his time in gainful employment and had very little time to devote to the plates, although at the beginning he had to work strenuously to keep thieves from stealing the plates. He and Emma were finally forced to move to Harmony, Pennsylvania to avoid the aggressive treasure seekers. For months he translated only in fits and starts, preoccupied as he was by the need to earn a living. At first he used his wife as a scribe to write out his dictation, and later an associate named Martin Harris. After more than a year of effort with only limited results,

---

9. Examples of writings claimed to be revealed from heaven are numerous. A recent example is Hunter, *Divine Messages*. The work (and other similar books by the same author) purports to come from "God, the Holy Spirit, my spirit team of guides, angels, and sometimes certain Archangels and Saints." The author is merely the "liaison" between these beings and the intended audience, for their "benefit, in order to live a happier, richer life." A glance through the book reveals a basic message of love, tolerance, the importance of taking care of the planet, and so on. *A Course in Miracles* is a well-known religious text which the author claims is mostly a direct transcription of the words given her by an inspired "inner voice," which she identifies as Jesus. So-called "automatic writing" was popular in the Victorian Age, including the text known as *Oahspe: A New Bible*. These texts can all be classed as wisdom texts, simply declaring how a person can be happier, have a better life, be closer to God, etc., and there is absolutely no way to prove their veraciousness; the reader is free to accept such material as a genuine divine message, a patent attempt at making money, or the product of the writer's own "higher consciousness," according to his or her predilections. It is impossible to either prove or disprove the truth of such writings—one either accepts them or not. Joseph's story stands quite apart from all such examples; it is at once more complex and concrete. This is true both of the story of the book's origin and of the content of the book itself. Not only did Joseph give a highly detailed and complex story of how he obtained the plates, but he actually produced a remarkably complex *history* of an actual people living in a specific time and place. This type of writing is infinitely more daring, because easier to disprove—in theory, at least. In practice, as I have stressed, one cannot do more than provide evidence one way or the other. Absolute proof one way or the other is pretty hard to come by. Scott C. Dunn has attempted to view the Book of Mormon through the lens of automatic writing in "Automaticity and the Dictation"; see the discussion by Robert A. Rees countering some of Dunn's conclusions, "Book of Mormon."

a schoolteacher named Oliver Cowdery moved into the area and began working as Joseph's full-time scribe. From that point the process took a huge leap forward, and nearly the entire book was completed in a period of two to three months. Although exactness is impossible to achieve, a reasonable reconstruction of the actual time of translation shows that whole process of translating a book of over 500 pages (the original edition had 590 pages) and over 250,000 words took place during 63 working days. The book was then printed and published, much to the scorn of many of his neighbors.[10]

We will consider shortly the possibility that the gold plates were an actual fraud. But could they have been the result of Joseph's imagination? Could he have *imagined* that he found gold plates in a stone box on a nearby hill? Were they a hallucination? It seems thoroughly implausible. And if we concede that Joseph actually possessed the plates, the theory that his revelations were a matter of traditional mystical insight or self-deception becomes awkward. Where, then, did he get the plates from, if not from an angel? Of course, he might have *pretended* to find plates and *pretended* to translate them, but that takes us into the realm of deliberate deceit, not hallucination. It is hard to imagine how he could have believed that he possessed gold plates that he did not actually possess, unless he was completely psychotic.

DID THE GOLDEN PLATES EXIST?

So the first question of order is, naturally: do we know for certain that Joseph Smith possessed gold plates? Consider the following evidence.

One of the peculiarities of Joseph's telling of his story is the degree of realistic, objective detail with which he describes various aspects of his supernatural experiences. For example, he gave a description of the angel Moroni in almost clinical detail:

> [W]hile I was thus in the act of calling upon God, I discovered a light appearing in my room, which continued to increase until the room was lighter than at noonday, when immediately a personage appeared at my bedside, standing in the air, for his feet did not touch the floor. He had on a loose robe of most exquisite whiteness. It was a whiteness beyond anything earthly I had ever seen; nor do I believe that any earthly thing could be made to appear so exceedingly white and brilliant. His hands were naked, and his arms also, a little above the wrist; so also were his feet naked, as were his legs, a little above the ankles. His head and neck were also bare. I could discover that he had no other clothing on but this robe, as it was open, so that I could see into his bosom.[11]

10. John W. Welch provides a detailed reconstruction of the timing of the translation in "Miraculous Translation." This article also includes a lengthy appendix which includes all the relevant primary source material.

11. *HOTC* 1:11.

After the vision, when he went to the hill to confirm what the angel had told him, he found the spot where the plates were located and recognized it instantly, "owing to the distinctness of the vision which I had had concerning it." He describes the stone under which he found them as "thick and rounding in the middle on the upper side, and thinner toward the edges," and the box in which the plates lay as having been "formed by laying two stones together in some kind of cement. In the bottom of the box were laid two stones crossways of the box, and these stones lay the plates . . ." The plates themselves he later described with a specificity that makes it hard to conclude that he saw them only in vision.

> These records were engraven on plates which had the appearance of gold. Each plate was six inches wide and eight inches long and not quite so thick as common tin. They were filled with engravings in Egyptian characters and bound together in a volume, as the leaves of a book with three rings running through the whole. The volume was something near six inches in thickness, a part of which was sealed. The characters on the unsealed part were small, and beautifully engraved. The whole book exhibited many marks of antiquity in its construction and much skill in the art of engraving.[12]

Another oddity is that Joseph did not shy away from revealing his own divine reprimands. On one occasion, before he actually took possession of the plates, he reported that Moroni told him that he had not been sufficiently engaged in the Lord's work. Afterwards he described this as "the severest chastisement I ever had in my life."[13]

Joseph always exercised great caution in showing the plates to others. The angel Moroni had charged him with a solemn responsibility for them, "that if I should let them go carelessly, or through any neglect of mine, I should be cut off." He states that before long he understood the basis for the solemn charge:

> I soon found out the reason why I had received such strict charges to keep them safe, and why it was that the messenger had said that when I had done what was required at my hand, he would call for them. For no sooner was it known that I had them, than the most strenuous exertions were used to get them from me. Every stratagem that could be invented was resorted to for that purpose.[14]

The primary motive for the sudden interest in the plates was naturally financial rather than spiritual. Even Joseph himself, when he first laid eyes on them at age seventeen, was prevented from picking them up and was told by the angel that he "had

---

12. Quoted in Givens, *By the Hand of Mormon*, 3.

13. Givens, *By the Hand of Mormon*, 21. Several additional divine reprimands of Joseph are memorialized in the Doctrine and Covenants; see esp. D&C 3; also sections 10 and 93:42. The Lord also referred specifically to Joseph having "faults" in 6:19 and "imperfections" in 67:5.

14. *HOTC* 1:18.

yielded to the temptations of Satan to obtain the plates for riches instead of having his eye single to the glory of God."[15]

Joseph did, however, show them to a small group of eight associates, on the understanding that they would serve as public witnesses to the reality of the existence of the plates. Their testimony is regularly printed in the preface to the Book of Mormon:

> Joseph Smith, Jun., the translator of this work, has shown unto us the plates of which hath been spoken, which have the appearance of gold; and as many of the leaves as the said Smith has translated we did handle with our hands; and we also saw the engravings thereon, all of which has the appearance of ancient work, and of curious workmanship. And this we bear record with words of soberness, that the said Smith has shown unto us, for we have seen and hefted, and know of a surety that the said Smith has got the plates of which we have spoken. And we give our names unto the world, to witness unto the world that which we have seen. And we lie not, God bearing witness of it."

Three other individuals also signed a separate testimony that they had not only seen the physical plates but also that the angel Moroni appeared to them and showed them the plates in detail.

> . . . we, through the grace of God the Father, and our Lord Jesus Christ, have seen the plates which contain this record . . . And we also testify that we have seen the engravings which are upon the plates; and they have been shown to us by the power of God, and not of man. And we declare with words of soberness, that an angel of God came down from heaven, and he brought and laid before our eyes, that we beheld and saw the plates, and the engravings thereon.

One of the most surprising things regarding these three witnesses is that each of them at different times became disaffected from the church. Two of them ultimately returned, but one did not. Yet none of them at any time in their life ever denied the truth of their testimony. David Whitmer became highly critical of some of the later teachings of Joseph Smith, and he was excommunicated in 1838. He went on to become city councilman and mayor of Richmond, Missouri. Yet he testified dozens of times over the years whenever he was asked, including on his deathbed, that he had actually seen the angel and the plates, and that his testimony was absolutely true.[16]

15. *Church History in the Fullness of Times*, 40.

16. His deathbed testimony went as follows: "I wish now, standing as it were, in the very sunset of life, and in the fear of God, once for all to make this public statement: 'That I have never at any time denied that testimony or any part thereof, which has so long since been published with that Book, as one of the three witnesses. Those who know me best, will know that I have always adhered to that testimony. And that no man may be misled or doubt my present views in regard to the same, I do again affirm the truth of all of my statements, as then made and published" (Whitmer, *Address to All Believers in Christ*). See further, Anderson, *Book of Mormon Witnesses*. The eight witnesses of the plates also reaffirmed their testimonies throughout their lives. John Whitmer, for example, declared in 1836: "To say that the Book of Mormon is a revelation from God, I have no hesitancy, but with all confidence have signed my name to it as such. . . Therefore, I desire to testify to all that will come to the knowledge

While Joseph was in the process of translating the plates, others of his family and associates reported hefting and feeling the plates, although he kept them wrapped up in a linen frock. He apparently would sometimes leave them lying on the table but wrapped up. Several family members later reported having felt the plates through the cloth and run their fingers along the side of the plates, which felt and which rippled and sounded like thin metal plates.[17]

If we take this historical evidence seriously, we must conclude that Joseph actually possessed metal plates essentially like the ones he described having, complete with rings running through them, and inscribed with peculiar figures. We actually have a transcription of a brief excerpt from the plates (roughly two hundred characters).

WERE THE PLATES A DELIBERATE FRAUD?

I think a strong case can be made, then, that the plates existed, and that if they were not what Joseph purported them to be, they were a deliberate, conscious fraud on his part. So we should now consider the question of whether the evidence points more to fraud or to authenticity.

Could Joseph have made the plates himself and made up the story of the angel out of whole cloth? Of course we can never say never, but it is hard to imagine how he might have done so—or *why*. The Smith family never had much money, and it is inconceivable that Joseph could have made them from gold. Could he have created them out of something else? It would have to be something heavy enough to pass for gold and also golden in color. Lead perhaps? Copper? Tin? It's not at all clear where would he have come by a large amount of any of those metals. None of them would be cheap, and they would somehow have to be treated to give them the appearance of gold. Copper and tin are nowhere near as heavy as gold. Whatever metal he used, he would then have had to hammer it smooth into many fine sheets of uniform size and appearance, punch even holes in one side, and form metal rings to link them together. Then he would have had to create many hundreds of lines of inscribed characters. That would by no means be impossible, but it would require considerable skill and time to make them look even reasonably authentic. Perhaps a highly skilled metal worker might have been able to pull it off, but there is no indication that Joseph had such skills.

Assuming that he somehow managed to do all that, a natural question is: Why? Why go to so much trouble when there were many other options available? He might have presented a document to the world with no plates at all, claiming that the words

---

of this address, that I have most assuredly seen the plates from whence the Book of Mormon is translated and that I have handled these plates, and know of a surety that Joseph Smith, Jr. has translated the book of Mormon [sic] by the gift and power of God." Quoted in Anderson, "Personal Writings," 54.

17. See a full discussion of this evidence in Mackay and Dirkmaat, *From Darkness unto Light*, 13–15.

had been given him by God. If he were determined to allege that he had dug something from the ground, it surely would have been easier to forge an ancient document on something other than metal—parchment, perhaps. And even if he somehow felt predisposed toward metal because of his treasure-seeking experiences, surely he would not have felt any need to create a large set of plates when just a few would have sufficed. If all he wanted to do was to trick some ignorant farmers and make a name for himself in his neighborhood, surely one or two or three plates, if well done, would have made just as much an impact as a whole book full of them. Even more striking is that a majority of the plates (two-thirds) were *sealed* in some way, perhaps with a metal band—i.e., the angel had forbidden him from translating them but said that their contents would come forth in the due time of the Lord. That is, according to Joseph, he was permitted to translate only *one-third* of the total set of plates. In other words, Joseph's story would have forced him to create far more metal plates than otherwise. For a fraudster, he seems to have been far too clever for his own good. Why in the world would he have created such a complex story that would force him into such an elaborate fraud?

If we extend the scope of our consideration to include Joseph's whole life, we might also ask why he spent his entire life from his mid-teens onward in the pursuit of a hoax. If we choose to view his entire life as one elaborate fraud, we have to conclude that he was willing to endure great tribulation, including persecutions and even the loss of his own life at age thirty-eight, for something he knew was just an ego trip.

Most fraudsters tend to be quite lazy people—they don't want to do a lot of work; they are trying essentially to get something for nothing, so they make stuff up. Some of the early detractors of Joseph Smith claimed that he was just that—a lazy young man, idle and shiftless. But Joseph was extremely and profoundly productive in his life, as we have seen. Was he really willing to place at risk his safety, freedom, and even his life, year after year, for a patent fraud? What was his motive for doing all that he did, ultimately going to his death, when all he had to do was to confess that the whole thing had been a joke?

QUESTIONS OF AUTHORSHIP

Let us turn our attention from the plates themselves to the book itself. Joseph did not merely claim to produce a book; he actually produced one—and a very long and elaborate one at that. As previously noted, the Book of Mormon is over 250,000 words. We might again wonder: why write such a long book when a much shorter one would do? Putting that question aside, let us consider the content of the book he in fact wrote. Does it seem likely—or even plausible—that it was a work of fraud?

At the beginning, of course, it was simply assumed by critics that Joseph must have written the book himself, from his own imagination. But the simple truth is that from everything we know about the twenty-four-year-old Joseph, it is extremely hard to believe that he was capable of such a feat. Emma's confidence in his prophethood was in great part based on the fact that the man she married had so little education that he could hardly compose a coherent letter. She had served as his first scribe, and she believed that his ability to dictate for hours and then, after stopping for a meal, "begin at once where he had left off, without either seeing the manuscript or having any portion of it read to him" was clear proof that he must have been inspired. "It would have been improbable that a learned man could do this; and for one so ignorant and unlearned as he was, it was simply impossible."[18]

There is little room for denying that Joseph had neither the knowledge nor the literary skills to produce a work as long and complicated as the Book of Mormon. As a consequence, critics have long sought to provide an alternative explanation of the book's origin. Either he was secretly in league with someone else more learned who wrote it for him, or he plagiarized most of the content of the book from one or more other works. Oliver Cowdery has been suggested as a possible conspirator, but he, though a schoolteacher, had only a rudimentary education himself and makes a poor candidate as a ghostwriter. Besides, his writing style was always very florid, while the Book of Mormon is written in a spare and plain style, much more like Joseph's. The only plausible alternative is Sidney Rigdon, a Campbellite preacher who became an early convert and quickly came to be one of Joseph's closest associates. Rigdon was well educated, knowledgeable about the scriptures, and a confident leader. The main difficulty with the Rigdon theory, however, is that according to all the evidence, he did not encounter the Book of Mormon until several months after its publication, when the earliest LDS missionaries brought it to Kirtland, Ohio. As a result, critics have been reduced to pure speculation to imagine how Joseph and Sidney might have secretly met several years earlier and conspired to produce the book. Apart from the chronological difficulties, it is hard to imagine that Rigdon, who was clearly a very proud man, would have been willing to allow Joseph to take all the credit for the book. He lived for three decades after the death of Joseph, yet adamantly insisted in later years that he had had nothing to do with the production of the Book of Mormon.

As for Joseph having a hidden source of plagiarism, the earliest suggestion was that the Book of Mormon bore a striking resemblance to an unpublished novel written by a certain Solomon Spalding (or Spaulding), a Congregationalist preacher from

---

18. "Last Testimony of Sister Emma," *Saints' Herald* 26, October 1, 1879, quoted in Vogel, *Early Mormon Documents*, 1:542. Emma also assured her son Joseph Smith III, regarding his father, that during the translation process, while "the larger part of this labor was done in her presence, and where she could see and know what was being done. . . during no part of it did Joseph Smith have any mss. or book of any kind from which to read, or dictate, except the metallic plates." See citation in Anderson, *Book of Mormon Witnesses*, 34 n. 25. The supposition that Joseph must have been dictating from a previously prepared manuscript was repeatedly denied by those closest to him. For example, the *Chicago Times* reported on October 17, 1881 that "Mr. [David] Whitmer emphatically asserts as did Harris and Cowdery, that while Smith was dictating the translation he had no manuscript notes or other means of knowledge save the seer stone and the characters as shown on the plates, he being present and cognizant how it was done." See Cook, *David Whitmer Interviews*, 92.

Connecticut. Spalding died in 1816, long before the publication of the Book of Mormon in 1830, but Spalding's brother and others declared years later that the story, called "Manuscript, Found," contained most of the story of the Book of Mormon, minus the "religious parts." The chief problem with this theory is that the manuscript of "Manuscript, Found" has never been found. The only such work by Spalding that is still extant is an unfinished, untitled romance that bears only the vaguest similarity to the Book of Mormon, so a fundamental question is whether Spalding actually wrote a second novel, one which bears much greater resemblance to the Book of Mormon but has never been located. In addition, it is not clear how Spalding's story, never having been published, could have come into the hands of the young Joseph. (Spalding lived in Ohio at the time he wrote it, where he remained until he died. Joseph was never in Ohio until 1831.) Finally, it is hard to believe that the Book of Mormon began as a non-religious historical romance when nearly every verse mentions God, Lord, Christ, faith, or righteousness. The theory has been discarded by most serious critics but continues to resurface—presumably in the hope that the "lost manuscript" will someday be found.[19]

A slightly better candidate for Joseph's supposed literary thievery is a work by a Reverend Ethan Smith (no relation to Joseph), *View of the Hebrews*. Although it was originally published in 1823, there is again no evidence that Joseph was familiar with the book until many years later. Nonetheless, critics over the last century have supposed that because it was published in a neighboring state (Vermont) and was in wide circulation, Joseph might have had access to it.[20]

This theory was popularized by a well-known biography of Joseph Smith by Fawn Brodie, *No Man Knows My History* (1945). Brodie, who was the niece of David O. McKay, the president of the LDS church at the time, presented a picture of Joseph as an idle young man with a tremendous imagination and a gift for storytelling and a remarkable talent for persuading others to believe the most outlandish things. This skill allowed him to persuade some gullible farmers that he could find underground treasures. According to Brodie's speculations,

> Sometime between 1820 and 1827 it occurred to the youth that he might try to write a history of the Moundbuilders [the early Indians who left large mounds of earth all over the eastern United States], a book that would answer the questions of every farmer with a mound in his pasture. He would not be content with the cheap trickery of the conjurer Walters, with his fake record of Indian treasure, although he might perhaps pretend to have found an ancient document or metal engraving in his digging expeditions. Somewhere he had

19. The complete text of the extant manuscript by Spalding has been published by BYU: Spaulding, *Manuscript Found*.

20. BYU has also published Smith, *View of the Hebrews*.

heard that a history of the Indians had been found in Canada at the base of a hollow tree.[21]

She quotes (though she does not exactly endorse) a hostile source who once related that, beginning with an idle remark to his family about possessing a golden bible, Joseph was amazed at their gullibility when they took him seriously, and he subsequently decided to keep up the pretense.

> Perhaps in the beginning Joseph never intended his stories of the golden plates to be taken so seriously, but once the masquerade had begun, there was no point at which he could call a halt. Since his own family believed him . . . why not the world?[22]

Brodie writes with a persuasive style, but it is essential to realize that she puts all sorts of thoughts in Joseph's head without the slightest evidence to support her conjectures. Note the first sentence quoted above: "Some time between 1820 and 1827 it occurred to the youth that . . ." What kind of source provided her with such insight into Joseph's thoughts, yet with such a vague chronological reference? None—it is pure inference. In any case, her Joseph simply stumbled awkwardly into his fraud—not maliciously, but merely because he was too embarrassed to admit to his family that he had told a casual fib. So rather than admit a minor fault, he decided to write a six-hundred-page book and dedicate his life to pretending that he was a prophet of God! Out of such inauspicious origins, she suggests, came not only the Book of Mormon but one of the most successful religious movements of the modern world. Just how plausible is such a theory of causation? Ultimately, she seems to suggest, he grew into his role as prophet, in essence believing his own deceit. This presumably explains why everything he did, and every word he spoke or wrote over the course of his life, seems so genuine and sincere.

It is notable that in contrast to her characterization of Joseph as a natural-born con man, Joseph's family considered him a very serious and truthful young man. According to the later recollections of Joseph's younger brother William, "Joseph Smith, at the age of seventeen years, with the moral training he had received from strictly pious and religious parents, could not have conceived the idea in his mind of palming off a fabulous story, such as seeing angels, etc. . . . There was not a single member of the family of sufficient age to know right from wrong but what had implicit confidence in the statements made by my brother Joseph concerning his vision and the knowledge he thereby obtained concerning the plates. Father and mother believed him; why should not the children? I suppose if he had told crooked stories about other things, we might have doubted his word about the plates, but Joseph was a truthful boy. That

21. Brodie, *No Man Knows*, 35.
22. Brodie, *No Man Knows*, 41.

father and mother believed his report and suffered persecution for that belief shows that he was truthful."[23]

In any case, Brodie rejected the Spalding theory as weak and supported by extremely questionable sources. When Philastus Hurlbut, an excommunicant from the church, searched for and finally discovered Spalding's manuscript, he discovered to his disappointment that the resemblance between the two books was limited to their both dealing with the question of the ancestors of the Native Americans, and that the two writing styles were utterly different.[24]

But *View of the Hebrews* was a somewhat different matter. That work's primary thesis is that the American Indians were of Hebrew origin, and Brodie found it plausible that it could have given Joseph "the idea of writing an Indian history in the first place" (p. 46). It is, of course, undeniable that the two books have that much in common. However, Ethan Smith's work is a semi-scholarly tome with a clear hypothesis and extensive analysis of biblical passages and supposed anthropological facts about Native Americans marshaled to prove his case, while Joseph's work was a purely narrative history of the presumed ancestors of the Indians. So it cannot be argued that Joseph actually plagiarized from *View of the Hebrews*. But assuming that Joseph had read *View of the Hebrews*, could he have been inspired by it to write his history? Could he have borrowed a few ideas from it? Conceivably, yes; but in reality all the ideas shared by the two books could have been obtained by Joseph from any one of a number of sources. The theory that the American aborigines were descended from the lost tribes of Israel was a common speculation of that time. Numerous books had argued the same, and there was doubtless extensive discussion in Joseph's surroundings. It was, so to speak, in the air.

It is quite notable, however, that despite the agreement on the general point of the Hebraic origin of the Indians, the specific approaches to this issue in the two books had almost nothing in common. Unlike *View of the Hebrews*, the Book of Mormon is *not* an attempt to explain the fate of the ten tribes. The question of what happened to the ten tribes after they were carried away captive to the North following their defeat by the Assyrian Empire in 721 BC is one that has intrigued mankind for many centuries. The notion that the native peoples of North America were descendants from those tribes is only one of many possibilities that have been considered, but one that had become quite well known in Joseph Smith's America. The Book of Mormon, however, does not really address the question of what happened to the ten tribes, though it does portray the Indians as having a Hebraic origin.

The Book of Mormon, as already noted, is the story of a small group of men and women who escape from the city of Jerusalem a few years before it was conquered by the Babylonians. This event is accurately dated in the book to the early sixth century (six hundred years before Christ). This group migrated down the coast of the

23. Backman, *Joseph Smith's First Vision*, 149.

24. Brodie, *No Man Knows*, 143–44. See her detailed analysis of the Spalding theory, 419–33.

Arabian Peninsula, and eventually built a ship that brought them to somewhere in the Americas (the exact location has been the subject of extensive debate). Now it just so happens that Lehi, the patriarch of this family, is briefly described in one verse in the middle of the book as a descendent of Manasseh, one of the early patriarchs in the book of Genesis, whose descendants became one of the ten tribes that were "lost." So it is technically correct that in the Book of Mormon the Nephites and Lamanites are the descendants of *one* descendent of *one* of the lost ten tribes. But the story of Lehi and his family has nothing to do with the lost ten tribes *per se*, who had been taken captive by the Assyrian Empire and disappeared from history more than a century earlier. Apart from the single reference to Manasseh, the ten tribes are not even mentioned. In other words, the story of the Book of Mormon presupposes a sophisticated understanding of the situation in Israel during this period. Lehi was a descendent of one of the ten tribes, but lived in Jerusalem over one hundred years after the ten tribes were "lost." Is this a gaffe? Hardly. Instead, it acknowledges the realistic view that while the ten tribes were led *en masse* away from their own native lands (this was a common practice of the Assyrians toward conquered peoples), some members of those tribes would have remained behind, perhaps because they had interbred with members of the southern kingdom of Judah (comprising the remaining two tribes.) What are the chances that Joseph Smith would have invented, out of thin air, a story with such historical sophistication?[25]

Critics have also argued that Joseph, like Ethan Smith, was concerned to bring the Christian gospel to the Indians.[26] Chapter 4 of *View of the Hebrews* argues at length that Isaiah and other Old Testament authors prophesied that nations of the West (i.e., America, or possibly Britain) would one day serve to save the tribes of Israel from the savagery and degradation into which they had fallen. One section of the Book of Mormon likewise suggests that the "gentiles" will one day serve God's purposes in bringing salvation to the "Lamanites." Notably, the Book of Mormon, like *View of the Hebrews*, makes extensive use of Isaiah's writings to show this.

Did Joseph Smith get his ideas from the other Smith? Every reader must decide for him- or herself (after, one would hope, a careful reading of both works!), but I suggest that the theory of plagiarism is implausible when considered in detail. For example, Brodie asserts that "both [books] quoted copiously and almost exclusively from Isaiah." This statement is accurate with respect to the Book of Mormon, but to describe Ethan Smith's use of Isaiah as "exclusive" is simply incorrect. He quotes more or less randomly from eight other Old Testament prophets, most notably Jeremiah, Ezekiel, Amos, and Zechariah. Moreover, if Joseph Smith decided to borrow the idea of quoting from the prophecies of Isaiah from *View of the Hebrews*, he did so in a

---

25. See Gardner, *Book of Mormon as History*, 6–8. Chadwick, "Lehi's House," 85–93, discusses in detail the place of the tribe of Manasseh (and other tribes from the north) in Jerusalem and surrounding areas prior to the fall of the kingdom of Judah.

26. See Persuitte, *Joseph Smith and the Origins*, ch. 9.

surprising way. A close comparison shows that in great part the two books quote different passages! One study has calculated that while the Book of Mormon quotes 407 verses from Isaiah, *View of the Hebrews* uses only 128 verses, but less than half of those 128 verses (56) were also used in the Book of Mormon. It is also worth noting that Ethan Smith places great emphasis on the prophecies of Isaiah 18, which are not mentioned in the Book of Mormon at all.

Most significant of all, I think, is that while each author made a sizeable number of modifications to the language of the King James Version of the Bible, Joseph Smith never made the same changes as Ethan Smith!

The very most one can accurately allege, then, is that Joseph Smith acquired the bare idea of quoting from Isaiah and used some of the same verses. On the other hand, he did not follow Ethan Smith's alternate translations, he used numerous verses that were not in *View of the Hebrews*, he omitted many verses that were used in the other volume, and he never quoted any of the other prophets that Ethan Smith repeatedly cited.

In other words, the conclusion that we would have to draw to make the case for borrowing is that Joseph read *View of the Hebrews*, noticed the connection between Isaiah and the American Indians, and decided to do the same himself. But rather than simply quote the same verses of Scripture, he would have had to study the verses quoted in that book, and then study at great length the rest of the book of Isaiah and find a large number of relevant verses that Ethan Smith happened to miss. Keep in mind that most readers find the book of Isaiah one of the most challenging books in the Hebrew Bible to understand, and Joseph would have had, *at most*, perhaps one biblical commentary and none of the other tools that modern scholars have at their disposal to assist him in sorting through the book and finding passages that would suit his purposes. It seems to me that he would have had to exercise superhuman restraint in *not* using the many verses that the other book does cite.

This would be true also for a large number of other details from *View of the Hebrews*. How many of us, if we were trying to write a long, detailed narrative of Hebrew immigrants to the Americas off the top of our heads, having no background at all in the subject but having one scholarly resource in our possession, would be able to resist using a sizeable number of the examples of evidence cited in the one book on the topic we did have? There are simply hundreds of details that Joseph might have borrowed but did not. If we suppose that Joseph had set himself the task of writing a lengthy history of the ancestors of the American Indians, how could he have resisted the temptation to simply crib dozens of details pointed out by Ethan Smith? Instead, according to Brodie, he preferred to invent nearly everything himself. The typical high school student or college freshman is as likely as not, when writing a research paper on some subject they know nothing about, to find roughly three sources and crib from each of them in rotating order. Serious research into dozens of sources takes a great deal of work! Brodie supposed that Joseph simply produced most of the details of the Nephites and Lamanites from his fertile imagination. But apart from the interesting correlations with legitimate ancient sources, try to imagine having as helpful a resource as *A View of the Hebrews* and then simply ignoring 99 percent of it. Brodie and her followers point out various other details that they suppose he found in Ethan Smith, for example, the presence of iron or steel among the ancient aborigines.

Even if we were to grant that Smith stole a few elements from outside sources, that would still leave, let us say, 98 percent of the content of the book, including the actual words themselves, that Joseph would have had to invent himself. (The actual writing is no small feat, though it is often underappreciated by non-writers, who often suppose that once one has a great idea, the book will practically write itself!) That Joseph, even with a bit of cribbing, could have written such a complex book with perfect consistency is, I still suggest, implausible.

I can't begin to do justice in this brief space to the huge number of critiques of the Book of Mormon and the complex analyses by its defenders. There are many other examples that could be discussed if I were less solicitous of the reader's patience. But they tend to follow a common pattern: the critics make accusations that seem plausible at first, especially to casual readers, but careful reading and detailed analysis tend to show that the accusations are at best highly misleading and often quite erroneous.

THE ARCHAEOLOGICAL STORY

The repeated attempts to dismiss the Book of Mormon by finding an alternative explanation of its origin have been essentially fruitless. Probably the most damning evidence against the historicity of the Book of Mormon is the *absence* of any concrete archaeological evidence demonstrating that the Nephites and Lamanites ever existed. While Joseph Smith and his associates were extremely gratified when they began to read accounts of ancient civilizations found in Mesoamerica just a few years after the publication of the Book of Mormon, modern developments in the field have not quite borne out the early promise of scriptural confirmation. Clearly there were numerous civilizations in the Americas at approximately the same time that the Book of Mormon says there were, and these civilizations had highly developed cultures. And scholars have found intriguing parallels between the ancient inhabitants and the Book of Mormon. But after numerous decades of archaeological searching (mostly by amateurs until recent years) not a single artifact has been uncovered that can be conclusively shown to be from Book of Mormon peoples.

The question is: just how damning is this lack of decisive evidence? In reality, perhaps not all that damning; as the saying goes, absence of proof is not proof of absence. Serious archaeological work is extremely slow, tedious, painstaking labor, not the romantic adventure it is often imagined to be. As a result, there are many thousands of promising archaeological sites that have never been excavated. There may also be many areas that are in fact quite valuable historically but have never been identified by scholars because there are no surface clues to indicate their promise. Many others are known but not excavated because of the limits of time and funding. So it is not at all a stretch to assume that there are still grand discoveries—even unknown civilizations—to be discovered.[27]

The region of the Middle East composed of Palestine, Syria, and Mesopotamia has probably been excavated more thoroughly than any other region of the world. Still there are many missing pieces. For example, Akkad, the capital of the Akkadian Empire (Mesopotamia) in the later third millennium BC, has never been identified; either the site has not been found at all or perhaps it has in fact been excavated but no identifying signs have been found to allow scholars to recognize it.

On the other hand, many stunning discoveries made in the last 150 years have revealed the existence of whole civilizations either completely unknown to researchers or believed to be legendary. The city of Troy, long believed by scholars to be a myth created by the Greek poet Homer, was shown by Heinrich Schliemann in the 1870s to have actually existed, as well as the early Greek Mycenaean civilization. Thirty years later Arthur Evans revealed the existence of the commercially powerful Minoan civilization, centered on the island of Crete.

Prior to their discovery in Turkey in 1908, it was commonly believed by scholars that the Hittites, mentioned briefly in the Old Testament, were a very minor people, if they had existed at all. Instead, to everyone's great surprise, Hittite civilization turned out to be one of the great civilizations of the ancient Near East, on a par with the Egyptians and Babylonians. Among countless other discoveries, innumerable tablets written in the Hittite language were discovered. Since the writing system was a form of cuneiform, the wedge-shaped writing used in Mesopotamia, it was naturally assumed that the Hittite language was a Semitic language akin to those of the Mesopotamian civilizations (e.g., Akkadian). Again to the experts' great surprise, it turned out that the Hittites spoke an Indo-European language related to Greek and Latin rather than Akkadian.

Prior to the 1920s there were few hints of a powerful early civilization in the basin of the Indus River. No one had any idea that a remarkably advanced civilization had existed in India in the third millennium BC. Then when the cities of Mohenjo-Daro and Harappa and thousands of other nearby sites were excavated, scholars realized that the area was host to one of the most remarkable civilizations in the ancient world. Their cities were built according to a strict grid pattern, carried on extensive international trade with Mesopotamia and China, and even had underground drainage and sewer systems that surpassed all others in antiquity. In the Americas, the spectacular Inca settlement of Machu Picchu, though located only fifty miles from the city of Cuzco, Peru, was not discovered until 1911.

Spectacular discoveries of new cities and civilizations have not been limited to the late nineteenth and early twentieth centuries. In the 1960s archaeologists discovered

27. See the discussion in Wenke, *Patterns in Prehistory*, 44–45.

the city of Ebla in Syria, which had previously been known only by a few mentions in inscriptions from Egypt and Mesopotamia. What their excavations revealed was a full-blown civilization in the third millennium BC with its own language. A formal library containing fifteen thousand clay tablets was discovered in 1974, and thousands more were excavated shortly afterwards. Prior to this discovery, the area of Syria in the third millennium was believed to be inhabited purely by nomadic peoples, contrasting with the urban civilization found in the Mesopotamian area to the east. Then, in the words of Giovanni Pettinato, "All of a sudden the area once considered the territory of nomads has changed into a center of advanced civilization, the place where a culturally and socially developed people lived, even a primary hub along with the other two previously known centers, Pharaonic Egypt and Sumerian Mesopotamia."[28]

Sarah Parcak, an expert in satellite archaeology (detecting potential settlement sites from satellite imagery), makes the guesstimates that perhaps 10 percent of the earth's land surface has been explored archaeologically and that there remain more than fifty million *unknown* archaeological sites of all sizes, huge, large, small, and tiny.[29] With respect to Central America alone, she notes that the Maya civilization was located in an area of more than three hundred thousand square kilometers, 43 percent of which is covered in dense vegetation. In 2018 a major discovery was made using lidar laser technology showing that several major Maya cities, including Tikal, were immensely larger than anyone had ever imagined—sixty thousand buildings previously unknown were mapped (identified through technology) which are hidden from view by jungle vegetation.[30]

The point of this brief catalogue is simply to show that by any reasonable estimation there are still untold treasures and surprises to be uncovered by archaeologists around the world. Whether one of these will ever produce a firm tie-in with the account of the Book of Mormon is anybody's guess. But the *absence* (so far) of any firm evidence is hardly conclusive.

ARCHAEOLOGICAL EVIDENCE IN YEMEN?

In fact, it appears that in recent years a discovery has been made that has plausibly been described as constituting "the first actual archaeological evidence for the historicity of the Book of Mormon."[31] The discovery was made not in Mesoamerica or anywhere in the Western Hemisphere, but on the Arabian Peninsula, in present-day Yemen. As already mentioned, the first chapters of the Book of Mormon tell of a family that escaped from Jerusalem around the year 600 BC, just prior to the capture of the city by the Babylonians. They fled southward, down the western coast of Arabia,

28. Pettinato, *Ebla*, 6.
29. Parcak, *Archaeology from Space*, 122.
30. Parcak, *Archaeology from Space*, 108–9.
31. Givens, *By the Hand of Mormon*, 120.

finally turning eastward before they reached the coast. One of their party died and was buried in that location, which they called Nahom. In the 1990s German archaeologists discovered an altar with an inscription referring to the tribe of Nihm. Since Semitic languages such as Hebrew, Aramaic, and Arabic pronounce but do not write out vowels, the emphasis is always on the consonantal patterns, or roots, so that *NHM* might have been pronounced by different peoples as "Nahom," "Nahum," "Naham," "Nihm," "Nehem," or "Nahm." The basic meaning of the root is typically preserved across many different languages, and the Hebrew name *Nahum* means comfort while the Arabic root means to sigh or moan. So when the Book of Mormon tell us that they named the resting place Nahom because "we have wandered much in the wilderness, and we have suffered much affliction, hunger, thirst, and fatigue; and after all these sufferings we must perish in the wilderness with hunger," it provides notable confirmation that the author of the book knew Hebrew.[32]

In addition to the absence of clear confirmation of the reality of Book of Mormon peoples, critics over the years have identified many apparent gaffes in the Book of Mormon, which seemingly proved that the book was written not in the ancient world but in nineteenth-century America. These are too numerous to discuss at any length, but it is notable that in many such cases scholars have uncovered evidence showing the polar opposite—that in fact those elements provide confirmatory evidence of the antiquity of the text.

For example, when Lehi, the patriarch of the family that left Jerusalem, was near his death, he declared that his body was about to be laid down "in the cold and silent grave, from whence no traveler can return." This phrase, critics claimed, was an obvious anachronism—a quotation from Shakespeare's *Hamlet*! In the famous soliloquy in that play, when Hamlet is contemplating suicide, he refers to death as "the undiscovered country from whose bourn no traveler returns." At first blush, this parallel seems like damning evidence indeed—how could an ancient document be quoting Shakespeare? Yet a broader knowledge of literature shows that similar phrases are found throughout history, particularly in the ancient world. In a Sumerian text dating to many centuries before the purported date of the Book of Mormon, the gatekeeper to the netherworld asks, "Why have you traveled to the land of no return? How did you set your heart on the road whose traveler never returns?"[33] Indeed, the phrase "land of no return" was a standard name for the underworld in ancient Mesopotamia. It can also be found in the Roman poet Catullus, dating to the time of Julius Caesar.[34]

---

32. Joseph Smith did learn some Hebrew later in life, but was completely ignorant of it when he dictated the Book of Mormon in 1829. Givens, *By the Hand of Mormon*, provides a nice overview of some of these matters.

33. Inanna's Descent to the Netherworld, ll. 82–84, in Black, et al., *Literature of Ancient Sumer*, 68.

34. Catullus, Poems 3.

One of the most famous witticisms about the Book of Mormon comes, appropriately enough, from the great humorist Mark Twain, who described the book as "chloroform in print."

> All men have heard of the Mormon Bible, but few except the "elect" have seen it, or, at least, taken the trouble to read it. I brought away a copy from Salt Lake. The book is a curiosity to me, it is such a pretentious affair, and yet so "slow," so sleepy; such an insipid mess of inspiration. It is chloroform in print. If Joseph Smith composed this book, the act was a miracle—keeping awake while he did it was, at any rate . . . Whenever he found his speech growing too modern—which was about every sentence or two—he ladled in a few such Scriptural phrases as "exceeding sore," "and it came to pass," etc., and made things satisfactory again. "And it came to pass" was his pet. If he had left that out, his Bible would have been only a pamphlet.[35]

To be sure, the Book of Mormon does not have the literary wit, charm, and polish of *Huckleberry Finn*. But then neither do many of the great historical works such as the *Epic of Gilgamesh*, *Beowulf*, or the Mesopotamian creation account known as the *Enuma Elish*. Even the Bible, stylistically speaking, was an object of shame to many of the great churchmen from late antiquity who had been steeped in classical rhetorical theory. St. Jerome, who lived in the late fourth and early fifth century and was one of the greatest biblical scholars of all times, insisted that educated readers should not be put off by the "soiled gown" of the Scriptures (i.e., their mundane style) and should instead focus on the beautiful body inside (i.e., their spiritual content). One has the impression that he was never really able to accept the Scriptures as they were. One day, he tells us, when he was on his way to Jerusalem, he felt impelled to go to the library at Rome, where he stayed up nights reading classical literature, his true passion. When he finally "came to his senses," he says, he forced himself to turn to the Scriptures, but "their uncouth style was dreadful." It was then that he had the famous dream in which Jesus appeared to him and made the pointed accusation: *Ciceronianus es, non Christianus*—"You are a Ciceronian, not a Christian!"[36]

As for the phrase "it came to pass that . . . ," its frequent use in the Book of Mormon is a bit difficult for even the book's most ardent admirers to endure. It occurs eight times in the first chapter alone, out of a total of twenty verses. Yet Mark Twain's conclusion that it was Joseph Smith's own lack of literary skill that was the basis for this repetition was premature. If he had been familiar with the original Hebrew of the Old Testament, he would surely have noticed how often the phrase *wayehi* occurs—which means "and it came to pass." It occurs about 1,200 times in the Hebrew text, although in the classic King James Version it is translated as "it came to pass"

---

35. Twain, *Roughing It*, 133. Apparently Twain, unlike Fawn Brodie, did not perceive Joseph's talent as a budding novelist.

36. Jerome, *Letters* 22.29–30, in NPNF 6:35.

only about 60 percent of the time.[37] The rest of the time it is translated in some other way ("it happened that") or is omitted entirely because it is so unnecessary in English prose.[38]

Book of Mormon names have proved to be a fruitful field for scholarly defenders of the faith.[39] The narrative is full of personal names of the characters and places. If Joseph Smith had written the book simply from his "fertile imagination" (Brodie), one would expect it to be full of very common modern names, biblical names, and perhaps a few ridiculous made-up names. Some of the names, to be sure, are from the Bible—such as Noah, Jacob, Sarah, and Laban—which is not surprising, since Lehi and his family lived in Jerusalem before migrating to the New World. But there are also many names that might seem absurd at first sight, such as Gidgidonnah, Coriantumr, and Jacobugath. Not all such names have been discovered to have credible derivations. But some have. Two very odd names, Paanchi and Pahoran, were confirmed by William F. Albright, dean of ancient Near Eastern studies in the twentieth century, as good Egyptian names (Egypt, of course, borders on Israel and the two lands have had constant intercourse for thousands of years). Korihor, a personification of the "Antichrist," is a direct equivalent of the good Egyptian name *Herihor*. Hermounts, the name given "that part of the wilderness which was infested by wild and ravenous beasts," bears a startling resemblance to Hermonthis, a town in Egypt named after the god Montu, whose name meant "nomad." Perhaps the most striking discovery in the area of names concerns the name Alma. To any Westerner, the name is obviously feminine. Alma means "soul" in Latin and Latin-based languages and is a common name in various languages. Yet in the Book of Mormon it is the name of two very prominent *men* in the narrative. Obviously Joseph made a peculiar blunder, no? Or so it seemed, until Yigael Yadin, an eminent Israeli scholar, found a document in 1961 on the shore of the Dead Sea which included the name "Alma, *son* of Yehudah."[40]

There are many other seeming anachronisms in the book that have been addressed intelligently, if not always conclusively, by Mormon scholars. Brief discussions of some of these can be found in chapters 4 and 5 of Terryl Givens's *By the Hand of Mormon*. Apart from such external evidence, Latter-day Saints often point to the

37. By comparison, it occurs some 1,400 times in the Book of Mormon, which is about 45 percent as long. But one should note that in both texts it occurs only in narrative prose, never in poetical passages. If one were to count only the pages of the Old Testament that were narrative, the phrase might well turn out to be *more* frequent in the Bible than in the Book of Mormon.

38. A very similar device is frequently used in Egyptian narratives as well. The phrase *khpr-n* also means "it happened that" or "it came to pass that." Hugh Nibley points out in *Since Cumorah*, 150, that in similar manner, speeches typically begin with "I opened my mouth." Nibley says they are grammatical necessities. Also note the argument that they acted as punctuation in ancient texts, where there was none. For a counterargument, see Finley, "Does the Book of Mormon Reflect," 350–51.

39. For an extensive collection of discussions of Book of Mormon names, see the "Book of Mormon Onomasticon" at https://onoma.lib.byu.edu/onoma/index.php/Main_Page.

40. Yadin, *Bar Kochba*, 176. The same name has also been identified in the texts from the ancient city of Ebla. See Szink, "Personal Name 'Alma.'"

fact that the Book of Mormon is not only a long text; it is also an extremely complex text with numerous narrative digressions and long quotations from other documents, including the Bible. And yet despite all these immense complexities, it is also remarkably self-consistent. Anyone who has ever written a long work of fiction knows how difficult it is to achieve perfect consistency. A character named John may be described as blond in one chapter and brunette in another, while Kate may be from California on page 10 and Oregon on page 73. Such authorial blunders can only be eliminated through extremely careful editing after the fact, preferably by another set of eyes. However, Joseph Smith, as we have seen, dictated the Book of Mormon roughly cover to cover in less than three months without any use of notes or any major editing of the manuscript before publication.[41] Yet all the dates and chronological references, all the names and identities, and all the narrative details coincide exactly. Even the narrative digressions always circle back exactly as they should.

Of course, none of these examples of confirmatory *evidence*, considered individually, can remotely be taken as firm *proof* that the book did not originate in the imagination of Joseph Smith. But their cumulative effect is significant. What are the chances that a young farmer with scarcely even an elementary school education, no matter how imaginative he may have been, could have written such a text and made virtually no blunders? Or made so many accurate guesses about the ancient world? Even the practice of writing on metal plates and hiding them away and burying them in stone boxes—a surprising oddity in 1830—turns out to have been an almost common practice in antiquity.[42]

THE TEACHINGS OF THE BOOK OF MORMON

Most Latter-day Saints probably have at most only a vague knowledge of the scholarly arguments, pro and con, we have been discussing. For them, the truth of the Book of Mormon is simply a matter of faith. More importantly, many of its stories are beloved examples of powerful religious faith in action. It also has many overt passages of preaching and theologizing. It stresses above all the importance of having a firm belief in Christ and of following the commandments of God. In fact, the book refers so frequently to Christ that Mormons can only scratch their heads in perplexity when they are accused of being non-Christian. The book concludes with the following exhortation:

> Yea, come unto Christ, and be perfected in him, and deny yourselves of all
> ungodliness; and if ye shall deny yourselves of all ungodliness, and love God

41. By "major editing" I refer to substantive changes, not changes in spelling, grammar, and punctuation, of which there were many hundreds. See Skousen, *Earliest Text*.

42. See Tvedtnes, *Other Hidden Books*.

with all your might, mind, and strength, then is his grace sufficient for you, that by his grace ye may be perfect in Christ.[43]

No brief synopsis can do justice to all the teachings it contains, so I will only attempt to summarize three of its most striking doctrinal passages. Probably the most notable one takes place shortly before the death of Lehi, the patriarch of the family. It essentially consists of a lecture by Lehi to one of his sons, and concerns the atonement of God's messiah and the forgiveness of sins. He emphasizes the essential importance of every person's freedom to choose between good and evil. For this choice to be meaningful, he says, there must be a clear opposition between good and evil in the world.

> It must needs be that there is an opposition in all things . . . [including] the forbidden fruit in opposition to the tree of life; the one being sweet and the other bitter. Wherefore, the Lord God gave unto man that he should act for himself. Wherefore, man could not act for himself save it should be that he was enticed by the one or the other.

Lehi also teaches what is sometimes called the doctrine of the "fortunate," or "happy," "fall of Adam."[44] Contrary to the traditional Christian doctrine of the fall of Adam as a disaster for the human race, by which paradise was lost, the Book of Mormon emphasizes the crucial importance of Adam's transgression for the *benefit* of humankind:

> And now, behold, if Adam had not transgressed he would not have fallen, but he would have remained in the garden of Eden. And all things which were created must have remained in the same state in which they were after they were created; and they must have remained forever, and had no end. And they would have had no children; wherefore they would have remained in a state of innocence, having no joy, for they knew no misery; doing no good, for they knew no sin. But behold, all things have been done in the wisdom of him who knoweth all things. Adam fell that men might be; and men are, that they might have joy.[45]

Certainly one of the most beloved passages in the book is that of the appearance of Jesus Christ to Book of Mormon peoples. This narrative takes place following Christ's resurrection in the Holy Land, and Christ shows the nail prints in his hands to the people and blesses their children. He repeats the Sermon on the Mount and other teachings made to the Jews, but he adds many additional instructions. One of the most notable of these is the injunction to have no contention or disputations among

43. Moroni 10:32.

44. This phrase has been used in Christian theology to describe teachings similar to the LDS position. The similarities and differences are discussed in Judd, "Fortunate Fall."

45. 2 Nephi 2:22–25.

the people: "For . . . he that hath the spirit of contention is not of me, but is of the devil, who is the father of contention, and he stirreth up the hearts of men to contend with anger, one with another."[46]

All three of these passages are in fact related to one of the underlying themes of the entire narrative—namely, mankind's divinely bestowed gift of moral agency and the fundamental importance of *learning to choose* what is good and right. There are countless examples of such choices—both good and bad—in the book. A superficial reading often concludes that the Book of Mormon is a simplistic morality play, a black-and-white struggle between the "good Nephites" and the "evil Lamanites." But a deeper exploration reveals a much subtler message. In numerous instances throughout the narrative, the "good Nephites" are depicted using their free will for ill—they turn evil, through pride or greed.

While there existed constant enmity between Nephites and Lamanites, most of the truly wicked people in the book are apostate Nephites, dissenters who have rejected the religious and moral teachings of their fathers, and are trying to undermine the religious and political institutions of their own people. Often they manipulate the traditional hatred of the Lamanites against the Nephites in order to attack and destroy the Nephites. On numerous occasions the contention among the Nephites themselves becomes so great that political rebellion and social chaos result. In the last segment of the book, the first two centuries following the visit of Jesus Christ are a near-utopian period in which all distinction between Nephite and Lamanite has disappeared. But things quickly turn dark as this political, social, and religious unity deteriorates into a conflict-ridden, polarized society, ultimately resulting in a vicious struggle that culminates in a massive war, once again between Nephites and Lamanites, and finally in the utter destruction of the Nephite people.

The curious thing, however, is that this division between Nephites and Lamanites had nothing to do with the old tribal divisions but was an entirely new social grouping. As class distinctions and political divisions sprang up and became hardened, one group began to call itself Lamanites, and the opposing group became known as Nephites, the two groups merely adopting the traditional names.[47] Mormon, the book's narrator, observes that in the space of a century "both the people of Nephi and the Lamanites had become exceedingly wicked one like unto another."[48] Ultimately, the Nephites become even more wicked and bloodthirsty than their foes, "seeking for blood and revenge" because of "the willfulness of their hearts."[49] To drive the point home, an abbreviated account of an earlier people is inserted towards the end of the story of the Nephites. This people, known as Jaredites, lived in exactly the same land,

46. 3 Nephi 11:28–29.
47. See, for example, 4 Nephi 1:20, 36; see also Helaman 4:22, Moroni 9.
48. 4 Nephi 1:45.
49. Moroni 9:23.

and were eventually wiped out to a man, for exactly the same reasons—contentions and wars brought about as the result of pride, greed, and the desire for power.

The inescapable conclusion is that contention, enmity, and hatred are diametrically opposed to the ways of God and must be avoided at all costs. Nonetheless, God allows his children to make their own decisions and to be accountable for the outcomes. Indeed, he prefers that mankind live in a free society—not to permit the pursuit of happiness, but to allow people to make their own choices, even if those choices prove to be evil ones. In a dramatic passage where the king has decided to abolish the kingship and institute a freer system in which the voice of the people is taken into account, King Benjamin declares:

> And if the time comes that the voice of the people doth choose iniquity, then is the time that the judgments of God will come upon you; yea, then is the time he will visit you with great destruction.[50]

This declaration turns out to be a kind of prophecy, for that is exactly what happens by the end of the book. The Nephites have made so many wicked choices that they are completely destroyed.

No one can prove the Book the Mormon either true or false. For some people, the bits of evidence discussed here, along with many others, which we do not have room to discuss, add up to an overwhelming case in favor of its historicity. For others, they are mere coincidences. It is a matter of personal impression. To me, the question boils down to whether the story of the angel and the plates seems so bizarre and off-putting that one is unwilling to pursue the investigation any further. If one does pursue it, however, some remarkable gems can be found—gems that would be so unlikely to be found in the work of a young farmer in 1830.

And when one examines the biography of Joseph Smith and reads his own words, it is much harder to conclude that his whole life from age fourteen on was one big pretense. To me, the following quotation from Joseph Smith (relating to his very first vision in 1820), in the simplicity and directness of his appeal, carries the ring of absolute sincerity.

> So it was with me. I had actually seen a light, and in the midst of that light I saw two Personages, and they did in reality speak to me; and though I was hated and persecuted for saying that I had seen a vision, yet it was true; and while they were persecuting me, reviling me, and speaking all manner of evil against me falsely for so saying, I was led to say in my heart: Why persecute me for telling the truth? I have actually seen a vision; and who am I that I can withstand God, or why does the world think to make me deny what I have actually seen? For I had seen a vision; I knew it, and I knew that God knew it,

50. Mosiah 29:27.

and I could not deny it, neither dared I do it; at least I knew that by so doing I would offend God, and come under condemnation.[51]

No one can truly know what is in the mind of another person. But private diaries and personal correspondence often provide us with the most revealing look into a person's true self.

Joseph Smith produced a great deal of written work, though he often used scribes to write for him, as he lacked confidence in his own abilities as a writer. However, we do have a number of documents in his own handwriting. He kept a journal intermittently during his life, though a relatively small percentage of the entries are in his own handwriting,[52] among which are the two following excerpts:[53]

> 4 December 1832
>
> this day I been unwell done but little been at home all day regulated some things this Evening feel better in my mind than I have for a few days back Oh Lord deliver thy servant out of temtations and fill his heart with wisdom and understanding.

> 19 November 1833
>
> from the 13th u[n]till this date nothing of note has transpired since the great sign in the heavins this day before my {h[ea]rt}is somewhat sorrowful but feel to trust in the Lord the god of Jacob I have learned in my travels that man is trecherous and selfish but few excepted Brother {Sidney} is a man whom I love but is not capable of that pure and stedfast love for those who are his benefactors as should possess the breast of a President of the Church of Christ this with some other little things such as a selfish and indipendence of mind which to often manifest distroys the confidence of those who would lay down their lives for him but notwithstanding these things he is {a} very great and good man a man of great power of words and can {gain} the friendship of his hearrers very quick he is a man whom god will uphold if he will continue faithful to his calling O God grant that he may for the Lords sake Amen the man who willeth to do well we should extoll his virtues and speak not of his faults behind his back a man who willfully turneth away from his friend without a

51. *HOTC* 8. Arthur Henry King was an internationally known poet and professor of literature who joined the LDS Church later in life. He served for twenty-eight years on the British Council, which oversees international educational and cultural affairs for Britain, and was twice decorated by Queen Elizabeth II for this service. He describes his initial reaction to Joseph's own account as follows: "When I was first brought to read Joseph Smith's story, I was deeply impressed. I wasn't inclined to be impressed. As a stylistician, I have spent my life being disinclined to be impressed. So when I read his story, I thought to myself, this is an extraordinary thing. This is an astonishingly matter-of-fact and cool account. This man is not trying to persuade me of anything. He doesn't feel the need to. He is stating what happened to him, and he is stating it, not enthusiastically, but in quite a matter-of-fact way. He is not trying to make me cry or feel ecstatic. That struck me, and that began to build my testimony, for I could see that this man was telling the truth." King, *Arm the Children*, 288.

52. I have kept most of the original spelling and (lack of) punctuation.

53. Jesse, *Papers of Joseph Smith*, 5, 11–12.

cause is not {easily forgiven} the kindness of a man {should} never be forgotten that person who never forsaketh his trust should ever have the highest place for regard in our hearts and our love should never fail but increase more and more and this [is] my disposition and sentiment &c Amen

We also have a wide variety of his correspondence. In a letter to his wife Emma, dated June 6, 1832, he wrote:

> my Situation is a very unpleasent one although I will be endeavor to be Contented the Lord asisting me I have visited a grove which is Just back of the town almost every day where I can be Secluded from the eyes of any mortal and there give vent to all the feelings of my heart in meaditation and prayr I have Called to mind all the past moments of my life and am left to morn [and] Shed tears of sorrow for my folly in Sufering the adversary of my Soul to have so much power over me and he has [had in times past] but God is merciful and has forgiven my Sins and I rejoice that he Sendeth forth the Comferter unto as many as believe and humbleeth themselves before him . . . it would have been very Consoling to me to have received a few lines from you but as you did not take the trouble I will try to be contented with my lot knowing that God is my friend in him I shall find comfort I have given my life into his hands I am prepared to go at his Call I desire to be with Christ I count not my life dear to me only to do his will[54]

Do these sound like the words of a fraud and cynic, someone who tangled himself up in a web of lies and deceptions, and kept going, ultimately to his death, because he enjoyed the exercise of power over his followers? Or are they more like the words of a man who was totally sincere in his beliefs, who had a deep faith in God and in the work he had devoted his life to? Moreover, do they read like the writings of a man with the necessary verbal skill to write the Book of Mormon? These are obviously subjective questions, which well-meaning people may disagree about. In any case, they are a few of the questions a good skeptic should consider when trying to decide the authenticity of the Book of Mormon.

I suggested earlier that Joseph's story of the origins of the Book of Mormon, no matter how implausible at first blush, is actually the most plausible of all available explanations. A brief summary of my argument may be in order. First of all, there does not appear to be any middle ground: Joseph was either a blatant liar or inspired of God. The plates are the key. There is substantial evidence that they in fact existed, and if they existed, Joseph must either have received them under the direction of an angel or he must have manufactured the whole thing deliberately. If he set out to create them deliberately, he would have needed to obtain the metal, create the plates (two-thirds of which would be sealed and untouched!), somehow cause the metal to look like gold, create his own writing system, and carefully inscribe many dozens

54. Jesse, *Personal Writings of Joseph Smith*, 264–65.

of plates with the characters he had invented. He would then have had to dictate an almost six-hundred-page book involving nearly three hundred named individuals, many with clear and distinct personalities, many with unusual names; and invent a complex series of plots, frequently interwoven with perfect consistency, not to mention chronological consistency (the book has frequent internal references to specific dates and passage of years). This dictation would take place over a period of roughly two years, but consist of only seventy-five days or so of actual dictation (note that most books of any complexity take much longer than two years to write), under highly unusual circumstances. He would somehow have had to do considerable research—in the Bible, biblical commentaries, and numerous other more obscure texts, to the degree that later scholars would be able to discover find many dozens of parallels. The text of this book would also include extensive religious passages, including some highly original discussions of theology. The book would have to be profound enough to inspire thousands of people not only to believe it had a divine origin, but also to embrace it to the point that they would be willing to dedicate their entire life, possessions, and security, and to endure repeated persecutions. It would likewise have to inspire many millions likewise after his death, for nearly two centuries. He would then somehow have had to convince three men that they had had an open vision of an angel who showed them the plates and other objects and declared to them that the translation was of God, so that they would cling to that conviction throughout their lives, even after being disaffected from Joseph and his church.

Readers are welcome to differ, but to me the idea that a young farmer/fraudster could accomplish all that (not to mention all the other things that Joseph Smith did during his life) is more miraculous than the simple story of the angel. Is there a single example in all of human history of another person who did anything comparable?

* * * *

One of the recurring themes of this book, I suppose, is that truth sometimes really is stranger than fiction. A few years ago I saw a news story about a window washer who fell eleven stories from the top of a building onto a *moving* car in the street, and was severely injured but quite conscious and lucid. Another news account from Russia tells of a young man who, trying to impress a girl with his bravery, fell twenty-three stories (230 feet) from a balcony onto a stationary vehicle and suffered only a bruised abdomen and lung, a tear in his liver and a broken shoulder. Such stunts are pulled in action movies all the time, and nobody takes them seriously. If we saw such a thing in a serious drama, we would all groan at the unbelievable script. And yet they actually happened.[55]

55. See "Window Washer Survives"; Barbash, "Siberian Youth."

10

The Witness of the Spirit—or, Why Latter-day Saints Say They Know the Gospel is True

We never can comprehend the things of God and of heaven but by revelation. We may spiritualize and express opinions to all eternity but that is no authority.

—JOSEPH SMITH[1]

Could you gaze into heaven five minutes, you would know more than you would by reading all that ever was written on the subject.

—JOSEPH SMITH[2]

EACH MONTH ON THE first Sunday, Latter-day Saints have a *testimony meeting* in which members get up spontaneously in front of the congregation and declare their beliefs and the reasons why they hold to those beliefs. These testimonies often take the form of stories of small but significant miracles—recent experiences in which they have perceived the hand of the Lord in their lives. Quite commonly, they state their beliefs in the language of *knowledge*—"I know that God lives." "I know that Joseph Smith was a prophet." "I know that Jesus Christ lived and died for our sins." Sometimes the language is even stronger—"I know as sure as I know the sun is shining that the Bible and the Book of Mormon are the word of God." What is it that leads Mormons to declare they have knowledge of things that seem to be inherently unknowable?

Rationalists and religious skeptics typically suppose that belief in God is entirely outside the realm of human reason. For them, faith is by definition an irrational belief—or at least an *a*rational one—and is therefore unacceptable. Faith is necessarily *blind* faith. Rationalists (so they suppose) ground themselves in logic and cold, hard fact; believers ground themselves in blind faith and wishful thinking.

---

1. Ehat and Cook, *Words of Joseph Smith*, 186.
2. *HOTC* 6:50–51.

This is a false dichotomy. We all use both rationality and irrationality every day of our lives. As useful as rational knowledge is, the reality is that no one lives their life on a purely rational basis. If we did, we would be more like the famous Mr. Spock than human beings. Reason is certainly a very important aspect of human life—it's what keeps us grounded in reality and keeps us from falling into the pit of gullibility. Science, which is based in great part on careful reasoning, has helped us discover many marvels about our world. But as we discussed in chapter 2, we should not fall into the trap of assuming that science or logical reasoning can provide a universal solution to all our questions and problems.

INTUITIVE KNOWLEDGE

How then *do* we solve our problems? How do we find answers to our questions, our problems, our dilemmas, large or small, that arise in our lives? Even if rational thought is not a panacea, where else can we go for answers?

One source is *tradition*. As a matter of reality, we all rely on tradition, whether we like it or not. Like the woman who cut off the ends of the ham because she had unreflectively copied the practice of her mother and grandmother, we all conduct much of our lives on the basis of custom, habit, and convention—i.e., we act as we do simply because *that is the way it is done*, in our family, our community, our country. And there is absolutely nothing wrong with that, in general, because we cannot analyze and reason through every detail of our lives. Even if there is no good *reason* for some of what we do, even if it is silly, like cutting off the ends of the ham, such traditions are mostly harmless and give us a sense of belonging to a human community.

But what other sources of knowledge and wisdom are there beside reason? Is there such a thing as knowledge that transcends reason—arational, or non-rational, knowledge?

We normally think of scientific research as the example *par excellence* of rational thought. Scientists engage in rigorous experiments to determine the nature of reality, and they conform their ideas to the outcomes of their experiments. Although they may have prior expectations (i.e., hypotheses) when they conduct their experiments, they have no personal commitment to those preconceived notions and are ready and willing to change their ideas as soon as the evidence shows that they were wrong. Most importantly, the outcome of an experiment is accepted as scientific truth only after it has been directly verified by multiple independent researchers repeating the experiment and reaching the same result.

Yet Michael Polanyi has pointed out that this is much more an abstract ideal of how scientific discoveries are made than it is a description of how science happens in real life. Exhibit number one to this argument is the story of how Einstein discovered relativity. It did not come about as the culmination of step-by-step accumulation of evidence and logical analysis, but began as a brilliant youthful insight. Einstein wrote in his autobiography that the basic essence of the special theory of relativity came to him intuitively at the age of sixteen. He writes that his discovery came

> after ten years' reflection . . . from a paradox *upon which I had already hit at the age of sixteen*: If I pursue a beam of light with the velocity c (velocity of light in a vacuum), I should observe such a beam of light as an electromagnetic field at rest though spatially oscillating. There seems to be no such thing, however, neither on the basis of experience nor according to Maxwell's equations. *From the very beginning it appeared to me intuitively clear* that, judged from the standpoint of such an observer, everything would have to happen according to the same laws as for an observer who, relative to the earth, was at rest. For how should the first observer know or be able to determine, that he is in a state of fast uniform motion? One sees in this paradox the germ of the special relativity theory is already contained.[3]

Somewhat later, he said of the same experience:

> During this year in Aarau the following question came to me: if one chases a light wave with the speed of light, then one would have before one a time independent wave field. But such a thing appears not to exist! This was the first child-like thought experiment related to the special theory of relativity. *Discovery is not a work of logical thought, even if the final product is bound in logical form.*[4]

Many scientific theories, like Einstein's, have begun with a momentary illumination—an intuition—followed by many years of painstaking effort to verify and work out the details. Note that this sequence of events is the direct inverse of the theoretical way of doing science just discussed. Moreover, Polanyi stresses that bare facts are essentially without meaning; their significance can only be grasped (by the scientist) when placed against a background of prior understanding. The researcher must *integrate* the new facts with everything else that he has previously learned, which may or not be correct. Thus, reaching a correct interpretation of the experimental results is directly dependent on the correctness of one's prior knowledge—or the lack thereof.

This should not lead us to conclude that science is pure speculation and unreliable, but merely that the rationalist's conviction that all valid knowledge comes through evidence and careful reasoning is wrong. It is a fantasy. Intuition, sudden insight (which by definition is inexplicable), and subjectivity all play an important part in science, as they do in all aspects of the human experience.

---

3. Einstein, "Autobiographical Notes," 53.
4. Quoted in Norton, "Chasing the Light, 130.

PARAPSYCHOLOGY

Many studies have been conducted to examine whether or not extrasensory perception (parapsychology or psi) is real. The field, as one might expect, is still quite controversial, in part because the results of studies have been ambiguous, but also because even serious researchers typically have strong biases for or (mostly) against the reality of psychic phenomena. Nonetheless, even skeptics have begun to acknowledge the validity at least of the value of studying such things, if not of the phenomena themselves.

The atheist philosopher Sam Harris, well known for his absolute opposition to all things religious, is rather more open to the possibility of psi. He acknowledges "a body of data attesting to the reality of psychic phenomena, much of which has been ignored by mainstream science." He also recognizes the importance of keeping an open mind:

> The dictum that "extraordinary claims require extraordinary evidence" remains a reasonable guide in these areas, but this does not mean that the universe isn't far stranger than many of us suppose. It is important to realize that a healthy, scientific skepticism is compatible with a fundamental openness of mind.[5]

Mario Beauregard, a neurologist and proponent of psi research, describes it as "a stable, *low-level* effect, typically a little too high to be chance." He adds that many dozens of studies regarding telepathy "show that people sometimes get small amounts of specific information from a distance that do not depend on the ordinary senses."[6]

For example, the common notion that we can sense when someone is staring at us has been repeatedly studied, and the conclusion seems to be, well, inconclusive. Numerous studies have suggested that there is a small but statistically significant positive correlation—not that it is an infallible sense by any means.[7] But attempts by experimental subjects to tell when they are being stared at seems to have a higher success rate than pure chance would allow for. Other experiments seem to show little or no correlation.

The problem with studies like these is that they attempt to take something that is inherently intangible and ephemeral and put it in a box, objectify it, and measure it. Extrasensory perception, assuming it exists at all, is clearly not the kind of thing that is easily proven. It's a little bit like trying to prove that so-and-so is in love with you. There might be certain concrete clues that you could list on a piece of paper if you were very rationally inclined. But even those elements—can they be measured?

---

5. Harris, *End of Faith*, 41.

6. Beauregard and O'Leary, *Spiritual Brain*, 169.

7. Sheldrake, *Science Set Free*, 225–26, tells of tens of thousands of simple tests that were carried out in which the subject indicates when he thinks he is being stared at. The results were fairly consistent, showing that roughly 55 percent of the guesses were correct. If mere chance were the cause, the results should have been 50 percent. Again, that is not a huge positive correlation, but it was a significant and consistent one. See also Sheldrake's *Sense of Being Stared At*.

For example, you might say that her eyes "sparkle" every time she sees you. But what exactly do we mean when we say that eyes "sparkle"? Can it be studied in a laboratory? Is it not true that eyes can sparkle even when love is not involved? Many of the clues would be purely intuitive—you can simply *sense* her (or his) feelings toward you.

Friendship is quite similar. Most people at some point will have had a quiet, deep conversation with another person during which you both felt an intangible but nonetheless very real bond or sense of unity. Similarly, stage performers report that they can sense, on certain occasions, when the audience as a whole is "with them." These experiences are not imaginary, and they are not just emotional, nor are they simply rational conclusions reached by an analysis of subtle physical clues. Friendship is real, even if it would be impossible to capture in a scientific study. Indeed, trying to objectify such things can often destroy them. Would you ever ask a person to *prove* beyond a reasonable doubt that they are really your friend? Such an approach might well ruin whatever friendship there was.

Is "intuition" just another word for emotion? Are we talking about making decisions based on emotions and feelings? No. Emotion is what you feel yourself individually when, for example, you contemplate seeing your lover (love) or when someone has wronged you (anger). What I am talking about is an intangible but real *connection* between two human beings that can only be described as "spiritual." It is a *communion between two spirits*.

SPIRITUAL KNOWLEDGE

But even if we grant that there are real limitations to logic and objective knowledge, and that there is something *real* about subjective, or intuitive, knowledge, is there any type of knowledge that transcends *both* of these? Is there such a thing as *spiritual* knowledge—knowledge that is communicated to us directly from some other realm or dimension?

Socrates, according to the common view, was the father of rationalism. J. B. Bury, one of the grand old historians of the early twentieth century, once described Socrates as "the first champion of the supremacy of the intellect as a court from which there is no appeal; he was the first to insist that a man must order his life by the guidance of his own intellect."[8] Bury also declared that while Socrates believed in some kind of god, he was agnostic about the nature of deity and rejected all forms of piety. Bury seems to be saying that Socrates believed in rationality at all costs.

Yet when we read Socrates' own words, we get a very different impression. In his defense before the Athenian court, he declared:[9]

8. Bury and Meiggs, *History of Greece*, 358.

9. I am, of course, cheating slightly when I quote the words of Plato as if they were Socrates' own. In reality, we have nothing written by Socrates himself, but only the writings of his followers, primarily Plato and Xenophon. Scholars are slowly coming to the realization that Socrates was "not

Gentlemen, what God seems to be saying through the oracle is this: that in reality it is God alone who is wise, whereas human wisdom is worth little or nothing. And when he names Socrates as the wisest man, it seems that he is not referring to me personally, but is using me as an example, as though to say that they are the wisest among you who, like Socrates, recognize that when it comes to wisdom they are in fact worthless.[10]

Socrates seems to have made a distinction between human and divine wisdom, between knowledge that we can find out for ourselves through human reason and that which is unknowable without recourse to divine assistance. We should not ask the gods, he says, for help in figuring out what we can figure out for ourselves. But things which are beyond human ken—for example, where the outcome of a particular action is uncertain—are a different matter.

Skill in carpentry or metalwork or farming or government, or critical ability in these subjects, or proficiency in mathematics or estate-management or military science—all these attainments he considered to be within the scope of human choice and judgment; but he said the most important aspects of those subjects the gods reserved for themselves, and none of them were revealed to mortals. A man who has sown a field well cannot tell who will reap the harvest; and a man who has built a house well cannot tell who will live in it. A general cannot tell whether it is to his advantage to hold his command, and a politician cannot tell whether it is to his advantage to be head of the State. The man who has married a beautiful wife for his pleasure cannot tell whether she will cause him pain, and the man who has secured influential connections in his native land cannot tell whether they will result in his banishment from it. To suppose that such consequences are all a matter of human judgment and contain no element of the divine was, he said, superstition; and he also said it was superstition to consult diviners about questions which the gods had

---

only a rational philosopher of the first rank, but a profoundly religious figure as well . . . who believed in gods vastly superior to ourselves in power and wisdom and shared many other traditional religious commitments of this sort with his fellow citizens." McPherran, *The Religion of Socrates*, 2.

10. Plato, *Apology* 21 (my translation). This passage is the origin of the erroneous idea that Socrates stated that "I know that I know nothing"—the ultimate paradox, as it were. But Socrates (as far as we know!) never made such an assertion. He does go on to say (referring to a conversation he had with a certain well-known Athenian politician), "I reasoned to myself, 'I am wiser than that man, for it is not likely that either of us knows *anything that is fine and good*; but while he supposes that he knows something, when he knows nothing, I, as I do not know anything [i.e., anything fine and good], do not suppose that I do. In this one small way, then, I appear to be wiser than he, that I do not suppose that I know what I do not know." But what he is saying here is simply that he is fully aware of his massive ignorance and does not pretend to know more than he knows. It is a statement of intellectual humility (as well as a put-down of arrogant politicians!), not a statement of a philosophical paradox. But as the quotation in the text makes clear, the basis of his humility was his awareness of the massive gap between the knowledge and wisdom of humans and that of God. For an in-depth discussion of this question (but with little awareness of the religious aspect of Socrates' thinking), see Fine, "Does Socrates Claim," 49–88.

enabled us to decide by the use of our wits (for example, supposing one were to ask whether it is better to engage a qualified or an unqualified driver for a carriage, or helmsman for one's ship, or to which the answers can be found by calculation or measuring or weighing). People who put this sort of question to the gods were, in his opinion, acting wrongly. He said that where the gods have given us power to act by the use of our intelligence, we ought to use it; but where the outcome is concealed from human beings, we should try to discover it from the gods by divination; for the gods communicate to those whom they favor.[11]

In fact, Socrates was particularly famous—or infamous—for his belief in a personal spirit, or *daimon*, which frequently spoke to his mind to give him guidance about how to act in certain circumstances. Specifically, this *daimon* told him how *not* to act when he was about to do something incorrect or improper. It had first spoken to him when he was a child, and he had learned that it was always right, even in fairly trivial matters. The ancient biographer and essayist Plutarch related a humorous example that on one occasion Socrates' personal deity told him to stop walking up the hill and to turn around. As always, he obeyed immediately, and most of his companions wisely accompanied him back down the hill. A small group of young followers, however, decided to put Socrates' inspiration to the test, and continued on up the hill. After a few minutes, they encountered a large herd of muddy pigs coming towards them. As there was no way to get around the pigs, the young men got knocked to the ground and covered with mud, while those who obeyed the divine prompting were spared the embarrassment.[12]

So it appears that Socrates regularly "heard voices" speaking to him. Does that mean he was crazy—a schizophrenic? Some have suggested as much. But surely if everyone who ever heard a bodiless voice speak in their minds were declared schizophrenic, half the population would need to be put away. One mental health expert has found "a *majority* of ordinary, well-adjusted people" have had the experience, at least once, of hearing a disembodied voice speaking to them.[13]

Even my skeptical mother occasionally told us the story of a voice she heard as a young mother, when she had gone to bed and my sister was supposedly asleep in her crib. She related that she suddenly heard a clear, distinct voice telling her to go check on my sister—immediately. She dismissed the thought at first, since she had just looked in on her before going to bed. But the voice came again, even more insistent, so she got up and went into my sister's room, only to find that she had somehow dislodged a piece of the mobile that was suspended over the crib, put it in her mouth, and was choking on it. Even that experience was not enough to make my mother believe in God or angels. But it did make her wonder.

11. Xenophon, *Memoirs of Socrates* 1.1.8–9, in Xenophon, *Conversations with Socrates*, 69–70.
12. Plutarch, "On Socrates' Personal Deity," quoted in Smith, *Muses, Madmen*, 141–42.
13. Watkins, *Hearing Voices*, 5.

Of course, merely hearing a few words in one's head is a far cry from the lengthy visions and revelations Joseph Smith claimed to have. What basis do we have to judge such claims?

Many Christians take the Bible as their foundation for judgment. If the teachings of Joseph Smith were biblical, they would accept them. But since (in their judgment) they are not, they must be false. But how can one know for sure that every word of the Bible is absolutely true? How can one know for sure that one's *interpretation* of the Bible is correct? There are countless Christian sects today, with many different varieties of doctrines. In the early Christian centuries there was an even greater variety of belief. Not all of them can be correct. How can a person determine which are correct and which not?

For most Christians prior to Martin Luther, the answer was that the church—specifically, the pope and the occasional church councils—was the ultimate arbiter of correct doctrine and interpretation of the Scriptures. The early Protestant divines, however, insisted that the Bible, rather than the Roman church, was the ultimate authority. This view was problematic, because individuals could, and did, read the Bible differently, and traditionalists argued that this approach would result in religious anarchy. Calvin confronted this problem head-on by arguing that those chosen by God possessed an inner illumination through God's spirit that would provide inspiration—i.e., not new revelation, but confirmation that all true revelation was to be found in the Bible. That same spirit would also provide a means for discerning the proper meaning of the Bible's words.[14]

If the Bible is not an ultimately reliable guide, what then is? The Mormon view is that there is only one ultimately reliable basis, which is God himself. Joseph Smith, as we have seen, prayed to God as a young man to dispel his confusion and skepticism over the question of religion. In the last chapter of the Book of Mormon, the following promise is given:

> And when ye shall receive these things, I would exhort you that ye would ask God, the Eternal Father, in the name of Christ, if these things are not true. And if ye shall ask with a sincere heart, with real intent, having faith in Christ, he will manifest the truth of it unto you by the power of the Holy Ghost. And by the power of the Holy Ghost ye may know the truth of all things.[15]

This is the "missionary promise" that countless Mormon proselytizers have presented to those whom they teach, insisting that they can receive direct divine confirmation of LDS teachings. Joseph Smith himself made a similar statement:

---

14. Popkin, *History of Scepticism*, 9–10. Many modern critics of Mormonism adhere to some type of Reformed Christianity, with John Calvin as the ultimate founder. But few recognize that Calvin acknowledged the need for divine inspiration in the interpretation of the Bible.

15. Moroni 10:4.

Search the scriptures—search the revelations which we publish, and ask your Heavenly Father, in the name of His Son Jesus Christ, to manifest the truth unto you, and if you do it with an eye single to His glory nothing doubting, He will answer you by the power of His Holy Spirit. You will then know for yourselves and not for another. You will not then be dependent upon man for the knowledge of God; nor will there be any room for speculation.[16]

Religious people throughout history have described a variety of encounters with God. Mystics of all stripes have reported experiences conveying a profound awareness of a transcendent reality. In most cases they find themselves completely unable to describe such experiences. They refer to being "engulfed" in God, or to attaining a "mystical union" with divinity. For example:

I felt . . . an inward state of peace and joy and assurance indescribably intense, accompanied with a sense of being bathed in a warm glow of light as though the external condition had been brought about by the internal effect. These highest experiences that I have had of God's Presence have been rare and brief—flashes of consciousness which have compelled me to exclaim with surprise—God is *here*—or conditions of exaltation and insight less intense . . . It was in these most real seasons that the Real Presence came, and I was aware that I was immersed in the infinite ocean of God.[17]

While such mystical experiences may involve a direct vision of God or an angel, rarely is there an indication that the mystic has received specific knowledge or revelation from deity that can be communicated to others. One of the greatest of all Christian mystics, Teresa of Avila, described one vision as follows:

Christ appeared before me, with a most severe expression, giving me to understand that this was something that grieved him. I saw Him with the eyes of the soul more clearly than I could have seen Him with those of the body, and it left such a deep impression on me that, though more than twenty-six years have passed, it still seems present before me. I remained very astonished and disturbed.[18]

One scholar of religion has described mysticism as follows:

Historic religions have used the word for a very specific experience, of an intimate relation to the Absolute Reality, the infinite, eternal and incomprehensible Ultimate that embraces all things at once. It is the One beyond all limits. It is God the Absolute, Brahman the incomprehensible, Allah the infinite, or the formless and eternal Tao that the mystic encounters in mystical experience . . . According to the mystics, this encounter is not really describable

16. *TPJS* 12.

17. J. Trevor, *Autobiography*, quoted in Jones, *Pathways to the Reality*, 29.

18. Teresa of Avila, *Libro de la Vida* 7:6, quoted in Zaleski and Zaleski, *Prayer*, 173.

because it is not experience in any usual sense of the word. It is not thinking or knowing because this experience takes a person beyond such limited states of consciousness. It may produce certain feelings or emotional states, but it is beyond mere emotions. It is not a seeing or hearing or touching, although metaphors based on sensation or sensory images can provide some poetic ways of speaking about it. The mystics attempt to describe it by saying it is a being-at-one with the One that is All. It is a momentary eternity, a few minutes or hours of identity with the Everything, in comparison with which the person is nothing. It is bliss; it is nothingness. It is ecstasy; it is emptiness. It is a rapture or utter peace. Then, when they have said all these things in an attempt to describe it, the mystics finally reaffirm that it is. Words might help point a person toward mystical union with the Absolute but only the experience of it can let a person "know" what it is.[19]

Thus, the most striking thing about the mystical experience is that it often leaves the mystic herself uncertain as to its precise meaning. On the other hand, is it possible to experience something more than an "overbrimming sense of presence"?[20] Can one actually receive a communication of *knowledge* from God, something that can be expressed in clear, precise language? Numerous accounts by converts to Mormonism have described the otherworldly but clear and specific divine witness that came to them when they sought understanding from God.

Lorenzo Snow, who later in life became president and prophet of the church, related the spiritual witness he received as a young man. He had gone to college at Oberlin at roughly the same time that his older sister Eliza had joined the fledgling LDS church. He became intrigued by the doctrines and on occasion even defended them in discussions with some of his theology classmates. Eventually he became dissatisfied with the Oberlin experience and went to join his sister at Kirtland, where he studied with Joseph Smith and other associates and quickly became convinced of the correctness of Joseph's teachings. He was then challenged to receive a spiritual witness to confirm his intellectual convictions, and when he knelt to pray, he immediately received an answer to his prayers.

> That will never be erased from my memory as long as memory endures . . . I received a perfect knowledge that there was a God, that Jesus, who died upon Calvary, was His Son, and that Joseph the Prophet had received the authority which he professed to have. The satisfaction and the glory of that manifestation no language can express! I returned to my lodgings. I could now testify to the whole world that I knew, by positive knowledge, that the Gospel of the Son of God had been restored, and that Joseph was a Prophet of God, authorized to speak in His name.[21]

19. Barnes, *Enduring Quest*, 133.
20. The words are from Jones, *Pathways*, 29.
21. Taken from a sermon entitled "The Grand Destiny of Man," by Lorenzo Snow, found in

But notions of revealed knowledge are not limited to the sphere of religion. The famous British astronomer Sir Fred Hoyle, though he never actually believed in a traditional idea of God, did come to believe in a great superintelligence in the cosmos. He attributed to this source the fortuitous "coincidences" in the physical realm that allowed life to exist in the universe. He also believed that this intelligent being was the source of much of the knowledge in the world—that is, that it was able to implant thoughts and ideas directly into the mind of mathematicians or musicians.[22] Hoyle reported the following conversation with the great physicist Richard Feynman about the experience of receiving such inspiration:

> Some years ago I had a graphic description from Dick Feynman of what a moment of inspiration feels like, and of it being following by an enormous sense of euphoria, lasting for maybe two or three days. I asked how often had it happened, to which Feynman replied 'four' [times], at which we both agreed that twelve days of euphoria was not a great reward for a lifetime's work.

Hoyle described with greater intimacy a particular occasion when he had been struggling to solve an extremely complicated mathematical problem. He decided to go on a hike in the Scottish Highlands with some colleagues.

> As the miles slipped by I turned the quantum mechanical problem . . . over in my mind, in the hazy way I normally have in thinking mathematics in my head. Normally I have to write things down on paper, and then fiddle with the equations and integrals as best I can. But somewhere on Bowes Moor my awareness of the mathematics clarified, not a little, not even a lot, but as if a huge brilliant light had suddenly been switched on. How long did it take to become totally convinced that the problem was solved? Less than five seconds. It only remained to make sure that before the clarity faded I had enough of the essential steps stored safely in my recallable memory. It is indicative of the measure of certainty I felt that in the ensuing days I didn't trouble to commit anything to paper. When ten days or so later I returned to Cambridge I found it possible to write out the thing without difficulty.[23]

In 1960, a young heart surgeon named Russell Nelson agreed with some reluctance to try to repair the heart of a gentleman with a heart defect that had previously been declared inoperable. The doctor and patient, both Latter-day Saints, prayed together before the operation, and Nelson prayed repeatedly for insight about how to carry out such an operation, which had never been done successfully. As the operation began, still at a loss as to how to proceed, he suddenly had a message impressed

---

Teachings of the Presidents: Lorenzo Snow, 22; see also Davies, *Mormon Culture of Salvation*, 23.

22. Compare the statement by Brigham Young quoted above on page 43: "Every discovery in science and art, that is really true and useful to mankind, has been given by direct revelation from God, though but few acknowledge it."

23. Hoyle, "Universe: Past and Present," 24–25.

upon his mind: "reduce the circumference of the ring." Although the strategy made sense, he still had no idea how to carry it out, until

> a picture came vividly to my mind, showing how stitches could be placed—to make a pleat here and a tuck there—to accomplish the desired objective. I still remember that mental image—complete with dotted lines where sutures should be placed. The repair was completed as diagrammed in my mind. We tested the valve and found the leak to be reduced remarkably. My assistant said, "It's a miracle." I responded, "It's an answer to prayer."[24]

Hoyle actually compares these kinds of experiences by rational scientists to the experiences of mystics, who report having "a direct and unmediated contact with a perceived ultimate reality." Kurt Gödel reportedly could achieve such insight by following actual meditative practices, lying down in a quiet place, and shutting out all sensual stimuli.[25] One might also consider the numerous scientific (and other) discoveries made in dreams. Mendeleev, for example, claimed that he saw the key to organizing the periodic table in a dream.

But I would stress the fundamental differences between the experiences of Hoyle and other scientists versus those of most mystics. Unlike the latter, they involved direct, clear, and instantaneous communications of specific knowledge from some unknown source—not merely a profound but vague awareness of one's place in the cosmos. Like Feynman and Hoyle, Lorenzo Snow also came away from his experience with absolute certainty regarding the knowledge he had been studying.

Joseph did not go into a mystical trance when he received a revelation but apparently was in full possession of his normal faculties, and the knowledge came to him directly. Parley Pratt was in the room on the occasion when Joseph received a revelation that became section 50 of the Doctrine and Covenants:

> After we had joined in prayer in his translating room, he dictated in our presence the following revelation. Each sentence was uttered slowly and very distinctly, and with a pause between each, sufficiently long for it to be recorded, by an ordinary writer in long hand . . . There was never any hesitation, reviewing, or reading back, in order to keep the run of the subject.[26]

On another occasion Joseph Smith briefly described the experience of revelation from the Holy Spirit as "enlighten[ing] your mind" and "fill[ing] your soul with joy," which is reminiscent of Feynman's description above of instantaneous intellectual enlightenment accompanied by "an enormous sense of euphoria."[27]

---

24. Nelson, "Sweet Power of Prayer," 7–9. See also Robinson and Hunter, "Discovering a Surgical First." In 1984, after many years as a noted heart surgeon, he became an apostle in the Church of Jesus Christ of Latter-day Saints; in 2018 he became president of the church.

25. See the discussion in Davies, *Mind of God*, 226–29, also 140–46.

26. Pratt, *Autobiography*, 62.

27. D&C 11:13.

Joseph also taught that such revelations were not the exclusive prerogative of prophets or church leaders, but were the right of every man, woman, and child who sought them.

> It is the privilege of the children of God to come to God and get revelation . . . God is not a respecter of persons; we all have the same privilege.[28]

> We believe that we have a right to revelations, visions, and dreams from God, our heavenly Father; and light and intelligence, through the gift of the Holy Ghost, in the name of Jesus Christ, on all subjects pertaining to our spiritual welfare; if it so be that we keep his commandments, so as to render ourselves worthy in his sight.[29]

FROM SKEPTIC TO BELIEVER

My own experience was not unlike that of Lorenzo Snow, if not quite so powerful. When I became interested in matters of religion as a seeking but skeptical fifteen-year-old, I quickly decided that there had to be a way of finding the truth. In other words, there had to be *a truth* out there somewhere, and there had to be some means of discovering it. This would be particularly true *if* God existed. After all, what God, what creator, with feelings of love, would place his creations in a world and then give them no guidance at all? I was convinced that there *had to be* an answer. The question, obviously, was how and where to locate that truth and how to identify it once found. And so I began my quest.

My friends, and the missionaries they invited to their home to teach me, stressed that they did not expect me to take their word for anything, but that I should pray to my Heavenly Father for knowledge and enlightenment regarding what they taught. That approach appealed to me immediately, because the opinions of human beings are so numerous as to be worth a dime a dozen. On the other hand, prayer was very foreign to me, and the idea of speaking to a being I didn't believe in, and who might well not even exist, made me extremely self-conscious.

My desire to *know*, however—to *understand*—pushed me forward. Although I had enjoyed the youth group I had attended a few times at a nearby Baptist church, traditional Christianity as a system was never very satisfying or plausible to me; it seemed full of logical holes, with no way to fill them in. But I had high hopes that Mormon Christianity would provide something more. I read the Book of Mormon and *A Marvelous Work and a Wonder*, a book by an old apostle, LeGrand Richards, so that I was already quite familiar with most of the doctrine by the time the missionaries

28. Discourse given by Joseph Smith about July 1839 in Commerce, Illinois; reported by Willard Richards, in Willard Richards, *Pocket Companion*; quoted in Turner, *Mormon Jesus*, 102.

29. Letter from Joseph Smith to Isaac Galland, March 22, 1839, found in *Teachings of the Presidents: Joseph Smith*, 132.

presented it to me, and I found the standard missionary discussions a bit dull. I wrote down the random, off-the-wall questions that occurred to me during my reading, which more than once stumped the missionaries. As always, my main focus was on big questions: How could I make sense of the idea of God? How could I know—for certain—that he in fact existed? How could I know that the Bible was his word? Or the Book of Mormon? How could I know that Joseph Smith really had the experiences he claimed he had?

Mormon missionaries have a standardized presentation of the plan of salvation, but I think they went a little deeper into the subject for me than they did for most people. It was good that they did, because that evening I had my first real flash of insight. I would not describe this experience as spiritual but as purely intellectual. I suddenly felt like I understood where Mormonism was coming from and what tied it all together, and had my first inkling that here was something different, something remarkable, and something that *just might* make sense. The concept that because we are the spiritual offspring of deity we have the natural potential of becoming deities ourselves was electrifying to me.

Slowly over the next few weeks I began to piece things together to see how the strange pieces of Mormon beliefs did indeed fit together into a meaningful whole, and I came *more or less* to the *tentative* conclusion that this was indeed *possibly* the Truth I had been searching for. Do I sound like an overly cautious person? That is what my son has often told me, but to me I am just being sensible. How could I commit my life to a belief unless I knew for certain that it was true? There are too many interesting (but not necessarily true) ideas out there in the world, and it is too easy to be sucked in by those that appear particularly attractive or enticing. I had to have a greater assurance that I was on the right track than just my own mind telling me that it *seemed* true. In any case, that was what the missionaries had promised to me from the beginning—that if I continued to pray sincerely, I could receive divine confirmation. Still tentative and self-conscious in my prayers, I continued to ask for guidance and insight, not even knowing exactly what form that confirmation would take, but determined to keep trying.

Everyone has had moments of emotional excitement, of euphoria even, when something you've longed for for years is suddenly yours—for example, when your proposal of marriage was accepted by the love of your life. Surely everyone has also had moments of intellectual insight, when the solution to a problem you've been struggling with for months suddenly becomes clear. I have had those and other similar experiences, yet the singular experience I had one particular evening at age seventeen far transcended all of them. The best way I can describe it is being "touched by the finger of heaven." It is a sudden, powerful insight that appears to come from outside yourself, almost as if you put your finger in a light socket and electricity courses through your body. Yet it is not a violent jolt like that; it is mild and gentle, yet at the same time surprisingly abrupt and powerful; subtle, yet with a profound and lasting effect.

It was more than a sense of oneness with the universe, of an "overbrimming sense of the presence of God," or of being "immersed in the infinite ocean of God." It included a specific communication of knowledge regarding the problem I was struggling with: whether the Book of Mormon and the "restored gospel" were true. The actual experience did not last long—less than a minute—although its aftereffects lasted for many days—indeed, for the rest of my life since then. I no longer had any doubts, only certainty. The ideas I had been pondering were no longer merely interesting or charming ideas, or even compelling, but they were *true*. I did not hear a *voice*, which is why I describe it as being *"touched* by the finger of heaven." I have had similar experiences a very few times in my life, in response to specific questions I was agonizing over. In a couple of instances, I heard actual, distinct words spoken to my mind or my soul.

Life is inherently filled with uncertainty. Rarely can we know with any real confidence that the road we are about to embark on is exactly the right path. That is how it should be, since we are on this earth to grow and to learn. We have to learn how to trust ourselves—our *best selves*—to make right choices, not rely on some divine answer book. We must stretch ourselves, plumb our very core, in order to reach an understanding of who we truly are. But I feel very blessed to have received, on rare and singular occasions, a clear and unmistakable confirmation about certain decisions in my life which have set me on the right road and given me the strength to remain on them through much adversity. Such experiences are life-transforming, for they give us insight into a different world—a hint of another reality—from the one we live in every day.

Joseph Smith once said, "Could you gaze into heaven five minutes, you would know more than you would by reading all that ever was written on the subject."[30] I have not *seen* heaven, but I'm quite certain that I have *felt* it.

30. *TPJS*, 324.

Conclusion

The Pearl of Great Price

IF GOD HAD A message for the world, would you be interested in hearing it?

That question is at the heart of the classic movie *Oh God!*, with George Burns as God and John Denver as his hapless, reluctant prophet who becomes the butt of jokes as a result of his decision to tell the world that God had spoken with him. He is fired from his job as a supermarket assistant manager, in part because his boss is jealous and thinks God should have spoken to him instead of to his lowly assistant. Even his wife begins to doubt his sanity. In the end, the divine message is uplifting but a tad simplistic: "Try not to hurt each other—there's been enough of that."

For reasons that should be clear from our earlier discussion, God does not make a habit of appearing to men and women in person. On the rare occasions when he has done so, it is because he has had a message of great significance. In the George Burns version, God's message consists of what we already know we should do but don't. The only striking part of the message is that God himself exists—he is *real*. He exists not only as a "spirit of love," as my mother would say, or as nice idea, or an uplifting influence, or even as a ubiquitous fog throughout the universe, but as a real being, who has concrete thoughts and actions and interacts directly with his children, very much in the way that we interact with each other.

The Latter-day Saints declare that they too have a message from God to the world, but one that is a little less shopworn, consisting of knowledge which the world has had no awareness of, or has completely lost sight of. At the risk of sounding arrogant, Mormons assert that they have found *the Truth*—the thing that everyone is seeking for but don't know where to find. This does not mean that they possess all the truth, nor that they are the only ones who possess any truth. Nor does it mean that they always do the best possible job at living their lives in accordance with that truth.

It does mean, however, that they believe they possess the purest and most complete version of the divine plan for humankind's eternal welfare. I like to think of it as the divine paradigm, a bare-bones sketch of the ideas, principles, and practices that will lead us back to God and to the happiness that is our right to inherit. There is an infinitely greater amount of knowledge to be gained beyond that—some of which we may acquire in this life, but most of it in the next.

We live today in a highly secular world. While surveys show that large numbers of people in the U.S. still believe in God, religion appears to be on the decline, and to play a limited role in most people's lives. Of course, we also live in a cynical age, one in which claims to know God's word are a dime a dozen. Worse still, there are many frauds out there who are actively trying to deceive people—in some cases to bilk them out of their money, and in the worst case to convince them to *drink the Kool-Aid*. How can anyone correctly distinguish between the frauds, the fools, the cranks, and the genuine prophets?

As a good skeptic, I have asked myself that question many times.

Logical reasoning based on clear and compelling *objective* evidence is important, but if we are looking for answers to ultimate questions, we must be willing to go a bit beyond. It is easy enough to conclude that because there is no absolutely decisive evidence for God, we should conclude either that he does not exist or that there is no way to know if he exists. On the other hand, millions of mystics and religious thinkers through the ages have found convincing *personal* evidence that he is real.

The Mormon message is not only that there is a truth out there, but that it is possible for the sincere seeker to know with a high degree of certainty that it is true. This is a remarkable claim, but it is one that has been verified by millions who have found in Mormonism the pearl of great price, for which they, like the merchant in the parable, were willing to sell all they had in order to possess it.[1]

1. See Matthew 13:45–46.

Appendix

A Comparison of Reports of Near-Death Experiences and Latter-day Saint Beliefs about the Life after Life

As I MENTIONED IN chapter 6, when I first read *Life after Life,* I was astonished at the parallels between the core NDE experience and LDS doctrine about the afterlife. I began writing an essay on the topic with the intention of sending it to Dr. Moody, and only a combination of my inherent shyness and my laziness kept me from doing so.

There had been an interest among Latter-day Saints in near-death accounts for many years long before the Moody book. Many of these were compiled by Duane Crowther and published in his *Life Everlasting.*

In the interest of space, I will not attempt to compare each of the basic elements of NDEs with Mormon doctrine, but instead confine myself to the most striking parallels.

1) SPIRIT BODIES

The first thing that struck me about Moody's discussion was the idea of a specific, distinct spirit body totally separate from our physical bodies.

> . . . all who experienced it are in agreement that the spiritual body is nonetheless *something,* impossible to describe though it may be. It is agreed that the spiritual body has a form or shape (sometimes a globular or amorphous cloud, but sometimes essentially the same shape as the physical body) and even parts (projections or surfaces analogous to arms, legs, a head, etc.).[1]

Attempts to describe this body can differ considerably—one woman even described her body during her NDE as similar to a jellyfish, but that she also had a neck and

---

1. Moody, *Life after Life,* 34.

ears![2] But descriptions that directly relate the shape of the new body to the old one seem to predominate.

> "To my surprise I found that I still had hands, and feet, and a body, for I had always regarded the soul as a something without shape and void . . . to find that though I was 'dead' I still had form, was new to me."[3]
>
> "During your experience, did you feel like you had a body like the one on this earth?"
>
> "No, it was lighter."
>
> "But you had arms and legs?"
>
> "Sure, I could touch the other children, and I could feel and smell. I played in the sand and made sand castles with my hands. As we were playing, sometimes I would walk, and other times, when we went as a group, we just floated."[4]

In one study reported in the *American Journal of Psychiatry*, 58 percent of those who reported a near-death experience said that they sensed themselves in a new body, of the same size and age as its physical counterpart, but lighter in weight.[5]

As we have seen, Mormonism teaches that we lived as a spirit body prior to our birth into this terrestrial world, and that we will return to that spirit world when we die (although ultimately, in the resurrection, we will receive our bodies once again but in a glorified form.) I have already emphasized how Mormons view this body as a definite, concrete entity that is shaped almost exactly like our physical bodies. A standard church manual for a young children's Sunday school class encourages teachers to use the following demonstration as a model of our spiritual bodies:

> Hold up your hand, and explain that it represents the spirit that is inside our bodies. The hand can move. Hold up the glove (or stocking), and explain that it represents the physical body. When we are born, the spirit and the body are temporarily joined together, and the spirit gives the body life. The body cannot move by itself. But just like when the glove is placed on the hand, the body becomes alive and can move when the spirit enters it. (Put the glove on your hand.) We all have a spirit and a body. Explain that when we die, the spirit separates from the body. (Remove the glove from your hand.) Can a body move or live without the spirit? After we die, is the spirit still alive and can it move? (Move your hand and fingers to illustrate.) At the time of the Resurrection the body and spirit are reunited. (Place the glove back on your hand.)[6]

2. Gibson, *Fingerprints*, 58.

3. Rogo, *Return from Silence*, 162.

4. Gibson, *Fingerprints*, 114.

5. Greyson and Stevenson, "Phenomenology," 1193–96.

6. "Lesson 45."

But the parallels do not stop there. Numerous reports of NDEs indicate that spirits can move and travel with lightning-like speed. George Ritchie reports that before he realized he was dead, he found himself travelling from Abilene, Texas to Richmond, Virginia "a hundred times faster than any train could take me."[7] Dr. Moody states that travelling in this spirit-state "is apparently exceptionally easy . . . Physical objects present no barrier, and movement from one place to another can be extremely rapid, almost instantaneous."[8]

In comparison, Brigham Young taught that spirit bodies "move with ease and like lightning. If we want to visit Jerusalem, or this, that, or the other place—and I presume we will be permitted if we desire—there we are, looking at its streets . . . If we wish to understand how they are living here on these western islands, or in China, we are there; in fact, we are like the light of the morning, or, I will not say the electric fluid, but its operations on the wires." Similarly, Orson Pratt, his contemporary, argued that because our bodies will be full of light, they will be able to travel at light-speed.[9]

One man who had been attacked and nearly murdered reported that "as my senses expanded I became aware of colors that were far beyond the spectrum of the rainbow known to the human eye. My awareness stretched out in all 360 degrees."[10] Orson Pratt speculated (based on his direct acquaintance with Joseph Smith's teachings) that our eyes (traditionally referred to as a window to the soul) literally allowed our spirit to interact with physical light and, therefore, see.

> The spirit is inherently capable of experiencing the sensations of light; if it were not so, we could not see. You might form as fine an eye as ever was made, but if the spirit, in and of itself, were not capable of being acted upon by the rays of light, an eye would be of no benefit. Then unclothe the spirit, and instead of exposing a small portion of it about the size of a pea to the action of the rays of light, the whole of it would be exposed. I think we could then see in different directions at once, instead of looking in one particular direction; we could then look all around us at the same instance.[11]

In a similar manner, spirit bodies are said to have an infinitely greater capacity for perceiving, understanding, and learning in general. One experiencer says:

> Knowledge and information are readily available—all knowledge . . . You absorb knowledge . . . You all of a sudden know the answers . . . It's like you focus mentally on one place in that school, and—zoom—knowledge flows by

---

7. Ritchie, *Return from Tomorrow*, 47.

8. Moody, *Life after Life*, 34

9. Top and Top, *Glimpses Beyond*, 68–69.

10. Ring, *Heading toward Omega*, 65.

11. *Journal of Discourses* 2:243.

you from that place, automatically. it's just like you had about a dozen speed reading courses.[12]

Orson Pratt again:

> There is a faculty mentioned in the word of God, which we are not in possession of here, but we shall possess it hereafter; that is not only to see a vast number of things in the same moment, looking in all directions by the aid of the Spirit, but also to obtain a vast number of ideas at the same instant. I believe we shall be freed in the next world from these narrow, contracted methods of thinking. Instead of thinking in one channel, and following up one certain course of reasoning to find a certain truth, knowledge will rush in from all quarters; it will come in like the light which flows from the sun, penetrating every part, informing the spirit, and giving understanding concerning ten thousand things at the same time; and the mind will be capable of receiving and retaining all.[13]

2) GOD IS A REAL BEING—OF LIGHT

We discussed at great length in chapter 6 the LDS view that traditional Christianity made a huge and unfortunate blunder in allying its notion of the greatness and supremacy of God with the absolutist notions of Greek philosophy regarding deity. Traditional Christianity has always viewed God as a spiritual (i.e., non-physical), transcendent essence that is present everywhere simultaneously. Mormonism, in contrast, sees God as a being with a real physical presence, even an actual physical body akin to ours. He has a mind not unlike ours, although his knowledge and wisdom are immeasurably greater. He is full of light, which is indicative both of his incomprehensible knowledge (physical light and the light of understanding are closely related) as well as his virtue, purity, and love.

The "being of light" as described in *Life after Life* and many other books on NDEs bears more than a considerable resemblance to this LDS notion of deity. According to Dr. Moody:

> What is perhaps the most incredible common element in the accounts I have studied, and is certainly the element which has the most profound effect upon the individual, is the encounter with a very bright light. Typically, at its first appearance this light is dim, but it rapidly gets brighter until it reaches an unearthly brilliance. Yet, even though this light (usually said to be white or "clear") is of an indescribable brilliance, many make the specific point that it does not in any way hurt their eyes, or dazzle them, or keep them from seeing other things around them.

12. Moody, *Life after Life*, 151.
13. Top and Top, *Glimpses*, 74.

Despite the light's unusual manifestation, however, not one person has expressed any doubt whatsoever that it was a being, a being of light. Not only that, it is a personal being. It has a very definite personality. He senses an irresistible magnetic attraction to this light. He is ineluctably drawn to it.[14]

One woman reported:

. . . then, this really bright light came. It did seem that it was a little dim at first, but then it was this huge beam. It was just a tremendous amount of light, nothing like a big bright flashlight, it was just too much light. And it gave off heat to me; I felt a warm sensation. . . It seemed that it covered everything, yet it didn't prevent me from seeing everything around me—the operating room, the doctors and nurses, everything. I could see clearly, and it wasn't blinding.

At first when the light came, I wasn't sure what was happening, but then, it asked, it kind of asked me if I was ready to die. It was like talking to a person, but a person wasn't there. The light's what was talking to me, but in a *voice*. . . from the moment the light spoke to me, I felt really good—secure and loved. The love which came from it is just unimaginable, indescribable. It was a fun person to be with! And it had a sense of humor, too—definitely![15]

The following is an excerpt from an interview of an experiencer by Dr. Moody:

Did this seem like a normal physical light?

No. It was nothing like I had ever seen before. It was what you might see if you looked up into the sunlight.

Did the light seem to hurt your eyes? Was it uncomfortable to look into it?

No. Not in any way.

Did it seem to have any particular color?

No. Nothing other than just a bright white light. It was like the sun—like looking into the sun.[16]

Although a large percentage of experiencers describe only this light with a personality rather than an actual being present *in* the light, some people do describe him quite clearly as a *being made of light*.

I stared in astonishment as the brightness increased, coming from nowhere, seeming to shine everywhere at once. All the lightbulbs in the [hospital] ward couldn't give off that much light. All the bulbs in the world couldn't! It was impossibly bright, like a million welder's lamps all blazing at once. And right in the middle of my amazement came a prosaic thought probably born of some biology lecture back at the university: *I'm glad I don't have physical eyes at this moment. This light would destroy the retina in a tenth of a second.*

14. Moody, *Life after Life*, 43.
15. Moody, *Life after Life*, 46–47.
16. Moody, *Life after Life*, 161.

No, I corrected myself, *not the light.*

He.

He would be too bright too look at. For now I saw that it was not light but a Man who had entered the room, or rather, a Man made out of light, though this seemed no more possible to my mind than the incredible intensity of the brightness that made up his form.[17]

A man who was an atheist described the being as "an image made of light particles in human form."[18]

Compare Joseph Smith's description of his first vision of God when he was fourteen:

I saw a *pillar of light* exactly over my head, *above the brightness of the sun,* which descended gradually until it fell upon me . . . When the *light* rested upon me I saw two personages *whose brightness and glory defy all description* standing above me in the air.

Next, compare his description of the appearance of the angel Moroni in his bedroom:[19]

I discovered a light appearing in my room, which continued to increase until the room was lighter than at noonday, when immediately a personage appeared at my bedside, standing in the air, for his feet did not touch the floor. He had on a loose robe of most exquisite whiteness. It was a whiteness beyond anything earthly I had ever seen; nor do I believe that any earthly thing could be made to appear so white and brilliant . . . Not only was his robe exceedingly white, but his whole person was glorious beyond description, and his countenance truly like lightning. The room was exceedingly light, but not so very bright as immediately around his person.

One of the striking things about Mormon scriptures is how often they refer to "light," both in the sense of knowledge and understanding as well as physical light. In fact, the two meanings of "light" are often blurred together so that there is almost no distinction.

He that ascended up on high, as also he descended below all things, in that he comprehended all things, that he might be in all and through all things, the *light* of truth; which truth shineth. This is the *light* of Christ. As also he is in the sun, and the *light* of the sun, and the power thereof by which it was made. As also he is in the moon, and is the *light* of the moon, and the power thereof by which it was made; as also the *light* of the stars, and the power

17. Ritchie, *Return*, 57–58.

18. Gibson, *Fingerprints*, 101.

19. Keep in mind that for Mormons angels are not special holy beings with wings but are merely messengers of God. They are human beings, either in premortal spirit existence, or resurrected and glorified.

thereof by which they were made; and the earth also, and the power thereof, even the earth upon which you stand. And the *light* which shineth, which giveth you *light*, is through him who enlighteneth your eyes, which is the same *light* that quickeneth your understandings; which *light* proceedeth forth from the presence of God to fill the immensity of space—The *light* which is in all things, which giveth life to all things, which is the law by which all things are governed, even the power of God who sitteth upon his throne, who is in the bosom of eternity, who is in the midst of all things.[20]

And if your eye be single to my glory, your whole bodies shall be filled with *light*, and there shall be no darkness in you; and that body which is filled with *light* comprehendeth all things.[21]

That which is of God is *light*; and he that receiveth *light*, and continueth in God, receiveth more *light*; and that *light* groweth brighter and brighter until the perfect day.[22]

As I noted in the main text, the being of light has not only a real personality but even a sense of humor.

I must tell you that God has a fantastic sense of humor; I never laughed so much in all my life![23]

D. Scott Rogo reports the following account as told to him by a man in a biker's bar relating what happened to another biker he knew. He says that his friend, who had been involved in a crash, died, and found himself in the tunnel, saw the light at the end, and then was engulfed by the light, and then sensed he was in the presence of God, even though he didn't see a being.

It was a kindly presence, a presence that loved him and accepted him completely and without judgment. Much to his surprise, the crash victim wasn't intimidated by the being, even though totally awed by it. Then the presence spoke to him and explained that everything would be all right and he would live. They also apparently discussed his life experiences and what changes he would make upon his recovery. "They just talked," the biker said to me. "Just like you and me, like friends. It was really great."

[Then another biker in the room added]: "Yeah . . . he said that God was really cool."[24]

---

20. D&C 88:6–12.
21. D&C 88:67.
22. D&C 50:24.
23. Long, *Evidence*, 132.
24. Rogo, *Return from Silence*, 11–12.

3) ENCOUNTERS WITH DECEASED RELATIVES AND LOVED ONES

One thing that clearly typifies this spirit world of the NDE is that it is populated with many spirits of the deceased, who often come to greet or otherwise interact with the new arrival. In the majority of cases these are one's relatives who had already passed.

A woman who "died" in childbirth related the following:

> I realized that all these people were there, almost in multitudes it seems, hovering around the ceiling of the room. They were all people I had known in my past life, but who had passed on before. I recognized my grandmother and a girl I had known when I was in school, and many other relatives and friends. It seems that I mainly saw their faces and felt their presence. They all seemed pleased. It was a very happy occasion, and I felt that they had come to protect or to guide me. It was almost as if I were coming home, and they were there to greet or to welcome me. All this time, I had the feeling of everything light and beautiful. It was a beautiful and glorious moment.[25]

In some cases, relatives who come to greet the "dead" person are not even recognized as such until sometime later:

> A woman held out her hand to me; she was lovely, and I felt that she loved me and knew who I was. I felt safe in her company. I didn't know who she was . . . One day a few years after the surgery my mother showed me a picture of my paternal grandmother, who had died giving birth to my father. It was the lovely woman who held my hand at the other side of the tunnel. I had never seen a picture of her before.[26]

One man remembered:

> Several weeks before I nearly died, a good friend of mine, Bob, had been killed. Now the moment I got out of my body I had the feeling that Bob was standing there, right next to me. I could see him in my mind and felt like he was there, but it was strange. I didn't see him as his physical body. I could see things, but not in the physical form, yet just as clearly, his looks, everything. Does that make sense? He was there but he didn't have a physical body. It was kind of like a clear body, and I could sense every part of it—arms, legs, and so on—but I wasn't *seeing* it physically.[27]

Like the great being of light, spirit bodies are sometimes described as "glowing." One woman named Theresa related:

25. Moody, *Life after Life*, 41.
26. Long, *Evidence*, 47.
27. Moody, *Life after Life*, 41.

> Looking at my hands I could see that they were white and they glowed—and I was dressed in a glowing white garment. I could feel the energy coming from me. It was coming from every part of my body.[28]

Again, compare Joseph Smith's description of the angel Moroni, above.

Note that this view of the afterlife—that we will reunite with our friends and loved ones—is a commonly held one in popular Christianity, but theologians find it much less certain. Protestant theology, of course, is tightly constrained by the doctrine of *sola scriptura*, reliance on the Bible alone. And as one standard theology declares, "We are told relatively little [in the Bible] about the activities of the redeemed in heaven." The emphasis is mostly on our relationship with God—specifically, worship of God—rather than with other people.[29]

4) SOCIABILITY IN THE SPIRIT WORLD

Along with the concept of meeting our relatives and loved ones when we pass beyond the veil of death, is that our relationships with other individuals is virtually the same as in this life. This emerges from countless NDE accounts.

A man named Jaime, who was undergoing surgery, met and spoke with his grandmother who had passed away after suffering from dementia.

> She invited me to sit and have coffee like we used to all the time at her house. Her table was there, the chairs. She looked like she did when she was in her thirties. She had on a purple dress, like a nice one she had with flowers on it, except that the flowers seemed to glow a fluorescent yellow . . . That's when she touched my hand, [and] I noticed that I looked down and could see my hand also. It was there, but it looked white, almost fluorescent, and she told me that it was all right. (All this conversation was in Spanish, by the way.) and she said, let's drink the coffee. I did. But I notice[d] that it was not hot and had no taste.[30]

A plumber who died when he fell off some scaffolding related an encounter with a group of people:

> As we came up to them, the closest member of the group approached me—a beautiful young woman dressed in the whitest, most brilliant robe of the finest material I've ever seen. Her complexion was white and creamy, her hair jet black in color. She was overjoyed to see me and threw her arms around me, embracing me fondly. She said she was my sister who had died when she was just three days old. Everyone else in the group was a relative who had

28. Lundahl and Widdison, *Eternal Journey*, 108.

29. Erickson, *Christian Theology*, 1130. With respect to whether we will be able to associate with or even to recognize our friends and loved ones, Erickson pleads "a certain amount of ignorance."

30. Long, *Evidence*, 95–97.

died. They were all extremely happy that I was there. We talked, it seemed, for hours. They thought I might be granted a second chance to go back.[31]

Joseph Smith wrote in D&C 130:2 regarding the afterlife:

That same sociality when exists among us here will exist among us there, only it will be coupled with eternal glory, which glory we do not now enjoy.

Emmanuel Swedenborg would have agreed absolutely:

Angels talk with each other just the way people in the world do, and they talk of various things—household matters, political matters, issues of moral life and issues of spiritual life, for example.[32]

5) PREEXISTENCE

We have already discussed at length the LDS belief in a premortal existence. Numerous sermons and books refer to death as "going home" to the world that we knew before birth. The notion of a preexistence, and of death as a homecoming, a return to a place one knew formerly, is not infrequent in accounts of NDEs. A man named Craig, who drowned while rafting on a river, said:

[I had] a sense of travelling a long distance and finally making it home. I sensed that I had been here before, perhaps before being born into the physical world.[33]

He saw an orange timeline stretching to infinity in either direction—

. . . and not simply the red area that was designated as my life in this world. It seemed to be telling me that I existed in some form before this lifetime, and that I would continue to exist after it ended.[34]

A Colombian woman reported:

[During the life review] I realized that I understood everything with a great clarity and superlucidity I had never experienced before. I discovered that I had personally chosen to take on a physical body and have the life experiences I was having. I realized I had wasted time in suffering, and what I should have been doing was using my freedom to choose true love, and not pain, in all that came into my life.[35]

31. Lundahl and Widdison, *Eternal Journey*, 177–78.

32. Quoted in Top and Top, *Glimpses Beyond*, 64. For Swedenborg, all angels were formerly living people—in complete human form. See McDannell and Lang, *Heaven*, 189.

33. Ring, *Lessons*, 14.

34. Ring, *Lessons*, 17.

35. Long, *Evidence*, 157.

One mother of a young boy (two years of age) who had an NDE said:

> I thought it was significant that several of your NDErs mentioned a feeling of
> homecoming, a familiarity, a feeling that they had always known everything
> they experienced. Is it possible that very young children retain some memory
> of having been there?[36]

6) SELF-JUDGMENT

Some traditional Christians have questioned the reality of NDEs on the grounds that
they do not sound biblical enough. Some have even declared them to be satanic in
origin. A major area of concern has been the lack of any sign of judgment by God
or condemnation either of non-Christians or of a person's sinful acts. A number of
accounts appear—at least at first glance—to reject the traditional notions of sin and
wrongdoing altogether.

Compared to the traditional notions of God and Christ, particularly the images
of the Last Judgment, the being of light seems downright easygoing. During the life
review, in which the "deceased" reports seeing something like a cinematic replay of
her deeds, the being of light (who is frequently present in such contexts) expresses no
overt criticism or condemnation of the person's past behaviors.

Raymond Moody addressed the question of divine judgment in his follow-up
book, *Reflections on Life after Life*. As he states, there is a clear element of judgment
in many NDEs, but it is more a matter of self-judgment than divine judgment—or
perhaps one might describe it as *divinely-led self-judgment*. As Moody points out, we
all, to one degree or another, wear a series of masks in life to keep from exposing our
true feelings and motives.

> However, in the moments around the time of death all such masks are neces-
> sarily dropped. Suddenly, the person finds his every thought and deed por-
> trayed in a three-dimensional, full-color panorama, If he meets other beings
> he reports that they know his every thought and vice versa. He finds that in this
> state communication is not mediated through words, but rather that thoughts
> are understood directly—to the point where, as one man put it, "You're too
> embarrassed to be around people who don't think the way you do."[37]

In numerous accounts it seems as though the being of light is prompting the
"deceased" to think about his or her behavior toward other people. The person is implicitly asked questions designed to prompt him to reflect upon his or her *actions* and
motivations and the *effects* they had on others. And at the same time, he is able to sense

36. Ring, *Lessons*, 98.
37. Moody, *Life after Life*, 167.

completely the feelings of people so that the impact of his actions is entirely open to him.[38]

> When I would see something, when I would experience a past event, it was like I was seeing it through eyes with (I guess you would say) omnipotent knowledge, guiding me, and helping me to see.[39]

> . . . when I got back, I had this overwhelming, burning, consuming desire to do something for other people . . . I was so ashamed of all the things that I had done, or hadn't done, in my life. I felt like I had to do it, that it couldn't wait.[40]

> When I got back from this, I had decided I'd better change. I was very repentant.[41]

These last two statements describe almost exactly the Mormon view of repentance: a sense of sorrow and even shame for one's acts—not the paralyzing kind of shame that depresses and drags down one's self-confidence, but one which provides a jolt of energy to do much better from now on.

Note that this repentance is often prompted by questions from the being of light. Dr. Moody tells of one man who stated that the being asked him "whether he had done the things he did *because* he loved others, that is, from the *motivation* of love. At this point, one might say, a kind of judgment took place, for in this state of heightened awareness, when people saw any selfish acts which they had done they felt extremely repentant. Likewise, when gazing upon those events in which they had shown love and kindness they felt satisfaction."[42]

Note that judgment in this context clearly takes a person's personality and disposition into account as well as their behavior. Consider the following contrasting accounts of life review:

> I would describe [the life review] as a long series of feelings based on numerous actions in my life. The difference was that not only did I experience the feelings again, but I had some sort of empathetic sense of the feelings of those around me who were affected by my actions. In other words, I also felt what others felt about my life. . . I had been somewhat of a troublemaker. I sometimes hurt other children when smaller and had taken to drug and alcohol abuse, stealing, crazy driving, bad grades, vandalism, cruelty to my sister, cruelty to animals—the list goes on and on. All of these actions were relived in

---

38. See the rather lengthy accounts in Greyson, *After*, 36–44.
39. Moody, *Life after Life*, 168.
40. Moody, *Life after Life*, 169.
41. Moody, *Life after Life*, 169.
42. Moody, *Life after Life*, 169.

a nutshell, with the associated feelings of both myself and the parties involved
. . . This feeling left me with a sense of having unfinished business in life.[43]

God asked if I was happy with how things went, and I said yes. He asked me
how I felt, and I said I was a little nervous. He explained that this was because
all my life I felt this way and it is sort of why I didn't handle [life] properly. I
was also told that if the bad outweighed the good you [are] left with the bad.
so if you were truly an awful person, you'd be feeling quite awful for your time
there. Alternately, if you have given out love and goodness and been kind and
caring, you'd be up there feeling sheer bliss and good. I was feeling no extreme
sense of badness, for lack of a better word. I was feeling happy, light, carefree
but a little nervous inside, like I'd been over a hill too fast or ridden on a roller-
coaster. but all in all, the balance seemed fair and just enough for what I had
just been shown. Mostly good stuff had outweighed the bad.[44]

As we discussed in chapter 6, the Latter-day Saint God, unlike the image of the
medieval God, which continues to influence many people's conceptions of God today,
is not a being that has the slightest interest in condemning any of his children. He is
willing and eager to exalt all of us, so long as they have demonstrated a willingness and
a desire to make the necessary effort to live a celestial lifestyle. If they are not willing
to live such a life, he knows they will be better off somewhere else, where they will feel
more comfortable, just as the amateur violin player would be embarrassed if she tried
to keep up with the professionals of the New York Philharmonic.

D&C 88:32 states that those who are not eligible to enter celestial glory shall
"enjoy that which they are willing to receive, because they were not willing to enjoy
that which they might have received."

The eagerness to condemn others for their real or perceived shortcomings is very
much a human trait, not a divine one, as Joseph Smith observed:

While one portion of the human race is judging and condemning the other
without mercy, the Great Parent of the universe looks upon the whole of the
human family with a fatherly care and paternal regard; He views them as His
offspring, and without any of those contracted feelings that influence the children of men, causes 'His sun to rise on the evil and on the good, and sendeth
rain on the just and on the unjust.'[45]

It is one evidence that men are unacquainted with the principles of godliness
to behold the contraction of affectionate feelings and lack of charity in the
world. The power and glory of godliness is spread out on a broad principle to
throw out the mantle of charity. God does not look on sin with the least degree
of allowance, but when men have sinned, there must be allowance made for

43. Long, *Evidence*, 108–9.

44. Long, *Evidence*, 112.

45. *TPJS* 218.

them . . . the nearer we get to our heavenly Father, the more we are disposed to look with compassion on perishing souls; we feel that we want to take them upon our shoulders, and cast their sins behind our backs . . . If you would have God have mercy on you, have mercy on one another.[46]

7) A SENSE OF PURPOSE IN ONE'S LIFE

As we have discussed at great length, a sense of purpose and direction in life is crucial to one's happiness—even if one is not quite sure what that purpose is. This is fundamental to LDS thinking, and it is also a common viewpoint of those who have experienced NDEs, as the following quotations show.

> I realize now that our time here is relatively short, and it makes me want to live my life to the fullest. I found that among the few things that people can take with them when they die, love is probably the most important. The only things left after one leaves his or her body are energy, love, personality, and knowledge. It seems like such a waste of precious time to become caught up in materialistic modes of thinking.[47]

> I wish I did [know what I am supposed to do with my life]. There is a feeling in me that somehow I am to help others.[48]

Many of those having undergone an NDE are extremely frustrated over the fact that they know they are supposed to accomplish something with their remaining life, but they cannot remember what it is. A few remember that they were told they would forget exact knowledge of their mission.[49]

8) SUFFERING IN LIFE HAS MEANING AND VALUE

Some people report having learned that there is a reason for everything that happens to us in this life, including the suffering we experience. A Jewish woman related speaking to the being of light about seeming injustices in this life:

> I'm sure that I asked the question that had been plaguing me since childhood about the sufferings of my people. I do remember this: there was a reason for *everything* that happened, no matter how awful it appeared in the physical realm. And within myself, as I was given the answer, my own awakening mind now responded in the same manner: "Of course," I would think, "I already know that. How could I ever have forgotten!" Indeed it appears that all that

46. *TPJS* 240–41.
47. Ring, *Light*, 17.
48. Gibson, *Fingerprints*, 48.
49. Gibson, *Fingerprints*, 68.

happens is for a purpose, and that purpose is already known to our eternal self.[50]

When I came back into my body I knew that everything had its place, its purpose, and there was a reason for everything. Even poor children that die of cancer at a young age, somebody's life that is taken; everything has a reason. But you don't know that until you are on the other side.[51]

Whatever we go through individually—or collectively as a nation and a world—it is all for a common . . . goal. That goal is to learn and improve so as to move closer to the source of the light of love . . . It's like a preschool preparing you for another school—and that's what life is. I don't know when those schools end, maybe never. And that's exciting to me . . . The experience of life is so profound and has so much more to offer than we normally think. Pain and suffering for example are an important part of life. One day of life is worth all the pain and suffering that we might have to go through. My death experience—if that's what it was—doesn't hold a candle to how I now value and get joy from each day.[52]

"Fear is a blessing . . . Fear is the key to unfolding what is within us. If we didn't have fear there would be nothing to propel us into the next adventure or experience. Without fear we would not be alert to the full measure of the experiences we pass through. Those experiences are vital for our growth. Tears and grief are what carve the opening for us to have joy and love. If we didn't have a cavity carved by fear, pain, and grief, we wouldn't be able to fully appreciate the love and joy that are within our reach."

"What about injury and illness?"

"That's a difficult question, because I don't like suffering. When I was suffering the most, though, I actually grew closer to those I loved than when I was well. Sometimes trauma and illness occur in order to help those who associate with the one having the trauma. We tend to feel that we come here and live our lives for ourselves—we are very selfish. In my life's review I understood that my life was lived, not just for me, but for others that I interacted with."[53]

As I argued in chapter 5, even severe cases of suffering can have beneficial aspects. An LDS experiencer who suffered from cystic fibrosis had a conversation with a voice and asked why he had died so young.

The voice answered: "You are here because you have earned the right to be here based on what you did on earth. The pain you have suffered qualifies you

50. Top and Top, *Glimpses*, 252.

51. Gibson, *Fingerprints*, 72.

52. Gibson, *Fingerprints*, 49.

53. Gibson, *Fingerprints*, 174.

to be here. You have suffered as much pain in 37 years as a normal person might have suffered in 87 years."

I asked: "It's pain that gets me here?" and the answer was yes.

This still puzzled me so I asked. "But why was it necessary for me to suffer so? . . .

He said to me, "You chose your disease and the amount of pain you would be willing to suffer before this life—when you were in a premortal state. It was your choice."[54]

9) QUEST FOR KNOWLEDGE—BOTH HERE AND IN THE HEREAFTER

Latter-day Saints often assert that the "only things that you can take with you from this life are the relationships you have made and the knowledge you have gained." In other words, nothing material goes with you, only knowledge, family, and friendships. In D&C 130:19–20 it says: "Whatever principle of intelligence we attain unto in this life, it will rise with us in the resurrection. And if a person gains more knowledge and intelligence in this life through his diligence and obedience than another, he will have so much the advantage in the world to come." As I have emphasized elsewhere in this book, there is great emphasis in Mormonism on the acquisition of knowledge. Joseph Smith also wrote, "It is impossible for a man to be saved in ignorance,"[55] and "the glory of God is intelligence, or in other words, light and truth."[56] This has reference to all types of knowledge, but particularly the knowledge of God and divine things.

A common theme in many NDEs is the almost overwhelming absorption of knowledge in the spirit world.

"My mind felt like a sponge, growing and expanding in size with each addition. The knowledge came in single words and in whole idea blocks. I just seemed to understand everything as it was being soaked up or absorbed. . . It was as if I had known already but forgotten or mislaid it, as if it were waiting here for me to pick up on my way by."[57]

All of a sudden [the knowledge] was just there, wham! I am not able now to retell and explain what I gained, but I have this memory that all of a sudden things made perfect sense and were clear, and I understood how everything came together in the universe, the reason for things being the way they are. And somehow math and geometry were seminal to understanding all of this puzzle. It became so clear, and I wondered how I could not have understood it

54. Gibson, *Fingerprints*, 176–77.
55. D&C 131:6.
56. D&C 93:36.
57. Ring, *Lessons*, 232.

before—it was now so simple, so beautiful. I was absorbing this knowledge as I floated towards the light.[58]

One experiencer emphasized the importance of learning as much as we can in this life even though our capacity for learning will be much greater on the other side:

You still want to seek knowledge even after you come back here [to earth life] . . . It's not silly to try to get the answers here. I sort of felt that it was part of our purpose . . . but that it wasn't just for one person, but that it was to be used for all mankind. We're always reaching out to help others with what we know.[59]

The following statement is from a man who prior to his NDE had little interest in learning or patience with scholars and those who devoted themselves to learning:

While the doctors were saying I was dead, this person I was with, this light, the Christ, showed me a dimension of knowledge, I'll call it . . . Now that was a humbling experience for me. You can say I don't scorn professors anymore. Knowledge is important. I read everything I can get my hands on now . . . It's not that I regret taking the path I did in life, but I'm glad that I have time now for learning. History, science, literature. I'm interested in it all. My wife fusses at me about my books in our room. Some of it helps me understand my experience better . . . All of it does, in one way or another, because, as I say, when you have one of these experiences, you see that everything is connected.[60]

This theme of the unity or connectedness of all knowledge is a theme that is stressed in both Mormonism and NDE reports. Dr. Ritchie summarized one of the main things that he learned from his experiences:

God wants us to search for truth in every area of life until we find it. This is not only true on the spiritual level but also in the mental and physical levels. Any time we learn a new truth in any field we are drawing close to God.[61]

By comparison, Joseph Smith stated that

When you climb up a ladder, you must begin at the bottom, and ascend step by step, until you arrive at the top; and so it is with the principles of the gospel—you must begin at the first, and go on until you learn all the principles of exaltation. But it will be a great while after you have passed through the veil before you will have learned them. It is not all to be comprehended in this world; it will be a great work to learn our salvation and exaltation even beyond the grave.[62]

58. Gibson, *Fingerprints*, 54.
59. Moody, *Life after Life*, 149.
60. Moody, *Light Beyond*, 44–5.
61. Quoted in Top and Top, *Glimpses Beyond*, 265.
62. *HOTC* 6:306–7.

Another experiencer stated:

> I came back feeling that I had to learn, that I had to absorb like a sponge as
> much as I could. It was as though I was charged with a duty to learn . . . when I
> was floating through the tunnel, I understood that it was important and duti-
> ful that I learn all that I could. I no longer could afford to be a superficial
> teenager. As a matter of fact, before my NDE, I was not all that excited about
> school. Within a few years of my NDE, I became, and remained, a 4.0 student.
> From that point on, I have been thirsty to read and learn about a variety of
> subjects.[63]

10) "REAL LIFE" IS BUT A PALE REFLECTION OF THE TRUE REALITY

Over 95 percent of respondents in a survey stated that they believed that their experience was entirely real. One woman said:

> This [world] is the dream world, the other one is the real world.[64]

Another woman:

> I was more alive in that realm than I am talking to you, here, now. Another
> way to relate to it is . . . like you and I are more awake now than when we are
> asleep at night. That's how much more aware I was in the other realm.[65]

> The experience of death has been the most real and physical experience of my
> life, and the world here [after his return] felt cold and heavy and unreal for
> some time afterward.[66]

One of many reasons for this sense of hyperreality, it seems, is the remarkable
vividness of everything.

> The colors on the other side are the brightest colors; our most fluorescent col-
> ors on this earth are muddy [compared] to the brightness and vividness of the
> colors that are in Heaven.[67]

> I was taken to a beautiful meadow with the most gorgeous plant life and colors
> so vibrant that I've never seen anywhere; it was amazing![68]

63. Gibson, *Fingerprints*, 67.

64. Gibson, *Fingerprints*, 71.

65. Gibson, *Fingerprints*, 72.

66. Long, *Evidence*, 54.

67. Long, *Evidence*, 58.

68. Long, *Evidence*, 59.

> What I saw was too beautiful for words: I was looking at a magnificent land-scape full of flowers and plants that I couldn't actually name. It all looked hundreds of miles away. And yet I could see everything in detail—even without glasses, although in real life I have bad eyesight. It was both far away and close. Exceptionally beautiful. The best way to describe it would be: a heavenly sight. I arrived in a royal realm, or at least that's what it smelled like. The atmosphere, insofar as you could call it that, was divine, a flowery, sweet-smelling environment, which was completely three-dimensional and about a thousand times more beautiful than my favorite holiday destination in spring.[69]

Plato, in the famous Allegory of the Cave in his *Republic*, described so-called real life as but a series of shadows cast by a fire onto the wall of a cave. Human beings, being confined and chained, as it were, to view only the cave wall, are unable to view the fire or the solid objects behind them that create the shadows, and so are convinced that the shadows themselves constitute reality. In truth, of course, they are no more real than a reflection of a solid object in a mirror. However, if one man, freed from his chains, were to turn and see the fire behind him, he would at first be blinded by the light, and want to revert to the world of shadows. And if he were then forced out of the cave into the sunlight, he would find the view even more painful until his eyes became adjusted to the new reality. Later, however, if he were to return to the dark cave, he would have trouble seeing anything, and if he attempted to explain to the others the new reality he had perceived, they would reject the true reality as absurd. Since the man who had been outside and seen the sun would be unable to see much in the darkness of the cave, the cave-dwellers would conclude that his vision had been destroyed and that any further attempt to "liberate" them from the cave was evil and wrong. Indeed, if anyone attempted to drag them out of the cave, they would likely attack and kill him.

Joseph Smith was no abstract philosopher, but implicit in his view of the world was that the eternal world of light, angels, and deity was more real than the dark reality that most men live in. The "fullness of the gospel" that he taught was "a light [which] shall break forth among them that sit in darkness . . . But [men shall] receive it not; for they perceive not the light, and they turn their hearts from me because of the precepts of men."[70] Unlike Plato, he did not denigrate the physical world, which was specifically designed by God for our benefit. But he clearly viewed it as a temporary world, of less permanence, than the other world. Heaven, in other words, is our true home.

We have already discussed how the LDS notion of eternity suggests that earthly life is a relatively small blip in our eternal existence, while eternity in the presence of God is our real life. Similarly, one man who experienced an NDE stated: "It was like

---

69. Van Lommel, *Consciousness Beyond Life*, 32.

70. D&C 45:28–29.

eternity. It's like I was always there and I will always be there, and that my existence on earth was just a brief instant."[71]

71. Ring, *Heading toward Omega*, 54.

Bibliography

"Advertising and Promotion of Alcohol and Tobacco Products to Youth." http:// www.apha.org/policies-and-advocacy/public-health-policy-statements/policy- database/2014/07/29/10/58/advertising-and-promotion-of-alcohol-and-tobacco- products-to-youth.

Albrecht, Stan L., and Tim B. Heaton. "Secularization, Higher Education, and Religiosity." In *Latter-day Saint Social Life: Social Research on the LDS Church and its Members*, edited by James T. Duke, 293–314. Provo, UT: Religious Studies Center, Brigham Young University, 1998.

Alcorn, Randy. *Heaven: A Comprehensive Guide to Everything the Bible Says about Our Eternal Home*. Carol Stream, IL: Tyndale House, 2004.

Alexander, Eben. *Proof of Heaven: A Neurosurgeon's Journey into the Afterlife*. New York: Simon and Schuster, 2012.

Alexander, Thomas G. *Mormonism in Transition: A History of the Latter-day Saints, 1890– 1930*. 3rd ed. Salt Lake City: Greg Kofford, 2012.

Allen, James B., and Glen M. Leonard. *The Story of the Latter-day Saints*. Salt Lake City: Deseret, 1976.

Allison, Gregg R. *Historical Theology: An Introduction to Christian Doctrine*. Grand Rapids: Zondervan, 2011.

Anderson, Richard Lloyd. *Investigating the Book of Mormon Witnesses*. Salt Lake City: Deseret, 1981.

———. "Personal Writings of the Book of Mormon Witnesses." In *Book of Mormon Authorship Revisited: The Evidence for Ancient Origins*, edited by Noel B. Reynolds, 39–60. Provo, UT: Foundation for Ancient Research and Mormon Studies, 1997.

Arrington, Leonard J. *Brigham Young: American Moses*. Chicago: University of Illinois Press, 1985.

———. "An Economic Interpretation of the Word of Wisdom." *BYU Studies Quarterly* 1:1 (1959) 37–49.

Arrington, Leonard J. "James Gordon Bennett's 1831 Report on 'The Mormonites.'" *BYU Studies* 10:3 (1970) 1–10.

Arrington, Leonard J., and Davis Bitton. *The Mormon Experience*. New York: Knopf, 1979.

"As It Turns Out We Really Are All Starstuff." https://www.universetoday.com/119541/as-it- turns-out-we-really-are-all-starstuff/.

Ash, Michael R. *Shaken Faith Syndrome: Strengthening One's Testimony in the Face of Criticism and Doubt*. 2nd ed. Redding, CA: Foundation for Apologetic Information and Research, 2013.

Bibliography

Athanasius, *On the Incarnation of the Word*. https://ccel.org/ccel/athanasius/incarnation/incarnation.ix.html.

Augustine, *Confessions*. Tranlated by R.S. Pine-Coffin. Harmondsworth: Penguin, 1961.

Aurelius, Marcus. *Meditations*. Translated by Robin Hard. Oxford: Oxford University Press, 2011.

Bachman, Danel, and Ronald K. Esplin. "Plural Marriage." In *Encyclopedia of Mormonism*. https://eom.byu.edu/index.php/Plural_Marriage.

Backman, Milton V., Jr. *Joseph Smith's First Vision: Confirming Evidences and Contemporary Accounts*. 2d ed., revised and enlarged. Salt Lake City: Bookcraft, 1980.

Baggini, Julian. *What's It All About?: Philosophy and the Meaning of Life*. London: Granta, 2004.

Baier, Kurt. "The Meaning of Life." In Klemke, *Meaning of Life*, 101–32. New York and Oxford: Oxford University Press, 2000.

Bailey, Lee W., and Jenny Yates, *The Near-Death Experience: A Reader*. New York: Routledge, 1996.

Barbash, Fred. "Siberian youth hangs over balcony to impress girl, falls 23 floors onto car—and lives." *Washington Post*, September 28, 2016. https://www.washingtonpost.com/news/morning-mix/wp/2016/09/28/siberian-youth-hangs-over-balcony-to-impress-girl-falls-23-floors-onto-car-and-lives/.

Bar-Ilan, M. "The Hand of God: A Chapter in Rabbinic Anthropomorphism." In *Rashi 1040–1990: Hommage à Ephraim E. Urbach, Congrès européen des études juives*, edited by G. Sed-Rajna, 321–35. Paris: CERF, 1993.

Barnes, Michael Horace. *The Enduring Quest for Meaning: Humans, Mystery, and the Story of Religion*. Winona, MN: Anselm Academic, 2015.

Baugh, Alexander L. "Joseph Smith's Athletic Nature." In *Joseph Smith: The Prophet, The Man*, edited by Susan Easton Black and Charles D. Tate Jr., 137–50. Provo, UT: Religious Studies Center, Brigham Young University, 1993.

Beauregard, Mario, and Denyse O'Leary. *The Spiritual Brain: A Neuroscientist's Case for the Existence of the Soul*. New York: HarperCollins, 2007.

Benedict, Jeff. *The Mormon Way of Doing Business*. New York: Warner Business, 2007.

Bennett, Bob. *Leap of Faith: Confronting the Origins of the Book of Mormon*. Salt Lake City: Deseret, 2009.

Bennett, James Gordon. "The Mormons—a Leaf From Joe Smith." *Times and Seasons* 3:13 (May 2, 1842). https://www.josephsmithpapers.org/transcript/times-and-seasons-2-may-1842.

Berger, Peter. *The Sacred Canopy: Elements of a Sociological Theory of Religion*. New York: Anchor, 1990.

Bettenson, Henry, ed. *The Early Christian Fathers: A Selection from the Writings of the Fathers from St. Clement of Rome to St. Athanasius*. Oxford: Oxford University Press, 1956.

Bickmore, Barry R. "Mormonism in the Early Jewish Christian Milieu." http://www.fairmormon.org/perspectives/fair-conferences/1999-fair-conference/1999-ormonism-in-the-early-jewish-christian-milieu.

Biskind, Peter. "Reconstructing Woody." *Vanity Fair*, December 2005. http://www.vanityfair.com/culture/features/2005/12/woodyallen200512.

Black, Jeremy A., et al., eds. *The Literature of Ancient Sumer*. Oxford: Oxford University Press, 2004.

Blackmore, Susan. *Dying to Live*. Amherst, NY: Prometheus, 1993.

Blomberg, Craig L. "Is Mormonism Christian?" In *The New Mormon Challenge*, edited by Francis J. Beckwith, et al., 315–33. Grand Rapids: Zondervan, 2002.

Bloom, Harold. *The American Religion: The Emergence of the Post-Christian Nation*. New York: Simon and Schuster, 1992.

Bogle, Kathleen. *Hooking Up: Sex, Dating and Relationships on Campus*. New York: New York University Press, 2008.

Bostock, Gerald. "The Sources of Origen's Doctrine of Pre-Existence." In *Origeniana Quarta: Die Referate des 4. Internationalen Origenskongresses*, edited by Lothar Lies, 259–64. Innsbruck: Tyrolia, 1987.

Boudry, Maarten, and Massimo Pigliucci, eds. *Science Unlimited?: The Challenges of Scientism*. Chicago: University of Chicago Press, 2018.

Bowman, Matthew. *The Mormon People: The Making of an American Faith*. New York: Random House, 2012.

"A Brief Introduction." https://www.skeptic.com/about_us/.

Brodie, Fawn. *No Man Knows My History*. New York: Knopf, 1945.

Brown, Peter. *The World of Late Antiquity, AD 150–750*. London: Thames and Hudson, 1971.

Brown, Samuel Morris. *In Heaven as It Is on Earth: Joseph Smith and the Early Mormon Conquest of Death*. New York: Oxford University Press, 2012.

Burnyeat, M. F. "Other Lives." *London Review of Books* 29:4 (February 22, 2007). https://www.lrb.co.uk/the-paper/v29/no4/m.f.-burnyeat/other-lives.

Bury, J. B., and Russell Meiggs. *A History of Greece to the Death of Alexander the Great*. 4th ed. New York: St. Martin's, 1975.

Bush, Lester E., Jr. "The Word of Wisdom in Early Nineteenth-Century Perspective." *Dialogue: A Journal of Mormon Thought* 14:3 (Autumn, 1981) 46–65.

Bushman, Claudia. *Contemporary Mormonism: Latter-day Saints in Modern America*. Westport, CT: Praeger, 2006.

Bushman, Richard Lyman. *Joseph Smith and the Beginnings of Mormonism*. Urbana: University of Illinois Press, 1984.

———. *Rough Stone Rolling*. New York: Knopf, 2005.

Buttrick, George Arthur, ed. *The Interpreter's Bible*. 12 vols. New York: Abingdon, 1952.

Calaprice, Alice, ed. *The Ultimate Quotable Einstein*. Princeton, NJ: Princeton University Press, 2011.

Carroll, Sean. "How Did the Universe Start?" *Discover*, April 27, 2007. http://blogs.discovermagazine.com/cosmicvariance/2007/04/27/how-did-the-universe-start/#.V40jFvkrKE0.

Catalano, Shannan, et al. "Female Victims of Violence." Bureau of Justice Statistics, Selecting Findings, September 2009. http://www.bjs.gov/content/pub/pdf/fvv.pdf.

Catechism of the Catholic Church. New York: Doubleday, 1995.

Cavett, Dick. "Enough with the Agony, Already." *New York Times*, September 30, 2011. https://opinionator.blogs.nytimes.com/2011/09/30/enough-with-the-agony-already/.

Cannon, George Q. *Joseph the Prophet*. American Fork, UT: Covenant Communications, 2005.

Chadwick, Jeffrey R. "Lehi's House at Jerusalem and the Land of His Inheritance." In *Glimpses of Lehi's Jerusalem*, edited by John W. Welch, et al., 81–130. Provo, UT: Foundation for Ancient Research and Mormon Studies, 2004.

Charlesworth, James H. *The Old Testament Pseudepigrapha*. 2 vols. New York: Doubleday, 1983.

Cherbonnier, E. LaB. "The Logic of Biblical Anthropomorphism." *Harvard Theological Review* 55:3 (July 1962) 187–206.

Church History in the Fullness of Times: The History of the Church of Jesus Christ of Latter-day Saints. 2nd ed. Salt Lake City: Church of Jesus Christ of Latter-day Saints, 2000.

Collins, Francis S., and Karl Giberson. *The Language of Science and Faith*. Downers Grove, IL: InterVarsity, 2011.

"Common Sense Is Nothing More than a Deposit of Prejudices Laid Down in the Mind before Age Eighteen." https://quoteinvestigator.com/2014/04/29/common-sense/.

Conkin, Paul, and Roland D. Stromberg. *Heritage and Challenge: The History and Theory of History*. Arlington Heights, IL: Forum, 1989.

Coogan, Michael D., ed. *The New Oxford Annotated Bible*. 3rd ed. New York: Oxford University Press, 2001.

Cook, Lyndon W. *David Whitmer Interviews: A Restoration Witness*. N.p.: Grandin, 1991.

Cooper, John M. *Plato: Complete Works*. Indianapolis: Hackett, 1997.

Couliano, I. P. *Out of This World: Otherworldly Journeys from Gilgamesh to Albert Einstein*. Boston: Shambhala, 1991.

Crawley, Peter L. *The Essential Parley P. Pratt*. Salt Lake City: Signature, 1990. Available at http://signaturebookslibrary.org/essential-parley-p-pratt/.

Crowther, Duane S. *Life Everlasting*. Salt Lake City: Bookcraft, 1967.

Csikszentmihalyi, Mihaly. *Flow: The Psychology of Optimal Experience*. New York: Harper, 1990.

Dahood, Mitchell. *Psalms 1:1–50*. Garden City: Doubleday, 1966.

Daniélou, Jean. *The Theology of Jewish Christianity*. Philadelphia: Westminster, 1964.

Davies, Douglas J. *The Mormon Culture of Salvation*. New York: Routledge, 2000.

Davies, Paul. *The Mind of God*. New York: Simon and Schuster, 1992.

———. *Superforce: The Search for a Grand Unified Theory of Nature*. New York: Simon and Schuster, 1984.

Davis, Stephen T. *Logic and the Nature of God*. London: Macmillan, 1983.

Dawkins, Richard. *The God Delusion*. New York: Houghton Mifflin, 2008.

Daynes, Kathryn M. *More Wives Than One: Transformation of the Mormon Marriage System, 1840–1910*. Urbana: University of Illinois Press, 2008.

Dickens, Charles. "In the Name of the Prophet—Smith!" *Household Words* 3 (July 19, 1851) 385. http://www.archive.org/stream/householdwords03dickmiss#page/385/mode/1up.

Dines, Gail. *Pornland: How Porn Has Hijacked Our Sexuality*. Boston: Beacon, 2010.

The Doctrine and Covenants of the Church of Jesus Christ of Latter-day Saints. Salt Lake City: Church of Jesus Christ of Latter-day Saints, 1981.

Doyle, Arthur Conan. "The Sign of Four." In *Sherlock Holmes: The Complete Novels and Stories*, 1:121–236. New York: Bantam Classics, 1986.

Drake, H. A. *Constantine and the Bishops: The Politics of Intolerance*. Baltimore: Johns Hopkins University Press, 2000.

Dunn, Scott C. "Automaticity and the Dictation of the Book of Mormon." In *American Apocrypha: Essays on the Book of Mormon*, edited by Dan Vogel and Brent Lee Metcalf, 17–46. Salt Lake City: Signature, 2002.

Durant, Will. *The Reformation: A History of European Civilization from Wyclif to Calvin, 1300–1564*. New York: Simon and Schuster, 1957.

Dyson, Freeman. "How We Know." *New York Review of Books* 58:4 (March 10, 2011).

Edelstein, David. "Mamma Mia! Woody Loves Soon-Yi." *New York Magazine* March 30, 2012. http://nymag.com/news/features/scandals/woody-allen-soon-yi-2012-4/.

Edwards, Jonathan. *A Dissertation Concerning the End for Which God Created the World.* https://www.monergism.com/dissertation-concerning-end-which-god-created-world-jonathan-edwards.

———. *Sinners in the Hand of an Angry God.* http://www.jonathan-edwards.org/Sinners.pdf.

Edwards, Mark Julian. *Origen against Plato.* Burlington, VT: Ashgate, 2002.

Ehat, Andrew F., and Lyndon W. Cook, eds. *The Words of Joseph Smith.* Provo, UT: Religious Studies Center, Brigham Young University, 1980.

Ehrman, Bart D. *God's Problem: How the Bible Fails to Answer Our Most Important Question—Why We Suffer.* New York: Harper, 2009.

———. *How Jesus Became God: The Exaltation of a Jewish Preacher from Galilee.* New York: HarperCollins, 2014.

———. *Misquoting Jesus: The Story Behind Who Changed the Bible and Why.* New York: HarperCollins, 2005.

Einstein, Albert. "Autobiographical Notes." In *Albert Einstein: Philosopher-Scientist*, edited by P. A. Schilpp, 1–95. Evanston, IL: Harper, 1949.

———. *The World as I See It.* Translated by Alan Harris. New York: Wisdom Library, n.d.

Eliade, Mircea. *The Myth of the Eternal Return or, Cosmos and History.* Translated by Willard Trask. 1954. Reprint, Princeton, NJ: Princeton University Press, 1971.

Emba, Christine. *Rethinking Sex: A Provocation.* New York: Sentinel, 2022.

Enstrom, James E. "Health Practices and Cancer Mortality among Active California Mormons." In *Latter-day Saint Social Life: Social Research on the LDS Church and Its Members*, edited by James T. Duke, 441–60. Provo, UT: Religious Studies Center, Brigham Young University, 1998.

Enstrom, James E., and Lester Breslow. "Lifestyle and Reduced Mortality among Active California Mormons, 1980–2004." *Preventive Medicine* 46 (2008) 133–36. https://www.sciencedirect.com/science/article/abs/pii/S0091743507003258.

Erickson, Millard J. *Christian Theology.* 3rd ed. Grand Rapids: Baker, 2013.

Eusebius. *The History of the Church.* Translated by G. A. Williamson. New York, Penguin, 1965.

Fackre, Gabriel et al. *What About Those Who Have Never Heard?: Three Views on the Destiny of the Unevangelized.* Downers Grove, IL: IVP Academic, 1995.

"The Family—a Proclamation." https://www.churchofjesuschrist.org/bc/content/shared/content/english/pdf/36035_000_24_family.pdf.

Ferris, Timothy. *Coming of Age in the Milky Way.* New York: Harper Collins, 2003.

Feynman, Richard. *The Character of Physical Law.* Boston: MIT Press, 1965.

Fine, Gail. "Does Socrates Claim to Know that He Knows Nothing?" *Oxford Studies in Ancient Philosophy* 35 (2008), 49–88.

Finley, Thomas J. "Does the Book of Mormon Reflect an Ancient Near Eastern Background?" In *The New Mormon Challenge*, edited by Francis J. Beckwith et al., 315–33. Grand Rapids: Zondervan, 2002.

Fisher, Helen. *Why We Love: The Nature and Chemistry of Romantic Love.* New York: Holt, 2004.

Flew, Anthony. *There Is a God: How the World's Most Notorious Atheist Changed His Mind.* New York: Harper, 2007.

Fluhman, J. Spencer. *"A Peculiar People": Anti-Mormonism and the Making of Religion in Nineteenth-Century America*. Chapel Hill: University of North Carolina Press, 2012.

Foster, Douglas, et al., eds. *The Encyclopedia of the Stone-Campbell Movement*. Grand Rapids: Eerdmans, 2004.

Fox, Mark. *Religion, Spirituality and the Near-Death Experience*. New York: Routledge, 2003.

Frankl, Viktor E. *Man's Search for Meaning*. Boston: Beacon, 2006.

Freedman, David H. "Lies, Damned Lies, and Medical Science," *The Atlantic*, November 2010.

Freitas, Donna. *The End of Sex*. New York: Basic Books, 2013.

Freud, Sigmund. *New Introductory Lectures on Psychoanalysis*. Translated by J. Stracey. New York: Norton, n.d..

Gardner, Brant A. *The Book of Mormon as History*. Salt Lake City: Greg Kofford, 2015.

Gaustad, Edwin S. *Liberty of Conscience: Roger Williams in America*. Grand Rapids: Eerdmans 1991.

Geirland, John. "Go with the Flow." *Wired*, September 1, 1996. https://www.wired.com/1996/09/czik/.

George, Timothy. *Theology of the Reformers*. Rev. ed. Nashville: Broadman and Holman, 2013.

Gibson, Arvin S. *Fingerprints of God: Evidences from Near-Death Studies, Scientific Research on Creation, and Mormon Theology*. Bountiful, UT: Horizon, 1999.

Gilpin, W. Clark. *The Millenarian Piety of Roger Williams*. Chicago: University of Chicago Press, 1979.

Givens, Terryl L. *By the Hand of Mormon: The American Scripture that Launched a New World Religion*. New York: Oxford University Press, 2002.

———. *Feeding the Flock: The Foundations of Mormon Thought: Church and Praxis*. New York: Oxford University Press, 2017.

———. *When Souls Had Wings*. New York: Oxford University Press, 2010.

———. *Wrestling the Angel: The Foundations of Mormon Thought: Cosmos, God, Humanity*. New York: Oxford University Press, 2015.

Givens, Terryl, and Fiona Givens. *The God Who Weeps: How Mormonism Makes Sense of Life*. Salt Lake City: Deseret, 2014.

Givens, Terryl, and Matthew J. Grow. *Parley P. Pratt: The Apostle Paul of Mormonism*. New York: Oxford University Press, 2011.

Gleiser, Marcelo. *The Island of Knowledge: The Limits of Science and the Search for Meaning*. New York: Basic Books, 2014.

Goode, Erica. "When Women Find Love Is Fatal." *New York Times*, February 15, 2000. https://www.nytimes.com/2000/02/15/science/when-women-find-love-is-fatal.html.

Gottstein, Alon Goshen. "The Body as Image of God in Rabbinic Literature." *Harvard Theological Review* 87 (1994) 171–95.

Graham, Franklin. *Billy Graham in Quotes*. Nashville: Thomas Nelson, 2011.

Grant, Adam. "The #1 Feature of a Meaningless Job," *Huffington Post*, January 30, 2014. http://www.huffingtonpost.com/adam-grant/the-1-feature-of-a-meanin_b_4691464.html.

———. "Three Lies about Meaningful Work." *Huffington Post*, May 6, 2016. https://www.huffingtonpost.com/adam-grant/three-lies-about-meaningful-work_b_7205036.html.

Grant, Robert M. *The Early Christian Doctrine of God*. Charlottesville: University of Virginia Press, 1966.

———. *Gods and the One God*. Philadelphia: Westminster, 1986.

———. *Second-Century Christianity: A Collection of Fragments*. London: SPCK, 1946.

Greene, Brian. *The Fabric of the Cosmos: Space, Time, and the Texture of Reality*. New York: Vintage, 2004.

Greyson, Bruce. *After: A Doctor Explores What Near-Death Experiences Reveal about Life and Beyond*. New York: St. Martins, 2021.

Greyson, Bruce, et al. "Explanatory Models for Near-Death Experiences." In *Handbook of Near-Death Experiences*, edited by Janice Miner Holden et al., 213–34.

Greyson, Bruce, and Ian Stevenson. "The Phenomenology of Near-Death Experiences." *American Journal of Psychiatry* 137:10 (October 1980) 1193–96.

Gunkel, Herman. "Influence of Babylonian Mythology Upon the Creation Story." In *Creation in the Old Testament*, edited by Bernhard W. Anderson. Philadelphia and London: Fortress, 1984.

Guth, Alan. *The Inflationary Universe: The Quest for a New Theory of Cosmic Origins*. New York: Basic Books, 1998.

Hales, Laura Harris, ed. *A Reason for Faith: Navigating LDS Doctrine and Church History*. Salt Lake City: Deseret, 2016.

Hammarberg, Melvyn. *The Mormon Quest for Glory: The Religious World of the Latter-day Saints*. New York: Oxford University Press, 2013.

Hanegraaff, Hank. *Christianity in Crisis: 21st Century*. Nashville: Thomas Nelson, 2012.

Harline, Paula Kelly. *The Polygamous Wives Writing Club: From the Diaries of Mormon Pioneer Women*. New York: Oxford University Press, 2014.

Harnack, Adolf von. *What Is Christianity?* 2nd ed. New York: Putnam, 1908.

Harper, Steven C. *Joseph Smith's First Vision: A Guide to the Historical Accounts*. Salt Lake City: Deseret, 2012.

Harris, Sam. *The End of Faith: Religion, Terror, and the Future of Reason*. New York: Norton, 2005.

Hartley, L. P. *The Go-Between*. New York: New York Review Books, 2002.

Hartshorne, Charles. *Omnipotence and other Theological Mistakes*. Albany, NY: SUNY Press, 1984.

Hatch, Edwin. *The Influence of Greek Ideas and Usages upon the Christian Church*. London: Williams and Norgate, 1897.

Haws, J. B. *The Mormon Image in the American Mind*. New York: Oxford University Press, 2013.

Hick, John. "Jesus and the World Religions." In *The Myth of God Incarnate*, edited by John Hick. London: SCM, 1977.

Hill, Marvin S. *Quest for Refuge: The Mormon Flight from American Pluralism*. Salt Lake City: Signature, 1989.

Holan, Angie Drobnik. "The Mormon religion has 'a plan that will see the Constitution thrown out and replaced by a theocracy.'" *Politifact*, January 8, 2008. https://www.politifact.com/factchecks/2008/jan/08/freedom-defense-advocates/no-evidence-to-support-conspiracy-theory/.

Holden, Janice Miner, et al., eds. *The Handbook of Near-Death Experiences: Thirty Years of Investigation*. Westport, CT: Praeger, 2009.

Hood, Brian. "Caroline: Getting Dumped by Rory Was Necessary Evil." *Page Six*, March 25, 2015. https://pagesix.com/2015/03/25/caroline-getting-dumped-by-rory-was-necessary-evil/.

Hoskisson, Paul Y. "Different and Unique: The Word of Wisdom in the Historical, Cultural, and Social Settings of the 1830s." *Mormon Historical Studies* 10:2 (Fall 2009) 41–61.

House, Patrick. "What Is Elegance in Science?" *The New Yorker*, August 17, 2015. https://www.newyorker.com/tech/elements/what-is-elegance-in-science.

"How Porn Can Change the Brain." http://fightthenewdrug.org/porn-is-like-a-drug/.

Hoyle, Fred. "The Universe: Past and Present Reflections." *Annual Review of Astronomy and Astrophysics* 20 (1982) 1–36. http://www.annualreviews.org/doi/abs/10.1146/annurev.aa.20.090182.000245

Hughes, Richard T., and C. Leonard Allen. *Illusions of Innocence: Protestant Primitivism in America, 1630–1875*. Chicago: University of Chicago Press, 1988.

Hunter, Kevin. *Divine Messages for Humanity: Channeled Communications from the Other Side of Death, the Afterlife, the Ego, Prejudices, Prayer, and the Power of Love*. Los Angeles: Warrior of Light, 2013.

Hurtado, Larry. *One God, One Lord*. 3rd ed. London: Bloomsbury T. & T. Clark, 2015.

"If He Found that Flower in His Hand When He Awoke — Ay! And What Then?" https://quoteinvestigator.com/2017/05/29/flower/.

Ioannidis, John. *Wrong: Why Experts Keep Failing Us—and How to Know When Not to Trust Them*. New York: Little, Brown, 2010.

Jaeger, Werner. *Early Christianity and Greek Paideia*. Cambridge, MA: Harvard University Press, 1961.

Jensen, Chris. "Shine as the Sun: C.S. Lewis and the Doctrine of Deification." *In Pursuit of Truth: A Journal of Christian Scholarship*, October 31, 2007. http://www.cslewis.org/journal/shine-as-the-sun-cs-lewis-and-the-doctrine-of-deification/.

Jesse, Dean C., ed. *The Papers of Joseph Smith*, vol. 2: *Journal, 1832–1842*. Salt Lake City: Deseret, 1992.

———. *Personal Writings of Joseph Smith*. Rev. ed. Salt Lake City: Deseret, 2002.

Jones, Rufus. *Pathways to the Reality of God*. New York: Macmillan, 1936.

Journal of Discourses. 26 vols. London: Latter-day Saints Book Depot, 1853–1884. Reprint, Salt Lake City, UT: Bookcraft, 1966.

Joyce, George. "The Blessed Trinity." *Catholic Encyclopedia*, vol. 15. New York: Robert Appleton, 1912. http://www.newadvent.org/cathen/15047a.htm#IV.

Judd, Daniel K. "The Fortunate Fall of Adam and Eve." In *No Weapon Shall Prosper*, edited by Robert L. Millet, 297–328.

Kaku, Michio. *Hyperspace: A Scientific Odyssey through Parallel Universe, Time Warps, and the Tenth Dimension*. New York: Doubleday, 1995.

Kaufmann, Walter, ed. *The Portable Nietzsche*. New York: Viking Penguin, 1954.

Keating, Daniel. *Deification and Grace*. Naples, FL: Sapientia, 2007.

Kellehear, Allan. *Experiences Near Death: Beyond Medicine and Religion*. New York: Oxford University Press, 1996.

Keller, Helen. *My Religion*. New York: Swedenborg Foundation, 1960.

Keller, Timothy. *The Reason for God: Belief in an Age of Skepticism*. New York: Dutton, 2008.

Kierkegaard, Søren. *Repetition and Philosophical Crumbs*. Translated by M. G. Piety. New York: Oxford University Press, 2009.

King, Arthur Henry. *Arm the Children: Faith's Response to a Violent World*. Provo, UT: Brigham Young University Studies, 1998.

Kirkham, Francis W. *A New Witness for Christ in America*. 2 vols. 4th ed. Salt Lake City: Utah Printing, 1967.

Klemke, E. D., ed. *The Meaning of Life*. 2nd ed. Oxford: Oxford University Press, 2000.

Kreeft, Peter. *Making Sense out of Suffering*. Ann Arbor, MI: Servant, 1986.

Kruger, Michael J. *Christianity at the Crossroads: How the Second Century Shaped the Future of the Church*. Downers Grove, IL: InterVarsity, 2018.

Kushner, Harold. *When Bad Things Happen to Good People*. New York: Anchor, 2004.

Landau, Iddo. *Finding Meaning in an Imperfect World*. Oxford: Oxford University Press, 2016.

Lang, Randy. "Stress in Dentistry—It Could Kill You!" *Oral Health*, September 1, 2007. https://www.oralhealthgroup.com/features/stress-in-dentistry-it-could-kill-you/.

Lanza, Robert, and Bob Berman. *Biocentrism: How Life and Consciousness Are the Keys to Understanding the True Nature of the Universe*. Dallas: Ben Berman, 2009.

Lawrence, Gary C. *How Americans View Mormonism*. Orange, CA: Parameter Foundation, 2008.

"Lawyers and Depression." http://www.daveneefoundation.org/scholarship/lawyers-and-depression/.

Layton, Bentley. *The Gnostic Scriptures: Ancient Wisdom for the New Age*. New York: Doubleday, 1987.

Lectures on Faith. Salt Lake City: Bookcraft, n.d.

Leff, Gordon. "The Making of the Myth of the True Church." In *Heresy, Philosophy, and Religion*, by Gordon Leff, 1–15. New York: Routledge, 2002.

Lennox, John C. *God's Undertaker: Has Science Buried God?* Oxford: Lion Hudson, 2009.

Leonard, Glen M. *Nauvoo: A Place of Peace, a People of Promise*. Salt Lake City: Deseret, 2002.

Lereah, David. *Why the Real Estate Boom Will Not Bust—and How You Can Profit from It*. New York: Doubleday, 2005.

Leslie, John. *Universes*. New York: Routledge, 1989.

"Lesson 45: The Book of Mormon Is a Witness of the Resurrection of Jesus Christ (Easter)." *Primary 4: Book of Mormon* (1997) 160–62. https://www.lds.org/manual/primary-4/lesson-45?lang=eng.

Lewis, C. S. *Mere Christianity*. New York: Harper, 1952.

Lewis, Michael. *The Big Short: Inside the Doomsday Machine*. New York: Norton, 2010.

Litwa, M. David. *Becoming Divine: An Introduction to Deification in Western Culture*. Eugene, OR: Cascade, 2013.

———. *We Are Being Transformed: Deification in Paul's Soteriology*. Berlin: De Gruyter, 2012.

Long, Jeffrey, and Paul Perry. *Evidence of the Afterlife: The Science of Near-Death Experiences*. New York: Harper, 2011.

Lovejoy, Arthur. *The Great Chain of Being*. Cambridge, MA: Harvard University Press, 1936.

Lundahl, Craig R., and Harold Widdison. *The Eternal Journey: How Near-Death Experiences Illuminate Our Earthly Lives*. New York: Warner, 1997.

Luo, Michael. "Crucial Test for Romney in Speech on His Religion." *New York Times*, December 6, 2007. http://www.nytimes.com/2007/12/06/us/politics/06romney.html?_r=0.

Luther, Martin. *Word and Sacrament I. Luther's Works*, vol. 35. Philadelphia: Fortress, 1960.

Lyon, Joseph L., and Steven Nelson. "Mormon Health." *Dialogue: A Journal of Mormon Thought* 12:3 (Fall 1979) 84–96.

Mackay, Charles. *The Mormons or Latter-day Saints, with Memoirs of the Life and Death of Joseph Smith, the "American Mahomet."* London: Office of the National Illustrated Library, 1851.

Bibliography

Mackay, Michael Hubbard, and Gerrit J. Dirkmaat. *From Darkness unto Light: Joseph Smith's Translation and Publication of the Book of Mormon.* Provo, UT: Religious Studies Center, Brigham Young University, 2015.

Maltz, Wendy, and Larry Maltz. *The Porn Trap.* New York: Harper, 2008.

Mansfield, Stephen. *The Mormonizing of America: How the Mormon Religion Became a Dominant Force in Politics, Entertainment, and Pop Culture.* Brentwood, TN: Worthy, 2012.

Markschies, Christoph. *God's Body: Jewish, Christian, and Pagan Images of God.* Translated by Alexander Johannes Edmonds. Waco, TX: Baylor University Press, 2019.

Mauss, Armand. *The Angel and the Beehive: The Mormon Struggle with Assimilation.* Urbana: University of Illinois Press, 1994.

Maxwell, Neal A. *Deposition of a Disciple.* Salt Lake City: Deseret, 1976).

McBride, Spencer W. *Joseph Smith for President: The Prophet, the Assassins, and the Fight for American Religious Freedom.* New York: Oxford University Press, 2021.

McDannell, Colleen, and Bernhard Lang. *Heaven: A History.* New Haven, CT: Yale University Press, 2001.

McGrath, Alister. *Reformation Thought: An Introduction.* 4th ed. Chichester, UK: Wiley, 2012.

———. *Surprised by Meaning: Science, Faith, and How We Make Sense of Things.* Louisville: Westminster John Knox, 2011.

McLanahan, Sara, and Gary Sandefur, *Growing Up with a Single Parent: What Hurts, What Helps.* Cambridge, MA: Harvard University Press, 1997.

McPherran, Mark L. *The Religion of Socrates.* University Park, PA: Penn State University Press, 1999.

Metzger, Bruce. *Canon of the New Testament.* Oxford: Oxford University Press, 1987.

Mickey, Paul A. *Essentials of Wesleyan Theology: A Contemporary Affirmation.* Grand Rapids: Zondervan, 1980.

Midgley, Mary. *Science as Salvation: A Modern Myth and Its Meaning.* London: Routledge, 1992.

Miller, J. Steve. *Near-Death Experiences: As Evidence for the Existence of God and Heaven.* Acworth, GA: Wisdom Creek, 2012.

Millet, Robert L., ed. *No Weapon Shall Prosper: New Light on Sensitive Issues.* Provo, UT: Religious Studies Center, Brigham Young University; Salt Lake City: Deseret, 2011.

Milton, John. *Paradise Lost.* Edited by David Hawkes. New York: Barnes and Noble, 2004.

Moloney, Karen. "Euphoric, Harmless, and Affordable: A Trend Analysis of Sex." *The Futurist,* May 1, 2014. Library. https://www.thefreelibrary.com/Euphoric%2c+harmless%2c+and+affordable+a+trend+analysis+of+sex.-a0370319923.

Moltmann, Jürgen. *The Trinity and the Kingdom of God.* Translated by Margaret Kohl. London: SCM, 1981.

Moody, Raymond A., Jr. *Life after Life.* Carmel, NY: Guideposts, 1975.

———. *The Light Beyond.* New York: Bantam, 1989.

———. *Reflections on Life after Life.* Carmel, NY: Guideposts, 1977.

Moore, R. Laurence. *Religious Outsiders and the Making of Americans.* New York: Oxford University Press, 1986.

Morris, Thomas V. *The Logic of God Incarnate.* Ithaca, NY: Cornell University Press, 1986.

———. *Making Sense of It All: Pascal and the Meaning of Life.* Grand Rapids: Eerdmans, 1992.

Morse, Melvin. *Closer to the Light: Learning from the Near-Death Experiences of Children.* New York: Random House, 1990.

———. *Transformed by the Light: The Powerful Effect of Near-Death Experiences on People's Lives.* New York: Villard, 1992.

"The Most and Least Meaningful Jobs." https://www.payscale.com/data-packages/most-and-least-meaningful-jobs.

Mulder, William, and A. Russell Mortenson, eds. *Among the Mormons: Historic Accounts by Contemporary Observers.* Lincoln: University of Nebraska Press, 1958.

Mullen, E. Theodore, Jr. *The Assembly of the Gods: The Divine Council in Canaanite and Early Hebrew Literature.* Chico, CA: Scholars, 1980.

Neill, Stephen. *Christian Faith Today.* Baltimore: Penguin, 1955.

Nash, Brittany Chapman. *Let's Talk about Polygamy.* Salt Lake City: Deseret, 2021.

Nash, Ronald H. *The Concept of God.* Grand Rapids: Zondervan, 1983.

Nauvoo Neighbor, April 10, 1844. http://boap.org/LDS/Nauvoo-Neighbor/1844/4-10-1844.pdf.

Nelson, Russell M. "Sweet Power of Prayer." *Ensign* 33:5 (May 2003) 7–9.

Nibley, Hugh. "Return to the Temple." In *Temple and Cosmos: Beyond This Ignorant Present*, edited by Don E. Norton, 1–41. Salt Lake City: Deseret; Provo, UT: Foundation for Ancient Research and Mormon Studies, 1992.

———. *Since Cumorah.* 2nd ed. Salt Lake City: Deseret; Provo, UT: Foundation for Ancient Research and Mormon Studies, 1988.

Noë, Alva. *Out of Our Heads: Why You Are Not Your Brain, and Other Lessons from the Biology of Consciousness.* New York: Hill and Wang, 2009.

Norris, R.A. *God and World in Early Christian Theology.* London: Black, 1965.

Norton, John D. "Chasing the Light: Einstein's Most Famous Thought Experiment." In *Thought Experiments in Philosophy, Science, and the Arts*, edited by Mélanie Frappier et al., 123–40. New York: Routledge, 2013. Available at http://www.pitt.edu/~jdnorton/papers/Chasing.pdf.

Nozick, Robert. "Philosophy and the Meaning of Life." In *The Meaning of Life*, edited by E. D. Klemke.

Ogden, Gina. *The Heart and Soul of Sex.* Boston: Shambhala, 2006.

Origen. *Homilies on Genesis and Exodus.* Translated by Ronald E. Heine. Washington, DC: Catholic University of America Press, 1982.

———. *On First Principles.* Translated by G. W. Butterworth. Gloucester, MA: Peter Smith, 1973.

"Our Beliefs." Community of Christ. www.cofchrist.org/basic-beliefs.

Packer, Boyd K. "The Play and the Plan." 1995. http://emp.byui.edu/huffr/The%20Play%20and%20the%20Plan%20--%20Boyd%20K.%20Packer.htm.

———. *Teach Ye Diligently.* Salt Lake City: Deseret, 1975.

———. "Why Stay Morally Clean." *Ensign*, July 1972. Available at https://www.lds.org/ensign/1972/07/why-stay-morally-clean?lang=eng.

Pagels, Elaine. *The Gnostic Gospels.* New York: Random House, 1979.

Palmer, Spencer J., ed. *Deity and Death.* Provo, UT: Religious Studies Center, Brigham Young University, 1978.

Papadopoulos, Loukia. "Dear Neil deGrasse Tyson, Thank You for Cosmos and All Your Poetry." *HuffPost*, October 29, 2015, updated October 29, 2016. https://www.huffpost.com/entry/dear-neil-degrasse-tyson-_b_5004912.

Parcak, Sarah. *Archaeology from Space: How the Future Shapes Our Past.* New York: Henry Holt, 2019.

Paton, W. R., and Michael A. Tueller, eds. *The Greek Anthology*. Cambridge, MA: Harvard University Press, 2014.

Paulsen, David L., and Martin Pulido. "'A Mother There': A Survey of Historical Teachings about Mother in Heaven." *BYU Studies Quarterly* 50:1 (2011) 70–97. https://scholarsarchive.byu.edu/byusq/vol50/iss1/7.

The Pearl of Great Price. Salt Lake City: Church of Jesus Christ of Latter-day Saints, 1981.

Pelikan, Jaroslav. *Jesus through the Centuries: His Place in the History of Culture*. New Haven, CT: Yale University Press, 1985.

Perego, Ugo A. "The Book of Mormon and the Origin of Native Americans." In *No Weapon Shall Prosper*, edited by Robert L. Millet, 171–216.

Persuitte, David. *Joseph Smith and the Origins of the Book of Mormon*. 2nd ed. Jefferson, NC: McFarland, 2000.

Peters, Edward. *Heresy and Authority in Medieval Europe*. Philadelphia: University of Pennsylvania Press, 1980.

Peterson, Christopher, and Martin E. P. Seligman. *Character Strengths and Virtues: A Handbook and Classification*. New York: Oxford, 2004.

Peterson, Daniel C. "'Ye Are Gods': Psalm 82 and John 10 as Witnesses to the Divine Nature of Humankind." In *The Disciple as Scholar: Essays on Scripture and the Ancient World in Honor of Richard Lloyd Anderson*, edited by Stephen D. Ricks et al., 471–594. Provo, UT: Foundation for Ancient Research and Mormon Studies, 2000.

Pettinato, Giovanni. *Ebla: A New Look at History*. Baltimore: Johns Hopkins University Press, 1991.

Pinnock, Clark H. *Most Moved Mover: A Theology of God's Openness*. Grand Rapids: Baker, 2001.

Plato. *Republic*. Translated by Robin Waterfield. New York: Oxford University Press, 2008.

———. *Symposium*. Translated by Walter Hamilton. New York: Penguin, 1951.

Pojman, Louis P. *Philosophy: The Quest for Truth*. 6th ed. New York: Oxford University Press, 2006.

Polanyi, Michael. *Personal Knowledge: Towards a Post-Critical Philosophy*. Chicago: University of Chicago Press, 1974.

———. "Scientific Outlook: Its Sickness and Cure." *Science* 125:3246 (1957) 480–84. http://science.sciencemag.org/content/125/3246/480.

Polkinghorne, John. *Quantum Physics and Theology: An Unexpected Kinship*. New Haven, CT: Yale University Press, 2007.

———. *Quarks, Chaos and Christianity: Questions to Science and Religion*. New York: Crossroad, 2005.

Popkin, Richard H. *The History of Scepticism: From Savonarola to Bayle*. Rev. ed. New York: Oxford University Press, 2003.

Popper, Karl. "Natural Selection and the Emergence of Mind." In *Evolutionary Epistemology, Rationality, and the Sociology of Knowledge*, edited by Gerard Radnitzky and William W. Bartley III, 139/–56. La Salle, IL: Open Court, 1987.

Porter, Roy. *The Greatest Benefit to Mankind: A Medical History of Humanity*. New York: Norton, 1997.

Pratt, Parley P., Jr., ed. *Autobiography of Parley Parker Pratt*. Salt Lake City: Deseret, 1980.

Price, Lucien. *Dialogues of Alfred North Whitehead*. Boston: Godine, 2001.

Randall, Lisa. "New Dimensions." In *Mind, Life and Universe: Conversations with Great Scientists of our Time*, edited by Lynn Margulis and Eduardo Punset, 297–303. White River Junction, VT: Chelsea Green, 2007.

Rappoport, Angelo S. *Myth and Legend of Ancient Israel*. Vol. 1. New York: Ktav, 1966.

Rakestraw, Robert V. "Becoming Like God: An Evangelical Doctrine of Theosis." *Journal of the Evangelical Theological Society* 40:2 (June 1997) 257–69.

Rees, Robert A. "The Book of Mormon and Automatic Writing." *Journal of Book of Mormon Studies* 15:1 (2006) 4–17.

Regnerus, Mark. *Cheap Sex: The Transformation of Men, Marriage, and Monogamy*. New York: Oxford University Press, 2017.

Renehan, R. "On the Greek Origins of the Concepts of Incorporeality and Immateriality." *Greek, Roman and Byzantine Studies* 21 (1980) 105–38.

Ring, Kenneth. *Heading toward Omega: In Search of the Meaning of the Near-Death Experience*. New York: William Morrow, 1984.

———. *Life at Death: A Scientific Investigation of the Near-Death Experience*. New York: William Morrow, 1982.

Ring, Kenneth, and Sharon Cooper. *Mindsight: Near-Death Experiences in the Blind*. Palo Alto, CA: William James Center for Consciousness Studies, Institute for Transpersonal Psychology, 1999.

Ring, Kenneth, and Evelyn Elsaesser Valarino. *Lessons from the Light: What We Can Learn from the Near-Death Experience*. Needham, MA: Moment Point, 2000.

Ritchie, George. *Return from Tomorrow*. Grand Rapids: Chosen, 2007.

Roberts, Alexander, and James Donaldson, eds. *Ante-Nicene Fathers*. 10 vols. Reprint, Peabody, MA: Hendrickson, 1994.

Roberts, B. H., ed. *History of the Church of Jesus Christ of Latter-day Saints*. 2nd ed., rev. Salt Lake City: Deseret, 1949.

Robinson, Austin A., and Curtis T. Hunter. "Discovering a Surgical First: Russell M. Nelson and Tricuspid Valve Annuloplasty." *BYU Studies* 54:1 (2015) 6–28.

Robinson, H. Wheeler. "Hebrew Psychology." In *The People and the Book: Essays on the Old Testament*, edited by Arthur S. Peake, 353–82. Oxford: Oxford University Press, 1925.

Robinson, Stephen E. *Are Mormons Christian?* Salt Lake City: Bookcraft, 1991.

Rodgers, Joann Ellison. *Sex: A Natural History*. New York: Macmillan, 2003.

Rogo, Kenneth. *The Return from Silence: A Study of Near-Death Experiences*. Wellingborough, UK: Aquarian, 1989.

Rollins, Kyle M., et al. "Transforming Swampland into Nauvoo, the City Beautiful: A Civil Engineering Perspective." *BYU Studies* 45:3 (2006) 125–57.

Rosenberg, Alex. *The Atheist's Guide to Reality: Enjoying Life without Illusions*. New York: Norton, 2011.

"Routine periodic fasting is good for your health, and your heart, study suggests." *Science Daily*, May 20, 2011. http://www.sciencedaily.com/releases/2011/04/110403090259.htm.

Rucker, Rudy. "Big Bang Bust." *Wired*, July 1, 1995. http://www.wired.com/1995/07/rucker/.

Russell, Norman. *The Doctrine of Deification in the Greek Orthodox Tradition*. New York: Oxford, 2006.

Sabom, Michael. *Recollections of Death: A Medical Investigation*. New York: Harper and Row, 1982.

Sanders, John. *No Other Name: An Investigation into the Destiny of the Unevangelized*. Grand Rapids: Eerdmans, 1992.

Saunders, Richard L. ed. *Dale Morgan on the Mormons: Collected Works. Part 1, 1939–1951*. Kingdom in the West: The Mormons and the American Frontier 14. Norman: University of Oklahoma Press, 2012.

Schaff, Philip, and Wace, Henry. *Nicene and Post-Nicene Fathers*. 1st and 2nd series. 28 vols. Peabody, MA: Hendrickson, 1994.

Schopenhauer, Arthur. "On the Suffering of the World," In *The Meaning of Life: Questions, Answers, Analysis*, edited by Steven Sanders and David R. Cheney. Upper Saddle River, NJ: Prentice Hall, 1980.

Schwartz, Howard. *Tree of Souls: The Mythology of Judaism*. Oxford: Oxford University Press, 2004.

Sextus Empiricus. *Selections from the Major Writings on Scepticism, Man & God*. Indianapolis: Hackett, 1985.

Sheldrake, Rupert. *Science Set Free: 10 Paths to New Discovery*. New York: Deepak Chopra Books, 2012.

———. *The Sense of Being Stared At: And Other Unexplained Powers of Human Minds*. Rochester, VT: Park Street, 2013.

Shipps, Jan. "Is Mormonism Christian?: Reflections on a Complicated Question." In *Mormons and Mormonism: An Introduction to an American World Religion*, edited by Eric A. Eliason, 76–97. Urbana: University of Illinois Press, 2001.

Sire, James W. *The Universe Next Door: A Basic Worldview Catalog*. 5th ed. Downers Grove, IL: InterVarsity, 2009.

Skousen, Royal. *The Book of Mormon: The Earliest Text*. New Haven, CT: Yale University Press, 2009.

Smith, Daniel B. *Muses, Madmen, and Prophets: Rethinking the History, Science, and Meaning of Auditory Hallucination*. New York: Penguin, 2007.

Smith, Emily Esfahani. "Is Sex Still Sexy?" *The Atlantic*, May 27, 2013. http://www.theatlantic.com/sexes/archive/2013/05/is-sex-still-sexy/275936/.

———. "Meaning Is Healthier than Happiness." *The Atlantic*, August 1, 2013. http://www.theatlantic.com/health/archive/2013/08/meaning-is-healthier-than-happiness/278250/.

———. *The Power of Meaning: Crafting a Life that Matters*. New York: Crown, 2017.

———. "There's More to Life than Being Happy." *The Atlantic*, January 9, 2013. http://www.theatlantic.com/health/archive/2013/01/theres-more-to-life-than-being-happy/266805/.

Smith, Ethan. *View of the Hebrews*. 2nd ed. Edited by Charles D. Tate Jr. Provo, UT: Religious Studies Center, Brigham Young University, 1996. Available at https://rsc.byu.edu/book/view-hebrews.

Smith, Howard. *Let There Be Light: Modern Cosmology and Kabbalah*. Novato, CA: New World Library, 2006.

Smith, Joseph. *Teachings of the Prophet Joseph Smith*. Salt Lake City: Deseret, 1976.

Sommer, Benjamin D. *The Bodies of God and the World of Ancient Israel*. Cambridge: Cambridge University Press, 2009.

Southwick, Stephen, and Dennis Charney, *Resilience: The Science of Mastering Life's Greatest Challenges*. 2nd ed. Cambridge: Cambridge University Press, 2018.

Sorell, Tom. *Scientism: Philosophy and the Infatuation with Science*. New York: Routledge, 1994.

Spaulding, Solomon. *Manuscript Found: The Complete Original "Spaulding Manuscript".* Edited by Kent P. Jackson. Provo, UT: Religious Studies Center, Brigham Young University, 1996. Available at https://rsc.byu.edu/manuscript-found/editors-introduction.

Speiser, E. A. *Genesis.* Garden City, New York: Doubleday, 1964.

Staniforth, Maxwell, ed. *Early Christian Writings: The Apostolic Fathers.* New York: Penguin, 1968.

Stead, Christopher. *Philosophy in Christian Antiquity.* Cambridge: Cambridge University Press, 1996.

Stott, Gerald. "Effects of College Education on the Religious Involvement of Latter-day Saints." *BYU Studies* 24:1 (1984) 43–52.

Svendsen, Lars Fredrik. *Work.* 2nd ed. New York: Routledge, 2016.

Swinton, Heidi. *American Prophet: The Story of Joseph Smith.* Salt Lake City: Shadow Mountain, 1999.

Szink, Terence L. "The Personal Name 'Alma' at Ebla." *Religious Educator* 1:1 (2000) 53–56. Available at https://rsc.byu.edu/archived/volume-1-number-1-2000/personal-name-alma-ebla.

Talbot, Christine. *A Foreign Kingdom: Mormons and Polygamy in American Political Culture, 1852–1890.* Urbana: University of Illinois Press, 2013.

Talmage, James E. *Articles of Faith.* Salt Lake City, Utah: Church of Jesus Christ of Latter-day Saints, 1977.

———. *Jesus the Christ.* Reprint. American Fork, UT: Covenant Communications, 2006.

Teachings of Presidents of the Church: Brigham Young. Salt Lake City: Church of Jesus Christ of Latter-day Saints, 1997.

Teachings of Presidents of the Church: Joseph Smith. Salt Lake City: Church of Jesus Christ of Latter-day Saints, 2011.

Teachings of the Presidents of the Church: Lorenzo Snow. Salt Lake City: Church of Jesus Christ of Latter-day Saints, 2012.

Tedeschi, Richard G., and Lawrence G. Calhoun. *Trauma and Transformation: Growing in the Aftermath of Suffering.* Thousand Oaks, CA: Sage, 1985.

Teicholz, Nina. *The Big Fat Surprise: Why Butter, Meat and Cheese Belong in a Healthy Diet.* New York: Simon & Schuster, 2014.

Top, Brent L. *The Life Before: How Our Premortal Existence Affects Our Mortal Life.* Salt Lake City: Deseret, 1988.

Top, Brent, and Wendy Top. *Glimpses beyond Death's Door: Gospel Insights into Near-Death Experiences.* Orem, UT: Granite, 2005.

Turner, John G. *Brigham Young: Pioneer Prophet.* London: Belknap, 2012.

———. *The Mormon Jesus.* Cambridge, MA: Harvard University Press, 2016.

Tvedtnes, John A. *The Book of Mormon and Other Hidden Books.* Bountiful, UT: Horizon, 2003.

Twain, Mark. *The Adventures of Huckleberry Finn.* New York: Signet, 1959.

———. *Roughing It.* Hartford: American, 1901.

Van Lommel, Pim. *Consciousness beyond Life.* New York: HarperCollins, 2010.

Vogel, Dan, ed. *Early Mormon Documents.* 5 vols. Salt Lake City: Signature, 1996–2003.

Von Rad, Gerhard. *Old Testament Theology.* 2 vols. Edinburgh: Oliver and Boyd, 1962–65.

Vujicic, Nick. *Life without Limits: Inspiration for a Ridiculously Good Life.* New York: Doubleday, 2010.

Waite, Linda J., and Maggie Gallagher. *The Case for Marriage: Why Married People Are Happier, Healthier, and Better Off Financially*. New York: Random House, 2000.

Wallace, Peter G. *The Long European Reformation: Religion, Political Conflict, and the Search for Conformity, 1350–1750*. 2nd ed. New York: St. Martins, 2012.

Waller, John. *The Discovery of the Germ: Twenty Years that Transformed the Way We Think about Disease*. New York: Columbia University Press, 2002.

Wardrop, Murray. "Man with No Arms or Legs Can Play Football, Swim, and Surf." *The Telegraph*, July 2, 2009. http://www.telegraph.co.uk/news/newstopics/howaboutthat/5716185/Man-with-no-arms-or-legs-can-play-football-swim-and-surf.html

Watkins, John. *Hearing Voices: A Common Human Experience*. Melbourne: Michael Anderson, 2008.

Webb, Stephen H. *Jesus Christ, Eternal God*. New York: Oxford University Press, 2012.

Welch, John W. "The Miraculous Translation of the Book of Mormon." In *Opening the Heavens*, edited by John W. Welch and Erick B. Carlson, 77–117.

———. "The Role of Evidence in Religious Discussion." In *No Weapon Shall Prosper*, edited by Robert L. Millet, 259–94.

Welch, John W., and Erick B. Carlson, eds. *Opening the Heavens: Accounts of Divine Manifestations, 1820–1844*. Provo, UT: Brigham Young University Press; Salt Lake City: Deseret, 2005.

Wenke, Robert J. *Patterns in Prehistory: Humankind's First Three Million Years*. 3rd ed. New York: Oxford University Press, 1990.

"What Is Repentance and Is It Necessary for Salvation?" http://www.gotquestions.org/repentance.html#ixzz3M9bFaDqH.

Whitmer, David. *An Address to All Believers in Christ*. Self-published, 1887. Available at https://archive.org/details/addresstoallbelioowhit/page/8/mode/2up?view=theater.

Widtsoe, John A. *A Rational Theology as Taught by the Church of Jesus Christ of Latter-day Saints*. Salt Lake City: General Priesthood Committee, 1915.

Wilber, Ken, ed. *Quantum Questions: Mystical Writings of the World's Great Physicists*. Boulder, CO: Shambhala, 1984.

Wilken, Robert L. *The Christians as the Romans Saw Them*. New Haven, CT: Yale University Press, 1984.

Williams, Richard N., and Daniel N. Robinson, eds., *Scientism: The New Orthodoxy*. London: Bloomsbury, 2015.

Williams, Wesley. "A Body Unlike Bodies: Transcendent Anthropomorphism in Ancient Semitic Tradition and Early Islam." *Journal of the American Oriental Society* 129:1 (January–March 2009) 19–44.

Wilson, Gary. *Your Brain on Porn: Internet Pornography and the Emerging Science of Addiction*. Margate, Kent, UK: Commonwealth, 2015.

"Window washer survives 11-story fall onto moving car in Calif." *Fox News*, November 29, 2015. http://www.foxnews.com/us/2014/11/21/window-washer-survives-11-story-fall-onto-moving-car-in-calif/.

Xenophon. *Conversations with Socrates*. Translated by Robin Waterfield. New York: Penguin, 1990.

Yadin, Yigael. *Bar Kochba: The Rediscovery of the Legendary Hero of the Last Jewish Revolt against Imperial Rome*. London: Weidenfeld and Nicholson, 1971.

Young, Brigham. *Discourses of Brigham Young*. Edited by John A. Widtsoe. Salt Lake City: Deseret, 1941.

Zaleski, Philip, and Carol Zaleski. *Prayer: A History*. Boston: Houghton Mifflin, 2005.

Index

Index

Randall, Lisa, 134n.

Rappoport, Angelo, 64

Real estate market, unexpected decline in
  prices of, 28–29

Remini, Robert, 9

Reorganized Church of Jesus Christ of Latter
  Day Saints. *See* Community of Christ.

Repentance, 93, 118, 138–40

Restored gospel of Jesus Christ. *See*
  Mormonism.

Rigdon, Sidney, 15, 205

Ritchie, George,
  near-death experience of, 101–102

Sabom, Michael, 108

Sacrifice, in LDS thought, 160–61

Sagan, Carl, 30, 50

Satan (Lucifer), fall of, 66–67

Schrödinger, Erwin, 41

Schopenhauer, Arthur, 93–94

Science, limitations of, 33–35
  intuitive nature of discoveries, 225–26

Scientism, 40–41

Service, in LDS culture, 158–60

Sex
  and hookup culture, 146
  and passion, 145–51
  and pornography, 146–47

Shakespeare, 46, 52, 214

Shipps, Jan, 1, 4, 196

Shoe that pinches, as example of suffering
  (Schopenhauer), 93–94

Skepticism, xi, xii-xiii, 26–27, 41

Skeptics Society, 26–27

Smith, Emma, 195, 199, 220–21

Smith, Ethan (*View of the Hebrews*), 206–211

Smith, Joseph, 138, 224, 238
  attitude toward other religions, xiv
  impressions of by non-Latter-day Saints,
    9–10, 17–18, 20–23
  journal of and correspondence with Emma
    Smith, 221–22
  martyrdom of, 18
  on death, 48, 53–54, 97
  on knowledge and salvation, 42
  on premortality, 61–62
  presidential campaign of, 17–18
  temperament of, 20
  tribulations in life, 80–81, 96
  vision of angel Moroni, 12
  vision of God and Jesus Christ, 12, 220
  youth of, 11–12

Smith, William, on his brother Joseph, 207–08

Snow, Lorenzo, 233

Socrates, 228–30

Spock, 225

Spalding, Solomon, 205–206, 208

Stone, Barton W. *See* Stone-Campbell
  movement.

Stone-Campbell movement, 15, 193–94

Suffering
  benefits of, 94–95
  classical (biblical) view of, 77–78
  in book of Hebrews, 79–80
  of Christ, 79
  necessity of in life, 91–95

Superforce, 134n.

Superstring theory, 37

Swedenborg, Emmanuel, 83, 84, 250

Talmage, James E., 44

Taylor, John, 161

Telepathy, 227

Teresa of Avila, 232

Tertullian (early Christian theologian), 186–87

Theodicy, 75–81

Theosis. *See* deification.

Three degrees of glory, 10 112–14

Three-dimensional view of life. *See*
  Mormonism

Tolstoy, Leo, 52, 90

Trinity, doctrine of the, 179–90
  See also God, nature of

Twain, Mark, 118, 215

Tyson, Neil DeGrasse, 50

Under the Banner of Heaven (Krakauer), 2

Universe, creation of, 131–35

Valentinus (early gnostic thinker), 170

View of the Hebrews (Smith), 206–211

Violinist, parable of, 120

Voices, phenomenon of hearing, 230

Voltaire, xiv

Vujicic, Nick, 85–86

Wallace, Mike, 138, 161

Warren, Rick, 139

Webb, Stephen, 5, 23n.

Weil, Simone, 7

Westminster Catechism, 54

Westminster Confession, 123

Whalen, William, 6

Whitehead, Alfred North, 40

Whitmer, David, 202

Whitmer, John, 202n.

Wyclif, John, 190, 192

Widtsoe, John A., 42

Williams, Roger, 13n., 192–93, 194

Woodruff, Wilford, 136–37

Word of Wisdom, 19, 141–43

Printed in Great Britain
by Amazon

59279643R00170